THE TEXTURE OF THE DIVINE

THE TEXTURE OF THE DIVINE

Imagination in Medieval Islamic and Jewish Thought

Aaron W. Hughes

INDIANA UNIVERSITY PRESS
Bloomington and Indianapolis

Publication of this book is made possible in part with the assistance of a Challenge Grant from the National Endowment for the Humanities, a federal agency that supports research, education, and public programming in the humanities.

This book is a publication of

Indiana University Press
601 North Morton Street
Bloomington, Indiana 47404-3797 USA

http://iupress.indiana.edu

Telephone orders 800-842-6796
Fax orders 812-855-7931
Orders by e-mail iuporder@indiana.edu

The paper used in this publication meets the minimum requirements of American National Standard for Information Sciences–Permanence of Paper for Printed Library Materials, ANSI Z39.48-1984.

Manufactured in the United States of America

Library of Congress Cataloging-in-Publication Data

Hughes, Aaron W., date
The texture of the divine : imagination in medieval Islamic and Jewish thought / Aaron W. Hughes.
p. cm.
Includes the text of an English translation of Abraham ben Meïr Ibn Ezra's Ḥai ben Mekits.
Includes bibliographical references and index.
ISBN 0-253-34353-4 (cloth : alk. paper)
1. Imagination–Religious aspects–Islam. 2. Imagination–Religious aspects—Judaism. 3. Avicenna, 980–1037. Risālat Ḥayy ibn Yaqẓān. 4. Ibn Ṭufayl, Muhammad ibn ʿAbd al-Malik, d. 1185. Risālat Ḥayy ibn Yaqẓān. 5. Ibn Ezra, Abraham ben Meïr, 1092–1167. Ḥai ben Mekits. 6. Image of God–Comparative studies. 7. Neoplatonism in literature. 8. Ascension of the soul. 9. Philosophy, Medieval. I. Ibn Ezra, Abraham ben Meïr, 1092–1167. Ḥai ben Mekits. English. II. Title.
BP190.5.I57H84 2004
181'.07–dc22

2003013824

1 2 3 4 5 09 08 07 06 05 04

To Lisa

and My Parents,
William and Sadie Hughes

Contents

Acknowledgments ix

Introduction 1

1. Reading the Divine: A User's Guide to the Initiatory Tale 13

2. Reading between the Lines: Text as Encounter with the Divine 48

3. Polishing a Dirty Mirror: The Philosophic Imagination 82

4. The Initiation of the Philosopher: Ritual Poetics and the Quest for Meaning 115

5. "God Is Beautiful and Loves Beauty": The Role of Aesthetics in Medieval Islamic and Jewish Philosophy 146

Conclusion 185

Appendix: *Ḥay ben Meqitz:* An Initiatory Tale by Abraham ibn Ezra 189

Notes 209

Bibliography 245

Index 267

Acknowledgments

I am fortunate indeed to have had the generous support of many individuals and institutions for this project. Here, I try to acknowledge, all too briefly, the intellectual and financial debts that have enabled this book to see the light of day.

This work reached its first stage of completion as a doctoral dissertation written under the expert guidance of Hava Tirosh-Samuelson at Indiana University. Her encouragement and acumen have helped me immensely, and I am grateful that she has always forced me to formulate and ask bigger questions of my material. Her model of scholarship and professionalism is something to which I aspire. I would also like to thank Warren Harvey of the Hebrew University of Jerusalem, with whom I first encountered the *philosophical* thought of ibn Ezra, and who encouraged me to pursue this topic at the dissertation level. I would also like to thank Elliot R. Wolfson, who has been supportive of my work from the time I was a graduate student. I greatly appreciate this support, especially since his work on the imagination in medieval Jewish mysticism has been instrumental in my own attempts to make sense of this faculty in medieval Islamic and Jewish philosophy. I am also grateful to Steven M. Wasserstrom, who has helped me see the connections between my data and the wider Islamicate world. Because of him, this is a better book. Individuals who have always been willing to talk about this project with me include: Barry Kogan, Scott C. Alexander, James G. Hart, John Walbridge, Robert Ford Campany, David Brakke, and the late J. Samuel Preus. I also have to thank Amram Tropper and Elisheva for their conversation and warmth around the Shabbas table in Oxford, when my own family was far away. Finally, I would like to acknowledge the editorial staff at Indiana University Press, especially Michael W. Lundell who believed in and encouraged this project from the beginning, and Joyce Rappaport for the care with which she copyedited the manuscript. Any shortcomings in this book reside solely with me.

As for institutions, I should like to acknowledge the generous support of the Department of Religious Studies at Indiana University. This department creates an ideal and friendly environment that does much to encourage creativity. Parts of this book were also written at the Hebrew University in Jerusalem, and the Oxford Centre for Hebrew and Judaic Studies. Thanks to the helpful librarians at both the Oriental Institute and the Bodleian Library, Oxford.

Granting agencies that have supported this project include the Inter-University Fellowship in Jewish Studies, the Social Sciences and Humanities Research Council of Canada (SSHRC), the Maurice Amado Foundation for Sephardic Studies at UCLA, and the Memorial Foundation for Jewish Culture. I would also like to thank the Dean's Office in the Faculty of Humanities at the University of Calgary for course release and the generous funding that it provides to new faculty.

Last, but certainly not least, I dedicate this book to those who are closest to me and who have, accordingly, suffered through its completion. In particular, I would like to thank my parents, William and Sadie Hughes, and my partners in crime, Tilley and Murphy. And it is to my dear wife, Lisa, whose faith in this project and in me has never wavered, that I am grateful beyond words.

THE TEXTURE OF THE DIVINE

Introduction

THE QUARREL BETWEEN PHILOSOPHY AND LITERATURE, INTELLECT AND imagination, according to Socrates in Book 10 of the *Republic*, is ancient and virulent. In its most severe representation, philosophy and literature are seen as occupying opposite ends of a continuum. Philosophy is about all that is unchanging, universal, and permanent; the purview of literature, on the other hand, is about the fickleness of specific characters making specific choices in response to localized contexts. Yet such a characterization is ultimately a false one because it ignores the finitude and specificity of our existence. Moreover, it does not adequately fit with the historical record of philosophy. Despite the criticisms of Socrates, we have never witnessed the construction of an impermeable border separating these two modes of discourse. Indeed, even Socrates' transcriber, Plato, did not hesitate to turn toward the mythic and the poetic to make a philosophical point.

Literature and philosophy utilize two different languages that ultimately allow access to the same world. The study that follows explores some of the various points of intersection between these two languages: the relationship between form and content, the attempt to textualize the ineffable, and the use of poetic images for philosophical purposes. In calling attention to these features, I attempt to recreate a paradigm of understanding that turned not only on the intellect, but also on the exercise of the imagination and the emotions. This paradigm gave priority to the perception of particular people and particular situations over abstract and analytical argumentation. Rather than regard this paradigm as irrational or prone to vagueness, many saw it as an important way to speculate about God and the divine world.

This study examines the broad theme of the relationship between philosophy and literature within the rich intellectual and cultural landscape of medieval Judaism and Islam. It argues that the key to understanding this relationship comes from both the imagination and aesthetics. Each of these is ultimately concerned with specifics and with articulating how such specifics lead to a proper understanding of universals. To make my argument, I focus on a set of philosophical texts written in a highly literary style. These treatises, which combine philosophy, poetry, and allegory, recount the journey of a protagonist through the ascending layers of the universe, with each segment of the journey described in literary as opposed to scientific terms. Each journey culminates in the imaginative apprehension of God, with the protagonist gazing into the divine presence. These texts are not only beautiful literary and poetic works; they also provide important insights into medieval philosophy and mysticism.

If one of the main themes of this study is that of the convergence between philosophy and literature, an equally important one is to show how a minority appropriates and thinks with the narratives of a majority culture. Such appropriation is not simple translation, but often involves adaptation and cultural hermeneutics. Even though the new narrative may share certain affinities with the original, it nonetheless must begin to confront and address the various intellectual, social, and cultural concerns of the minority group. If not, why not simply read the original? As a case study, I explore some of the ramifications of what happens when a Jew (who spoke and wrote Arabic) living in Muslim Spain decided to take over an Arabic narrative and the various processes by which he went about this. My study, unlike many devoted to medieval Jewish and Islamic philosophy, does not deal solely with ideas, but also seeks to bring to light the various concerns of cultural and religious identity.

In examining these narratives within the history of both medieval poetics and philosophy, my goal is to demonstrate that Jewish and Islamic philosophy when approached in new ways can yield new critical insights. For instance, the iconographic and mythic dimensions of philosophy, and the ritualistic and visionary aspects of Neoplatonism, are often ignored or downplayed in studies of this type of philosophical literature. My goal is to bring such features into the conversation to see how they can help us reframe some of the traditional assumptions of the field. In thus re-orienting the traditional approach to medieval Jewish and Islamic philosophy, I hope to provide a different vantage point from which to illumine the beauty, timelessness, and multidimensionality of but one aspect of medieval Jewish and Islamic civilization.

The data I use to enter into this discourse consist of various *Ḥayy ibn Yaqẓān* (lit. "Living, the Son of Awake") narratives written in medieval Jewish and Islamic thought.[1] In particular, I focus on three versions:[2] the famous Arabic texts by Avicenna (980–1037) and ibn Ṭufayl (ca. 1116–1185),[3] and the less well-known Hebrew text of Abraham ibn Ezra (1089–1164).[4] All three are highly literary accounts that offer elaborate descriptions of the structure of the universe and the changing role of the individual within it.[5] All three texts poetically describe the protagonist's intellectual and mystical ascent, and all culminate in the protagonist's imaginative apprehension of the divine.

Although studies have examined each of these as individual texts, there has yet to be an analysis of the entire cycle. Since all of the texts share a similar set of literary and philosophical assumptions, my contention is that they are not *ad hoc* creations, but represent a distinct genre. My analysis grounds these texts in a particular historical moment, showing how they represent, locally, the intersection of the various cultural, intellectual, poetic, and aesthetic trajectories of medieval Islamicate civilization.[6]

What follows is devoted to offering a fresh interpretation of these texts. Previous studies have shown diverging opinions about how to classify them. Some regard them as nothing more than philosophical primers and, thus, of no real intellectual importance; yet others see them as the epitome of medieval philosophical speculation, an attempt to offer an "Eastern" alternative to the standard Aristotelian system. The direction of my study, *The Texture of the Divine,* differs from both of these approaches by making the argument that these treatises provide important insight into two traditionally marginalized aspects of medieval Islamicate philosophy: the imagination and aesthetics.

Traditionally, the overwhelming interest of historians of medieval Islamicate philosophy has been in metaphysics, ontology, and epistemology. These grand themes are sounded often by many of the philosophers themselves in their explicit condemnation of the imaginative faculty: "imagining is no more than the mind's projection of images belonging to sense objects no longer present."[7] Similar strains reverberate among innumerable historians of Islamic and Jewish philosophy who, to cite but one recent example, argue that "imagination and reason represent two distinct levels of consciousness and, therefore, two distinct thinking processes."[8] The result has been the almost ubiquitous denial of the imagination within the medieval philosophical enterprise. If philosophy is about the august contemplation of divine and ephemeral truths, the imagination becomes the faculty that has the potential to undermine this activity, thereby corrupting the individual and banishing him or her to the dreamy obfuscations of mysticism.

Aesthetics is part and parcel of the imagination. By aesthetics I mean a theory of beauty that is primarily interested in delineating the pleasure that arises in the soul of an individual upon viewing an object or hearing a poem or harmony. This pleasure, according to the medieval Islamicate philosophers, occurs because physical beauty (often defined in terms of order and harmony) is regarded as participating in a higher order. Such a theory, of course, had its origin in Plato's theory of beauty,[9] which made its way into medieval thought through the conduit of Plotinus. But the thinkers who are the subject of this study did not simply copy this discussion; on the contrary, they created their own discourse to address specific monotheistic concerns. One of the key features of medieval aesthetics is that it was not simply about artistic sentiment, but rather was inseparable from ontic concerns. The beauty to be found in an object or heard in a harmony pointed beyond itself, thereby situating the object or harmony within an ontological hierarchy. Aesthetics thus takes on an important role in directing the soul of the individual to its true home in the celestial world.

Both aesthetics and the imaginative faculty concern themselves with the particulars of sense perception and how the structure of the sensual world reveals the immateriality of the divine world. The medieval philosophers worked within an intellectual framework in which the only way to grasp something was to abstract a formal structure encased within a material substratum. Although knowledge is not about sensual particulars, the latter become necessary because they function as prolegomena to all understanding. Within this context, the divine world is taxonomically unique because it does not conform to the materiality of this world. The divine world is essentially closed to sense perception and, thus, to intellection. The only way in which the individual can apprehend the divine world is by means of experiencing it, not just by describing it in terms of something else. This is why the imagination is so important to the philosophical enterprise: it is the faculty that is ultimately responsible for the creation of images or symbols that capture certain perspectives of the divine's ineffability. The imagination now becomes the primary vehicle whereby the individual grasps that which exists without matter. Aesthetics fits into the puzzle because it is primarily concerned with how concrete particulars reflect a universal and spiritual beauty. Like the imagination, aesthetics is concerned with delineating how the incorporeal is experienced in terms of the corporeal. Both the imagination and aesthetics revolve around the interface between the visible and the invisible, the particular and the universal, and the transcendent and the ephemeral.

The intimate relationship between the imagination and the role of aesthetics is, in turn, related to a much larger theme that runs throughout the religious civilizations of Islam and Judaism. This theme is, for want of a better term, the "monotheistic paradox" between God's absence and presence.[10] On the one hand, both of these traditions regard God as completely other, a deity who is unsusceptible to any sort of iconic or corporeal representation; yet, on the other hand, humans have a basic need to encounter God's presence in order to ascertain His providence at work in their lives.[11] Even if the theological traditions of both Islam and Judaism wanted, often with unintended and awkward consequences, to have the best of both worlds, the Islamicate philosophical tradition was extreme in its negative theology and the need to protect God's complete uniqueness.[12]

This has led some to argue that whereas "Greek culture" and understanding is defined by its emphasis on the visual, "Semitic culture" is primarily defined by its aurality.[13] Such civilizational reifications, which were particularly in favor at the beginning of the twentieth century, are thankfully becoming rarer today. The unfortunate by-product of such assumptions, however, still remains. It rises to the surface in the claim that both Islam and Judaism are somehow devoid of the visual,[14] especially when it comes to the visualization of the divine. It is beyond the parameters of this study to offer a history of this visual representation of the divine in Islam and Judaism. Nevertheless, the tension between the iconic and the aniconic, visualization and the prohibition against such an act, created a series of reverberations in the authors who are the subject of this study. This tension will essentially form the basis of what follows.

This study seeks to situate the *Ḥayy ibn Yaqẓān* cycle against the broader backdrop of medieval aesthetics. In particular, it investigates the historical origins, intellectual moorings, and philosophical implications of these texts. Accordingly, I argue that these three tales and the way they incorporate both the imagination and aesthetics are not unique. On the contrary, they are indicative of a larger though much neglected aspect of medieval Neoplatonism; namely, the importance of beauty and the notion of visualizing or imaginatively apprehending it. Where appropriate, I show how these three treatises and their denouements relate not only to Neoplatonism but also to the larger corpora of the authors concerned. These texts, I contend, are not *ad hoc* creations written by different authors in different temporal and spatial locations. Rather, they represent a distinct genre of medieval philosophical literature. This study, then, is an attempt to treat thoroughly the various problems associated with the imagination as they appear in a distinct group of texts.

My major focus is on the imagination, for this faculty, occupying a distinct place in the psychic hierarchy, is the pivot around which revolve all the features I here discuss. It is, for instance, the imagination that becomes the locus of vision that permits the initiate to experience and visualize the divine world. In many ways, this is paradoxical because the divine is regarded as incorporeal and that which does not possess spatial extension cannot physically be seen. Yet the function of the imagination is to provide three-dimensional extension to that which exists without body. It does this by taking the information that is stored from the individual's sensual encounter with this world and projecting it on the spiritual world. As a result, the imagination ultimately becomes responsible for giving the transcendental an appropriate phenomenality. But this is not simply a translation of something ineffable into a communicable form. Rather, the imagination's gaze is the main component of the experience. Here I am influenced by the work of Elliot Wolfson, the historian of Jewish mysticism, who argues

> What scholars have not always duly noted is that recourse to sensible images and symbols is part of the mystical experience itself and is not restricted to the description of an ineffable experience in oral or written communication. Mystical vision is such that the suprasensible world is experienced in sensory imagery and not simply described in terms of the sensible.... In traversing the barrier between the visible and spiritual worlds, the mystic experiences the latter in terms of the modalities of the former. There is no passage in which the cognitive and epistemological categories of the sensory world are consumed by the fires of spiritual reality. On the contrary, those very conditions are upheld, for they allow for an experience of the divine matters that figure prominently in the mystical vision.[15]

This approach differs from typical treatments of mystical vision, which contend that the actual experience transcends all categories and that only *after* the individual has returned to his or her "normal" state does he or she search for the appropriate image to try to describe this otherwise ineffable experience.[16] The utility of this new approach is such that the vision and its images now become the only phenomena by which the initiate can have access to the transcendent. In other words, the divine world is all but inaccessible without the various categories of everyday sense experience. This shift in emphasis now puts the imagination at the center of the visual experience. It becomes an active faculty whose main goal is to provide the initiate with the currency by which he or she experiences the otherwise ineffable.

The primary function of the imagination is hermeneutical. It is responsible for presenting one thing (i.e., the spiritual) in terms of another (i.e., the sensual), thereby making the unknown known. The imagination is thus central to the initiate's ability to visualize spiritual entities, including God, which would otherwise be unknowable because they are unavailable to sense perception.

Although the major focus of this work is the imagination and its relationship to experience and aesthetics (chapters 3 through 5), the first two chapters seek to chart the various modalities and trajectories needed to understand this. Chapter 1 in particular offers a "user's guide" to the *Ḥayy ibn Yaqẓān* cycle. Here, I provide brief biographies of the three authors, in addition to giving synopses of their respective treatises. In so doing, I offer an overview of this genre that I have decided to call, for reasons to be elaborated in that chapter, the "initiatory tale." What do these diverse texts have in common? How do they fit within both medieval Islamicate Neoplatonism and the larger corpora of these authors? There is a tendency to regard these tales in the secondary literature from one of two competing hermeneutical perspectives, what I here call the "minimalist" and the "maximalist." The former regards these texts as nothing more than philosophical primers, whereas the latter contends that these texts are part of an amorphous "Oriental Wisdom." I argue that both approaches ultimately prove unhelpful. In their stead, I opt for a reading that seeks to ground these texts in the intellectual categories of Neoplatonism that tended to blend so well with the rich religious and mythic vocabularies of monotheism.

The second chapter builds naturally on the first in that it seeks to analyze certain features of Neoplatonism that bear specifically on these texts. I focus, in particular, on the crucial nexus between language and embodiedness. One of the central paradoxes of Neoplatonism, one that the authors who are the subject of this study share, is that although Truth is outside of language, the latter becomes one of the few mechanisms we have at our disposal to contextualize the former. Within this context, and using the vocabulary of modern phenomenology, it is language that makes ontology possible since one of its primary goals is to articulate meaning and bring the ineffable to light. This gives way to a type of writing that is double-edged, one that seeks to conceal as it reveals. A large part of this paradox stems ultimately from the problem the body poses for Neoplatonism in particular and philosophy in general. The body, composed of matter and thus corruptible, is the main stumbling block in our quest for impermanence. Yet it is a feature that must be accounted for if the initiate is ultimately to transcend this world. For this reason, the body and the senses become important loci for philosophical activity. Indeed, the imagination uses the sensual data of human corporeality in order to give phenomenal expression to that which exists without corporeal extension. Rather than subscribe to the traditional assumption that the medieval philosophers denigrated the body and matter, I contend that they realized that they could not dispense with these features and, thus, used them as one of the primary means at their disposal to apprehend the transcendental. And it is precisely within this framework that we must contextualize the rich sensual descriptions of the initiatory tales.

I am well aware that my discussion of Greek philosophy in this chapter is not particularly original. Despite this, my goal in discussing the Greek philosophers is twofold. First, I aim to show one of the two main sources whence the medieval philosophers derived their ideas. (The other, of course, is the sacred scripture, either the Hebrew Bible or the Qur᾽ān, depending upon one's tradition.) Second, I am not necessarily concerned with the "real Plato" or the "real Aristotle," but rather with such figures as seen from the vantage point of the eleventh- and twelfth-century Islamicate world. From this perspective, the ideas of Plato or Aristotle were often intermingled through the prism provided by the Neoplatonic commentators of late antiquity.

Chapters 3–5 represent the core of the study. In chapter 3, I focus particularly on the role and function of the imagination. This faculty represents something of a paradox in the history of Western philosophy. On the one hand, many follow Plato and condemn it as mistrustful, the part of our psyche that threatens ratiocination since it creates its own reality by making things absent appear as present, in dreams or even while one is awake. Yet, on the other hand, this ability to present the absent is also one of the imagination's greatest virtues. In this regard, it now becomes the faculty responsible for representing the spiritual world in terms of the categories of the sensual one. Without the imagination, knowledge of the divine is impossible. We see this at work in Neoplatonism in general and in the treatises that are the subject of this study in particular, especially when it comes to the denouement of the philosophical quest. Without wanting to mystify or de-rationalize this denouement, it becomes readily apparent that these texts culminate in a vision of the divine wherein the initiate must see through his or her inner eye. This, I contend, is a code word for the imaginative faculty.

To begin the process of rehabilitating the imagination, I have found it useful to employ some of the terminology of the German philosopher Martin Heidegger. Within this system, the imagination now becomes the locus that allows the individual to experience modes of Being that are otherwise inaccessible. The imagination becomes the faculty that enables us to apprehend the transcendental by means of the phenomenality by which it shows itself. Images, the epistemological currency of the imagination, are not simple translations of the ineffable into three dimensions; in effect, they become part and parcel of the divine. To use the language of Heidegger, there can be neither logos nor an appreciation of it without phenomena.

The *Ḥayy ibn Yaqẓān* cycle exploits this use of imagination not only in the initiate's textual protagonist but in the reader as well. In effect, the reader is invited into the narrative and encouraged to experience the journey through the eyes of the protagonist. This role of a journey that includes (especially in the versions of Avicenna and ibn Ezra) encounters with sacred springs and all-consuming fires, culminating in a distinct telos, led me to conceptualize these narratives as symbolic rituals. In the fourth chapter, therefore, I examine these treatises from the theoretical perspective of ritual studies. In particular, I analyze these texts through the prism of the tripartite scheme developed by van Gennep and Turner, and nuanced by later theorists such as Grimes. Such an approach enables us to envisage these texts from the perspective of the history of religions. For we see at work in them some of the classic paradoxes and tensions that are foundational to human experience, and that religion in general and ritual in particular seek to mediate: sacred and profane, pollution and purification, death and rebirth, ignorance and gnosis, mortality and immortality. By examining medieval texts from this disciplinary perspective, I hope to show how the philosophers who are the subject of this study cannot be neatly categorized. Furthermore, these texts are not simply about what we today call philosophy; rather, they are also concerned with the religious life and how it relates to human felicity. These authors used as many means, textual and supratextual, at their disposal to describe the quest of an individual to move beyond the inherited way of apprehending the world.

The final chapter is devoted to the philosophical content of these three treatises. My main contention is that the medieval Islamic and Jewish philosophers developed aesthetics as a distinct sub-field of philosophy and that these texts represent the literary expression of this. Until now, historians of medieval literature have primarily studied this material. I argue, however, that the analysis of such material needs to be viewed against the broader background of the history of philosophy. All of the medieval Neoplatonists worked on the Platonic assumption that anything beautiful in this world participated in and derived its harmony and order from a formal and celestial beauty. The subsequent result was the elucidation of an ontological relationship between intelligible and sensible beauty, in which the latter is necessary for the apprehension of the former. For these individuals, the only justifiable purpose of artistic enjoyment resided in the fulfillment of some basic psychological or noetic need that in turn could enable the individual to fulfill his or her true telos. As a result, the medieval philosophical conception of beauty was rarely treated as a distinct subject of philosophical inquiry. Rather, it was often subsumed within other discussions, particularly those relating to ontology, epistemology, metaphysics, and ethics. Despite this, all agreed that the philosophical importance of beauty resided in its centrality to the noetic development of the individual. Finally, I attempt to address why Avicenna, ibn Ezra, and ibn Ṭufayl—all important philosophers in their respective traditions—would choose to write philosophical treatises in this literary form. What was it about this genre that provided them with something that more discursive prose could not?

The Courtly Ideal in Muslim Spain (al-Andalus)

Since two of our three authors were born on Spanish soil and since its cultural and intellectual presence looms large in this study, let me devote the remainder of this introduction to a brief overview of both the Jewish and Muslim context there. Although what follows is certainly not meant to be exhaustive, it does seek to emphasize the main cultural and intellectual trajectories that form the backdrop against which much of the rest of my analysis takes place. When the Muslims conquered Spain in 711,[17] they brought with them the grandeur of Islamicate culture and civilization. In 929, the process of consolidation having reached its peak, Abd al-Raḥman III declared himself caliph and asserted his own legitimacy over the Abbasid caliphal court at Baghdad.[18] By maintaining economic ties with Muslim lands from the East and North Africa, Spain (al-Andalus) became a true cosmopolitan center. Its capital, Cordoba, had more than seventy libraries, a factor that encouraged many great architects and scientists to settle there; the caliphs and rich patrons, in turn, established schools to translate classical philosophic and scientific texts into Arabic.[19] Although the center at Cordoba gradually fragmented into a number of courts,[20] the result was a rich intellectual, cultural, and social landscape that was grounded on the notion of *adab,* the polite ideal of cultured living that developed in the courts of medieval Islam. The *adīb* (pl. *udabāʾ*) was defined by social graces, literary tastes, and ingenuity in manipulating language. *Adab* proved to be very attractive to the local population, many of whom adopted the ideals of Islamicate culture, including the use of Arabic.[21]

By the third Islamic century, there existed an oft-quoted saying that the *adīb* differed from the *ᶜālim,* scientist, in that the latter specialized in only one branch of knowledge (*ᶜilm*) whereas the former dabbled in various branches of knowledge.[22] The *adīb* was someone who was intimately familiar with, and involved in, the courtly etiquette of Muslim centers of power. He was someone who both partook of and was supported by the lavish tastes and urbane lifestyle that the various courts—both in Andalus and in the East—offered. The *udabāʾ* were a class who occupied a high social standing and produced a fairly uniform high culture despite the heterogeneous nature of the Islamic Empire.[23] They were learned, wrote poetry, composed works of literary criticism, dabbled in philology and various other sciences, and read the latest philosophical treatises that made their way from the eastern domains of the empire. They tried to maintain a purity of diction and improvised on a set of stock literary motifs whenever a proper social situation arose.

This aesthetics had tremendous repercussions for all of those who found themselves within the cultural and intellectual orbit of Islam. Jews, in particular, were attracted to these themes. Subsequent contact with Islam led to ground-breaking developments in the areas of Jewish philosophy, Hebrew grammar, poetry, and poetics, to name but a few disciplines. As Jews assimilated Arabic paradigms of beauty, rhetoric, and eloquence, they began, as Ross Brann has documented, to translate them into autochthonous Jewish forms.[24] This fusion of biblical and humanistic horizons created a rich, flexible vocabulary in which the Andalusi Jews expressed themselves.

Although Jews lived for the most part on the margins of Andalusi society, they did not simply mimic the culture and values of the dominant culture.[25] Simply to adopt these values would lead to assimilation of Jewish culture to its Arabo-Islamic model. On the contrary, the Jewish courtier class effectively lived in two competing worlds and served as the fault line between these worlds, producing a creative, though often tense and ambiguous, synthesis. For example, rather than simply write Arabic poetry, these Jews adopted Arabic prosody, yet composed poetry in Hebrew and with motifs that resonated with biblical imagery. In like manner, rather than jettison the biblical narrative, the Andalusi exegetes read the sacred text through the lenses that the new culture provided.[26] As Jews learned Arabic and its various literary models, they nevertheless remained steadfast to their traditions. Unlike the Arab poets, the Hebrew poets not only wrote secular love poetry, but they composed sacred poetry (much of which comprises part of the Jewish liturgy to this day), wrote philosophical treatises, were often the religious leaders of their communities, and were the jurists who administered the religious law (*halakhah*). However, an underlying nationalistic framework linked all of these disciplines. This allowed the Andalusi Jewish philosopher-aesthetes to demonstrate the superiority of Hebrew over Arabic and, based on this, that of Judaism over Islam. As a result, the Hebrew of the Bible, the language the Hebrew literati employed in their poetry—and, in the case of ibn Ezra with philosophy as well—became the aesthetic and rhetorical standards of the age.[27] This led to a situation in which, as Dan Pagis noted, the Andalusi-Jewish poets modeled themselves on the biblical prophets.[28]

In drinking from the cultural stream of medieval Islam, Jews suddenly found themselves with a new discourse and rhythm with which to mine the depths of the religious life.[29] The repercussions of this encounter were manifold. In expressing themselves in Arabic using the categories of Islam, the Jews internalized a culture different from their own. This did not just involve writing Hebrew poetry in a meter learned from the Arabs or composing philosophical treatises in Arabic. We need to be aware of a fundamental tension here: How did a group absorb both the cultural and the linguistic expressions of another group and still retain its own identity? How, then, do we understand the Andalusi-Jewish cultural expression?[30] Is it a reflection of "the anxiety of influence"?[31] Is it imitative?[32] Or, should we situate it against a polemical background as Jews tried to overcome the ambiguities associated with their cultural, social, and linguistic assimilation of Arabo-Islamic ideals?[33]

Ross Brann has recently attempted to re-examine, correctly in my opinion, the traditional answers to such questions. He argues that the Andalusi-Jewish intelligentsia created a "discourse of power" by which they not only stressed their own superiority over other Jewish communities, but also subversively appropriated Arabic culture for their own ideological purposes.[34] It is important not to lose sight of the fact that the language the Andalusi-Jewish intellectuals spoke molded the questions that they asked, the categories they employed to answer such questions, and the answers they considered to be satisfactory or not. In the study that follows, I shall examine this in greater detail as it relates specifically to ibn Ezra's *Ḥay ben Meqitz* and its relationship to Avicenna's Arabic text. In so doing, I will focus on the way in which Jews thought with the categories of Arabo-Islamic civilization and how they were able to participate in the pluralistic and multi-cultural Andalusi intellectual life.

The year 1147 sounded a death knell to much of this way of life, for it marked the invasion of the puritanical Almohades into Spain from North Africa. This dynasty was determined to put an end to what they perceived to be the religious laxity that they witnessed among the Andalusian intellectual and courtier classes. They demanded, *inter alia,* the conversion of all Christians and Jews to Islam.[35] It was during this period that many Jews left Spain: the majority went north to Christian territories.[36] The Almohade invasion signaled the end of one of the most fascinating and eclectic eras of world history.

This period in which Jews partook of Islamic culture and literature in al-Andalus was, in hindsight, relatively brief. Despite this brevity, however, it was a period to which later generations always looked and indeed continue to look back at with fondness. Although ibn Ezra spent only the first half of his life in Spain, he never fails to remind his readers that that is the place from which he came. The dynamic cultural and literary traditions that the Jews encountered and adopted as their own in Muslim Spain would live on even when its reality had receded to become nothing more than a distant memory. What follows is meant as a testament to the shared literary and philosophical categories of Judaism and Islam.

1

Reading the Divine: A User's Guide to the Initiatory Tale

Anyone who approaches texts necessarily brings to them certain questions and interests that, in turn, determine what of significance will be found. This is certainly the case with the *Ḥayy ibn Yaqẓān* cycle. Those who emphasize the Aristotelian component of medieval Neoplatonism tend to regard these texts as little more than simple allegories, a form of philosophy for the masses, or a type of philosophical primer. I have chosen, for heuristic purposes, to refer to this way of looking at these texts as the "minimalist" position. Occupying the opposite end of the continuum is a hermeneutical approach emphasizing the mystical dimensions of medieval Neoplatonism and that, in the process, downplays or marginalizes the philosophical component. According to the scholars who subscribe to this position, these texts become quasi-mystical treatises, texts in which the medieval philosophers were able to develop most fully their insights into the unfolding of the universe and the relationship of the individual soul to this process. For reasons that I hope are obvious I have called this approach the "maximalist." In the present chapter, I attempt to walk the middle ground between these two hermeneutical strategies or approaches. My argument is that these texts are neither marginal nor at the center of medieval Islamic and Jewish thought. On the contrary, they are important philosophical treatises and, in order to understand them properly, it is necessary to connect them to some of the broader intellectual and cultural trajectories of medieval Islamicate civilization.

Since these three texts share a similar set of literary, aesthetic, and philosophical assumptions, I argue that they are not *ad hoc* creations, but represent a distinct genre of medieval Islamicate philosophical literature. It is for this reason that I bring ibn Ezra's *Ḥay ben Meqitz* into this study since, even though written in Hebrew, it nonetheless partakes of the dynamic intellectual milieu enjoyed by the other two philosophers. Consequently, unlike previous approaches that tend to view these texts as individual narrative units, I contend that there exist very good reasons for reading them together. This chapter paves the way for such a reading and, within this context, attempts to articulate a framework in which we can begin to re-examine and rethink the *Ḥayy ibn Yaqẓān* cycle.

Significantly, each one of our authors did not necessarily know of the existence of the others. Obviously Avicenna, who was born about a generation before the other two and in the eastern Islamic world, could not have known of either ibn Ezra or ibn Ṭufayl. Despite this, these two latter authors were intimately familiar with Avicenna's work.[1] As far as his *Ḥayy ibn Yaqẓān* is concerned, ibn Ezra's *Ḥay ben Meqitz* so closely follows its structure that it is obvious he knew Avicenna's text well. In like manner, the stated goal of ibn Ṭufayl's *Ḥayy* is to unlock the secrets of Avicenna's work. Moreover, since ibn Ṭufayl seems to have written his text between 1177 and 1182,[2] obviously ibn Ezra (d. 1164) could not have read it. Similarly, even though ibn Ṭufayl was an older contemporary and countryman of ibn Ezra, it is highly unlikely that he would have known Hebrew. My goal in bringing these three narratives into conversation with each other is not simply historical or to establish a series of influences between either the eastern and western Islamic worlds, or medieval Islam and Judaism. On the contrary, my analysis seeks to ground them in a particular historical moment, showing how they represent, on a small scale, the intersection of some of the various cultural, intellectual, and aesthetic features that were defining elements of medieval Islamicate civilization.

Despite the fact that I envisage these texts as a genre, I have no desire to downplay their differences. Indeed, according to J. Z. Smith, comparison is much more productive and meaningful when it takes difference and complexity into consideration.[3] For this reason, Smith stresses the importance of a "third-term" type of comparison over the more traditional "two-term" variety. For instance, the latter (e.g., *x* resembles *y*) is often based on extra-historical categories and is, therefore, often predicated on ideological or political concerns. A "third-term" type of comparison (*x* resembles *y* more than *z* with respect to . . .), by contrast, is desired.[4] Within this context, ibn Ṭufayl's narrative, for example, departs radically from those of Avicenna and ibn Ezra, especially when it comes to the role of political science within the noetic development of the individual. Moreover, ibn Ezra's narrative absorbs the basic philosophical and mystical presuppositions of his Arab Muslim colleagues, yet renders them in a very poetic Hebrew to appeal to a Jewish audience. It is, thus, important not to regard ibn Ezra's work as a simple Hebrew translation of Avicenna's Arabic text; rather, it is necessary to ask about the specific concerns, Jewish or otherwise, that his text seeks to address.

Of particular concern to me is the way in which these tales are of fundamental human significance. What follows, both in this chapter and in this study as a whole, is not meant to be a technical discussion of medieval Islamic and Jewish philosophy. Certainly this text will address such philosophical concepts as the role and function of the imagination and the relationship between ontology and epistemology. Yet my overarching concern is to articulate a way in which we can yield fundamental insight into why, in any culture or period, people might compose texts such as these. Why did our authors, some of the most important philosophers of the Middle Ages, write at such length about the mythological and poetic journey of the individual soul? Why, in their world, was this a compelling thing to do? What were the questions of the day that these texts seek to answer? What sense can we, today, make of such texts?

The key to begin understanding the *Ḥayy ibn Yaqẓān* cycle resides in the eclectic mélange of eleventh- and twelfth-century Neoplatonism. Although this produced a dynamic intellectual environment, it is one that is potentially difficult to grasp due to the fact that individual Neoplatonists had many divided and competing loyalties. Conceptual, not to mention taxonomic, difficulties arise whenever one has a loyalty to disciplines as diverse as poetry and philosophy, or religious law (Ar. *sharīʿa;* Heb. *halakhah*) and astrology. How, for example, do we make sense of our authors' disparate disciplinary allegiances? Are these various loyalties arbitrary or is there something that unifies them? Did they have so many divided and potentially fracturing loyalties that those loyalties ultimately cancel each other out? Or is there some principle or overriding purpose that abrogates them?

Furthermore, there is an inherent tension in the terms "Muslim Neoplatonist" and "Jewish Neoplatonist." Within Neoplatonism, a number of "disciplines"—for example, logic, astronomy, astrology, literary criticism, aesthetics, and mysticism—sit together, often uncomfortably.[5] We compound this once we attach to it the adjective "Jewish" or "Muslim," both of which ostensibly entail another set of loyalties, to a particular law, a particular mythos, and a specific language. This becomes even more complicated in the case of the Jewish philosophers once we add to this the specific Arabo-Islamic notion of *adab* (courtly ideal of cultured living) that many found so attractive. Can there be any doubt, then, that these individuals had many allegiances? The difficult question, of course, is how to make sense of such allegiances.

Within this context, it is important to remember two key features. First, Neoplatonism, as I just mentioned, was extremely interdisciplinary. Indeed, the more disciplinary perspectives used to illumine Truth the better. Second, Neoplatonism, like many of the philosophical schools of late antiquity, did not regard philosophy simply as an intellectual commitment, but rather as what Pierre Hadot calls a "way of life."[6] The complexities of life thus demand a complex, interdisciplinary methodology. One turned to philosophy in order to receive a broad-based scheme or pattern of life, which was the *sine qua non* of the good life or human felicity.

Some of the central concerns of Neoplatonists, and these are themes that I will articulate more fully in the next chapter, are the limitations of language, the awakening of the soul to its true home in the heavens, and the personal, experiential component of wisdom. The goal of the medieval Neoplatonists was not the construction of a system based only on internal coherence and derived solely from propositions. The Neoplatonic text, on the contrary, attempts to foster in the reader the capacity for vision, insight, and self-awakening. In order to do this, Neoplatonists applied a number of textual strategies and employed a variety of disciplinary commitments.

The overarching concern of Neoplatonism was the purification of the soul. This was an endeavor that involved the imagination, the senses, and the emotions, in addition to the intellect. All of these various faculties therefore have philosophical importance. Significantly, though, one cannot affect the imagination or the senses in the same way as one does the intellect. This is one of the reasons why the Neoplatonists employed so many different loyalties: as a way to speak to the entire individual in order to transform him or her in his or her entirety.

Within this context, Neoplatonism admits of no disciplinary allegiances. There exists only one allegiance: the purification of the soul so that it can ascend to its true home. All other concerns are secondary. One can be a poet, a mathematician, a geometrist, a metaphysician, or an astrologer. Each one of these sciences provides a particular perspective on, or insight into, Truth that the other sciences might not. However, this can, at least from our perspective today, create certain difficulties. For example, how can ibn Ezra be committed to both the science of astrology that admits of determinism on the one hand, and the Law that mitigates against this, and, in its stead, demands freedom of choice, on the other? Despite such difficulties, the point is that the more sciences or disciplines that one can bring together, the better the chance of arriving at Truth. Unlike philosophers today, the Neoplatonists in their interdisciplinarity were not worried about doing each discipline justice.

Neoplatonism was more than just a philosophical system; rather it represented a hybrid—part philosophy, part mysticism, part poetry, part aesthetics—that included elements from a variety of cultural sources. In what follows, I argue that we need to situate these texts precisely within this interdisciplinary context. In order to do this, I attempt to define what an initiatory tale is, begin the process of articulating its component parts, and explore the manner in which these parts contribute to a broader meaning. This will lead into a discussion about some of the features that the *Ḥayy ibn Yaqẓān* cycle share: What assumptions do they have in common? How do the various authors articulate these assumptions?

Why Initiatory Tale? Toward Defining a Genre

In the secondary literature, these tales have been called many things. In the *editio princeps* of the Arabic text by ibn Ṭufayl, Edward Pococke referred to the text as an autodidactical treatise.[7] Since that time, the initiatory tale has also been referred to by the following names: "philosophical tales,"[8] "philosophical treatises,"[9] "philosophical novels,"[10] "visionary recitals,"[11] and, of course, "allegories."[12] Each of these terms, however, implies something quite different and each, in one way or another, potentially obfuscates by narrowing the scope of these rich narratives.

Implicit in the aforementioned terms that include the adjective "philosophical" is the assumption that these treatises are primarily about philosophy. Indeed, the fact that they were written by some of the best-known philosophers in both Islam and Judaism—Avicenna, ibn Ezra, ibn Ṭufayl—immediately alerts us to the fact these should be, in some way, designated as philosophical works. However, "philosophy" of the eleventh- and twelfth-century Neoplatonic variety, as I have already indicated, means something considerably different than what we today mean by this term. While the philosophical component can certainly not be ignored, we must equally not lose sight of the mystical, or, perhaps more accurately, the trans-philosophical dimensions of these tales. It is for precisely these reasons that it is necessary to view these tales against a broader cultural, literary, intellectual, and religious background than is traditionally done. Such an approach should, ideally, emphasize the various disciplinary perspectives that are at work in the way these tales construct and generate meaning.

But if these texts are not simply about philosophy, how do we understand their literary dimensions? Does one study them as literary works? Their form and structure are, after all, highly literary and poetic. Yet, on the other side of the coin, if we do this, do we risk marginalizing their content? These tales do, certainly, concern themselves with the career and fate of the soul, the structure of the universe, knowledge of God, and similar topics worthy of philosophical analysis. Consequently, we must avoid simply reducing them to the literary.

Following the lead of Martha Nussbaum, I contend that we need to envisage these tales at the interface of philosophy and literature.[13] They represent a style of philosophy that is at odds with the abstract, detached style and structure of what we customarily call philosophical prose. Such prose, according to Nussbaum, is a mode of discourse meant to reflect a God-like activity with the assumption that, by engaging in it, we are able to transcend our humanity.[14] This mode of analysis, however, is informed by the *a priori* notion that reason is a transcendent feature of the universe and that when we engage in it, we somehow become disembodied, distinct from the peculiarities of our bodies.[15] This approach to philosophy, however, is detached from specific contexts, thereby ignoring the genius of what it means to be human. It is the fragility of the human condition—both the joyful and painful awareness that we possess bodies, senses, emotions, imaginations—that provides us with the desire to philosophize in the first place.[16]

Because we are humans, not gods, we tell stories. Stories provide us with narratives through which we both encounter and interact with the uncertainties and vicissitudes of our existence. Philosophy, with its discursive and abstract reasoning, seeks to free us from the complexity and desires of our particularity.[17] Literature, on the contrary, sees in the messiness of this complexity a key to unlock the meaning of our encounter with this world. The initiatory tale, then, is not about "philosophy" versus "literature." Rather, it is a form of philosophical literature that attempts to combine the universal and abstract quality of philosophy with the particular concerns that are the provenance of literature. It is certainly no coincidence that these tales were written, as I shall argue throughout this study, in a milieu that stressed the interplay and correspondence between phenomenon and logos by means of an emanative ontology.

We witness this most clearly in the denouement of the tales. For although the majority of these texts recount in allegorical fashion the standard teachings of medieval Islamicate Neoplatonism, each one culminates in the protagonist achieving a goal that is ultimately outside of both the text and the realm of reason.[18] On a fundamental level, then, these tales are not just about philosophy, even though the author of each of these tales is a well-known philosopher. Each one intimates that the philosophical sciences will only take the hero so far, and that the ultimate moment involves a mystical vision (Ar. *mushāhada*) and taste (Ar. *dhawq*) of the divine.

For this reason, and after much reflection and recidivism, I have opted to refer to narratives that comprise the *Ḥayy ibn Yaqẓān* cycle by the term "initiatory tale."[19] The adjective "initiatory" conveys a ritualistic meaning, intimating that the textual protagonists undergo profound existential changes in the course of their textual journeys. In other words, they are *initiated* into the secrets of the universe.[20] Even though these secrets are philosophical (and here I depart from the likes of the maximalists), they ultimately culminate in a vision of the divine world. So although this vision comes about through the study of the various philosophical sciences, it cannot simply be reduced to such sciences. The textual protagonists undergo the classical ritual paradigm that is characterized by the tripartite structure of separation (from their customary existence), marginalization (from their traditional mode of Being-in-the-world) and ultimately aggregation (back into society as new and changed individuals).[21]

What are the advantages of employing the term "initiatory tale"? First, the scope becomes wider if we can avoid using the adjective "philosophical." (To reiterate, though, philosophy is obviously important here precisely because well-known philosophers wrote the texts.) Secondly, "tale" as a translation of the Arabic *qiṣṣa* (literally, a "story," or "narrative"),[22] or even *risāla* (lit. a "tract," "small treatise," "discourse," or even "recital")[23] is more appropriate than the term "novel," which is essentially a word with a modern provenance. Third, there is a distinct initiatory aspect to these tales. The protagonist must undergo a journey (in some of the tales it is literal, whereas in others it is metaphorical) through various sciences and cosmological levels. At the interface between these sciences/levels, the protagonist is initiated into those of the next level. Within this context, there exists a clever transference between the protagonist and the reader, in which the latter must identify with the former.

Ḥayy ibn Yaqẓān: Three Variations on a Theme

The three texts that are the subject of this study all share a similar plot, structure and characters. My goal in the present section is twofold: first, to provide a brief, non-exhaustive, biography of each of the three thinkers, showing how and where they fit into the broader picture of medieval Islamic and Jewish thought; second, to provide a short plot-summary of each of the three narratives to ensure that we are all in agreement about their basic outlines. I include mentions of their similarities and differences. This is also meant to be non-exhaustive, as the rest of this study will be devoted to an in-depth analysis of these narratives.

Avicenna and His Ḥayy ibn Yaqẓān

Unlike many of the other medieval Islamic philosophers, we know a great deal about Avicenna (ibn Sīnā), since he is one of the few philosophers, either ancient or medieval, who wrote an autobiography.[24] Avicenna was born in 980 near Bukhārā, in a town called Afshana. He spent a good part of his earliest years studying the various sciences, and claims to have mastered them by the age of eighteen.[25] As an adult, he was employed as a courtier and a physician, spending the majority of his life in the royal courts of the area, many of which were rampant with political intrigue. Within this environment, he often traveled among the courts seeking patronage and employment from their rulers. This was, by all accounts, a rather vicarious way to make a living, and there is evidence that, in several near-disastrous reversals, Avicenna spent time in jail where he was threatened with execution.

Avicenna is not only one of the greatest of all the Islamic philosophers, but also one of the most important figures in the history of Western philosophy. Avicenna was a true polymath. He composed treatises in virtually all of the sciences: Logic, Psychology, Medicine, Metaphysics, Poetics, and Rhetoric, to name but a few. His *magnum opus* is the monumental *al-Shifāʾ* (The healing), the majority of which is written as a commentary to the Aristotelian corpus. He also wrote different compendia of *al-Shifāʾ*, for example, *al-Najāt*, *ᶜUyūn al-ḥikma*, and *al-Hidāya*, and composed a famous treatise on medicine, *al-Qānūn fī al-ṭibb*, that became the standard textbook for medicine in the West for well over five hundred years.[26]

Avicenna's *Ḥayy ibn Yaqẓān*, chronologically the first of our three tales, tells of an unnamed protagonist and his three friends who encounter a beautiful, old, yet youthful-looking man outside an unspecified city. The protagonist, intrigued by the peaceful countenance of this man, sojourns toward him, seeking out his company. In the presence of three companions, the protagonist asks the man his name and place of origin, to which he replies: "My name is Ḥayy, son of Yaqẓān, my home is the city of the holy dwelling (*madīna al-bayt al-muqaddas*)."[27]

Ḥayy subsequently informs the protagonist of the true nature of his three traveling companions, who, if left unchecked, will mire him in the world of bodily and sensual desires.

Ḥayy encourages the protagonist to temper the negative effects of these companions by playing them off one another. However, in order to become like Ḥayy, he must abandon them entirely. Although this can be done intermittently, it can only be achieved completely at corporeal death. Ḥayy then offers to sketch for the protagonist a map of what his potential initiation will ideally look like. After the protagonist bathes in a sacred spring, Ḥayy points out two paths, one moving toward the East and the other toward the West. Ḥayy first describes the contents of the Western path. This path is divided into distinct regions: following an area of "perpetual darkness," in which there exists no inhabitant, Ḥayy describes various regions in which different races of people dwell, some of whom are wise and kind, others of whom are ignorant and cruel. Finally, at the end of this path, there exists a kingdom whose inhabitants are described as spiritual angels (*al-rūḥānīyūn min al-malāʾika*).[28] From this kingdom, "the Divine Command (*al-amr al-ilāhī*) and Destiny (*al-qadar al-ilāhī*) descend upon all those who occupy the degrees below."[29]

Ḥayy then describes the contours of the Eastern path. This is a path that, although initially full of the objects with which we are familiar, quickly gives way to angels and demons who are constantly at war not only with one another, but also with humans. Proceeding further along this path, there exist spiritual angels who are responsible for guiding the initiate to the correct path that subsequently leads to the King (*al-malīk*), who is beyond all description and comprehension. The tale finally culminates in a rich vision, in which the initiate is able to apprehend and experience the divine.

Ibn Ezra and His Ḥay ben Meqitz

In ibn Ezra, we witness all of the glories and tensions that the life and times of the Andalusi Jewish philosopher-aesthete embodied. Drawn to the universal themes of Arabo-Islamic culture on the one hand, he was nonetheless aware of the particularities of the Jewish people on the other. It is the synthesis of these two trajectories that makes ibn Ezra's work representative of Jews who shared his class, time, and geography. Ibn Ezra was born in 1089 in the town of Tudela, in the northeastern region of Castille, the same place as his older contemporary Judah Halevi. As a son of a wealthy Jewish family, ibn Ezra received a rich and variegated education: the Bible, Talmud, and other traditional subjects, as well as the literature, science, philosophy, and culture of the Arabs.

With the fall of Tudela to the armies of Alfonso I, the king of Aragon, in 1115, ibn Ezra left the city of his birth and began what would prove to be a lifetime of peregrinations. In the years immediately following his departure from Tudela, he traveled throughout Spain, both Muslim and Christian. On these journeys, he met many other famous Jews of his generation: Joseph ben Jacob ibn Ẓaddik,[30] Judah Halevi,[31] Abraham ibn Daud,[32] and Moses ibn Ezra.[33] Unfortunately, we know relatively little about his encounters with such individuals or, for that matter, many of the facts surrounding the first half of his life.[34]

Following these travels in Spain, ibn Ezra crossed the Mediterranean and wandered throughout North Africa, visiting the Jewish communities in, among other places, Tunis, Fez, Marrakesh, and Algiers. In Tunis he stayed with the wealthy ibn Jamᶜa family. And it was in response to a request from Samuel ben Jacob ibn Jamᶜa, a like-minded poet and philosopher, that ibn Ezra wrote his *Ḥay ben Meqitz.*[35]

Meanwhile in Spain, the fate of the Jewish communities worsened, as they were essentially caught between the armies of the Christian Reconquista on the one hand and the fanaticism of the Muslim Almoravids on the other. In 1140—the same year Judah Halevi set sail for the land of Israel—ibn Ezra left Spain never to return.[36] He left for Rome, penniless and full of fear. From 1140 until his death in 1164, he traveled to Luca, Pisa, Verona, Southern France (where he met the grandsons of Rashi), and London. He witnessed the great sufferings of the Jewish communities throughout Europe,[37] yet nevertheless constantly taught the universalism of Judaism, its correspondence to truth and the various sciences, and the need for individuals to perfect their rational faculties.

Despite his constant traveling, this period was amazingly productive for ibn Ezra. He wrote commentaries (often at least two) to many biblical books;[38] he also wrote mathematical, astronomical, astrological, grammatical, and philosophical treatises. Ibn Ezra's scholarship had a tremendous impact on later Jewish thought and mysticism. His biblical commentaries, to this day, remain an indispensable tool for clarifying texts.[39] In addition, many later Jewish and non-Jewish scientists of the Middle Ages cite his astronomical and astrological treatises.[40] Despite this, ibn Ezra's position as a Jewish philosopher has never been firmly established, largely due to the unsystematic nature of his writings. This, compounded with the fact that he never wrote a philosophical treatise *per se,*[41] often leads to the charge that he was nothing more than a philosophical dilettante.[42]

Ibn Ezra's *Ḥay ben Meqitz* is, in terms of the characters and the plot, almost identical to Avicenna's. This, however, is not to say that it is simply a copy of the earlier work. Ibn Ezra, for instance, seems to have been much more interested in the literary and poetic dimensions of the text. This may stem from the fact that either ibn Ezra was an accomplished poet or because he was aware of contemporaneous theories governing the notion of plagiarism (Ar. *sariqa*), in which originality was not defined by who says what first, but by the embellishment of traditional, well-known motifs (Ar. *ma*ᶜ*ānī*).[43]

Whereas Avicenna's text only describes what the journey might be like, ibn Ezra's protagonist actually undergoes the journey. Since the journey in ibn Ezra's *Ḥay* is actual, the structure is somewhat different: ibn Ezra is more interested in the vertical structure of the universe, and he ignores the horizontal dimensions. For this reason, ibn Ezra does not divide the cosmos into an East–West horizontal axis.

Another feature of ibn Ezra's *Ḥay* that is lacking, for obvious reasons, in the other narratives, is the Jewish and Hebrew component. For instance, ibn Ezra uses the sacred scripture of his tradition in a way that Avicenna does not. His *Ḥay* is essentially a pastiche of biblical words, phrases, and verses. It is not *other* than the Bible; indeed, it is essentially a retelling of the Bible that describes the Neoplatonic career of the soul. In so doing, ibn Ezra takes the themes and motifs of Avicenna's narrative and makes them into a Jewish and Hebrew narrative.

Ibn Ṭufayl and His Ḥayy ibn Yaqẓān

Of the three authors, we know the least about ibn Ṭufayl. He was born in 1116 in Guadix (Wādī Āsh), about fifty kilometers from the important intellectual and cultural center of Granada. We know very little about his family, education, or upbringing other than that his father was a scholar from Marchena.[44] He worked as a physician and in 1154 became a secretary to the governosr of Ceuta and Tangier.[45] He eventually caught the attention of the Muwaḥḥid caliph Abū Yaᶜqūb Yūsuf, who appointed him as court physician in 1163. He resigned this post in 1182 because of ill health and was replaced by the young Averroes. According to some accounts, ibn Ṭufayl was responsible for both introducing the young Averroes to court and encouraging him to write his commentaries to the Aristotelian corpus.[46] According to al-Andalusī, when Abū Yaᶜqūb died, ibn Ṭufayl was jailed under the suspicion of poisoning him.[47] Whether or not this actually happened, ibn Ṭufayl himself died the following year, 1186, and was given the equivalent of a state funeral.[48]

The philosophical milieu into which ibn Ṭufayl was born was, as he himself admits, relatively undeveloped. In a famous and oft-quoted passage, ibn Ṭufayl claims that the first generation of Andalusi thinkers were interested primarily in the study of mathematics, and the second generation had progressed to logic. It is only in the third generation, that of ibn Bājja, that Andalusis began to get "closer to the truth."[49] Part of this evolutionary schema may be due to historical circumstances: philosophy and philosophical inquiry were mistrusted and roundly criticized by the political and religious leaders of Spain and the Maghrib.[50] This gave way to a situation that Lawrence Conrad characterizes as follows:

> It is perhaps not surprising to find, then, that in Spain and the western Maghrib philosophy was a field of study that was pursued not as an established comprehensive discipline or under the aegis of a "school," but rather in limited special topics by individuals who often knew little about each other's work and had great trouble gaining access to seminal works of earlier writers.[51]

Luckily for ibn Ṭufayl, he lived in the enlightened age of Abū Yaᶜqūb Yūsuf who, as Vincent Cornell argues, was the only Muwaḥḥid caliph to display any interest in philosophy.[52] Ibn Ṭufayl, according to his own prologue, seems to have been familiar with the main thinkers and trajectories of Islamic philosophy, since he quotes from the work of Alfarabi (esp. *Al-Siyāsat al-madaniyya*, and a now lost commentary on Aristotle's *Nichomachean Ethics*), Avicenna (esp. *K. al-ishārāt wa al-tanbīhāt*), and al-Ghazali (esp. *Mishkāt al-anwār* and *Al-Munqidh min al-ḍalāl*). Despite this, however, we must not lose sight of ibn Ṭufayl's relationship to Sufism. Although he criticizes earlier Sufis such as Bisṭāmī (d. 874) and Hallāj (d. 922) for their willingness to disclose secrets, he nonetheless seems to be aware of the states to which they refer. Moreover, as Cornell has shown, ibn Ṭufayl actually studied with Abū al-Ḥasan ibn ᶜAbbād, himself a student of Aḥmad ibn Muḥammad al-Ghazali (d. 1126), the brother of the famous Abū Ḥāmid al-Ghazali (d. 1111).[53] These last two points should alert us to the danger of reducing the complex thought of ibn Ṭufayl simply to the "philosophical."

Unlike either Avicenna or ibn Ezra, we only possess the one work, *Ḥayy ibn Yaqẓān*, of ibn Ṭufayl. Despite this, his text is certainly the most complex and detailed of the three writers in our study.[54] Ibn Ṭufayl begins his narrative with a prologue, in which he provides us with an overview of the history of Islamic philosophy as he understood it. Following this, he moves into the narrative proper, relating two possible accounts of the birth of an individual named *Ḥayy ibn Yaqẓān*. In this respect, ibn Ṭufayl departs significantly from his two predecessors, who gave this name to the old sage. The rest of the narrative essentially relates Ḥayy's growth on a deserted island: he uses his intelligence to master his environment and subsequently learn all of the sciences by observing natural phenomena. He thus proceeds naturally from the physical and biological sciences to the astronomical sciences until he reaches the supreme science of metaphysics.

In observing the multiplicity of the natural world, Ḥayy gradually comes to appreciate that there must exist a unified, incorporeal principle that acts as a causal agent. This leads him to posit the existence of God, a figure that Ḥayy tries to emulate in his actions by means of various ascetic exercises. This finally gives way to a rich mystical experience, in which Ḥayy's self appears to be annihilated (*fanāʾ*) into God. Aware of the problems that such a statement poses for orthodox Islam, ibn Ṭufayl informs us that Ḥayy was mistaken and that rather than be a form of annihilation it was really one of conjunction (*ittiṣāl*).

Following this, the focus of the narrative shifts rather quickly and dramatically. One day an individual by the name of Absāl arrives on Ḥayy's island with the intention of escaping civilization. He has heard of the solitary Ḥayy and hopes to learn from him. They encounter one another and, after a tense introduction, eventually become friends. Absāl teaches Ḥayy how to speak and soon thereafter Absāl informs Ḥayy of religion. Ḥayy is intrigued, thinking religion approximates the truths that he has experienced, and wants to go to Absāl's island to learn more. When the two individuals arrive on the island, ruled by Salāmān, Ḥayy is ultimately disappointed: he realizes that the religion of the island, like all religions, is essentially a pale imitation, a set of symbols, of the truths that he has learned directly. So Ḥayy sets out to inform the island's inhabitants about what they are missing; needless to say, he is met with resistance and scorn. Ḥayy thus comes to the rather quick conclusion that most people are unable to fathom the true secrets of the divine, and that they prefer to think of God in simplistic and anthropomorphic terms. He nevertheless realizes that organized religion plays an important political role.

Other Genres, Other Tales

Despite the fact that this study deals with the initiatory dimension of the *Ḥayy ibn Yaqẓān* cycle, the genre of initiation is by no means unique to these texts. Indeed, my goal in examining these specific treatises is to illumine but one aspect of a much broader and wide-ranging phenomenon. The theme of initiation was, for example, a common one among the mystery cults of late antiquity.[55] Many of these themes were translated into an Arabo-Islamic idiom by way of the Ismāᶜīlīs and eventually they made their way into Sunni Islam and Judaism.[56] In this section I examine, briefly and generally, several contemporaneous and closely related initiatory genres that help us contextualize the *Ḥayy* cycle.[57] Of especial importance is the role of initiation and esoteric gnosis (*maᶜrifa*) in Ismāᶜīlī thought and praxis.[58] A central component of this religious movement was the initiation of the neophyte or adept into the mysteries of the tradition, whereby he or she would progress through various intellectual and cosmological stages.[59] Both pro- and anti-Ismāᶜīlī literature frequently makes mention of the role of initiation.[60] From such literature, we observe that initiates were sworn to observe esoteric (*bāṭin*) secrets by means of a special oath (*ᶜahd*).[61]

The *Ikhwān al-Ṣafāᵓ*, one of the most famous of all philosophical "brotherhoods," is believed by most scholars to be associated, in some way, with the Ismāᶜīlīs.[62] The *Ikhwān* were a group of men who probably lived in Basra sometime in the late tenth or eleventh centuries. Their writings, the *Rasāᵓil* (Epistles), emerged from meetings (*majālis*) of like-minded individuals, and eventually came to exert a large influence on subsequent Islamic and Jewish thought.[63] From these Epistles, we learn that the Brethren were very much a "secret society," in much the same manner as the Pythagoreans, and were open only to those initiated into the secrets of the group. Only initiates could attend their meetings, which were held at set, pre-arranged times.[64] Such meetings were supposed to be held every twelve days.[65]

Although philosophers, the Brethren were intimately concerned with non-discursive and symbolic textual strategies (e.g., allegories, anecdotes, Qurᵓānic quotations). As their name suggests, the Brethren were a select group of individuals who constantly emphasized the importance of purity (*ṣafāᵓ*), and only those who possessed such purity were allowed entrance into the group's teachings. Each individual had to undergo some form of initiation before he (and presumably they were only males) could be part of the Brethren:

> When they reach this stage and achieve the position [of exalted knowledge, noble deeds, and independence from others in their material needs], we are right to call them Ikhwān al-Ṣafāᵓ. Know, O brother, that the real truth (*haqīqa*) of the name is the special quality actually, not figuratively, inherent in those who are worthy of it. Know, O brother, may the most high God help you, that purity of soul only comes when the soul has reached a state of complete tranquility in both religious and earthly affairs. . . . The man who is not thus cannot be counted as one of the People of Purity (*ahl al-ṣafāᵓ*).[66]

Presumably, the neophyte's initiation into purity and tranquility occurred by means of a special liturgy and a regimen of spiritual praxes.[67] The *Ikhwān* also seem to have been particularly fond of the genre of the initiatory dialogue. Throughout the *Rasāʾil* we encounter various dialogues, the most famous of which is the *Epistle of the Animals.*[68] Another important Ismāʿīlī dialogue, or series of dialogues, is Jaʿfar ibn Manṣūr al-Yaman's *Kitāb al-ʿālim wa al-ghulām* (The master and the disciple).[69] This work, written in the tenth century, recounts a series of dramatic conversations between various neophytes seeking truth and those who have already been initiated into such matters.

Much like the *Ḥayy ibn Yaqẓān* cycle, the *K. al-ʿālim wa al-ghulām* is a highly literary text with a dramatic and full-scale narrative. Significantly, this tale, albeit in somewhat different terms, also revolves around the notion of three cosmological levels. The first level, that of the *ẓāhir,* represents this world and its mundane, exoteric realities; the second level, that of the *bāṭin,* refers to the inner secrets of this exoteric reality; and the final level, that of *bāṭin al-bāṭin,* "the innermost spiritual," refers to the "essential realities" of the universe.[70] Only "true humanity" (*ādamiyya*) has access to such cosmological secrets; this group, in turn, is divided into those who have already attained such gnosis, and those who are seeking it.[71] It is against this backdrop that the neophyte is initiated into the *bāṭin al-bāṭin:*

> So the Master (*al-ʿālim*) began to recite the oath (*ʿahd*) to the young man (*al-ghulām*), and he slowly repeated it and bound himself by it. The young man couldn't control himself because of his emotions, and his tears were streaming down because of the intensity of that moment, until [the Master] brought him to the end of the oath. So he praised God and glorified Him and gave thanks for all that had reached him, knowing with certainty that he was henceforth part of the party of God (Qurʾān 5:56; 58:22) and the party of God's friends because he had accepted the obligation of their oath. Then he finished his praises and became silent, and the Master began his explanation and clarification.[72]

In order to gain access, as this passage makes clear, the initiate was required to take an oath of allegiance. It was this oath that made certain that those unable to grasp the highest echelons of the cosmos, and the various esoteric sciences associated with it, were unable to gain access.

The spiritual autobiography was yet another genre that attempted to encode textually the initiatory process. Again, this was a genre that seems to have been fairly popular among the Ismāʿīlī missionaries (*dāʿīs*).[73] One of the most famous of Ismāʿīlī autobiographies is that of Naṣīr al-Dīn al-Ṭūsī (1201–1274). Ṭūsī describes his spiritual growth as a form of ascent, each level of which is accompanied by the lifting of a veil. Such a journey, however, is not something that one can undertake on one's own. One must begin as a novice, since, as he argues, it

> becomes clear that without the instruction (*ta*ᶜ*līm*) of a teacher (*mu*ᶜ*allim*), and the bringing to perfection (*ikmāl*) by an agent of perfection (*mukammil*), the attainment of the truth is not possible; that mankind, with its great number and differences of opinion, is mistaken in its claim that the truth can be reached solely through the intellect and reason.[74]

For Ṭūsī, then, the initiate can only proceed on the path with the guidance of one who has already been on it.[75] This role of the master–disciple relationship can also be seen in the initiatory genre of epistolary treatises.[76] Indeed, some of the most famous medieval philosophical texts were written in such a way that stressed the individual nature of the teaching. For instance, Maimonides' (d. 1204) *Guide of the Perplexed* and ibn Ṭufayl's *Ḥayy ibn Yaqẓān* are both written as teachings directed toward specific individuals in order to facilitate their journey along the path of intellectual perfection.[77] Maimonides, in his frame letter to the *Guide,* writes to his pupil Joseph ben Judah:

> When you read under my guidance texts dealing with astronomy and prior to that texts dealing with mathematics . . . I let you train yourself in that science, knowing where you would end. . . . I saw that you are one worthy to have the secrets of the prophetic books revealed to you so that you would consider in them that which perfect men ought to consider. Thereupon I began to let you see certain flashes and to give you certain indications. Then I saw that you demanded of me additional knowledge and asked me to make clear to you certain things pertaining to divine matters. . . . Then when God decreed our separation and you betook yourself elsewhere, these meetings aroused in me a resolution that had slackened. Your absence moved me to compose this Treatise, which I have composed for you and those like you, however few they are. I have set it down in dispersed chapters. All of them that are written down will reach you where you are, one after the other. Be in good health.[78]

Although Maimonides certainly does not have in mind the same kind of literal initiation that the Ismāᶜīlīs did,[79] one cannot deny that this quotation indicates a process of symbolic or intellectual initiation. For Maimonides, like the great majority of medieval Islamicate philosophers, knowledge was only for the intellectual elite and one had to do all that one could to prevent such knowledge from reaching the "masses."

It is against this background of "initiation" that we need to situate the *Ḥayy ibn Yaqẓān* narratives that form the core of this study. These initiatory tales had a relatively short career in Islamic and Jewish philosophy. These narratives flourished for about one hundred and fifty years before the Sufis—undoubtedly appreciating this genre's use of allegory and its ability to function on multiple narrative levels—adopted many of the motifs for their own epic poetry.[80] For all intents and purposes, the initiatory tale in Islamic philosophy entered the mainstream with Avicenna,[81] who wrote two other treatises in addition to *Ḥayy ibn Yaqẓān: The Story of Salāmān and Absāl* and *The Epistle of the Bird* (*Risāla al-ṭayr*).

Salāmān and Absāl[82] unfortunately exists only in a brief plot summary provided by a figure whom we have already encountered, Nasīr al-Din al-Ṭūsī (d. 1274).[83] According to his account, Absāl is the handsome and unmarried younger brother to Salāmān, who is the leader of an unnamed kingdom. One day, Salāmān's wife falls in love with Absāl and does everything in her power to seduce him. With the aid of her sister, she seeks to trap him on his wedding night, but is prevented from doing so because of an auspicious flash of lightning. Absāl subsequently flees with an army and meets with tremendous military success against the enemies of Salāmān. He returns to the kingdom to find Salāmān's wife's passion still unabated. He flees her advances so she arranges to have him killed in battle by paying his soldiers to abandon him. They do and he is injured and left for dead. However, a wild animal suckles him and nurses him back to health.[84] Salāmān's wife, realizing her love for Absāl will never be returned, finally devises a plan whereby a chef will poison him. Upon learning of his brother's death, Salāmān abandons the kingdom and becomes an ascetic. One day, when Salāmān is deep in contemplative prayer, God reveals to him the true nature of his brother's death. He subsequently returns to his kingdom and has his wife and the cook poisoned.

The Bird, by contrast, exists in a much fuller form.[85] This treatise, to use the words of Alfred Ivry, is "more personal, even poignant. It is written more in the first person, and conveys more emotion than Avicenna reveals in his other allegories."[86] The structure of this work consists of a prologue, main body, and epilogue. In the prologue, Avicenna expresses himself in paradoxical fashion:

> Brothers of truth, strip yourselves of your skins as the snake casts his. Walk like an ant, the sound of whose step none hears. Be like the scorpion that ever bears its weapon at the end of its tail, for it is from behind that the demon seeks to surprise men.[87]

The narrative consists of the story of a bird, once free, now captured in the snares of hunters. One day, the bird is part of a group that is able to escape from their cages after they learn of a land far away where they will be free. They are afraid to land on any of the mountains that they fly over, however, lest they be tempted to stay before completing their journey. They eventually arrive at a place whose resident birds inform them of a king who resides in a city just beyond the mountain. They arrive at this city and make their way to the king's castle, where they are granted an audience with him. They gaze at him and his great beauty, and ask him to remove the chains that are still fastened to their legs. He informs them that only those who locked them can open them. Nevertheless, he provides the birds with a messenger to accompany them back. At this point the narrative comes to an end.

These two texts are remarkably similar to his *Ḥayy ibn Yaqẓān*. They are, I contend, composed of a similar structure and, therefore, need to be conceived as occupying the same genre. Space prevents me from examining these two other treatises in any great detail, but suffice it to say that much of my analysis could easily be applied to illumine these other two narratives.

In addition to ibn Ezra's and ibn Ṭufayl's narratives, there are also a number of commentaries to Avicenna's *Ḥayy ibn Yaqẓān*. These responses to the original are useful because they reveal the manner in which the text was received. Despite this, if one assumes, as I do, that the form of these narratives is as significant as the content, the best a straightforward interpretation can do is connect the narrative to broader Avicennian themes; it can, however, do little in the way of explicating the form.[88] This is also in keeping with Avicenna's own theory of poetics: we assent to imaginative syllogisms through a process that is based on wonder and pleasure, not necessarily on truth or falsity. As a result, one cannot simply translate a poetic utterance into a literal or analytical one.

The two most influential commentators, ibn Zaylā and al-Jūzjānī,[89] both pupils of Avicenna, bring to full expression the philosophical dimensions of Avicenna's work. The fact that Avicenna's pupils wrote such commentaries is ample proof that his *Ḥayy ibn Yaqẓān* was meant to be more than just a philosophical text for the masses. Its narrative progression, its indeterminacy as regards philosophical vocabulary, its denouement—all demand interpretation on different levels. This is one of the central goals of these narratives: to force the individual to respond to the text, to anticipate its meaning.[90]

Ḥayy ibn Yaqẓān and the Enigma of "Oriental Wisdom"

Before proceeding, now is probably as good a time as any to discuss the infamous concept of "Oriental Wisdom" (*al-ḥikma al-mashriqiyya*) that plagues the study of medieval Islamic Neoplatonism in general and Avicennian scholarship in particular. Significantly, this controversy, for reasons that will shortly become apparent, is ultimately rooted in the *Ḥayy ibn Yaqẓān* cycle. The controversy revolves around how to define and what subsequently to do with the phrase. For how one interprets it ultimately affects one's understanding not only of these texts in particular, but of Islamic thought generally. In order to understand exactly what Avicenna might mean by the term "Oriental Wisdom," it is necessary to examine the various places within the Avicennian corpus that we encounter it. For example, in his prologue to *al-Shifāʾ*, Avicenna writes:

> I also wrote a book other than these two, in which I presented philosophy as it is in itself and as required by an unbiased attitude. . . . This is my book on Eastern philosophy (*al-ḥikma al-mashriqiyya*). But as for the present book, it is more elaborate and more accommodating to my Peripatetic colleagues. Whosoever wants the truth without indirection (*majmaja*), he should seek the former book; whoever wants the truth in a way that is somewhat conciliatory to colleagues, elaborates a lot, and alludes to things which, had they been perceived, there would have been no need for the other book, then he should read the present book.[91]

This passage, in turn, is often coupled with one from his introduction to "The Easterners" (the so-called "Manṭiq al-mashriqiyyīn"):

> We have resolved to compile a treatise on matters about which researchers have disagreed. In it we shall not proceed by following partisan considerations, our own fancy, customary practice, or personal habit. Nor shall we be concerned about any apparent departure on our part both from what those who study the books of the Greeks are accustomed to out of unmindfulness and obtuseness, and from what our position has been understood to be in books which we composed for the philosophers, who are infatuated with the Peripatetics and who think that no one else was ever guided by God or attained to His mercy.[92]

According to these two passages, Avicenna seems to intimate that there exists a path to truth other than the standard Aristotelian one. The actual contours of this "other path" are the object of extreme and one could say virulent debate. This controversy is further compounded by the fact that there exists an uncertainty about the exact number of works penned by Avicenna and the fact that some have been lost. Even though we do not possess these "other works" in which Avicenna outlines his so-called "Oriental Wisdom," this has not stopped many from either arguing that they did exist at one time or from trying to reconstruct it themselves.[93]

Further contributing to the controversy is ibn Ṭufayl's *Ḥayy ibn Yaqẓān*. In the prologue to this work, ibn Ṭufayl claims that it is his intention to explain "the secrets of the oriental wisdom (*asrār al-ḥikma al-mashriqiyya*) as mentioned by the prince of the philosophers, Avicenna."[94] He subsequently proceeds to discuss the importance of mystical vision (*mushāhada*) and taste (*dhawq*) of the divine, in addition to a quasi-mystical union (*ittiṣāl*) with God. This has led many to use ibn Ṭufayl's comments in order to project them back onto what "Oriental Wisdom" would have meant to Avicenna.[95]

These few statements have created a virtual cottage industry concerning the "real" Avicenna and the contents of his "real" philosophical system. This is an industry that continues unabated to this day. It has not only created an artificially schizophrenic Avicenna, but has obfuscated the true nature of his *Ḥayy ibn Yaqẓān*. The debate over "Oriental Wisdom" turns on what various interpreters make of the term "Oriental" (*mashriqiyya*). There exist, for all intents and purposes, two competing and diametrically opposed "camps" in this debate.[96] One camp, the "maximalist," probably best epitomized in the work of Henry Corbin (d. 1978), argues that when Avicenna refers to "Oriental Wisdom," he means an immediate and experiential system of gnosis (*ma^{c}rifa, ^{c}irfān*) that is juxtaposed against a more plodding and intellectual form of philosophy (*falsafa*).[97] Before I discuss the other camp, I think it worthwhile to try to articulate Corbin's larger project, one that is often missed in critiques of his work.

For Corbin, the "Orient," not necessarily used in its geographical sense, seems to represent the Heideggerian notion of "authenticity," the point at which we are most at home with ourselves. Accordingly, Corbin argues that the student of religion must not reduce religious data to history, sociology, psychology, and so on;[98] rather, he or she must understand this data as it originally uncovers itself to practitioners.[99] In order to do this, according to Corbin, the interpreter must participate in this uncovering. This is possible because the uncovering is not idiosyncratic or religion-specific; rather, it represents a specific manifestation of Being.[100] Just as Heidegger went all the way back to the Presocratics in an attempt to capture true philosophical thinking, the oriental gnostics provided Corbin with a similar source.[101] It was for this reason that Corbin was so interested in Persian thinkers such as Avicenna and Suhrawardī: they were the phenomena by which he could return to the logos of the ancient Persian sages.[102] Indeed, where Heidegger had argued that in order to break free of the traditional encrusted concepts of philosophy it was necessary to engage in their destruction, Corbin vociferously opposed the reductionism and historical positivism of the

Western academy.[103] Avicenna, Suhrawardī, and the other *Ishrāqī* thinkers thus provided Corbin with a way not only of critiquing the contemporary academic discourse, but also a way of recovering our authentic relationship with Being.

This led Corbin to emphasize the importance of the imaginal world and the concomitant notion of the imagination.[104] The imaginal world (alternatively known as the *mundus imaginalis* or *ᶜālam al-mithāl*) is qualitatively and quantitatively different from the historical and temporal world: it is the realm of "fundamental reality between mind and matter."[105] Within this realm, there exists an inner, esoteric history ("hierohistory").[106] Since this world is not bound by historical or causal connections, one can grasp intuitively the connections between, say, an Avicenna or Suhrawardī, on the one hand, and a Swedenborg or followers of Mithras or even those who search after the Holy Grail, on the other. It is at this point that the imagination becomes so important for Corbin. For this is the faculty that takes us into the immediate presence of the imaginal world. For it is ultimately the imagination that perceives the logos to which phenomena in this world point.[107] Departing from Heidegger, then, Corbin argues for the existence of an ontological realm that is independent of the world of form and matter wherein the individual has immediate access to Being. Moreover, this logos only reveals itself non-discursively to the faculty of the imagination.

It is precisely for this reason that Corbin takes an interest in these narratives, which he calls "visionary recitals." These recitals provide an access into Being that is not possible in other, more analytical works. Corbin argues that Avicenna substitutes "a dramaturgy for cosmology [and] the recitals guarantee the genuineness of the universe; it is veritably the place of a personally lived adventure."[108] Avicenna's *Ḥayy ibn Yaqẓān,* then, essentially presents Corbin with what he considers to be the proof of his methodology. For in this work, as I mentioned above, Avicenna divides the cosmos according to an East–West axis. He associates the West with matter, that is, with darkness and non-existence. The East (the infamous "Orient"), on the other hand is associated with form or light. Based on these comments and the ones that I already mentioned above from the prologue to the *Shifāʾ* and the "Easterners," Corbin feels justified in trying to articulate and re-create Avicenna's *ḥikma al-mashriqiyya.*

Corbin, it seems to me, ultimately reads too much into the sources and, as a result, creates a falsely bifurcated Avicenna. Despite this, Corbin is correct to regard these narratives as more than just a form of popular philosophy (in contrast to the other camp). In so doing, he shows that philosophy for the medieval Neoplatonists was not simply an intellectual system, but a "way of life" that was ultimately meant to be transformative to the entire individual.

The other camp, the "minimalist," argues that by "Oriental Wisdom," Avicenna does not mean a system different from his other works, but one that complements it and takes it in slightly different *intellectual* directions. For some scholars, most notably Dimitri Gutas, what Avicenna means by "Eastern" (*mashriqī*) is a school of Peripatetic philosophy located in the East, that is, Khurasan.[109] In other words, when Avicenna uses the term "Oriental Wisdom," he means to signal his frustration with the traditional Western (i.e., Baghdadi) form of Aristotelianism.[110]

Gutas is steadfastly opposed to any attempt that seeks to argue that there exists an experiential or mystical side to the thought of Avicenna. He claims that the approach of Corbin and his disciples (whom Gutas refers to as "hierophants") is a "non-issue" and accuses them of perpetuating a "scholarly hoax."[111] Unlike Corbin et al., Gutas spends very little time on works such as the "notorious" *Ḥayy ibn Yaqẓān.*[112] He locates treatises such as this within Avicenna's "symbolic method" (i.e., allegory):

> The symbolic method of presentation consisted for Avicenna in presenting Knowledge in images (*amthāl*) and symbols, either singly or in aggregates (*ramz/rumūz*), that corresponded one to one to the philosophical concepts in which this Knowledge was expressed when it reflected the syllogistic structure of the universe. By its very nature, this method of presentation was inferior to the demonstrative, and constituted the lowest possible denominator in which Knowledge could be communicated. It needs to be emphasized that the symbolic method *did not* communicate knowledge that was different, more true, or more profound than that communicated through the demonstrative method.[113]

Gutas is certainly correct to try and situate works such as *Ḥayy ibn Yaqẓān* within Avicenna's larger philosophical corpus. I also agree with him that what Avicenna presents in his narratives is not qualitatively different from that found in his more analytical treatises. However, I am not always convinced that there exists a "one-to-one" correspondence between these two methods of communication. In this regard, I hesitate to go so far as he does to assert that these narratives were written solely for "mentally inferior people."[114]

Moreover, Gutas downplays, and too easily marginalizes, the mystical dimensions of medieval Neoplatonism. In so doing he is too quick to equate the problems surrounding the thorny notion of "Oriental Wisdom" with the concept of intellectual mysticism in the thought of

Avicenna. This, of course, is obvious by the very title of Gutas's major work, *Avicenna and the Aristotelian Tradition.* For Gutas, in order to understand Avicenna properly it is essential to regard him primarily as an Aristotelian. In so doing, Gutas downplays the other aspects of Avicenna's commitment to Neoplatonism (e.g., theurgy, poetics, mythopoesis), a tradition that permitted many seemingly contradictory loyalties.

According to Gutas, Avicenna's system is rationalistic through and through. He claims that Avicenna

> used symbol and allegory, and some terminology from Sufism, in order to convey this knowledge that grants salvation to those best disposed to receive it in such a medium. Otherwise the symbols and Sufi terms correspond *exactly* to the philosophical concepts of his system. The *ᶜāref* mentioned in the final chapters of *Eshārāt,* for example, refers to the person whose soul has reached the stage of the acquired intellect.[115]

Here Gutas overstates his case.[116] Certainly, Avicenna is not a Sufi; despite this, however, one must not lose sight of the type of intellectual mysticism that so many of the medieval Neoplatonists found attractive. Indeed, Gutas all but ignores Avicenna's own statement in the *K. al-ishārāt,* wherein he talks about the various spiritual exercises that the *ᶜārif* must undergo in order to attain the level of vision. Moreover, Avicenna also states in the closing pages of this work that the imagination plays an important role in the acquisition of knowledge.

Perhaps I should briefly and explicitly restate my own position here. I contend that these texts are *not* part of some amorphous and undefined "Eastern Wisdom." Despite this, they need to be situated against a distinct strain of mystical vision that is inseparable from the telos of medieval Neoplatonism. Indeed, this emphasis on vision, imagination, and its ability to apprehend the divine is not an Eastern phenomenon; on the contrary, it is something that is firmly grounded within the history of Western philosophy, beginning with the likes of Plato and Aristotle and culminating in the intellectual-mystical thought of Plotinus.[117]

Allegory and Allegoresis in the Initiatory Tale

In order to appreciate fully the *Ḥayy ibn Yaqẓān* cycle, it is necessary to situate it within the Arabo-Islamic philosophical tradition of allegory and allegoresis. Before I do this, allow me a few comments on the nature of allegory and its relationship to allegoresis. Allegory is derived from *allos* (other) and *agoreuein* (to speak publicly; lit., in the agora). Allegory is, thus, characterized by "otherness," by the strange, by a narrative's ability to say one thing yet ostensibly mean something completely different.

Allegory is, to use a well-known definition by Northrop Frye, a genre that turns on a perceived relationship between a fictional narrative and a "simultaneous structure of events or ideas, whether historical events, moral or philosophical ideas, or natural phenomena."[118] In its simplest terms, allegory is an oblique way of writing, a literary form or genre that seeks to conceal and reveal at one and the same time.[119] It is a type of writing that turns on aesthetic contradiction. What appears on the surface is ostensibly different from, and potentially subversive of, the real intentionality. Allegoresis, in turn, is interpretive as opposed to compositional. It designates the actual allegorical exegesis of a narrative regardless of whether or not such a meaning was intended by the authors of the text being interpreted.

Allegories always try to tell stories. There exists, then, a distinct narrative dimension to an allegory, whether this occurs in the literal meaning, the non-literal meaning, or the way in which both of these play off against each other. In many ways, an allegory is a battleground of competing texts, meanings, and interpretations. For in it, the non-literal or the indirect meanings sit, often uncomfortably, beside the literal or direct meaning. This gives way to a host of questions that are inseparable from allegory: From where is a reader provided with the clues to ascertain the allegorical nature of a text? Does each generation read the allegory in the same manner? Can the allegorical meaning replace the literal meaning to such an extent that the latter is erased?

Allegory and allegoresis thrive on ambiguity. The world that the allegory opens up before the reader is often one that is the opposite of what it narratively appears to be. Whereas the narrative is concerned with specific, yet often vaguely defined, individuals and/or places, allegory itself forces the reader into the "recovery of the pure visibility of the truth, undisclosed by the local and the accidental."[120] This creates an omnipresent tension between the actual plot and structure of the narrative and a telos that always lies just beyond it. As a genre, then, allegory is always trying to come to terms with its own provisionality.[121] In like manner, the reader of allegory finds between its lines the search for meaning, immortality, and ultimately redemption.

In some ways, allegory is elitist. Under the threat of persecution, medieval philosophers, with the fate of Socrates always in the background, wrote in such a manner that those uninitiated into philosophy would bypass the deeper truths.[122] Despite this, however, allegory is also potentially democratic, its polysemous nature offering meaning to virtually every potential reader. Allegories seem to be popular in one of two, seemingly contradictory, types of environments. The first is in an era of political totalitarianism, where freedom of expression is sharply curtailed.[123] Within such a context, allegories provide an outlet of expression. The second such environment is, according to Peter Heath, one whose *épistème* combines a philosophical idealism with a certain cultural sophistication.[124]

Allegory nourishes the imagination. This is because the reader must be an active participant in reading the text, since the surface of the narrative simultaneously reveals and conceals its truths. This encourages the participation of the reader actively to create meaning within the work, to experience it aesthetically and not just passively.[125] The allegory, like the work of art, is a complex imitation of reality: just as the artwork mimics the reality around us, it is not reality; its meaning ultimately resides not in the sum of its parts, but in its ability to point beyond itself. As such, the reader must articulate a meaning in the allegory or else he or she risks stumbling and arriving at a situation of unmeaning.

Allegory works so well because it represents a synergy between the imagination and the intellect. But many mistrust this synergy. Philosophers often denigrate or marginalize allegories by writing them off as "merely literature." This despite the fact that literature, as Nussbaum clearly demonstrates, is inseparable from the philosophical enterprise.[126] But if philosophers are critical of allegories, poets and literary critics often denounce the plodding simplicity of allegory. Many moderns, in particular critics like Coolidge and Poe, fault allegory for its dearth of adequate plot structure and its employment of flimsy narrative techniques.[127]

But allegory and allegoresis are not universal. Although virtually all cultures engage in allegory at different periods, the contents are proportionally related to the hermeneutical strategy of a specific community with a particular social, cultural, and historical identity. Despite the fact that Islamic allegory comes in a variety of forms and contents, it nonetheless represents a cohesive literary tradition.[128] Interestingly, Arabic lacks a term for allegory. Nevertheless, it does possess many nouns that are used to designate what Western literary criticism has come to denote as allegory. For example, *ramz* (symbol), *ishāra* (allusion), and *isti*ᶜ*āra* (metaphor) all have similar connotations to "allegory." In like manner, the Arabic term *ta*ᵓ*wīl* (often translated as "allegorical interpretation") comes remarkably close to the term *allegoresis.* Rather than conclude that this lack of exact correspondence admits the failure of the enterprise or that my employment of the term "allegory" is tantamount to an Orientalist imposition, I concur with Heath that the concept, if not the actual name, of allegory has a lengthy indigenous history in the Islamicate world.[129]

However, in using the term "allegory" we must be cautious of the Romantic assumption that claims this genre is characterized by a static and artificial mode of language.[130] As a consequence of this assumption, to this day an allegory is often regarded as a functional narrative in which the reader attempts to substitute awkwardly the concrete for the abstract.[131] An allegory, based on this reading, is regarded as possessing a flimsy narrative in which the significance of people, things, or happenings resides in their symbolic or moral meaning. Implicit in this assumption is that the allegorist has coded an intellectual or moral system into a story and it is the reader's goal to decode this in order to arrive at *the* "proper" understanding. Within such a narrative, the form is regarded as dispensable: the first-level order of meaning is jettisoned once the reader has arrived at the second-level order of meaning.[132]

In a recent study, John Walbridge has argued that we need to distinguish between "closed" and "open" allegories in philosophical writings.[133] An "open" allegory is a work that "tells how people enter life, make choices, and are blessed and ruined by the choices they make, but it concerns real people and the real universe, or at least it purports to."[134] He cites Platonic myths as the foremost examples of this type. The "closed" allegory, on the other hand, is a "coded set of symbols" in which "we are not expected to suspend disbelief or identify with the characters."[135] For Walbridge, all of the Islamic philosophers wrote, with the possible exception of ibn Ṭufayl, "closed" allegories. Walbridge's distinction between these two types of allegory is ultimately based on his contention that these tales are essentially pedagogical treatises:

> Philosophical allegories seem to have been written as a way of popularizing philosophy and should thus be ranked with vernacular philosophical encyclopedias and abridgments as literature produced for the use of the educated public, particularly the bureaucratic class.[136]

In what follows I want to avoid reducing these tales in such a functional or utilitarian manner. Although the characters Ḥay ben Meqitz or Ḥayy ibn Yaqẓān can, on one level, be associated with the Active Intellect, they are both ultimately more than this. For example, the relationship between an initiate and a master has deep cultural and intellectual resonances in both medieval Islam and Judaism. In particular, the various tropes and imagery that these authors employ, as I will demonstrate shortly, are drawn from their religious traditions and evoke a much wider set of symbols. Moreover, the actual language employed to describe this master, especially in ibn Ezra's *Ḥay ben Meqitz*, is extremely rich in terms of its evocation of the biblical account of both Moses in Deuteronomy and the Beloved of the Song of Songs. It is my contention that initiatory tales are more than simple allegories; rather, they represent a distinct genre that employs poetic techniques in order to aid the reader to grasp certain supertextual truths.

Allegory implies interpretation and, not surprisingly, those who see these tales as simple allegories focus their attention on exegesis. Relatively little time, however, has been spent on the language of these texts: the rhetorical, metaphorical, and poetic modalities that make such interpretation possible. Walbridge further argues that one of the characteristics of "closed allegories" is a guide who explains the meaning of all the items in the narrative. In *Ḥay ben Meqitz,* however, the guide (Ḥay) does very little explaining. On the contrary, it is the unnamed protagonist who encounters the mysteries of the world firsthand. All of these mysteries, quite significantly, are encountered on the narrative level: they are not phenomena that are beyond or outside of the text. For ibn Ezra both the first-order and the second-order levels of meaning are represented by the biblical text. The first-order, therefore, cannot be jettisoned once one has arrived at the second-order.

Walbridge also claims that these works are unemotive and, as a result, we do not relate to them on either a human or aesthetic level.[137] In what follows, I wish to argue the exact opposite. These works do speak to us on both levels precisely because we, as readers, are able to grasp the universe in its entirety through the protagonist's eyes. We essentially follow in the footsteps of the protagonist's revelatory ascent through the universe. Such a journey is transformative not only for the protagonist, but also for the reader. In the case of *Ḥay ben Meqitz,* for example, this journey takes us not only through the various worlds that compose the universe, but also through the various levels of the biblical narrative. The culmination of both these intertextual and supratextual journeys is the visual apprehension of God. In other words, both the beauty of the intelligible world and the interpretive act consist in the art of seeing. And these texts seek to awaken the potentiality of such vision within the reader.

Within this context, there exists a distinct performative aspect to this genre. The text is in many ways a metaphor of divine reality. As the reader enters the world of the text and proceeds along its path, she finds herself at the center of an unfolding drama describing the ascent of the soul. There is an intimate correspondence between the protagonist of the journey and the reader, as both are invited to participate in an initiation that takes place against the backdrop of a specific cosmology. My analysis proceeds from the notion that the literary-aesthetic form and structure of these texts are as important as their intentionality. It is not so much the message that is encountered in these texts, but the actual experience of the reading that is so important. To reduce texts such as *Ḥayy ibn Yaqẓān* or *Ḥay ben Meqitz* simply to the allegorical is akin to claiming that the works of Milton or Shakespeare are purely symbolic or functional while ignoring their poetical structure, use of imagery, and other features.[138]

The goal of the text, therefore, is not to arrive at a level of meaning that is solely supratextual. Rather, the glory that the protagonist of each tale encounters is also *in* the text, not necessarily *outside* of it: the word and the world thus become two strands of the same fabric. Consequently, there exists an intimate connection between reading and religious activity. Hermeneutics, according to Daniel Boyarin, becomes a practice that allows the exegete to recover the vision of God.[139] This visionary experience of God can only occur within a rich narrative setting such as that which the reader encounters in the *Ḥayy ibn Yaqẓān* cycle.

In sum, although I believe it is important to contextualize these tales against the broader background of Islamicate allegory, it is essential that we not lose sight of their rich literary and aesthetic components. Though this theme runs throughout this study, I will develop it in detail in the final chapter. Suffice it to say here that allegory is not the only option that our three authors had at their disposal to generate meaning through literary techniques. All three were heirs to rich literary, poetical, mythopoetical, and cultural traditions—and all three of our authors freely drew upon these traditions. It is essential, then, not to ignore the way in which these texts generate philosophical truth by means of the images that they create. To reiterate: although it is necessary to situate these initiatory tales within the broader context of philosophy, it is also important to examine them from a literary perspective.

The Mythic Structure of the Initiatory Tale

The fact that not many of these tales were written throughout the period of either medieval Islamic or Jewish philosophy mitigates against "maximalist" readings of these texts, such as the one provided by the likes of Corbin. Despite this, "minimalist" readings, such as those given by Gutas or Walbridge, also fail to account for the various intellectual and cultural reasons behind their composition. Why, for example, did these tales flourish in the eleventh and twelfth centuries? How do they relate specifically to the Neoplatonic (as opposed to a more Peripatetic or Aristotelian) milieu of the Islamicate world? What did our authors find so attractive about this genre that other philosophers, writing in different temporal or spatial locations, did not?

Neoplatonism provided an important framework that coincided naturally, and at times effortlessly, with monotheism. For foundational to Neoplatonism is a narrative—that of the career and adventures of the soul as it makes its way from the quagmire of this world of form and matter to its original and celestial home. Furthermore, a central feature of Neoplatonism is its rich use of highly visual imagery and its employment of both a mythic narrative and a mythopoeic vocabulary to articulate this journey. All three authors choose, in their respective *Ḥayy ibn Yaqẓān* narratives, to give this narrative a full-blown, highly literary, and aesthetic treatment. These tales, then, essentially occupy the interface between the mythic worlds of Neoplatonism and that of monotheism (be it Islam or Judaism). In other words, both the structure and the mythic details of these tales draw their impetus not only from the Neoplatonic system, but also from the basic religious framework provided by the religious affiliations of the author. For at the heart of both of these traditions is the soul's ascent through the various heavenly spheres, a journey that ultimately culminates in the majestic vision of God.

This concept of a journey through a structured and hierarchical cosmos is central to the religious understanding of both Judaism and Islam. In the latter tradition, for example, one of the defining features of Muḥammad's prophetic career, indeed the event that, according to later Islamic theology, distinguished him from all previous prophets, was his night flight (*isrāʾ*) and subsequent ascension (*miʿrāj*) into heaven. This journey has it seeds in the Qurʾān:

> Glory be to Him, who carried His servant by night from the Holy Mosque to the Further Mosque the precincts of which we have blessed, that We might show him some of Our signs.[140]

This verse, although sparse in details, was often read with other verses dealing with ascent and vision:

> By the star when it plunges, your comrade is not astray, neither errs, nor speaks he out of caprice. This is not but a revelation revealed, taught him by one terrible in power, very strong; he stood poised being on the higher horizon, then drew near and suspended hung, two bows' length away, or nearer, then revealed to his servant that he revealed. His heart lies not of what he saw; what, will you dispute with him what he sees? (53:1–12)

Such verses, however, received full-fledged narrative expansions in subsequent articulations.[141] According to these later accounts, Muḥammad encountered on this journey the previous prophets associated with Judaism and Christianity (e.g., Abraham, Aaron, Moses,

Jesus). These prophets, who are now associated with each of the spheres, remain on fixed levels. As Muḥammad ascends through these spheres, he is the only one that is granted a certain mobility. The other prophets acknowledge his prophethood and, because he ascends to levels that they cannot, ultimately attest to the supremacy of Muḥammad's prophecy. The entire journey, however, culminates in Muḥammad's vision of God. For Tustarī, a ninth-century Sufi, the night journey and ascension of Muḥammad represents the prototype of the mystical vision (*mushāhada*) that every Sufi has the power to re-enact. In his mystically inspired *tafsīr* (Qurʾānic commentary) to chapter 53, Tustarī writes as follows:

> "By the star when it plunges" (53:1) refers to Muḥammad when he returned from heaven (*samāʾ*). "Your comrade is not astray neither errs" (53:2) means, in no case was he astray from the reality of the profession of God's Oneness (*ḥaqiqa al-tawḥīd*), neither did he in any event follow Satan. "Nor speaks he out of caprice" (53:3): by no means did he utter falsehood (*bāṭil*)... "His heart lies not what he saw" (53:11) namely what he (Muḥammad) saw at the mystical vision (*mushāhada*) of his Lord (*rabb*), as he face to face encountered Him with the sight of his heart (*baṣar qalbihi*).[142]

It should be apparent that this notion of ascent and vision of the divine was not something that ended with Muḥammad. Indeed, what was originally an unspecified and rather vague account mentioned in the Qurʾān subsequently provides a topography of the divine world, becoming the paradigm by which later mystics could understand and compare their own mystical ascents. According to the Islamic mystics, Muḥammad's *miʿrāj* becomes the ideal to which every Sufi should aspire. With Muḥammad as their prototype, the Sufis acknowledge that each individual was essentially a battleground of competing desires and forces. The heart (*qalb*) of the Sufi desires God, to contemplate Him, and, ultimately, to become like Him. Juxtaposed against this are the desires of the lower self (*nafs*) that pull the heart in the opposite direction. This battle is often described in mythical terms,[143] and was something that could easily fit with the imagery and vocabulary of Neoplatonism.

Many of the later accounts of the *miʿrāj* offer increasingly elaborate accounts of the various celestial levels. In the following account, al-Ghaiṭī, a fourteenth-century thinker, described it thus:

> There then came over [Muḥammad] a cloud containing every color. Gabriel stayed behind, but he—upon whom be God's blessing and peace—was taken up to a lofty place where he heard the scratching of pens [that are

> writing God's decrees]. There he saw a man [sitting] concealed in the light of the Throne. Said he: "Who is this? Is it an angel?" The answer came: "No." "Then who is it?" The answer came: "This is a man whose tongue in the world was always moist with the mentioning of God, whose heart cleaved to the mosque, and who never at any time abused his parents." Then he saw his Lord—glorified and exalted be He—and the Prophet—upon whom be God's blessing and peace—fell on his knees in obeisance.[144]

In other words, Muḥammad's night flight and ascension are not simply historical relics or unique religious events. On the contrary, they establish a paradigm for every potential Muslim. There is also evidence that Sufis did not regard the *mi*^{c}*rāj* solely as a physical ascent, but also as an internal one into the inner self.[145] In so doing, this event provided a symbolic and mythical code that came to be used and reused by every subsequent generation to understand, or mediate, their experiences. Even when Muḥammad's ascent is not explicitly mentioned in these later accounts, it nonetheless remains, in Michael Sells's words, "a continual subtext, evoked by subtle allusions to inspiration, vision of the divine, and the gaze of the contemplator."[146]

A similar structure exists in Judaism. The twin concepts of ascent and vision are central to the prophetic experience, which, as in Islam, became the paradigm for subsequent mystical speculation. The biblical narrative, the foundational document of Judaism, frequently mentions a divine journey, one that culminates in some kind of vision of the divine palaces (*hekhalot*) or chariot (*merkabah*). Even though the religion of ancient Israel forbade the making of images, the basic need to depict God, according to Elliot Wolfson, manifested itself in the prophetic vision of Him.[147] In Ezekiel, for example, we read:

> Above the expanse over their heads was the semblance of a throne, in appearance like sapphire; and on top, upon this semblance of a throne, there was the semblance of a human form. From what appeared as his loins up, I saw a gleam as of amber—what looked like a fire encased in a frame; and from what appeared as his loins down, I saw what looked like a fire. There was a radiance all about him. Like the appearance of the bow which shines on the clouds on a day of rain, such was the appearance of the surrounding radiance. That was the appearance of the semblance of the Presence of the Lord. When I beheld it, I flung myself down on my face. And I heard the voice of someone speaking (1:26–28).[148]

Or, again, in the book of Daniel, we encounter the following:

> Thrones were set in place, and the Ancient of Days took His seat. His garment was like white snow, and the hair of His head was like lamb's wool. His throne was tongues of flame; Its wheels were blazing fire. A river of

> fire streamed forth behind Him; Thousands upon thousands served Him; Myriads upon myriads attended Him. The court sat and the books were opened (7:9–10).[149]

This creates a paradox in subsequent Jewish thought. Although God is deemed to be completely transcendent and ultimately unrepresentable in human form, the visualization of the divine presence on a throne is central to the early Jewish mystical tradition, as embodied in the Apocalyptic writings.[150] These writings, dating anywhere from ca. 250 B.C.E. to ca. 250 C.E., are characterized by a journey through the heavenly or celestial world that culminates in a vision of the enthroned form.[151] Such a vision, in turn, is related to the revelation of divine secrets.[152] Central to the visual speculation associated with the Apocalyptic traditions is the character of Enoch (cf., Gen. 5:24) who, according to later Jewish tradition, was said to have been transformed into the angelic Metatron. In 2 Enoch, for example, we read that the protagonist, having ascended to the tenth heaven, apprehends the divine presence:

> And on the tenth heaven, Aravoth, I saw the view of the face of the Lord, like iron made burning hot in a fire and brought out, and it emits sparks and is incandescent. Thus even I saw the face of the Lord. But the face of the Lord is not to be talked about, it is so very marvelous and supremely awesome and supremely frightening.... Who can give an account of his beautiful appearance, never changing and indescribable, and his great glory? And I fell down flat and did obeisance to the Lord.[153]

One could multiply such examples exponentially. Rather than do this, however, I simply draw attention to the fact that at the very center of this literature is a vision of God that represents the culmination of a heavenly ascent. This is a feature that also figures prominently in the pre-Kabbalistic Hekhalot and Merkabah works.[154] In particular, the goal of the *yored merkabah* (one who ascends—literally "descends"—to the celestial chariot) is to contemplate the King on His throne.[155] The *yored merkabah,* according to *Hekhalot Rabbati,* is able to envisage the celestial King on His throne:

> Bear witness to them of the testimony you see in Me regarding what I do to the visage of Jacob, your father, which is engraved upon My throne of glory, for when you say before Me, Holy, I bend down over it, clasp it, embrace it, and kiss it, and My hands are on its arms, thrice daily, for you say before Me Holy, as it says "Holy, holy, holy."[156]

The twin phenomena of ascent and visualization, therefore, are central to early Jewish mystical speculation. As in the Islamic mystical tradition, the heavenly ascent of a protagonist is intimately associated with the notion of gnosis that derives from the quasi-mystical apprehension of the divine. As should now be apparent, the *Ḥayy ibn Yaqẓān* cycle is anything but foreign to the monotheistic heritages of Islam or Judaism. On the contrary, these tales essentially absorb many of the linguistic, conceptual, and symbolic categories of earlier Muslim and Jewish literature. The basic structure and plot of these tales coincide naturally and almost effortlessly with both the traditions and vocabularies of monotheism. This is further evidence against the reductionist claim that these tales are transparent, simplistic, or devoid of any emotional content. Indeed, these tales represent an abstract canvas wherein the mythic, the poetic, the philosophic, and the religious intersect. The level on which one chooses to read each tale is, as I will argue in a subsequent chapter, ultimately dependent upon one's expertise.

These tales integrate the religious and mythical worldviews of Judaism and Islam with the scientific and philosophical theories that were in favor at the time. This task, as I shall argue in chapter 2, was made easier by the mythical structure of the basic Neoplatonic narrative. This synergy between the religious and the philosophic reinforces the claim of Islamicate philosophers that to engage in science was a religious obligation.[157] In order to understand the narratives of people like Muḥammad, Enoch, or Moses properly, one first had to engage in philosophical pursuits. So, even though our three authors use the vocabulary and the conceptual framework of their respective traditions, rather than privilege certain secret gnosis, they nonetheless naturalize the path, making it potentially open to everyone. In many ways this was in keeping with the intellectual climate of al-Andalus, wherein intellectuals combined the mystical and the philosophical to mine the depths of the religious life.

The Philosophical Component of the Initiatory Tale

Despite the centrality of these tales' literary and mythic qualities, it is equally important not to lose sight of their philosophical dimensions. Following the lead of the philosophers of late antiquity, Islamic and Jewish philosophers included Aristotle's *Poetics* as part of his logical system (the so-called *Organon*).[158] For these individuals, poetics represented one component of a more comprehensive theory devoted to the human capacity to reason.[159] Literature was not simply a form of entertainment; following Aristotle, the medieval Islamicate philosophers recognized that literature played a potentially positive role in the noetic and emotional development of the individual. For implicit in the Aristotelian analysis of literature, according to Nussbaum, is the notion that the emotions and the imagination ultimately influence the rational decisions that humans make.[160]

Avicenna, who articulated one of the richest discussions of medieval Islamicate poetics, emphasizes that demonstrative and poetic utterances share a similar logical structure. Although the poetic utterance, unlike its demonstrative counterpart, is ultimately unconcerned with the truth or falsity of a statement, it nevertheless requires an assent (*taṣdīq*) that is based on the pleasure (*ladhdha*) and awe (*ta^c^ajjub*) that we experience in it.[161] The crucial difference between the poetic and the demonstrative utterance is that the former relies for its validity on the pleasure and wonder that it evokes in the soul. In short, the goal of the poetic or allegorical utterance is not to produce the intellect's assent to specific conclusions, but to stimulate the faculty of the imagination to apprehend truths that are beyond the surface.[162] In his *Kitāb al-majmu^c^*, Avicenna clarifies this notion further:

> Poetical syllogisms are syllogisms that occur to the soul imaginatively and not by assent. The imagination (*al-takhayyul*) is aroused by amazement (*ta^c^ajjub*), glorification (*ta^c^zīm*), disparagement (*tahwīn*), diminution (*tasghīr*), affliction (*ghamm*), and ardor (*nashāṭ*) without conviction (*i^c^itiqād*) being the object of the utterance. It is not one of the conditions of these syllogisms that they be true or false, commonly-held or deceptive, but that they evoke the imagination.[163]

It is within this context that we need to situate not only Avicenna's tale, but also those of ibn Ezra and ibn Ṭufayl. For in all three of these narratives, we encounter the allegorical treatment of the ascent of an unnamed protagonist's soul through an imagined cosmos. This ascent, though described in a rich literary and aesthetic manner, turns on the philosophical enterprise. In other words, our authors realize that there exists a distinct philosophical component to both literature and aesthetics. Guided by the enigmatic Ḥayy ibn Yaqẓān, each protagonist learns of the true composition of his soul, its relationship to the body, and the impending journey. In chapter 3, I suggest that the mechanism facilitating this intimate connection between poetics and philosophical discourse is the faculty of the imagination. For it is the imagination that enables us to encounter, at a pre-rational yet ratiocinative and self-reflective level, the images of our experience.[164] These images—which the faculty of imagination (*takhayyul*) manipulates and the related faculty of estimation (*wahm*) further abstracts and judges[165]—constitute the building blocks of our ability to comprehend universals, the subject matter of philosophy.[166] The imagination thus becomes central in virtually all noetic activity; without it, conception (*tasawwur*) and assent (*taṣdīq*) are impossible.

Conclusions

In his study of ibn Ṭufayl's *Ḥayy ibn Yaqẓān,* Sami Hawi argues that "Ibn Ṭufayl seems to have adopted the names and nothing more from Avicenna. Any attempts to find more significant resemblances between the two authors in this respect is an overplay of scholarship."[167] As should be obvious from what I have argued in this chapter, I disagree with such a statement. Not only do these three tales share the same name and protagonist, but they also share a basic literary, poetic, and mythological worldview against which the protagonist's journey takes place. These similarities are anything but coincidental; rather, they are part and parcel of a shared concern for the ineffability of the divine and the inability of the embodied human to gain access to Truth without the mediation of indirect and non-propositional discourse.

These three tales are not simply the ad hoc creations of three different authors who happen to have all lived at roughly the same time. Rather, these tales share not only similarities in terms of their main characters and plots, but also literary assumptions. The goal of the text that follows is to begin to articulate the reasons behind these assumptions and to show how they connect to the broader context of eleventh- and twelfth-century Neoplatonism. As will gradually become apparent, these tales seek to challenge fundamentally the way in which we traditionally perceive the universe and our relationship to it. The rhythmic use of language, the invocation of prophetic and mystical categories from each of the two traditions, and the suprarational culmination of the protagonist make these tales more than simple philosophical stories. The transformative aspect of these tales is also meant to influence the reader who must essentially undergo the same journey as the protagonist. This process involves the reader focusing his or her gaze on the narrative's unfolding, the understanding that the intellect will only take one so far, before it must give way, paradoxically, to the imagination. Before I examine this faculty, however, it is important to situate these tales within the broader literary context of Neoplatonism.

2

Reading between the Lines: Text as Encounter with the Divine

IN CHAPTER 1, I ARGUED THAT THERE IS A TENDENCY TO REGARD THE INITIATORY tale from one of two competing and ultimately contradictory perspectives. For the sake of convenience, I referred to these as the maximalist and the minimalist positions. The former contends that these tales are *sui generis*, the apogee of medieval philosophy. The mistake of this position, to reiterate briefly, is to see in these tales something that is impossible to verify by independent means. Those who follow the minimalist position, by contrast, argue that these tales are trivial and not worthy of serious philosophical attention. In this chapter, I want to move beyond these two characterizations by looking at the late antique antecedents of the initiatory tale. I will show that these tales are genetically related to the visionary, non-discursive, and symbolic textual universes of Neoplatonism. The argument of this chapter is that unless we contextualize these tales within this tradition of Neoplatonism, we risk overlooking their contribution to medieval philosophy.

What follows is not an introduction to Neoplatonism but an analysis of certain themes and trajectories of this tradition that made their way into medieval Islam and Judaism; these aspects found concrete expression in the genre of the initiatory tale. Unlike those who take the maximalist position, I argue that there is nothing unique about these initiatory tales. Indeed, they share the same literary, textual, and linguistic assumptions that were developed by Plotinus and elaborated upon by his successors. Where they do differ from such earlier texts, however, is in their basic monotheistic frameworks and vocabularies. Both the literary account of a heavenly ascent and the rich use of mythic language provided by the religious narratives of Islam and Judaism offered the individuals who are the subject of this study an ideal framework to connect, and subsequently explore, the counterpoints between philosophy and religion. Once we analyze the philosophical underpinnings of Neoplatonic literary criticism, we will see that these tales are in fact philosophically significant. Indeed, they presuppose a certain aesthetics, ontology, and epistemology—and only make sense when understood against this background.

In so doing, I draw attention to and focus on the form and style of the Neoplatonic text in general, and the initiatory tale in particular. The literary, mythic, and aesthetic presentation we encounter in this type of writing is inseparable from a specific way of doing philosophy. Within this philosophical worldview, form and style are not incidental. According to Martha Nussbaum,

> Certain truths about human life can only be fittingly and accurately stated in the language and forms characteristic of the narrative artist. With respect to certain elements of human life, the terms of the novelist's art are alert winged creatures, perceiving where the blunt terms of ordinary speech, or of the abstract theoretical discourse, are blind, acute where they are obtuse, winged where they are dull and heavy.[1]

It is important not to minimize the genre, formal structures, and vocabulary of philosophical treatises that are presented non-discursively. Within the context of medieval Jewish and Islamic thought, these initiatory tales are among the few philosophical texts written in such a manner. This alone should encourage us to pause in order to examine their mode of expression, which is ultimately inseparable from the search for, and ultimate presentation of, truth. In the present context, I examine certain themes and trajectories that were basic to the Neoplatonic worldview in order to show why it was no accident that Avicenna, ibn Ezra, and ibn Ṭufayl choose to compose their tales in such a manner. Rather than assuming that the narrative dimension of Neoplatonism—whether ancient or medieval, Islamic or Jewish—is unphilosophic, non-analytic, or prone to mystical opaqueness, I contend that it challenges the logocentric assumption that philosophical thinking is somehow image-free or that there even exists such a phenomenon as imageless thinking.[2]

Language is not simply a means of communication, but the vehicle that makes ontology possible since it is ultimately responsible for bringing phenomena to light. This property of disclosure led Heidegger to refer to language as one of the original events of unconcealment.[3] I am influenced by his discussion and contend that it is language that reveals the world, in all of its fullness, to the individual. Language is intimately connected to art (especially literature) since both are attempts to articulate the relationship between presence and absence and, in the process, both delineate the parameters of truth. For Heidegger, poetry, as a work of art, clears a space for the individual and opens his or her gaze onto a new world.[4] All art is ultimately poetic since it is essentially the "setting-into-work-of-truth."[5] The reader must essentially remove him- or herself from everyday existence and enter into the world that is disclosed by the work of art.

A central feature that weaves throughout this chapter, and one that is intimately related to the notion of art as a form of clearing, is that of embodiedness. Since we are not simply intellects, but a composite of form and matter, we are incapable of constant intellection. Consequently, we cannot separate ourselves from our bodies or reason as if they did not exist. Our bodies help define the way we interact with and perceive the world around us. This concept of embodiedness, in turn, implies a certain aesthetics. The world is not simply a pale imitation of a transcendent truth. Rather, it is the locus where our emotions, our feelings, our perceptions, and our imaginations are activated and upon which they project conceptual apparati in the quest for truth. A work of art—in particular, a work of fiction—possesses an important ontological value. Literature, in particular, is based on the experiences of our mundane existence in such a manner that these experiences are arranged into a story that gives them an epistemic significance and clarity.[6] Literature, like all art forms, restructures our interaction with the world: better defining it, highlighting certain instances of it, and attempting to push us cognitively beyond it.

It is within such a context that we must situate the initiatory tale. It is, in a very real sense, a work of art that is concerned with the things, emotions, and concepts that we value in the particularities of our embodied, everyday existence. What is our origin? Our destiny? What does it mean to be human? What constitutes happiness? What are the contours of our relationship with God? These tales deal with such concerns by putting them into an organic, aesthetic, and interconnected whole. Ibn Ezra, for instance, writes:

> The Torah speaks according to the language of men (*ha-torah diberah ki-leshon benei adam*) . . . For man is not able to speak about things that are either above him or below him, only about what is in his image. Thus we talk about "the mouth of the earth" (Num 16:30), "the hand of the Jordan" (Num 13:29), and "the first clumps of clay" (Prov 8:26; lit. "the head of the earth of the world"). Heaven forbid that this is an image for God! Thus it says "To whom will you liken me?" (Is 40:25).[7]

Here ibn Ezra seems to intimate that the philosophical disclosure of ultimate reality requires the use of images. In other words, we can only understand the higher articulations of the universe because they are founded on the lower, and it is the latter that are ultimately responsible for illuminating the former. Therefore, even though the universe has an elemental embodied level of meaning, the articulation of the world cannot be merely reduced to us as articulators of the world. The end result of this is that we do not experience or apprehend truth in an unmediated way, but only through the mediation of other phenomena. Since we are limited by our bodies, we require stories, metaphors, and other such objects to help us encounter and negotiate that which exists without corporeal extension. We thus experience truth by means of hermeneutics.[8]

The philosopher becomes an artist who creates a portrait of the soul and subsequently defines its relationship to the One or God. The language of myth and poetry is crucial to this process since it forces the reader to engage in the hermeneutical act. The reader must become an active participant in the narrative, taking away from the text what he or she has put in. Literature in general and the initiatory tale in particular offer artistic representations that provide a way of helping the individual confront and transcend his or her particularity.

Text as Locus of Visionary Experience

More than any other ancient philosophical school, the Neoplatonists argued that Truth[9] lay outside both texts and language. Despite this, the Neoplatonists had no qualms about writing philosophical texts. This created a dilemma since the Neoplatonists had essentially to write about that which cannot be confined to writing. Important questions emerge from this paradox: What does it mean for experience to exist independently of language? How does one write or speak about the quest for Truth without confining it? Successive attempts to grapple with these questions have resulted in a fundamental tension that runs throughout Neoplatonic texts. Although Truth is ineffable, language is all that we possess to delineate it. Neoplatonic texts thus represent a curious amalgam of presence and absence, logic and non-discursivity, representation through non-representational propositions, and appeals to both the intellect and the imagination.

Within this context, however, a twofold problem immediately presents itself. First, the very term "Neoplatonic" is notoriously slippery. Since it was originally coined in the nineteenth century, none of the thinkers that we today label as such would have considered themselves to be "Neoplatonists" or individuals who belonged to a distinct school that engaged in something called "Neoplatonic" philosophy.[10] Historically, by the close of the fifth century the study of Aristotle had become inseparable from the exposition of Plato's thought. Indeed, by the time we get to John Philoponus in the sixth century, Aristotle's philosophy had been used as the standard introduction to Plato for at least two centuries. The philosophical commentators of late antiquity, convinced that the thought of Aristotle was reconcilable with that of Plato,[11] envisaged themselves as working within the Platonic tradition and making explicit what was therein. Although they wrote commentaries, it must be kept in mind that commentary writing was one of the main ways of exploring philosophy in this period. The result was, as Sorabji claims, an "Aristotle transformed."[12]

Second, there exists a potential danger in the desire to regard Neoplatonism simply as a philosophical school.[13] As soon as we do this, we marginalize a number of other disciplinary aspects[14] that were regarded as an important part of intellectual speculation. Yet those very disciplines are today considered to be outside the pale of the standard philosophical repertoire (e.g., astrology, theurgy).[15] Neoplatonism was, to reuse the phrase of Hadot, "a way of life," a form of holistic intellectual inquiry that had a distinct religious ideology complete with liturgical and ritual praxis.[16] In many ways, this categorization simply compounds the problem mentioned in the previous paragraph because whenever we label a thinker as Neoplatonic, we assume that he shares much in common with other thinkers labeled by the same term. A Neoplatonic school, in theory, implies a greater doctrinal uniformity (e.g., *the* Neoplatonic ontology, *the* Neoplatonic metaphysics) than existed in reality. To cite but one example, the theurgical rituals of the Neoplatonic Iamblichus were completely anathema to the Neoplatonic Porphyry.[17] Whereas the latter contended that theurgy was degenerate and superstitious, an attempt to manipulate the gods, the former regarded it as the culmination of an individual's philosophical development.[18]

Despite such differences, however, we can articulate a set of concerns and a series of commonalities that many individual Neoplatonists shared. For instance, the great majority of Neoplatonists contended that although Truth can never be fully disclosed, everything somehow participates in it. Central here is the notion of emanation, or the way in which the One gradually becomes manifest through successive stages of corporealization.[19] Since the One is essentially unknowable, the only way to gain access to the One is through the phenomena of this world that are ontically related to It.[20] In phenomenological terms, access to the logos is inseparable from the phenomena by which it reveals itself. Consequently, mythic and poetic images provide a vehicle by which not only the One manifests Itself, but also by which the individual recognizes the logos-nature of the image. Images are so central because they are, in part, transparent: one sees not only the image, but also the reality that exists behind it.

Within this context, the language of Truth must, by its very nature, be non-representational, metaphorical, paradoxical, and even contradictory. For the Neoplatonist, Truth is ineffable, residing outside of human comprehension and therefore being immune to linguistic categorization. Despite this ineffability, we ultimately require the text's horizon not only to develop a series of concerns deemed worthy of philosophical analysis, but also to situate ourselves against such concerns so as to chart our intellectual ascent. Moreover, many of the authors we today deem Neoplatonists seemed to have shared an assumption that the reader of a philosophical text must be an active participant. The meaning of the text can only be understood when the reader clarifies his or her own situation in the light of the text. The hermeneutical act, the primary philosophical act, forces the reader to measure his or her life experiences against that of the text. A Neoplatonic reading, therefore, must be an active reading because one reads not so much for the message but for the experience. To put a modern spin on this, one could argue that the hermeneutical experience resides in the space that opens up during the encounter between the text and the reader. This experience, although ultimately supralinguistic, must occur in and through language. According to Hans-Georg Gadamer,

> The interpreter dealing with a traditionary text tries to apply it to himself. But this does not mean that the text is given for him as something that is universal, that he first understands it per se, and then afterward uses it for particular applications. Rather, the interpreter seeks no more than to understand this universal, the text—that is, to understand what it says, what constitutes the text's meaning and significance. In order to understand that, he must not try to disregard himself and his particular hermeneutical situation. He must relate the text to this situation if he wants to understand at all.[21]

Admittedly Gadamer is not a Neoplatonist. Moreover, he is writing approximately a thousand years after the authors who are the subject of this study. Despite this, he does bring to the forefront the centrality of hermeneutics to human understanding. Although he might use different terminology than our authors, it seems to me they would all agree that meaning is ultimately mediated through a variety of signs and symbols that humans encounter in their intersubjectivity. In other words, we never experience Truth head-on; rather, we always encounter it indirectly, obtusely. Even though Truth can be limited by language, it is ultimately the process or the mechanism by which it emerges. The text, thus, must not be read literally or on the surface; we only encounter the text, and ultimately ourselves, by interpreting and decoding its signs. Or, as Wolfson argues, "insofar as the visionary experience is hermeneutically related to the text, it may be said that the way of seeing is simultaneously a way of reading."[22]

The reader must become a part of the text, a participant in its literary unfolding. Although I will explore the performative aspect of Neoplatonic texts in chapter 4, suffice it to say here that the text's use of metaphor and symbol creates an important hermeneutic situation. In effect, imaginative vision and the phenomenology of experience are given priority over descriptive, and ultimately inaccurate, accounts of the universe.[23] This is why the motif of self-knowledge is so important to Neoplatonism.[24]

This principle of self-knowledge is readily apparent in the *Ḥayy ibn Yaqẓān* cycle. In both Avicenna's and ibn Ezra's accounts, the journey or pilgrimage occurs on an internal or spiritual plane for both the protagonist and, ideally, the reader. Although ibn Ṭufayl presents this pilgrimage in a somewhat different manner, it is, like the others, primarily experiential: Ḥayy unlocks the mysteries of nature as they relate specifically to him and his embodied condition as opposed to engaging in purely theoretical or disembodied speculation. The fact that the terminus of all three tales culminates in a visionary and quasi-mystical experience indicates that these tales are not just about the acquisition of theoretical, discursive knowledge. Although this knowledge certainly has its place, especially in understanding the phenomenal world, the basic Neoplatonic system stresses not only the essential organicism that interlocks the various sciences, but also that, to reiterate, at the highest level Truth is beyond linguistic or conceptual representation.

In the Neoplatonic universe, every thing occupies a distinct place on the ontological hierarchy. In particular, the One occupies the top of the chain and matter the bottom, to form an ontological pyramid. Despite this rigidity, everything within the universe is, on a fundamental level, interconnected. Consequently, the individual self is not necessarily something that stands over or against the rest of the universe. Indeed, Plotinus seems to intimate that we should not regard the world solely as an external phenomenon, but as something that can also be apprehended internally by the individual mind.[25]

In *De Anima* III.8 Aristotle argues that thinking creates an identity between the knower and the known since the former becomes identical with the abstracted form of the latter. Although Plotinus agrees that the thinking mind requires mental images of the forms, he nevertheless contends that discursive thinking still creates a fundamental disconnect between the thinking self and the objects thought.[26] In other words, the mind of the individual engaged in discursive analysis may possess certain structural parallels with the form of the thing known, yet such activity does not make the intellect identical with the object.

A common theme or trope that runs throughout the history of Western philosophy and mysticism is that of the mirror. The mirror is regarded as a symbol of both the receptivity and reflectivity of the universe. Here it is important not to lose sight of the actual manufacture of the medieval mirror:

> Such mirrors had to be kept polished in order to preserve their reflective qualities and, furthermore, it required great skill by the craftsman to make a perfectly flat surface. With such a mirror, therefore, there was always the possibility of surface deterioration and distortion. Thus, so long as the mirror was perfectly polished and flat, the observing subject might see his own form or image perfectly reflected on its surface, in which case the otherness of the mirror itself is reduced to minimum in the observing consciousness, or even effaced completely. To the extent, however, that the mirror reflects a dulled or distorted image, it manifests its own otherness and detracts from the identity of image and subject.[27]

Implicit in the metaphor of the mirror, according to Richard Rorty, is the assumption that for human knowledge to be true it must be regarded as an accurate representation of Nature.[28] The universe, in other words, is the locus of Truth, and the soul when properly polished reflects these truths. The goal of the philosophical enterprise is to break down the soul's reliance on the body, thereby making the soul mirror-like.[29] Just as a polished mirror both becomes and reflects what is in front of it, so, too, should the soul reach a state where it reflects the higher principles of the universe. For many Neoplatonic thinkers, discursive thinking can impede this process. The aim is to make the soul mirror-like by moving beyond the state of discursivity. Avicenna, in his *Kitāb al-ishārāt wa al-tanbīhāt* (Book of hints and admonitions), argues that

> When he passes from spiritual exercise (*al-riyāḍa*) to attainment (*al-nayl*) then his heart (*sirr*) will resemble a polished mirror (*mirʾā majluwa*) with which he faces in the direction of truth (*shatra al-ḥaqq*). Then the sublime pleasures are poured on him and he rejoices in his soul owing to the traces of Truth. For he has a perception (*naẓar*) of Truth and a perception of himself.[30]

We witness similar passages in our other two thinkers. Ibn Ezra, for example, regards the soul as a *tabula rasa* (*luaḥ ḥalaq*) that is gradually inscribed with universal truths. In his *Yesod Mora,* for example, he writes that

> Man's soul (*neshamah*) is singular; when God [initially] provides it, it is like a tablet (*luaḥ*) upon which one writes. When God's writing—which consists of the general principles derived from the four elements, the knowledge of the spheres, the throne of Glory (*kisse ha-kavod*), the secret of the chariot (*merkabah*), and the knowledge of the Most High (*ha-eliyon*)—is inscribed on this tablet the soul cleaves to the Divine Name (*shem ha-nikbad*) while it is yet in man and also afterward when its power is removed from the body.[31]

In order to gain immortality, ibn Ezra here argues that one must let the soul become like a tablet upon which all of the various physical and metaphysical sciences are inscribed. Although this is somewhat different than the metaphor of the mirror, it nonetheless is based on the same principle since the perfect soul reflects the same truths that are inscribed in both the natural and supernatural worlds. Likewise, if one ignores the soul and its perfection, the tablet will become scratched and what is written on it illegible.

Ibn Ṭufayl employs similar imagery in his *Ḥayy ibn Yaqẓān.* When he describes the pinnacle of Ḥayy's experience, he frequently resorts to the metaphor of the mirror: "As the form of the sun appearing in a polished mirror is neither sun nor mirror, and yet distinct from neither."[32] Similarly, when ibn Ṭufayl describes the various spheres that Ḥayy apprehends, he writes:

> Thus for each sphere he witnessed a transcendent immaterial subject, neither identical with nor distinct from those above, like the form of the sun when reflected from mirror to mirror with the descending order of spheres.[33]

He subsequently describes the various classes of human souls. The souls of the enlightened are like bright, polished mirrors that are able to reflect the beauty of the cosmos. The souls of the unenlightened, on the contrary are

> like tarnished mirrors, covered with rust, their faces averted and their backs to the brilliant mirrors in which shone the image of the sun. They were ugly, defective, and deformed beyond imagining.[34]

The goal of so many Neoplatonic texts—whether from late antiquity or the medieval Islamic and Jewish period—is to get the soul to move beyond discursive thinking, to make it mirror-like. To achieve such a goal, the individual must begin to realize, much like the mystic does, that truth and being do not exist independently of the individual. The philosophers intimated at this, as we will see in the remaining sections of this chapter, by employing a variety of textual strategies.

For Plotinus, a description of the ultimate source of all life cannot be a discursive description but an attempt to create a textual situation based on the sensual experiences of the reader. He writes:

> The emergence of [all things] is from a single source, so to speak, but the source is not like some one particular breath or like a single feeling of warmth. Rather, it is as if a single quality contained all qualities in itself, and actually preserved them, so that [the quality of] sweetness [would be preserved] together with the [quality of] fragrance, and this single quality were [to become] simultaneously the taste of wine, and all of the modes of taste, and sights of colors, and all the sensations of touch. The quality would bring about whatever sounds are heard, all songs and every rhythm.[35]

In this passage, Plotinus intimates that the only recourse we have to understanding the source of everything is by an indirect account that relies on the sensory data of everyday experience. The reader, in effect, must juxtapose Plotinus's textual account with his or her own bodily experiences in order to approximate, insofar as it is possible from a limited and embodied perspective, first principles. The sources describe this as a form of "seeing"—something that our three authors will all pick up on. Marinus, the pupil and biographer of Proclus (d. ca. 485), writes that his teacher

> Saw directly with his eyes the blessed visions of reality, no longer obtaining knowledge through the detail and demonstration of discursive reasoning, but looking at it as if by direct vision and by the simple conceptions of the intellective activities. Thus he acquired both the paradigms in the divine Intellect and the virtue which can no longer be called practical reasoning (*phronêsis*) in the strict sense but rather wisdom, or by another even more reverent name.[36]

Here the emphasis is on the experience of the upper levels of the universe by means of the sense of vision. There is an explicit acknowledgment that in order to penetrate to the uppermost echelons of the cosmos, one must ultimately rise above the discursive principles of analytical thought; one must pass from discursivity to non-discursivity, from deduction to induction, from intellect to imagination.

This feature of non-discursivity, pointing to the truth without fully disclosing it, is apparent throughout the *Ḥayy ibn Yaqẓān* cycle. The author most interested, at least most explicitly, in pushing beyond the confines of traditional linguistic categories is ibn Ṭufayl. Essentially, he attempts to set up a text that reveals as it conceals so that only the reader with the proper training and background can enter into it. The text becomes a hermeneutical locus wherein one activates his or her visual experience. Most important for our immediate purposes is the author's dedicatory preface. Here he writes to an unnamed pupil[37] who has asked for the secrets of "Oriental Wisdom." Ibn Ṭufayl informs him that these secrets have to do with the experience as opposed to the simple deduction or intellection of the Ineffable. Indeed, the terms that ibn Ṭufayl employs will take him decidedly in the direction of both mystical speculation and praxis:

> Your question to me put in motion a sublime thought leading me, praise God, to a vision (*mushāhada*) I had not observed (*ashahadu*) before. It brought me to a wonderful (*gharāba*) place that the tongue cannot describe or assess because it is of another state and from a different world. This state includes such splendor (*bahja*), happiness (*surūr*), pleasure (*ladhdha*), and joy (*hubūb*) that one who has united (*waṣala*) with it or has been brought to its borders is unable to keep it secret or conceal it. For its delight (*ṭorab*), ardor (*nashāṭ*), mirth (*maraḥ*), and joy (*inbisaṭ*) prevent disclosure without proper estimation. Unless one is skilled in the sciences (*ᶜulūm*) one may speak of it without proper attainment.[38]

With this passage, ibn Ṭufayl signals that the true telos of philosophy in general, and his tale in particular, is experiential. This, in turn, intimates that what is to follow in the rest of the treatise is linked to the aforementioned proscriptive statement. Ibn Ṭufayl does not attempt to reveal what this union (*waṣl*) is like, but to show how the philosophical sciences (*ᶜulūm*) relate to it and ultimately lead to it.[39] Indeed, ibn Ṭufayl continues:

> You may ask me what the people of vision (*ahl al-mushāhada*) and direct mystical experience (*dhawq*) and divine presence behold in the way of mystical saintship (*wilāya*). This cannot be adequately put down in a book. Whenever one tries to do so and takes the pains of talking or writing about it in books, then its essence changes (*istahālat*) and shifts to the other order, the speculative one. For if it is clothed in letter and sounds and brought near to the visible world, it does not in any way remain what it was.[40]

Following the Neoplatonists of late antiquity (they themselves following the lead of Plato), ibn Ṭufayl here argues that the ineffable nature of Truth prevents even the individual who has experienced it from confining it to linguistic categories. For as soon as one attempts a definition of either the Truth or the experience of it, such a statement immediately refracts its essence. Ibn Ṭufayl further writes that

> The experience is so extraordinary that only some individuals grasp a slight portion of it here and there. And whoever has grasped something of it does not talk about it except in symbols (*ramzan*). For the people of pristine monotheism (*al-ḥanīfiyya*) and the genuine Sacred Law forbid one to delve into it and warn against it.[41]

It is significant that ibn Ṭufayl's comments on both the vision (*mushāhada*) and the taste (*dhawq*) of the Ineffable arise from the unnamed disciple's query into the secrets (*asrār*) of Avicenna's "Oriental Wisdom" (*al-ḥikma al-mashriqiyya*). Ibn Ṭufayl subsequently claims that if one simply read Avicenna's Peripatetic writings, one would not arrive at perfection (*lam yuwaṣilu bihi ilā al-kamāl*).[42] Although the term "Oriental Wisdom" is, as I indicated in chapter 1, extremely problematic, we cannot ignore the fact that Avicenna wrote certain treatises that seem to differ in both their scope and tenor from many of his other works. In particular is the last section of his *K. al-ishārāt* (Book of hints). As the name suggests, this is a work that is based on indirect communication, and in it Avicenna stresses the experiential component of accessing Truth. After describing a number of "spiritual exercises" (*al-riyāḍāt*) designed to bring the individual to an arrival (*waṣl*) at Truth, he writes that the culmination of such exercises is that the individual

> withdraws from himself so that he only apprehends the side of Truth. If he apprehends himself he apprehends the Truth not as it is decorated. Here he has reached the state of arrival (*wuṣūl*).[43]

In this passage, Avicenna signals that in order to apprehend the Truth one must not resort solely to intellectual activity and preparation; rather, one must also engage in praxis. Such praxis, according to Avicenna, includes asceticism (*zuhd*), listening to appropriate musical harmonies (*al-alḥān*), and worship (*ᶜibāda*). Such activities render the soul (including the imaginative faculty) tranquil so that it can pursue holy matters (*al-amr al-qudsī*).[44] Avicenna nowhere in this treatise provides a detailed account of what this arrival at truth consists of. He is content to offer hints and admonitions that point the way because, as he himself acknowledges, this entire process is experiential, taking place outside of language.[45]

This premise of the inability of language to signify the Ineffable, and the reliance on experience in addition to analysis also runs throughout ibn Ezra's biblical commentaries. Indeed, he is famous for his claim that *ha-maskil yavin* (the wise will understand)—a phrase that occurs at practically every occasion where he deals with a philosophical issue or a problematic notion (e.g., *ma^caseh bereshit;* lit., the account of creation). Many modern commentators point out that ibn Ezra resorts to this claim as a convenient way to avoid creating a more comprehensive system. They prefer to regard ibn Ezra as a dilettante who, although influenced by "popular Neoplatonism," was unable to provide a full-scale philosophical or scientific analysis.[46]

I disagree with this claim. It is my contention, as I hope to show throughout this study, that we have to examine ibn Ezra firmly within the many trajectories that compose Neoplatonism. Rather than regard him as someone who was intellectually unable to provide detailed philosophical analyses, we need to situate him within this trope of indirect communication. Following the argument in this section, we need to understand ibn Ezra's silence when it came to weighty philosophical issues against the broader backdrop of the epistemological and ontological claims of Neoplatonism. Rather than reveal his philosophical gnosis forthrightly, he opted to provide various signposts whereby individuals with the requisite intellectual capacity could mark their intellectual progress. In this regard, ibn Ezra's approach is very similar to that which we have already encountered in both Avicenna and ibn Ṭufayl.

In sum, all three of our authors contend, in various ways, that Truth is something that exists outside of the purview of the text. The text functions as a type of indirect communication. The role of the text is not to confine Truth, but to open it up to the reader's gaze. It does this by employing non-discursive language in order to encourage the soul to move beyond discursive thought, which operates on the assumption that there exists an ontological distinction between knower and object known. This, in turn, is related to a fundamental aesthetics in Neoplatonic thought, which acknowledges that even though the divine world is beyond our noetic grasp, we are nevertheless able to apprehend certain aspects of it by means of the phenomenal world.

The *Ḥayy ibn Yaqẓān* cycle represents the literary expression of such an aesthetics. In many ways, these tales use the familiar language of scriptural monotheism for philosophical purposes. The protagonist in each tale begins firmly in the world of form and matter, in many ways at the mercy of the bodily senses; gradually, however, this protagonist begins to emerge from this world by perceiving its structure and the principle of unity that underlies this structure. Through a process of self-knowledge and a growing recognition that the lower world holds the key to unlocking the secrets of the upper world, our three authors composed literary-philosophical treatises that attempt to embody these features. The result is a set of texts that attempt to unconceal the ineffability of Truth.

The Celestial Guide

The cultural and sociological resonances of the *Ḥayy ibn Yaqẓān* cycle rarely figure highly in the secondary treatments of this literature. In both Avicenna's and ibn Ezra's tales, Ḥayy ibn Yaqẓān is described as graying, yet imbued with youthful energy and countenance. He has a beautiful appearance and, in ibn Ezra's account, combines the characteristics of the Beloved from the Song of Songs with those of Moses from the closing chapters of Deuteronomy.[47] If we return momentarily to our minimalist and maximalist approaches to these tales, we see that both, albeit in diametrically opposed ways, downplay these descriptions. The minimalist approach sees the figure of Ḥayy or Ḥay as an allegorical personification of the Active Intellect.[48] On one level, this is certainly true as both Ḥayy and Ḥay, much like the Active Intellect, are responsible for bringing the unnamed protagonist (a personification of the soul) from potentiality to actuality. However, such an approach also ignores other features, like that of the revelatory experience and the master–disciple relationship, both of which play an important role in these two religious traditions.

The maximalist approach, by contrast, regards the character of Ḥayy or Ḥay as another variation on an Eastern gnostic prototype. Corbin, in one of his many different attempts to articulate the various functions of Ḥayy, argues that

> the epiphanic forms and the names of this Guide . . . [are] always recognizable. It may be the feminine Angel Daēnā in Mazdaism, Daēnā again or Manvahmed in Manichaeism; it may be the Perfect Body (*sōma teleion*) of the Liturgy of Mithra, to which the Perfect Nature (*al-ṭibā*ᶜ *al-tāmm*) corresponds among the Ishrāqīyūn, the "philosopher's angel"; it may be *Ḥayy ibn Yaqẓān,* the *pir*-Youth, corresponding to the *spiritus rector* of the Cathari; it may be the crimson-hued Arch-Angel of one of Suhrawardī's recitals.[49]

Although Corbin is correct to connect the figure of Ḥayy to broader cultural, religious, and intellectual forces, he is too quick to posit a Persian or Eastern prototype. I think it highly unlikely that groups such as the Cathari would have influenced our authors. Certainly, the various groups that Corbin mentions were familiar with the notion of an intimate relationship that forms between a spiritual master and a disciple.[50] But rather than posit such a tenuous connection or attempt to move toward a Jungian archetype, I prefer to look for more immediate and pressing cultural and religious significances. What, for example, was the relationship between the master and the disciple in the religions of our authors?

It is also important to examine the Neoplatonic literature of late antiquity for phenomenological parallels. For within this tradition, an important motif was that of philosophical knowledge given in the form of revelation.[51] In particular, a divine figure (often a philosopher of historical provenance) is sent down by one of the gods (usually Eros) in order to lead the individual soul back to its divine home in the celestial world.[52] Implicit in this is that a guide was indispensable for this journey home because without such a guide the soul was ignorant of the forces that ailed it, and was thereby prevented from ascending to its true abode. Iamblichus (d. ca. 330 C.E.), for instance, argues that Pythagoras was sent down by the gods in order to lead individual souls back to their original home. This was not the Pythagoras of history, however, but the Pythagoras created by Iamblichus to fit his goal of introducing mathematics into theurgical ritual. Pythagoras was able to do this because he himself had knowledge of the intelligible world and was able to transmit this knowledge to other embodied souls.[53]

A similar account comes from fourth-century Hermias, who was a disciple of Syrianus and a contemporary of Iamblichus. Although Hermias writes of the importance of a celestial figure who is responsible for imparting divine knowledge to individuals, the identity of this figure now becomes Socrates as opposed to Pythagoras. According to Hermias,

> Socrates has been sent down to the world of becoming to benefit mankind and the souls of the young. Since souls differ greatly in character and practices, he benefits each in a different way... turning them to philosophy.[54]

In other passages, Hermias refers to Socrates as a "saviour"—the person responsible for bringing the individual out of darkness and into light. Socrates is able to do this because, although unsullied by his contact with embodiedness, he is also able to communicate in embodied terms. So within the parameters of late antiquity Neoplatonism, to reiterate, is a philosopher who takes on, at least in monotheist parlance, the role and qualities of a quasi-religious prophet.

If at the center of Neoplatonism resides the drama of the ascent of the soul, then at the heart of this ascent is the intimate relationship between the master and the disciple. This relationship between a superior, divine revealer of gnosis and a human in need of guidance is readily apparent in Avicenna's *Ḥayy ibn Yaqẓān* and ibn Ezra's *Ḥay ben Meqitz*. Both Ḥayy and Ḥay appear as real individuals—people whom the unnamed protagonists see, converse with, and interact with on a personal level. To regard Ḥayy or Ḥay solely as a personification of the Active Intellect is to marginalize other important features of this character. On the contrary, the concept of a celestial guide represents other historical, literary, and cultural symbolic universes that would not have been lost on the reader of these tales.

First, as mentioned, is the literary parallel of the philosopher-guide in the Neoplatonic texts of late antiquity. This individual—whether Socrates, Pythagoras, or Ḥayy—is someone who has an active knowledge (both theoretically and experientially) of all the philosophical sciences, thereby embodying that which the unnamed protagonist must aspire to. In both ibn Ezra's and Avicenna's tales the goal of the unnamed protagonist *and* the reader is to become like Ḥayy or Ḥay. Significantly, in ibn Ṭufayl's tale, Ḥayy is now the name of the protagonist, and the reader must essentially go on the journey with him.

Secondly, the way in which the conversation takes place has structural parallels with the prophetic transmission of knowledge that is the cornerstone of both Judaism and Islam. Although I will have more to say about this in chapter 4, the knowledge that the unnamed protagonist receives in both Avicenna's *Ḥayy* and ibn Ezra's *Ḥay* borders on the prophetic. Indeed, in ibn Ezra's tale the language used is that of the biblical prophets.[55] Likewise, ibn Ṭufayl describes one of Ḥayy's birth narratives in a manner that draws important parallels with that of Moses in chapters 20 and 28 of the Qurʾān.[56] In like manner, his use of Qurʾānic quotations increases as the narrative proceeds and, by the end of the tale, he employs them frequently. The Ḥayy of all of these tales is a quasi-prophet who imparts knowledge of the universe not only to other characters in the tales, but also to the reader. The individual cannot of his own accord ascend up the Neoplatonic hierarchy without this guide. Significantly, however, the figures we encounter in these tales ascend up the *scala naturae* not by supernatural means, but naturally. The implication seems to be that any individual, given the proper intellectual capacity and requisite understanding of the sciences, can ascend to a level similar to that of the biblical or Qurʾānic prophets.

Thirdly, the master–disciple relationship has many obvious parallels in both the Islamic and Jewish mystical traditions. Within both of these contexts, the initiate is unable to proceed without the spiritual guidance of a master (Ar. *shaykh*). This master must invest the disciple with a spiritual roadmap, as it were. At the heart of both medieval Islamic and Jewish philosophy and mysticism is this relationship. Obviously, in the philosophical tradition, the teacher–student relationship is central. The student requires initiation into the philosophical sciences by one who has already undergone this. I do not mean anything esoteric about this "initiation"; only that, as all three of our authors state at the beginnings of their tales, the philosopher has around him a number of students, some of whom subsequently "graduate" from his company and then attract their own disciples. The master–student disciple is, thus, central to the transmission of philosophy.

If the relationship between the philosopher and his students is utilitarian or functional, that between the mystic and his disciple is distinctly spiritual. In medieval Islamic and Jewish mysticism, the role of the master is paramount. Without a master one is unable to learn the proper techniques of mystical praxis, which in turn make the mystical experience possible. The master is the individual responsible for receiving his students, and choosing the select few (i.e., those with the potential of mystical gnosis) among hundreds. The subsequent relationship that forms between the *shaykh* and his disciples is a charismatic one, in which the disciple must surrender himself to the master with the hope of transforming the manner in which he or she views the world.

It is important that, as readers of these tales, we be aware of and acknowledge the various nuances that the relationship between Ḥayy or Ḥay and the unnamed protagonist represents. The problem with the minimalist position is that it restricts this relationship solely to that between the Active Intellect and the human soul. In so doing it tends to downplay any other types of cultural, social, or intellectual significations, thereby ignoring the multidisciplinary forces that are at work. On the other side of the coin, however, it is important that we also avoid the more extreme conclusions of the maximalist approach to this relationship, which rarely moves beyond the archetypal relationship between master and disciple. In this section, I have attempted to walk a middle ground, a space that seeks to establish these tales within *specific* cultural and intellectual contexts.

Ontological Counterpoints: Between Literature and Philosophy

So far, I have been exploring specific points of contact between the various *Ḥayy* narratives and the Neoplatonic literature of late antiquity. My goal in doing this was to show that these tales, like much of medieval Islamicate philosophy, have precursors in the earlier philosophical tradition. The key themes are certainly those of Neoplatonism: the ineffability of the One, the paradox between text and the supratextual experience, and the celestial guide. None of these are unique to the *Ḥayy ibn Yaqẓān* cycle. This is not to reduce these tales, however, for they are much greater than the sum of their parts. Indeed, the various processes that these tales go through to become Muslim or Jewish is ultimately much more important and interesting than the fact that they show parallels. In what follows, I still want to stay with this dynamic relationship between late antique Neoplatonism and that of medieval Islamicate civilization. However, the focus will now switch to more general themes that reinforce my larger thesis of the counterpoint between philosophy, religion, and literature.

The Career of the Soul

At the center of virtually all Neoplatonic speculation resides a narrative unfolding documenting the career of the soul. We see this in Plato,[57] Plotinus,[58] and virtually all of the other thinkers of late antiquity. This narrative of the soul's career, in turn, made its way into both medieval Islamic and Jewish philosophical speculation. Indeed, the entire *Ḥayy ibn Yaqẓān* cycle is essentially a mythic re-enactment of this narrative, with each tale stressing a different emphasis of this psychological re-enactment. Before proceeding, it is worthwhile to define briefly what I mean by the term "myth." In employing it, I do not intend something that is false or untrue; rather, I refer to a narrative account that attempts to portray that which we are unable to experience literally. Because mythic discourse is non-objective, thereby providing a non-discursive narrative, it is able to probe the limits of human finitude. Since it does not rely upon unembodied, abstract, or analytical categories, myth effectively demonstrates how we experience the world that it presents.[59]

Mythic discourse, with its rich and suggestive vocabulary, allows the individual to encounter the transcendent realm on a level that is not divorced from more experiential claims. It is not the job of myth to portray the world accurately; rather, myth works by simplifying this world into a coherent system of categories that can subsequently be projected onto the entire spectrum of lived emotion and experience.[60] Today we tend to equate myth with either that which is untrue or that which aids in the education of the young. Consequently, many modern commentators take this use of the term and project it back onto medieval philosophy.[61] This results in the assumption that whenever a philosopher resorted to the mythic, as our three authors did with their tales, it was for the sake of popularizing philosophy. Such an assumption, however, overlooks the fact that none of these authors admitted that this was their intention in composing treatises such as these. On the contrary, all three seem to intimate, some more explicitly than others, that it was only after much prodding from their disciples to reveal certain secrets that they agreed to compose these tales.[62]

Neoplatonic literary criticism frequently discusses this use of myth and its employment in the service of Truth. According to Proclus, there exist two types of myths, the *paideutic* and the *entheastic*.[63] The former is an educative myth that aids in the *Bildung* of the student. The latter, by contrast, is a mythic representation of the entire universe and is geared for the philosopher.[64] Whereas the *paideutic* presents a simple one-to-one correspondence between signifier and signified, in the *entheastic* myth this correspondence is much more complex because it points to the entire structure of reality.[65] In other words, the latter type of myth uses a narrative format to articulate all of the complexities within the universe.

The myth of the soul that we encounter in all three of these tales needs to be understood in light of what Proclus calls an *entheastic* myth. Rooted in the Platonic dialogues,[66] the myth of the soul seeks to provide an account of the nature of the individual, the danger of succumbing to the corporeal appetites, and, most importantly, the telos that awaits the philosopher. These subjects, especially the last, go back to both the experiential and the ineffable claims that, as I argued above, characterize the Neoplatonic system. Since the apprehension of Truth cannot be confined to either linguistic or conceptual categories, it is essentially indemonstrable and does not readily lend itself to discursive analysis. Myth, however, with its non-discursive properties, allowed the philosopher to speculate on such matters by providing both a vocabulary and a narrative in which to express this. Moreover, it provided a way of discoursing about the fate and the career of the soul that was suggestive, but not meant to be unphilosophic.

Avicenna, for example, does more than simply present a quaint mythic account of the career of the soul.[67] On the contrary, what we encounter in *Ḥayy ibn Yaqẓān* and his other tales reveals a close correspondence with his more technical writings.[68] Avicenna, therefore, struggles with his mythic accounts on a philosophical level: they enable him to leave behind the conventional philosophical vocabulary for what Heath calls "likely stories."[69] Furthermore, the mythic and poetic dimensions of these tales allow each author to present a portrait of the superlunar world based on the images drawn from lived experience.

By focusing as much on the mode of expression as on the content, these tales create a mythic narrative that works on two distinct levels. The first resides in the basic narrative level, which as I argued above is still not as simple as it appears on the surface since it ultimately connects to the cultural, aesthetic, and religious worlds of the authors in question. The other, one could say trans-textual, level is opened up by these tales' use of suggestive and allusive language that subsequently forces the reader to engage the narrative, to take an active part in it. In so doing, these tales use a form of expression that acknowledges the inexpressible and ungraspable and which subsequently presents this by means of the phenomena of this world.

Let me illustrate this with an example from ibn Ezra's *Ḥay ben Meqitz.* The mythic and poetic setting of the work provided ibn Ezra with a context to speak about matters that were not open to him in his other writings, especially his commentaries. For example, a common motif in his commentaries is the notion that the individual with the proper intellectual and religious development cleaves to God.[70] Significantly, though, nowhere in his commentaries does ibn Ezra mention the content of this "cleaving" (*devequt*).[71] In *Ḥay,* however, he not only mentions the internal processes of this phenomenon, but also the manner in which it culminates in the vision of God. He writes:

> I said, "Please, my Lord [i.e., Ḥay], listen to my plea for mercy
> To you I turn my eyes.
> Upon you I cast my troubles
> To your hand I entrust my spirit.
> Tell me with what shall I approach Him?
> How shall I know Him?
> I have truly longed to know Him
> I yearn to see Him."
> He replied, "Uphold my words
> Keep my teaching.
> Walk in my path, and do not depart from me.
> You will know your spirit
> As is fitting to your ability and your strength.
> Then you will be able to know Him
> To apprehend (*laḥazot*) Him."[72]

The narrative structure of the initiatory tale, with its mythic and poetic dimensions, enables him to present, and subsequently speculate, on matters otherwise closed to discursive speculation. In this regard, the structure of the narrative prevents those who are unable from understanding the content of the myth. Likewise, in his *Ḥayy ibn Yaqẓān* (or in his other tales), Avicenna speaks of the denouement of the philosophical-visionary journey in ways that he does not in his more discursive treatises.

Why did our authors find the myth of the soul's ascent/descent so conducive to their philosophical outlooks? These mythic narratives seem to have been especially attractive because they were readily adaptable to monotheistic concerns. Although this myth had its origin in the Platonic writings, and found its subsequent narrative expansion in Plotinus and the other non-monotheist Neoplatonists, it reached its height of expression in the thinkers of medieval Islam and Judaism. This was the case because the mythic structure of the soul's career coincided nicely with the mythic dimensions of the narrative traditions of these two religious traditions.

Neoplatonic Literary Criticism

The Neoplatonic commentators of late antiquity developed a complex theory of literary analysis founded upon the same principles that guided their ontological and metaphysical speculation. Within this context, the literary text essentially becomes the universe in microcosm: the text, like the phenomenal world, participates in, and ultimately presents, a transcendental and ineffable order. It is up to the reader or interpreter to attempt to apprehend or imagine the latter through the former. The text thus becomes the center of philosophical activity. For example, Olympiodorus, a late-sixth-century commentator, writes:

> As he (i.e., Plato) says in the *Phaedrus,* "A literary composition must resemble a living thing." Consequently, the best-constructed composition must resemble the noblest of living things. And the noblest living thing is the cosmos. Accordingly, just as the cosmos is a meadow full of all kinds of living things, so, too, a literary composition must be full of characters of every description.[73]

It is the job of the reader to understand that a veil stands between him- or herself and the text. Just as sensible phenomena signify that which is beyond themselves, so, too, does the text reveal a dimension that is supertextual.[74] Since the structure of the literary text mirrors the structure of the universe, it is essential to understand how the text's surface relates to broader truth claims. Within the literary universe every detail is significant because it not only reflects, but also points back toward, the order of the whole. This led the Neoplatonic literary critics, according to James Coulter, to posit that the text, just like the universe, is made up of form and matter—with the poet functioning as a quasi-demiurge.[75] It is within this context that the author of the *Anonymous Prolegomena to Platonic Philosophy* wrote:

> We must now mention the reasons why Plato used this literary form (i.e., the dialogue). He chose it, we say, because the dialogue is a kind of cosmos. For in the same way as a dialogue has different personages, each speaking in character, so does the universe comprise existences of various natures expressing themselves in various ways; for the utterance of each is according to its nature. It was in imitation then that he did this.[76]

If the text is a microcosm, then the reader must proceed through the text in much the same manner as the philosopher journeys through the different stages of the universe. In both types of journey, the individual starts out firmly in the sensible world and proceeds slowly up the *scala naturae.* The key to ascension is that one must gradually unlock the secrets, much as the protagonists in the *Ḥayy* narratives do, of the (textual) universe. On a fundamental level, then, the reader and the philosopher are one and the same. It is for this reason that the act of reading is, like the philosophical enterprise itself, essentially a hermeneutical act.

How does all of this influence the initiatory tale? Because this is Neoplatonism—a philosophical system with a distinct view that Truth reveals itself in a way that is external both to textual and linguistic parameters—this process is necessarily non-discursive. One cannot just read a descriptive account of this. Rather, the text must be written in such a manner that it includes an experiential and imaginative dimension. My contention is that the Muslim and Jewish authors that are the subject of this study intentionally created a performative and non-discursive text whose very structure was modeled on what they perceived to be the structure of the universe.

We witness this, for example, in Avicenna's commentary to Aristotle's *Poetics.* In this work, Avicenna claims that the literary text provides a vehicle that is well suited to the understanding of the human condition because of its ability to engage in mimesis (*muḥākā*):

> If the imitation of a thing which is untrue moves the soul, then it is no surprise that the depiction of a true thing as such moves the soul too. The latter is even more necessary. But humans are more amenable to imaginative representation (*takhayyul*) than to conviction (*taṣdīq*); and many of them, when hearing the demonstrable truths, respond with aversion and dissociation. Imitation (*muḥākā*) has an element of wonder (*ta*ᶜ*jīb*) that truth lacks.[77]

The literary text invites the reader into its universe, thereby creating a textual map that allows the reader to pursue the path that unfolds within. The poetic or the mythic is particularly amenable to this process because, as Avicenna intimates, it creates a sense of wonder in the individual. The text is more than just an object that one reads and discards; rather, it becomes the fundamental arena in which the reader encounters and experiences Truth.

Furthermore, the concept of the veil (*ḥijāb*) is a prominent feature in ibn Ṭufayl's narrative. This idea is most clearly presented in the epilogue to his tale, wherein he writes that he has intentionally constructed his work as a veil, allowing only the learned into its secrets (*asrār*):

> We decided to intimate to them some of the secrets in order to attract them to the Truth and to divert them from the way [of error]. For this reason we deposited secrets in these few pages with a delicate veil (*ḥijāb*) and a light curtain (*sitr*) that will be easily lifted by one who is able but will solidify before one who is unworthy to pass.[78]

The text does not reveal its secrets to every potential reader, only to those who are able to unlock its secrets. Moreover, the secrets that are to be found within the text are, paradoxically, not simply textual. Rather, the meaning that the ideal reader is to derive from a text such as this is also beyond the text. One needs the text because it points the way to proper understanding, providing the correct intellectual environment in which the individual can begin to contemplate the secrets of the universe. If one is unable to penetrate the surface of the text, one is left with simple allegory that is inoffensive because the surface is *not* the only part of the narrative. However, if one goes beyond the surface, one is presented with the opportunity to grasp or apprehend the divine. Just as the locus of the text is inward rather than external, the place of the spiritual vision, which is the goal of the text and the reading, is not physical but internal. For the text, just like the imagination, foregrounds or presents transcendental truth. The text is thus not only a mirror of the universe, but also of the individual.

The Use of Metaphor

Since language is primarily creative, it is responsible for bringing meaning to light. It does so by articulating a framework that enables us to engage the world.[79] Language, in phenomenological terms, is that which points out, reveals, lets something appear. Language thus reveals the possibility of Truth. The connection between language use and

Truth is, as I have been stressing throughout this chapter, at the very heart of Neoplatonism. Because of the awareness that language, although imprecise, is all that we possess to delineate, demarcate, and communicate, many Neoplatonists tried to incorporate this into the very writing of philosophical discourse, writing in such a manner that both reveals and conceals at the same time.

A crucial vehicle that made this possible was the metaphor. Metaphor, simply put, is a figure of speech in which a name or descriptive term is transferred to some object different from, but analogous to, that to which it is properly applicable. Metaphors are neither simple literary devices nor the exclusive domain of the poet. On the contrary, we employ metaphor to both engage and interact with the world around us. Metaphors, according to cognitive scientists, are not simply linguistic constructions, but the very fabric of our conceptual systems.[80] Metaphors and similar tropes are, in turn, responsible for the construction and maintenance of both social and cultural reality.[81]

In terms of Neoplatonism, the metaphor is based on an incongruity that opens the reader's gaze upon a new horizon, thereby expanding his or her ability to perceive and understand the world. It is so effective because it forces the reader to make connections between sensual perception and emotion on the one hand, and intellection on the other. Furthermore, metaphors create meaning by dint of their suggestiveness as opposed to making explicit connections.[82] As a result, they demand an active engagement with the narrative: the reader must become a participant in its world of meaning if he or she is to come away with understanding.

The Arabs did not simply copy Greek literary theory about the metaphor. Rather, they adopted and adapted those ideas that were relevant, or could be made relevant, to their own concerns.[83] Greek ideas on poetry and literary criticism were used only insofar as they could help explicate and analyze the canons of Arabic poetry that had already been long established. What Greek thought did provide them, however, was both a conceptual and categorical apparatus with which to connect literature to a thorough philosophical analysis. One of the primary ways to accomplish this theoretically was by writing commentaries to Aristotle's *Poetics* and *Rhetoric*.[84] All of the Islamic philosophers who wrote such commentaries agreed that the importance of the poetic arts resided in their ability to arouse wonder (Ar. *ta*ᶜ*jīb*) and pleasure (Ar. *ladhdha*) in the listener/reader.

In his commentary to Aristotle's *Poetics*, Avicenna, following Alfarabi, argues that a metaphor is based on the comparison (*tashbīḥ*) between two objects. The ideal comparison is one that is both "close and suitable."[85] According to Avicenna, the metaphor (interestingly, he uses the generic *naql* as opposed to *tashbīḥ* or *istiʿāra*)[86]

> applies to a name with a given sense the sense of another, but not to the extent that the one becomes the name of the other and the distinction is lost between the first and the second. The transfer is sometimes from genus to species, or from species to genus, or from species to species, or the analogy of a thing is transferred from its like in relation to a fourth, as when old age is called the evening of life or the autumn of life.[87]

For Avicenna, the metaphor has a syllogistic structure that resembles more demonstrative utterances. As Heath notes, this is based on Avicenna's strategy "to invert our empirically based sense of reality so that we can come to regard the abstract realm of the intellect as more vivid and more genuine than that formulated by sensual apperception."[88]

In one of the finest expressions of medieval Hebrew poetics, Moses ibn Ezra (ca. 1055–1138), another poet-philosopher with a commitment to Neoplatonism, argued that the metaphor is foundational to human understanding. In his *Kitāb al-muḥāḍara wa al-mudhākara,* he claims that the metaphor is the most important of all devices employed by the poet.[89] It is, however, much more than simply a poetic device, it is the central feature of the biblical narrative.[90] He also contends that the metaphor has more than just linguistic significance: it is what enables us to function properly as humans (*bal lā ghanā ʿanhā;* lit. "it is indispensable"),[91] and is the device that allows us to understand that which we otherwise could not (*wa-maʿnā al-istiʿāra al-kalima lam yuʿraf bi-shay qad yuʿraf*).[92]

Metaphors thus provide a segue into the narrative. They do so by creating a textual moment that forces the reader to use his or her imagination in order to make connections between the language used and the reality that exists beyond such language. This is why the metaphor is the concern of both ontology and aesthetics. Metaphors and other such literary devices enable the reader to acknowledge that the text is not what it seems. Behind the language is a reality that the metaphor forces the reader to confront. Such linguistic devices allow the reader to move beyond linguistic categories by enabling him or her to engage the imagination in such a manner that the imagination moves from particulars grounded in the sensible world to a universal, non-corporeal reality. As I will show in chapter 3, this theory is predicated on the assumption that the faculties of the imagination and the intellect have a common goal, and that it is essential that they work in tandem. The initiatory tale makes sense only after we place it against this background.

Practical Expression

What are the concrete ramifications of this Neoplatonic epistemology and psychology of language? What is the practical value of employing metaphors and other tropes in the service of Truth? Is language simply a vehicle, something to be disposed of once one arrives at a proper understanding? Many commentators downplay the Neoplatonic use of metaphors and symbols, claiming that these devices simply retell, or tell in a slightly different manner, that which is described more discursively in a surrounding context.[93] Sara Rappe, however, has recently begun to question such a view. She argues that metaphors help us

> to distance and even to abandon, habitual ways of thinking. Plotinus's metaphors attempt at once to describe how things are, so that they succeed in being reality depicting, and at the same time to diverge from normal descriptive use by telling us how to see things. His metaphors push us outside of the semantic system in which a word is exchanged for some conceptual equivalent, by partially denoting some feature of the world or indeed of experience itself.[94]

By employing metaphors, Plotinus and his successors attempt to force us to reflect on language and its ultimate failure to grasp adequately the One. He uses metaphor and other poetic devices to push us to the limits of language's ability to signify. Rather than resorting to discursive, precise language, he often shifts to the poetic and the mythic. Both of these genres, as argued above, force us to become active participants in the text (and ultimately the universe) by encouraging us to look at the word and the world in new ways.

A common motif is to speak of the First Principle, or the One, as a spring (or a fountain or waterfall). This image works by forcing us to understand that what is above is responsible for nourishing what is below. Experience tells us that water flows from a spring in such a way that the source (i.e., the spring) does not diminish. By applying this to the One and emanation, the concept of nourishment and sustenance is placed within a coherent metaphorical system; its meaning, in turn, derives from its role in this system.[95] In the following passage, Plotinus describes the process of emanation:

> Imagine a spring that has no source outside itself; it gives itself to all the rivers, yet is never exhausted by what they take, but remains always integrally, as it was; the tides that proceed from it are at one within it before they run their several ways, yet all, in some sense, know beforehand down what channels they will pour their streams.[96]

Although the One theoretically transcends language, we must ultimately have recourse to such language if we are to speak of the One. As a result, this language must be indefinite, allusive, and non-discursive.[97] It is for this reason that the metaphor is so important: it facilitates a motion from that which is sensible to that which is intelligible.[98] Only a certain type of language should allow us to speak about (*ti peri autou*) the One in such a way that does not let us confine it.[99] We witness this paradox in a description of Plotinus of the One: it "is all things yet no thing; the source of all things is not all things."[100]

Because the One is beyond all attributes or accidents, any propositional statement threatens to limit It. When Plotinus compares emanation to a spring, he effectively says what this process is like, not that it is literally a spring. In doing this, he invokes a sensual image in the reader that approximates, but does not confine, the process of emanation.[101] Lest one mistake the metaphor for the reality, Plotinus immediately switches images:

> Think of the Life coursing throughout some mighty tree while yet it is the stationary Principle of the whole, in no sense scattered over all that extent but, as it were, invested in the root: it is the giver of the entire and manifold life of the tree, but remains unmoved itself, not manifold but the Principle of that manifold life.[102]

The use of the spring and tree metaphors is so effective because although they have different implications, they nevertheless make similar claims. Whereas the spring implies a certain downward movement, the root of the tree works from below to nurture the trunk and branches. This use of metaphor, once again, draws its potency from our embodied experience. Now, however, the conceptual system is somewhat different: the metaphor works only if we understand that which is below gives life to what is above. Although these two metaphors are based on different assumptions, both imply a coherent metaphorical system. Implicit in both is the notion that the spring and the root give of themselves without diminishing themselves in any way.[103] To insure that the reader does not get too attached to one metaphor, Plotinus supplies another one with different implications. The tension between these two images is not coincidental; on the contrary, it mirrors the tension between experiential concerns and philosophical inquiry. Plotinus seems to mediate this tension by appealing to metaphorical or poetic forms of expression that, paradoxically, acknowledge the contextualization of human existence, while trying to overcome it.[104]

This use of the metaphoric as a common element in both the poetic and the mythic found favor with virtually all of the Muslim and Jewish thinkers who subscribed to Neoplatonism's basic ontology. It became especially attractive to the Jewish poet-philosophers who lived in al-Andalus. In particular, it is noticeable in the work of Shlomo ibn Gabirol, one of the first Jewish poet-philosophers in this region.[105] We see the convergence between philosophy and poetry most clearly in his *Keter Malkhut*,[106] a work that had considerable influence on ibn Ezra's *Ḥay ben Meqitz*.[107] In it, ibn Gabirol weaves a rich tapestry in which biblical consciousness overlaps with both the unfixed meter and rhyme of the Arabic *maqāma*[108] and the philosophical themes of Neoplatonism. At the beginning of the poem he establishes God's Oneness and, in Plotinian fashion, claims that this principle lies beyond the human capacity to comprehend:

> You are One,
> prior to all computation
>   and ground to all figuration
> . . .
> You are One.
> and my speech can't establish your boundary or line
> therefore I said I would guard my ways
>   so as not to sin with my tongue
> And you are One,
> sublime and exalted above all that might fall—
>   that One might fall is impossible . . . .[109]

Much like Plotinus before him, ibn Gabirol uses allegories and metaphors to get his point across. God is beyond all capacities of human understanding. Yet, despite this, it is necessary for a Jewish philosopher to mediate this concept with the vivid descriptions of God that are found in the biblical narrative. Although on one level God is beyond all logical categories, ibn Gabirol nevertheless tries to convey with his poetry that God is not completely removed from human concerns. So, again, we witness the tension between philosophical inquiry and lived experience. The result is that ibn Gabirol appeals to mythic and poetic presentation to convey this tension, without completely wanting to mediate it.

In another passage, ibn Gabirol combines metaphoric images to point to the origin of the human soul. Again, the language that he uses is appropriate to an event that is essentially beyond all particular descriptions. In other words, because the soul's origin—essentially ungraspable like the nature of the One or the process of emanation—is beyond human comprehension, he resorts to metaphors that attempt to point to an event that is essentially non-objective and non-discursive:

> Who could grasp your intensity
> in forming the radiance of purity

from the glow of your glory
from a rock the Rock has hewn,
from the hollow of a clearness withdrawn?
You sent the spirit of wisdom along it
and gave it the name of soul,
and formed it out of the fire
of intellect's ardor
whose spirit burned on inside it;
and you sent it out through the body
to serve it and guard it—
and you watch as it acts like a flame within it,
though the body isn't consumed
which was formed from the spark of soul
and was brought into being from nothing
when the Lord came across it in fire.[110]

Since it is impossible to know how the human soul originated, the reader is able to grasp what the poet thinks the soul is like. The soul's point of origin is similar to a sculptor who brings a work of art into actuality from rock. Again, lest the reader get too attached to this metaphor, ibn Gabirol immediately switches to a different figure of speech: the soul now becomes like a flame that emerges from a fire. Both of these images convey that the individual human soul is ontically connected to, and is a particular manifestation of, the world soul just as the flame is to the fire; originally non-existent, the soul makes the human alive just as the sculptor does the stone.

Although these examples could be greatly multiplied,[111] these should suffice to show that language and images are not secondary to Neoplatonism. They are not something that one uses and then divests once one has acquired "proper understanding." On the contrary, such language is inseparable from this philosophical worldview: it is not only the vehicle that presents Truth, but language is also inseparable from Truth itself.

These examples have dealt primarily with metaphoric expression and have showed the way in which an adequate understanding of the transcendent realm is inseparable from poetic expression. I now want to draw attention to the mythic dimension of this tradition. In order to do this, it is necessary to go to the initiatory tales, which, as I argued above, provide a sustained narrative setting of the drama of the soul. Plotinus, for example, frequently alludes to this drama, but nowhere presents it as systematically as we find it in the tales. Furthermore, the presentation that we encounter in the tales provides a complex and multivalent narrative that not only hints at deeper truths beyond its own signification, but also gives a sustained sequential narrative. The latter, in particular, allows the authors to create an unfolding drama, replete with images and metaphors, that makes use (especially in the case of ibn Ezra) of the structures of one's own religious system. In his description of the protagonist's first encounter with Ḥayy, Avicenna writes:

> When I had seen this sage, I felt a desire to converse with him. From my inmost depths arose a need to become intimate with him. So, with my companions, I went in his direction. When we had approached, he took the initiative. He wished us peace and honored us with his salutations. Then, smiling, he addressed us in words that were sweet to our hearts.[112]

In this mythic enactment, the soul encounters the divine guide. There is no discussion of the intellectual or epistemological principles involved in this process. Rather, Avicenna presents us with a discussion that uses the terminology of desire. Seeing the paradoxical youthful old age of Ḥayy, the protagonist and his companions move toward him. This motion toward is caused by the desire to be in the immediate vicinity of Ḥayy. When Ḥayy speaks to them, his words are pleasant, appealing to the hearts of the listeners. This intangible noetic process by which the individual intellect begins its move from potentiality to its actuality is here given a narrative format. This is not an impersonal description of logic (as ibn Zayla describes it), the point of entry for all subsequent philosophical speculation, but a rich account of the quasi-mystical attraction that is propaedeutic to the spiritual quest.

We also see this principle at work in ibn Ezra's *Ḥay ben Meqitz,* which again puts the basic images of Neoplatonism into mythic terms that subsequently give narrative elaboration to the standard philosophical descriptions. For example, in the following passage ibn Ezra recounts the nature of the relationship between the soul and the body:

> While we were talking
> his words opened up.
> Extended to those who desire to understand
> the true nature of things and to searchers of the straight path.
> He said, "The countenance of your face speaks
> Your form attests to your sincerity
> Your ears are open to receive admonitions.
> Your soul has the ability
> To acquire wisdom and understanding.
> This is the art which I examine and research
> It never lies nor cheats.
> It is to the truth like scales
> Like the eyes are to vision
> He who relinquishes it will grope at noon.
> These friends
> Who rule over you
> They are not companions

They are rebellious.
They are not friends
They are evildoers.
They are not lovers
But rather enemies.
They hunt and destroy
Spreading their snares and traps.
They arrest and torture
The heroic and the mighty.
Blessed is the man who is rescued from them
Happy is the sinner trapped by them."[113]

In this description, ibn Ezra, like Avicenna before him, stresses the importance of physiognomy.[114] By looking at and into the unnamed protagonist's face, Ḥay acknowledges the individuality of the protagonist by examining his fixed and determined form.[115] Ḥay learns from this that the unnamed protagonist is noble, that he has the inherent capacity to learn and, therefore, the ability to undertake the journey that is still in front of him. What follows the examination of the face is a description wherein the corporeal appetites are given human qualities. Rather than provide abstract descriptions of these appetites, ibn Ezra personalizes them, describing them as being voracious like a lion and as deceitful as a thief. These two companions[116] have duplicitous personalities: feigning friendship with the protagonist, they are ultimately responsible for his lengthy sojourn in the world of generation and corruption. These descriptions provide a much more effective account of the process than any abstract account could. In so doing, ibn Ezra puts these companions into a mythic narrative of the soul's career, thereby presenting them in concrete, particularistic terms that derive their potency from the biblical narrative. For instance, he employs the original intent of Deuteronomy 28:29 ("he will grope at noon. . . ."), which refers to those who disobey the commandments, to signal the consequences of those who disobey reason.

Such descriptions are neither devoid of emotive content nor of the richly textured possibilities of lived experience. As a result, the individual is able to interact with these descriptive categories not on an abstract level, but on the level at which the uncertainties and dangers that define the human condition and its unfolding story.[117]

Continuing with a description of the protagonist's "companions," ibn Ezra writes:

"You desire to follow them
Your heart lusts after them.
You do not understand that he who walks in their company
Fails to survive their corruptible influences.

Can a man rake embers into his own bosom
Without burning his clothes?
Can a man walk on coals
Without scorching his feet?
This is the lot of he who is swayed by the
sweetness of their mouths.
To the one who is tempted
By the pleasantness of their words.
My son, do not walk in this path with them
Keep your feet from their path.
They have struck dead many
They subdued the mighty and the powerful.
Their way is the way to hell
Their road is the road toward death.
Rule over them!
Master them!
Subdue the fool with the use of desire and use desire against the fool!
Judge them with justice
Do not deviate from judgment!
As for he who speaks nonsense
Do not assent or give heed to him.
Though he be fair-spoken
Do not trust him for seven abominations are in his heart.
Do this, my son, and extricate yourself!
Before the day blows gently and the shadow flees!
Heed my words! Do not forget them
Never abandon them!
Always keep them close to you
Inscribe them upon your heart's tablet.
They will be yours alone
Others having no part with you.
Let them be as a graceful wreath upon your head
A necklace about your throat.
You will spend your days in happiness
Your years in delight."[118]

In this passage, ibn Ezra weaves together the narrative dimension of Neoplatonism with the images and mythic themes of the biblical narrative. Not only does he recount the dangers of succumbing to the corporeal passions, but he also gives Ḥay a vocabulary that is associated with the literature of the Proverbs. Ḥay's words allude to the importance of following Wisdom, personified as a woman, and of avoiding those who are led astray by wickedness, personified as a prostitute. Moreover, this passage compares the "friends" to false prophets, a phrase whose original context comes from Deuteronomy 13:9. Finally, the last sentence of this quotation evokes Job's mythic struggles and his eventual prosperity.

Ibn Ṭufayl is also fond of imbuing his tale with Qur'ānic imagery and language. This is especially evident near the end of his tale where he describes Ḥayy's and Absāl's realization that the inhabitants of Salāmān's island are ultimately ignorant and that this ignorance impedes their ability to experience Ultimate Reality:

> In the end Ḥayy despaired of helping them and gave up his hopes that they would accept his teaching. He saw *every faction delighted in its own* (23:55; 30:31). *They had made their passion their god* (25:43) and desire the object of their worship. They destroyed each other to collect the trash of this world *distracted by greed until they went down to their graves* (102:1–2). Preaching is no help, fine words have no effect on them. Arguing only makes them more pig-headed. Wisdom they have no means of reaching; they were allotted no share of it. They are engulfed in ignorance. *Their hearts are corroded by their possessions* (83:14). *God has sealed their hearts and shrouded their eyes and ears, Theirs will be an awesome punishment* (2: 6–7).[119]

Why are these mythic and poetic images so central to Neoplatonism? As I have suggested, one of the central features of its worldview is the embodied nature of the individual. The dichotomy between soul and body, the transcendent and the ephemeral is ontically connected to the dichotomy between logos and mythos. Since the soul exists within a body, access to the transcendent and/or the logos is impossible without taking into consideration specific contexts. Consequently, truth is not something that exists solely "out there" ready to be apprehended abstractly; rather, truth is inseparable from the phenomena of this world in which it reveals itself. The individual requires mythic and poetic images because the images attempt to mediate the various dichotomies of lived experience.

Conclusions

This chapter has presented an overview of the major themes and trajectories of Neoplatonism that find concrete expression in the initiatory tales composed by our three authors. These tales presuppose many of the features of Neoplatonic literary criticism, textuality, and the creative and dynamic counterpoint between literature and Truth. Because of these features, I have argued that it is important not to regard the genre and the use of language as incidental to these tales. On the contrary, these tales push the ideal reader in a certain direction and in a manner that is different from more analytical treatises. This, of course, is not to argue that the actual telos of these tales is qualitatively different from the latter, only that they use a different mode of communication that should not be regarded, *pace* the minimalists, as inferior to standard, discursive philosophical works.

A dominant theme running through this chapter has been that of *embodiedness*. Our bodies, to reiterate, are what enable us to interact with the world around us. One of the primary mechanisms that allows us to do this is literature since it organizes our experiences into an aesthetic whole. The hermeneutical act permits us to engage the incorporeal; it is what gives form and concrete expression to an otherwise transcendental truth. Consequently, the text becomes the locus of visionary experience, the vehicle of ocular desire. For this reason, the real meaning that occurs in the encounter between reader and text is not in front of the text or even in the readerly activity itself; on the contrary, it occurs in the space that opens up between the lines of the narrative. For in this area, one is afforded access to that which cannot be circumscribed by means of verbal communication.

It is for this reason that the hermeneutical act is so important. For the initiatory tale is not simply the description of a journey or an experience; rather, the images and the symbols are part and parcel of the experience itself. In it, to use the words of Wolfson, "the suprasensible world is experienced in sensory imagery and not simply described in terms of the sensible."[120] In other words, the initiatory tale allows the reader to experience the incorporeal world in terms of the imagery that the sensible world provides. The goal is to be able to make the cognitive leap from the latter to the former by means of the hermeneutical act. It is for precisely this reason that the imagination plays such an important role in this task. And for this reason I now turn attention to this faculty that, I contend, is central to our understanding the initiatory tale.

3
Polishing a Dirty Mirror: The Philosophic Imagination

VISION, THE STRONGEST OF OUR SENSES, IS CENTRAL TO OUR ENGAGEMENT WITH and in the world. Without vision, we encounter the world in only two dimensions, unable to process the fullness of the world in all of its richness and diversity. Since the currency of the imagination is images, its main activity is often associated with a type of visualization. This vision, however, is not external and directed toward what physically exists before us; rather it is internal, bringing into existence that which is no longer present. For this reason, the medieval thinkers often refer to the imagination as the inner eye (Ar. *al-ayn al-baṭiniyya;* Lat. *oculus imaginationis*). The imagination is, thus, a creative faculty responsible for the formation of images of things or concepts that the senses have apprehended but that are now no longer visible.

This presencing of the absent is both the blessing and the curse of the imagination in the history of Western philosophy. Because of its ability to make the absent present, many philosophers in both the ancient and medieval worlds regarded this faculty as unreliable and unpredictable, responsible for the formation of inauthentic expressions. For example, the image of a beautiful object is not the same thing as the object itself, which, in turn, is but a pale imitation of a formal and incorporeal beauty. Images, then, are twice removed from the really real. For reasons such as this, philosophers distrusted the productive or mimetic aspect of the imagination: in a system that gives priority to intellection, production must always be derivative. To imagine something, then, is secondary (or even tertiary) and inferior to our ability to encounter it physically and in such a manner that we can study, analyze, and know it.

But if this is the curse of the imagination, the philosophers who are the subject of this study also appreciated that this faculty could, in phenomenological parlance, grant access to a mode of being otherwise inaccessible. When properly conditioned and when working in tandem with the intellect, the imagination has the potential to bring forth our engagement with the world in such a manner that we can experience and apprehend that which exists without form. The imagination, in other words, becomes the faculty with the potential to create internal impressions of that which exists incorporeally. The imagination, thus, becomes the locus in which the individual can experience the divine presence.[1]

As I conceptualize it here, the imagination is essentially a hermeneutical faculty. Presenting one thing in terms of another, it translates the unknown into the known, the unfamiliar into the familiar. It does this by actively producing images that permit the individual to visualize and conceptualize spiritual entities. The imagination is not simply a passive faculty; rather, it enriches the individual's engagement with the world, mediating his or her experience with the divine. I concur with Elliot Wolfson who, in his analysis of the role of the imagination in ancient and medieval Jewish mysticism, argues: "In the absence of imagination there is no form, and without form there is no vision and hence no knowledge."[2] So even though the medieval philosophers were critical of the imagination, I think it is no coincidence that the telos of many of their systems is often an elaborate discussion of the philosopher's gaze into the divine, which is described in terms of rich and highly *visual* imagery. This is made all the more telling by the fact that these philosophers argued that God was neither a body nor bound by corporeal extension. From where do these images to describe the divine come? Are they metaphors used to suggest what the experience might be like? Do they represent the translation of the encounter with the Ineffable? Or do they constitute the quiddity of the actual experience?

The goal of the present chapter is to examine the role and function of the imagination as it specifically relates to the initiatory tale. In particular, I wish to examine how our three authors made sense of the philosophical import of the imagination in light of a specific ontology and epistemology. The problematic that these philosophers faced and that this chapter investigates is: How can an individual in this ephemeral world gain access to the eternal world that exists above the moon? Or, put somewhat differently, how can a non-material entity become accessible to a material entity?

It is difficult to address the role and function of the imagination from the vantage point of the twenty-first century without addressing the importance of phenomenology.[3] This is because phenomenology, as developed by Edmund Husserl, emphasizes the centrality of the imagination for the intuition of essences and its ability to reveal human consciousness to itself.[4] This, in turn, allows one to avoid the thorny issue of attaching valuational terms such as "true" or "false" to imagined forms of consciousness. According to Wolfson, "One cannot speak of an intentional object that is imaged without an intentional act of imaging, just as one cannot speak of an act without the object."[5]

According to the formulation of Martin Heidegger, one of the main goals of phenomenology is to investigate the way in which the structures of Being are revealed through the structures of human existence,[6] both of which are inseparable from modes of temporality. Because of this temporality, whenever an individual understands Being, he or she can only do so in time. As a result, all ontological understanding is ultimately rooted in temporality.[7] Hermeneutical phenomenology becomes important here since both of these structures ultimately require interpretation. Hermeneutical phenomenology is, therefore, inseparable from the uncovering of truth (*aletheia*).[8] Indeed, because truth does not exist apart from the phenomena of this world,[9] the goal of phenomenology is to reveal or uncover the nature of Being as it shows itself temporally to individuals rooted in their own temporality. Significantly, in his later writings, Heidegger acknowledged that this could best be done in works of art, in particular poetry.[10]

This discussion proves helpful in dealing with the imagination because it provides one with a framework with which to treat seriously the imagination and its workings. Rather than posit that the images created by the imagination are chimerical, reduced to the exercise of the senses, a phenomenological approach suggests that images not only represent the disclosure of reality, but that they can also become reality itself. The image thus becomes a translucent symbol through which an otherwise unapprehendable reality shines forth.

But this line of inquiry has the potential to create almost as many problems as it solves. If we simply read the imagination of phenomenology onto the medieval thinkers, how can we understand the medieval thinkers on their own terms? Such a question is made difficult owing to the extreme hermeneutical difficulties associated with examining a temporal and spatial order different from our own. Although objectivity is my aim, I am also extremely self-conscious of Gadamer's claim that the goal of interpretation is not simply to bring out the so-called "literal meaning" of the past but also to analyze the manner in which the past confronts the present and the various modalities whereby this confrontation manifests itself. Gadamer, for example, argues that

> every encounter with tradition that takes place within historical consciousness involves the experience of a tension between the text and the present. The hermeneutic task consists in not covering up this tension by

> attempting a naive assimilation of the two but in consciously bringing it out. This is why it is part of the hermeneutic approach to project a historical horizon that is different from the horizon of the present.[11]

My goal, then, is not only to try to re-create and describe the medieval philosophical imagination so as to place it within the various psychic and somatic hierarchies, but also to speculate as to *why* these medieval philosophers were so interested in this faculty despite their criticisms of it. The former allows for a historical study: How did the medievals think about the imagination? What did it allow them to do? What is the nature of the relationship between the intellect and the imagination? The latter permits us to examine the intentional structure of the imagination's content as it is, regardless of its causal origins. Why, for example, do all of these philosophers ultimately fall back on the concept of an inner vision, which implies the creation or formation of highly visual images?

Both of these approaches should, ideally, allow me to present the imagination as an important philosophical faculty. What do I mean by a "philosophical faculty"? Such a term could mean (1) an internal faculty that is relevant to philosophy; (2) an internal faculty capable of producing philosophical knowledge; (3) an internal faculty that translates philosophical knowledge. For the purposes of this study, I shall confine my use of the term to (3). The reason for this is that (1) is too vague and is, at any rate, pre-supposed by (3). Also, (2) would go against much of the philosophers' own comments, which, for the most part, treat the imagination with great suspicion.

The imagination's task, as I have already stated, is essentially hermeneutical. It is the faculty responsible for the creation of forms or images. These forms and images, however, are experienced and not simply described in symbolic terms. Although these forms and images are ultimately reflective of sensory experience, they cannot simply be confined to such experience. The imagination, in its engagement with the sensual world, translates particulars into images that the intellect uses.[12] Thought, as Aristotle claimed, is impossible without our ability to form images, which essentially become the raw data of our higher intellectual processes. Images and the imagination, therefore, represent the prolegomena to noetic activity. For even if, as many of the ancient and medieval philosophers formulated it, the goal of intellectual activity is to comprehend the imageless and the formless, human consciousness is impossible without either image or form. But even more than this: the imagination becomes the locus within the individual soul that allows access to the incorporeal through an intricate process of symbolization.[13]

How does this discussion bear on the initiatory tale? Initiatory tales challenge the assumption that the human mind is somehow distinct from the world and that it is capable of grasping reality by means of formless and imageless principles and that it is independent of the natural order. Based on this assumption is the concomitant notion that thinking is somehow distinct from imagining. The former, in theory existing without corporeal extension and, thus, independent of ephemeral matter, is deemed most real, least susceptible to corruption. The latter, in contrast, relies on the spatial and geometric extensions associated with matter because the imagination's function is to engage in pictorial representation. To a certain extent, however, this juxtaposition is misleading: even the most abstract thought is ultimately dependent upon images that are supplied to it.

Initiatory tales work so effectively because of the Neoplatonic picture of the universe, in which the ontological gap between the One and the many is bridged through emanation.[14] Such an ontology is what ultimately makes epistemology possible. Within this context, non-objective and non-discursive literary images create a clearing wherein the individual imagination is allowed to experience and apprehend specific manifestations of Being. They provide the imagination with a set of symbols—drawn from the cultural, religious, and intellectual trajectories of the day—that enable this faculty to form images of what is essentially formless. As such, these images provide the individual with a framework by which he or she can fathom the transcendent world that is beyond the ken of human experience. When, for example, our authors provide an imaginative account of the various celestial spheres, they realize that such accounts cannot pretend either to be discursive or descriptive. Although the intellect cannot provide a rational description of this superlunar world, the imagination can gain access to this world, giving it a spatial extension that is based on human experience. The mind, accordingly, yields to such images precisely because they are non-discursive or non-objective and such language is potentially able to trigger a sudden intuition.[15]

Greek Precedents

Before I move onto the role of the imagination in Avicenna, ibn Ezra, and ibn Ṭufayl, allow me to provide a brief overview of the philosophical discourse that they inherited from the ancients. The imagination, as I already alluded, occupies an ambiguous position in the history of Western philosophy.[16] Occupying the interface between the rational soul and the animal soul, it is, more often than not, regarded as part of the latter, yet, at the same time, its processes are deemed instrumental for the proper functioning of the former. Important questions that revolve around the function of the imagination are the following: Is the imagination a faculty or a capacity that serves other faculties of cognition? Is the role of the imagination to receive material from the higher soul, to convey information to it, or both? This, in turn, is related to the question of the source/s of the images that are produced in the imagination. Is the imagination simply a function of the body (i.e., the sum of the senses)? If not, what is its relationship to the intellect?

Plato's discussion of the imaginative faculty is brief, cursory and, for the most part, negative.[17] In the *Timaeus,* Plato argues that within the body the appetitive part of the soul, in which the imagination is located, is geographically far away from the rational part because the former does not understand the deliberations of the latter. The appetitive part is incapable "of paying attention to rational argument even if it became aware of it" and that it is "especially led by phantoms and images night and day."[18] Plato faults the imagination for many of the same reasons that he is critical of mimesis: both concern themselves with pale representations that obfuscate and lead astray.

Paradoxically, however, Plato presents the *Timaeus* in the form of a myth.[19] He is conscious of a tension between the concealment of Being and lived experience. Although he contrasts the imagination (*phantasia*) with the intellect, the functioning of the latter is impossible without the former.[20] Plato, then, cannot completely condemn the imagination for it is the faculty responsible for gaining access to the Ideas. In this regard, the imagination is related to the Platonic notion of intuition or the non-rational discovery of rational principles.[21]

In the *Philebus,* another late dialogue, Plato mentions almost in passing that the senses bring in the data and that the memory recalls this data in such a way that images arise. In typical fashion, Plato gives a simile of the "workman in our soul" who paints pictures for us.[22] Although Plato ultimately claims that these images are the core of opinions, which are to be contrasted with true belief, he does acknowledge that some images and opinions are truer than others.[23] Those images that appear to a healthy soul, one that has the proper balance, are more likely to be true or beneficial, presumably because such an individual can differentiate between good and bad, truth and opinion.

Unlike Plato, Aristotle attempts to provide a more adequate philosophical account of the role and function of the imagination.[24] Although it will play an important role in his accounts of action, memory, dreaming, perception, and thought,[25] Aristotle's only systematic treatment of the imagination is found in *De Anima* III.3, which is universally considered to be highly obscure.[26] Within this section, Aristotle situates the imagination between sense perception and discursive thinking. On the one hand, imagination is not found without sensation, since we are unable to produce images without prior sensory experience;[27] on the other, the imagination produces images by which we think.[28] Despite this, Aristotle is quick to distinguish imagination from knowledge or intelligence (which are never in error to him).[29]

Aristotle offers the following as his main definition of the imagination:

> But since when one thing has been set in motion another thing may be moved by it, and imagination is held to be a movement and to be impossible without sensation, i.e. to occur in beings that are percipient and to have for its content what can be perceived, and since movement may be produced by actual sensation and that movement is necessarily similar in character to the sensation itself, this movement cannot exist apart from sensation or in creatures that do not perceive, and its possessor does and undergoes many things in virtue of it, and it is true and false.[30]

Imagination is a movement that is produced by, and presupposes, the activity of the senses. It is the faculty in virtue of which images (*phantasmata*) arise in us.[31] This production of images is, in turn, common to both animals and humans. It is also connected to the body and its activities. Aristotle claims that it is not possible to think without images.[32] This is in keeping with his empiricism, which stresses the acquisition of knowledge through the sensible world. The sensibles that our senses perceive are the building blocks of our ability to know phenomena; once the perception has passed, we are still able to recall the image in order to think.

Like Plato before him, Aristotle sees in the imagination an ambiguous, yet very important, faculty. It is ambiguous because its subject matter is sensibles and not universals. Furthermore, the imagination can be deceptive: because it stores images, the imagination often produces illusions, especially during sleep or sickness.[33] However, images are also crucial to our ability to interact with the world and form knowledge about it.

It is for precisely this reason that Aristotle argues that literature is a valid domain of philosophical enquiry. Whereas Plato had always stressed the deceptive character of mimesis,[34] Aristotle now transforms mimesis from the simple reproduction of particular realities to the ability of embodying universals.[35] This stems from the fact that, according to Aristotle, humans, by their natures, engage in and take pleasure in mimetic activity.[36] This pleasure, he claims, is tantamount to the natural exercise of our faculties.[37] Aristotle, then, recognizes in mimesis the ability to improve our understanding; mimesis is a crucial vehicle that allows the intellect to move from particulars to universals.

Significantly, the majority of the commentators that came after Aristotle, even though they attempted to harmonize his work with that of Plato, stressed the Aristotelian justification for the relationship between literature and philosophy. However, they went beyond Aristotle in integrating his theory of poetics into a general theory of emanation and aesthetics, wherein images facilitate the upward movement of the intellect and its ability to cognize the supralunar world.

One of the key figures in introducing Aristotelian psychology into Platonic philosophy was Plotinus, who on the whole was much less suspicious of the imagination than his predecessors.[38] One of his overwhelming interests was in imaging: the One gradually becomes manifest through successive and increasingly corporealized images. The perception of truth is thus ontologically connected to images since it is the latter that make the former accessible. By appealing to certain types of language, Plotinus attempts to textualize the One's ineffability. Whereas ontologically the One manifests itself by dint of images, Plotinus tries to use images to point back beyond themselves.

For Plotinus, the soul is a reflection of higher being. When the soul is functioning properly—that is, according to its higher nature—the lower parts are subsumed into the higher. The higher parts, which include the imagination, are responsible for the upward progression of the individual. But the imagination is problematic. If left to its own devices, it will further enmesh the individual in this world. The imagination therefore needs to be harnessed and its subversive potential redirected so that it may be used for the philosophical enterprise.

In a famous passage, Plotinus compares the imagination to a mirror:

> When the intellect is in the upward orientation (the lower part of it) which contains that life of the soul is, so to speak, flung down again and becomes like the reflection resting on a smooth and shining surface of a mirror. When the mirror is in place, the image appears; but if the mirror is absent or out of place, all that would produce an image still exists. In the case of the soul, when there is peace in that part that is capable of reflecting images of the rational and intellectual principles, these appear.... When, on the contrary, the internal mirror is shattered through some disturbance of the body, reason and the intellectual principles are unpictured. Intellect is unattended by imagination.[39]

In other words, when this mirror is smooth, polished, and bright, it projects images "back beyond themselves."[40] We are thus able to know intelligibles as if we had perceived them through the senses. This activity occurs, according to Plotinus, when the mind operates non-discursively.[41] In *Ennead* IV.4.4.10–11, Plotinus writes, in typical paradoxical fashion:

> Even if the soul imagines this world before she enters it, yet she imagines it intellectually, and this act is ignorance not cognition; yet that ignorance is more sublime than any cognition, because the mind is ignorant of what is above it, with an ignorance more sublime than knowledge.[42]

Here the imagination is something that, tied to the intellectual faculty, provides beautiful images of its existence before the descent into the corporeal body. According to Plotinus,

> Memory (*mneme*) begins from heaven, because when the soul becomes like heavenly things she remembers them and knows that they are the ones she knew before entering the lowly world.[43]

The imagination is the faculty that allows the soul to realize that there exists something beyond this world of sense perception. It is responsible for apprehending the relationship between representation and object or appearance and reality. As a result, the imagination has the ability to take concrete particulars and show the way they represent specific disclosures of Being.

Plotinus complicates matters by arguing for the existence of two imaginations within the individual. This stems from his position that each part of the soul—both the rational and the irrational parts—possesses its own imagination. The lower imagination is associated primarily with the lower, sensual memories, whereas the higher imagination, which can also use the data of the lower imagination, departs, along with the upper soul, the body upon corporeal death.[44] When tied to the intellectual faculty, the imagination thus provides beautiful images of its existence before the descent into the corporeal body.

The impact of Plotinus on subsequent Arabic and Jewish Neoplatonists was significant, albeit indirect through works such as the *Theology of Aristotle*. Broadly speaking, he gave them a mythic narrative for charting the career of the soul. More specifically, he provided them with a language of vision to aid the reader's imaginative apprehension of the intelligible world.

Although medieval philosophers never developed what could be called a full-fledged discourse of the imagination, implicit in their discussion is a combination of Plato's theory of knowledge, Aristotle's theory of literature, and Plotinian psychology. The Platonism articulates a position in which our intuition of truth (the forms) occurs through the pale images present in this world.[45] The Aristotelian component, by contrast, argues that the mimetic dimension of literature improves our understanding and is a crucial vehicle that allows the intellect to move from particulars to universals.[46] By interpreting Plato's and Aristotle's concept of mimesis in terms of the functions of the imaginative faculty, the medieval philosophers developed a distinct theory of aesthetics.

Locating the Medieval Imagination

Of the three authors who are the subject of this study, Avicenna presents the clearest and most comprehensive discussion of psychology in general and the imagination in particular. I begin my analysis with him and then show how both ibn Ezra and ibn Ṭufayl either subscribe to or deviate from his writings. Although Avicenna's basic psychology is Aristotelian, his soul–body dualism is distinctly Platonic.[47] Despite this, however, he disagrees with the basic Platonic position that the soul pre-exists the body; rather, for Avicenna, the soul comes into existence with the body.[48] For Avicenna, the human soul is a unity made up of one substance. This substance, however, is divisible into three distinct parts:

> The soul's powers are divided (*inqasama*) into three categories (*ajnās*). The vegetative soul (*al-nafs al-nabātiyya*), which is the first entelechy of a natural body from the perspective of reproduction, growth, and nourishment . . . The animal soul (*al-nafs al-ḥaywāniyya*) which is the first entelechy of a natural body with respect to desire and movement . . . The human soul (*al-nafs al-insāniyya*) which is the first entelechy of a natural body with regard to thought and opinion.[49]

The relationship between these three souls is hierarchical,[50] with each soul subdivided into faculties. Since the vegetative soul is concerned with reproduction, growth, and nourishment, its three faculties are nutrition (*al-qūwa al-ghāthiyya*), growth (*al-qūwa al-munamiyya*), and reproduction (*al-qūwa al-muwallida*).[51]

The animal soul is divided into two main faculties, each of which is subdivided into other faculties. The two main faculties are the motive (*muḥarrika*) and the perceptive (*mudrika*).[52] The former is subdivided into active (*fāʿila*) and impulsive (*bāʿitha*) motions.[53] The former corresponds to instinct,[54] the latter to concupiscence and irascibility. Impulsive motions are related to the imagination because they either attract or repel the body through images supplied by this and related faculties.[55] The perceptive faculty is also divided into two—the external and internal senses—each of which has five subdivisions. The external senses are the traditional five senses: sight (*al-baṣar*), hearing (*al-sam*ᶜ), smell (*al-shamm*), taste (*al-dhawq*), and touch (*al-lams*).[56]

The internal senses receive data from the five senses and subsequently transfer this to the intellect.[57] The internal senses thus play a crucial role in linking the body to the rational faculty, the outer world of sense with the inner world of intellection. The lowest of the internal senses is the faculty of common sense (*al-qūwa al-mushtaraka*), which functions as a general storehouse for all of the incoming sensations. This faculty, which is located in the "forepart of the front ventricle of the brain," receives sensual data directly from the senses.[58] Above this is the faculty of representation (*qūwa al-khayāl* or *qūwa al-muṣawwara*). This is responsible for retaining the representations from the faculty of common sense, even when the actual object is absent.

The next faculty is called the imaginative (*qūwa al-mutakhayyila*) with regard to animals and the cogitative (*al-mufakkira*) with regard to humans.[59] This faculty, which is in the middle ventricle of the brain, combines and/or separates the various data in the faculty of representation.[60] The imagination, then, is primarily responsible for recombining various images that are not immediately present to the senses or do not exist in reality. This ability is ultimately responsible for the creation of myths, fables, and fictions.[61]

The fourth of the internal senses is the faculty of estimation (*qūwa al-wahm*), which is located in the far end of the middle ventricle of the brain. This is responsible for the perception of the intentions that are in sensible objects.[62] The example that Avicenna always cites in this regard is that one always knows to flee from a wolf. This faculty also is what judges the images of the imagination to determine whether or not they are believable.

The fifth, and final, of the internal senses is the recollective faculty (*al-qūwa al-dhākira*), located in the rear ventricle of the brain.[63] This is responsible for retaining the intentions that the faculty of estimation perceives.

In addition to possessing vegetative and animal souls, humans also possess a rational soul. This soul is divided into two faculties or intellects: the practical (*al-qūwa/al-*ᶜ*aql al-*ᶜ*āmila*) and the theoretical (*al-qūwa/al-*ᶜ*aql al-*ᶜ*ālima*).[64] The former is intimately connected to the imagination in serving as an intermediary between the lower souls and the theoretical intellect. For example, it uses the faculties of imagination and estimation to deduce transient activities and arts.[65] When the practical intellect has proper control over all of the lower faculties, the person is said to be ethical.[66] This intellect, however, is superior to the animal soul because it is able to induce premises with the help of the theoretical intellect in the ethical and political sciences.

The final faculty and the epitome of the individual is the theoretical intellect, whose function is to receive the impression of universals that exist outside of matter. The theoretical intellect has different relations to these universal forms: it can be completely potential, relatively potential, or active. When the rational faculty is completely potential, it is called the material intellect (*al-ᶜaql al-hayūlānī*); this stage of the intellect is common to all humans. As soon as this intellect acquires the primary intelligibles or axioms (e.g., the concept that the whole is greater than its parts), it becomes the habitual intellect (*al-ᶜaql bi al-malaka*). Once this intellect begins to acquire the secondary intelligibles (deduced through syllogisms), it becomes the actual intellect (*al-ᶜaql bi al-fiᶜl*). When the theoretical intellect is actively engaged in syllogistic inquiry and is aware of this activity, Avicenna calls this the acquired intellect (*al-ᶜaql al-mustafād*).

According to Avicenna, there are primarily two ways to acquire knowledge. One is through the external world, the world of particulars; the other is through the celestial world (more specifically, through the tenth celestial intellect, called the Active Intellect). The latter form of knowledge, since it is not based on particulars or matter, is regarded as superior to the former. Crucial to the acquisition of knowledge from the external world is the faculty of the imagination. This faculty is able to abstract the material accidents from something (e.g., a particular person named Zayd) and subsequently recombine them to create an image that may not exist in reality (e.g., a man with no head). Such an image, however, will nevertheless remain a particular, since the image that is imagined will still resemble an individual person.[67] Because the internal senses are confined to bodily organs, they can only perceive particulars.[68] For this reason, all sensually produced knowledge requires the body.[69]

Juxtaposed against this is the intellect, which in theory does not require the body, since it has immediate contact with universals. If the intellect were confined to an organ, Avicenna informs us, it would not be able to understand itself.[70] The intellect does not abstract form from matter in the Aristotelian sense;[71] rather, it receives forms directly from the Active Intellect:

> And we say that the theoretical faculty (*al-qūwa al-naẓariyya*) also moves from potentiality (*al-qūwa*) to actuality (*al-fiᶜl*) by means of the illumination of a substance (*jawhar*) that is already in this state. This is because a thing cannot move from potentiality to actuality by its own essence, unless another thing gives it actuality. This actuality that it gives is the intelligible form.[72]

The animal soul, including the faculty of imagination, thus plays a negligible role in this form of knowledge. Despite this, Avicenna does acknowledge that the imagination can help the rational soul acquire knowledge. First, since part of the imaginative faculty's function is to abstract attributes from particulars, the imagination aids the rational soul in the abstraction of single universals.[73] Second, it (along with the faculty of estimation) provides affirmation or negation about these single universals.[74] Third, this faculty aids in the discovery of empirical premises (e.g., if it is light, it is day; if it is not day, it is not light).[75] Fourth, the imagination is useful in the assent (*taṣdīq*) of traditional information (*shidda al-tawātur;* lit., the force of tradition).[76]

Within this Peripatetic paradigm, the imagination fairs rather poorly since it cannot provide the rational soul with universals. Indeed, the best that the faculty of the imagination can do is initiate the process of intellection; once this process has begun, however, the imagination actually gets in the way of the intellect's proper operation.[77] In other works—most notably in his *Kitāb al-ishārāt wa al-tanbīhāt,* his last major philosophical composition—Avicenna puts a somewhat different emphasis on the imagination. This is particularly apparent in his ninth section of the fourth part, entitled *Fī maqāmāt al-ᶜārifīn* (On the stations of the knowers). Although he nowhere identifies who these *ᶜārifūn* are, historically this term is used to designate the Sufis who possess *maᶜrifa* or *ᶜirfān*.[78] What Avicenna seems to be doing here, then, is equating the love of God with the wonder that is to be derived from philosophy broadly defined. To begin to undertake this, however, one must properly align one's soul. Music, poetry, as well as thoughtful worship, are the preparatory stages through which the *ᶜārif* begins a process that culminates in the conjunction (*ittiṣāl*) with God.[79] The reason one performs these spiritual exercises, according to Avicenna, is to harness the imaginative and estimative faculties to the rational soul.[80] In other words, such exercises enable the individual to rationalize the imagination, to make it into a faculty that is relevant to philosophy.

Avicenna also recognizes a more other-worldly function of the imagination. He argues that it is the faculty responsible for making the visions of dreams and other inspirations sensible, audible, and visible.[81] For in such dreams and inspirations, Avicenna claims, the individual's imaginative faculty makes contact with an external source that "draws" within the imagination "pictures of things that do not exist but that may be found in the future."[82] We see here that dreams and inspirations are not internal phenomena confined to the body; rather, they represent the contact between the imagination (significantly not the intellect) and the divine world.[83] Within this paradigm, the imagination does not simply recall or (re)combine past sense data; rather, it actively creates symbols that translate the encounter with the spiritual, incorporeal world.

The imagination is responsible for transferring the data that the intellect receives from its contact with the Active Intellect into the faculty of common sense. Avicenna writes,

> If the sense perceptions are reduced and fewer preoccupations remain, it is not unlikely for the soul to have escapes that lead from the work of the imagination to the side of sanctity. Thus, apprehensions of the invisible world are imprinted on the soul, which then flow to the world of the imagination and are then imprinted in the common sense.[84]

This data can then be used either by the intellect or the imagination. The imagination becomes important within this context because of its hermeneutical function. It essentially possesses the ability to focus the attention of the individual on the divine by expressing the incorporeal in corporeal form.

Avicenna further argues that what the rational soul learns in its conjunction (*ittiṣāl*) with the divine Intellect is beyond demonstration.[85] Indeed, Avicenna seems to imply that the imagination is the faculty that is responsible for conveying knowledge of the individual's direct experience with the divine: *wa lā yakshifu al-maqāl ᶜan-hā ghayra al-khayāl* ("the intellect cannot uncover it, only the imagination").[86] Knowledge of this experience therefore unfolds through the imagination. Even if the knowledge that one gains from this contact is ultimately syllogistic, rationality cannot fully explain the details of the contact.

Ibn Ezra is, for the most part, primarily interested in this second, less Peripatetic and more intuitive, of Avicenna's two paradigms. However, when we look at ibn Ezra's psychology, we immediately face a number of hermeneutical difficulties. Generally speaking, Jewish thinkers were forced to confront the biblical text in the light of the various philosophical paradigms that they inherited.[87] Consequently, it is often difficult to know just how these Jewish thinkers employed, let alone engaged, the terminology of the philosophical tradition. Did, for example, they use it unequivocally or metaphorically? Such usage is made even more difficult in ibn Ezra's *oeuvre*, which, for all intents and purposes, lacks a systematic vocabulary. In particular, it is often impossible to discern, even when he does use technical terms (e.g., *devequt, kavod*), whether he employs them technically, as metaphors, or simply as part of a common set of phrases that would have been in vogue among twelfth-century intellectuals.[88]

It is also difficult to isolate a philosophical topic or issue in an author who never wrote a philosophical treatise. Indeed, this is made even more difficult by the wide array of sources that ibn Ezra drew upon.[89] For example, ibn Ezra knew well the work of Saadya Gaon, yet Saadya's work has a set of theoretical assumptions that are radically different from those of thinkers who drew heavily from the work of Plotinus.[90] Although ibn Ezra's work is certainly greater than the sum of its parts, it is nevertheless unarguable that he took from a number of sources, both Jewish and non-Jewish, and that often these sources sit together uncomfortably in his work, often showing little or no attempt by the author at systematization.[91] To cite one example relevant to the imagination, ibn Ezra must essentially reconcile the philosophical system he inherited from the Greeks that potentially represses the visual with the biblical-rabbinic tradition stressing that God can be seen in the text.[92]

Now what are the repercussions of this for ibn Ezra's theory of the imagination? Or, perhaps more forcefully, does ibn Ezra even have a theory of the imagination? For obvious reasons, I assume that he does and that it can be retrieved. The way that I go about this is to examine various statements he made in his biblical commentaries and in his poetry and then to situate them in the light of my preceding analysis of Avicenna's discussion of the imagination. In doing this, my goal is not to present an exhaustive survey of ibn Ezra's psychology;[93] rather, I shall compare and contrast his comments on the imagination with those of Avicenna.

Ibn Ezra did not simply take over Avicenna's account. To argue this would be too reductive and would ignore the contribution of his other sources. The reason that I have chosen to emphasize the Avicennian dimension is because of ibn Ezra's initiatory tale *Ḥay ben Meqitz*. To understand this treatise fully, we must, in part, put it in counterpoint with its precursor, Avicenna's *Ḥayy ibn Yaqẓān*. One important distinction between the two thinkers, however, is that ibn Ezra is not particularly interested in exploring the nature of the relationship between the imagination and logic. We thus do not encounter in his writings the discussion of mimesis, which was so important to Avicenna. This could be the result of two factors: he was not interested in logic; or he was an accomplished poet, for whom the nature and power of the poetic image on the individual's imagination would have been obvious. Ibn Ezra, however, was particularly interested in how the embodied individual is able to grasp the uppermost world (*ha-olam ha-eliyon*). Indeed, his concern with this seems to be constant throughout many of his diverse writings. Avicenna, on the contrary, only alludes to this in his later works, such as the concluding sections of *K. al-ishārāt* and his Commentary to the *Theology of Aristotle*.

Of central importance for ibn Ezra is the nature of the relationship between the human soul and the divine world[94] and, more precisely, the question of how the human soul can know that world. In the cosmological system we encounter in *Ḥay ben Meqitz*, ibn Ezra recounts ten spheres in ascending order: the Moon, Mercury, Venus, the Sun, Mars, Jupiter, Saturn, the sphere of the fixed stars, the all-encompassing diurnal sphere which contains no stars, and the sphere of the unembodied angels.[95] This last sphere, which he alternatively calls glory (*kavod*),[96] is of crucial importance for understanding ibn Ezra's discussion of the imagination.

It is also worth noting that ibn Ezra's ontology also consists of a huge gap between the sublunar and superlunar worlds. Indeed, following Avicenna, ibn Ezra claims that God does not know particulars, except in a universal way.[97] Despite this claim, however, ibn Ezra is ambiguous about the way in which the embodied individual can attain knowledge of the divine world. In some of his comments, he argues that we can only know this by means of the created order (i.e., through the divine attributes of action).[98] Yet in other places, he claims that one can receive a direct, almost inspirational, form of knowledge if one's soul separates from the body and cleaves to the upper world.[99]

Although common to both of these modes of knowledge is the impossibility of knowing God's essence, they do nonetheless have rather different implications. The first form of knowledge is discursive and is based on rational, empirical, and scientific assumptions. The second form, however, implies a more experiential mode of knowledge. In other words, the latter cannot be grounded in an objective explanation because it is ultimately disclosed by means of non-objective and elliptical tools. It is this non-objective form of knowledge, I contend, that *Ḥay ben Meqitz* attempts to portray with its use of allegory and myth.

Let me briefly situate the imagination within ibn Ezra's psychology. In his commentary to Qohelet 7:3, ibn Ezra distinguishes, as did Avicenna before him, among three souls.[100] The lowest soul is the vegetative (*ha-nefesh ha-ṣomeḥet;* or, alternatively, the *nefesh*); the intermediate soul is the animal (*ha-nefesh ha-behema;* sometimes referred to as the *ruaḥ*); and the highest is the rational soul (*ha-neshamah,* or *ha-lev*). The function of the animal soul is both to act as an intermediary between the higher and lower souls and then to interact with the sensual world through the five senses and process the data associated with this. The animal soul is crucial since it can either fall victim to the passions of the body or be used in the service of the intellect. Through a combination of theoretical and practical wisdom, one is able to perfect oneself in such a manner as to achieve a union (Heb. *devequt;* Ar. *ittiṣāl*) with the Active Intellect:

> Wisdom (*ᶜaṣa*) and ethics (*musar*) lead an individual to put God before him both day and night and thus his *neshamah* cleaves to the Creator before separating from the body [i.e., at the death of the body].[101]

In other passages, ibn Ezra claims that it is the heart (*lev*) that cleaves to the upper world.[102] For the heart, as the essence (*ᶜiqqar*) of the individual,[103] is the locus in which one loves God and experiences His presence. However, since the heart (=soul or *nefesh*) exists within a corporeal body, it is unable to know the upper world without recourse to vision. It is at this juncture that the imagination, the "eye of the heart" (*ᶜein ha-lev*) becomes important.[104] For it is this "eye" that allows us to see visions of the upper world: it is the faculty responsible for giving corporeal forms to incorporeal phenomena.

This upper world, the world of the unembodied angels, cannot be perceived by corporeal beings without the aid of a certain faculty. Corporeality thus puts limits on our ability to discern the structure of abstract reality. However, images provide a non-explanatory contact with this reality. For example, ibn Ezra claims that

> When the soul is directed toward the glory[105] then it receives new images, forms and visions by the word of God.[106]

Here ibn Ezra seems to be arguing that when the soul of the righteous cleaves to the upper world, it is able to encounter that world in an unmediated way. This disclosure, however, can occur only through the mediation of the imagination, with its images becoming the symbols by which reality reveals itself. As a result, an intelligible portrait of the celestial realm can only occur through the familiar images of the world that is lived and experienced. The human soul is able to perceive the celestial world because it is composed of the same essence of the disembodied angels.[107] However, it cannot do this without the images provided by the corporeal world, for these images represent the sum and substance of our experience with the world. This is why, for example, ibn Ezra portrays the Active Intellect in *Ḥay ben Meqitz* as an old man with a youthful appearance. But, of course, one must try to present this in such a way that the image is not mistaken for the reality behind it.

According to his commentary to Psalm 139:18, there are open to the individual two paths by which to obtain divine knowledge: one occurs through the various channels associated with the ratiocination that we engage in while awake; the other, by contrast, occurs during special dreams:

> [This] is like the appearance of God when the body sleeps and when man's *neshamah* cleaves to the upper *neshamah* so that it sees beautiful images (*temunot nifla*ᵓ*ot*) . . . and this is not the path of all dreams.

These special dreams are those in which the soul of the wise man cleaves to the beings associated with the upper world (*ha-eliyonim*) that exist without bodies. In *Ḥay ben Meqitz,* ibn Ezra makes this explicit when he claims that one can only experience this world internally, through the "eye of the heart":

> It happened that when we came to its borders
> We approached to cross it.
> I saw wonderful forms (*ṣurot mufla*ᵓ*ot*)
> Awesome visions (*mar*ᵓ*ot nora*ᵓ*ot*).
> Angels stood guard
> They were mighty ones.
> Cherubim
> Enormous and many.
> Seraphim standing
> Praising and announcing His unity.
> Angels and ofanim
> Lauding and singing.
> Souls (*nefashot*)
> Consecrating.
> Spirits (*ruḥot*)
> Glorifying.
> I was afraid and said
> "How awesome is this place that I see."
> He replied: "From your feet
> Remove the sandals.
> From the matter of your corpse
> Lift your soul.
> Forsake your thoughts
> Relax your eyelids!
> See by the eyes of your interior
> The pupils of your heart (*be-ishonei levavekha*)."[108]

It is up to the imagination to give these incorporeal entities an appropriate form. This is something that the intellect cannot do since its epistemological currency is that which exists without image.

What ibn Ezra intimates, then, like Avicenna and others who came before him, is that the intellect needs the imagination because it is the faculty responsible for supplying images necessary for thought. These images, to quote his commentary to Psalm 17:15, do not occur through a "vision of the eye" (*mar*ᵓ*eh ha-*ᶜ*ein*), but through a "vision of wisdom" (*mar*ᵓ*eh shiqqul ha-da*ᶜ*at*). This latter vision is the vision that occurs when the imagination, in close association with the intellect, encounters the Active Intellect and subsequently transfers the perceived images to the intellect. In typical fashion, ibn Ezra only alludes to his sources: "These are truly visions of God (*mar*ᵓ*ot elohim*) and these are matters that are not appropriate to reveal except to one who has studied psychology (lit., the science of the soul)."

Of our three authors, ibn Ṭufayl's discussion is probably the most straightforward—only because he does not write very much about the imagination in *Ḥayy ibn Yaqẓān*. We should not be surprised to find that he is, at first blush, generally mistrustful of this faculty. Despite this, however, his entire tale is premised on the notion that the intellect is ultimately closed to the highest echelons of knowledge. At the beginning of his treatise, ibn Ṭufayl acknowledges that he decided to compose this tale in order to intimate to a disciple "a state so wonderful that the tongue cannot describe or explain it, for it belongs to another order of being, a different world."[109] He describes this state in rich experiential, as opposed to discursive, terms: it is full of splendor (*bahja*), happiness (*surūr*), pleasure (*ladhdha*), and joy (*ḥubūr*), and it is a state that (here he employs a Sufi term) is characterized by taste (*dhawq*).[110] Ibn Ṭufayl subsequently claims that on one level this state is certainly similar to the one that philosophers (here symbolized by ibn Bājja) mention:

> The level to which Abū Bakr [ibn Bājja] refers is reached by speculative science (*ᶜilm al-naẓarī*) and mental investigation (*al-baḥth al-fikrī*). No doubt he reached it—*but he did not surpass it.* The level of which I spoke at the outset is something quite different, although the two are alike in that nothing revealed here contradicts what is revealed by reason. The difference is an increase *in what is seen* and in the fact that this is experienced through what I must, only figuratively, call a faculty. For neither in popular language nor in specialized terminology can I find an expression for it.[111]

If the line between mysticism and philosophy was a fine one in the thought of Avicenna and ibn Ezra, we see it here very much in a state of collapse.[112] In particular, ibn Ṭufayl stresses the concept of *dhawq*, the direct experience of the divine, that was so central to the medieval mystics.[113] Although he nowhere addresses directly the concept of the imagination, he alludes to it once he begins to emphasize this metaphorical "faculty," whose function is to create a metaphorical "seeing" (*mushāhada*) in the individual.[114] For as ibn Ṭufayl is at pains to remind the reader, his intention in writing *Ḥayy ibn Yaqẓān* is essentially to discuss the nature of this "seeing" in a non-discursive manner.[115]

Once we progress beyond ibn Ṭufayl's prologue and enter into the narrative, our first encounter with the imagination is primarily negative. It occurs when Ḥayy comes to the realization that, although the world must have an incorporeal (*laysa bi-jism*) cause, such a cause can neither be perceived nor imagined:

> But if He cannot be perceived He cannot be imagined (*yatakhayila*) either, since imagining (*takhayyul*) is no more than the mind's projection of

sensual images (*al-ṣūr al-maḥsūsāt*) that are no longer present. Furthermore, if He is not a material body, then it is impossible to apply to Him any of the predicates of physical things.[116]

Although this passage is generally quite critical of the imagination, as Ḥayy progresses up the *scala naturae* he comes to a fascinating realization: in order to know God, he must essentially become like the imaginative faculty! As Ḥayy ascends the various cosmological levels, he understands that his body is a hindrance. He describes it as dark (*zulam*), dull (*kathīf*), and beholden to sensory phenomena.[117] In order to try to free his soul from his body, Ḥayy realizes that he must engage in mimetic activity (*tashbiḥ*), the main function of the imagination:

> Ḥayy had learned that his ultimate happiness (*saᶜāda*) and triumph over misery would be won only if he could visualize (*mushāhada*) the Necessarily Existent Being (*al-mawjūd al-wājib al-wujūd*) so continuously that nothing could distract him from it for an instant. He had wondered how this might be achieved and now came to the conclusion that the means would be to practice these three forms of mimesis (*tashbiḥāt*).[118]

While ibn Ṭufayl is quite critical of the imagination, he also acknowledges that mimesis is the only way embodied creatures can apprehend the divine. Most significant for my present purpose is his description of the third and final type of mimesis, which is an attempt to become as like the Necessarily Existent Being as possible:

> The third sort of imitation (*tashbiḥ*) is the attainment of a pure and all-consuming vision (*mushāhada al-ṣirf wa al-istighrāq*) of Him alone Whose existence is necessary. In this vision the self vanishes; it is extinguished, obliterated—and so are all other subjectivities. All that remains is the One, the Truth, the Necessarily Existent—glory, exaltation, and honor to Him.[119]

In order to achieve such a state, here described in highly *visual* terms, one must engage in ascetic praxis. This type of mimesis leads Ḥayy to the height of human perfection, a stage described in terms of a metaphorical "seeing." Although I will describe the content of this vision in the following section, suffice it to say here that ibn Ṭufayl is ultimately forced to fall back on the activities of the imaginative faculty:

> Still I shall not leave you without hints (*ishārāt*) as to the wonders Ḥayy *saw* (*shāhad*) from this height, not by pounding on the gates of truth, but by coining symbols (*mithāl*), for there is no way of finding out what truly occurs at this plateau of experience besides reaching (*wuṣūl*) it [yourself]. So listen now with the ears of your heart (*samᶜ al-qalb*) and look sharp

> with the eyes of your mind (*baṣar al-ᶜaql*), for what I shall try to convey to you. Perhaps in what I say you will find guideposts to set you on the main road. My only condition is that you now demand of me no further oral explanation (*mushāfaha*) than what I have set down in these pages. For it is dangerous to make pronouncements on the ineffable, and the margins in which I work are narrow.[120]

The faculty that is ultimately responsible for this—for interpreting the unknown, putting it into corporeal images—is the imagination, not simply the intellect. Here it is worth reiterating that the imagination is an active faculty, one that is ultimately responsible for the creation of images that embody the individual's experience with the intelligible world. As such, the imagination is able to invest or divest images, as the case may be, that mediate between the corporeal individual and the incorporeal spiritual world. The imagination, in other words, mediates, puts into form, an otherwise unknowable encounter. The "ears of the heart" and the "eyes of the mind" here work as synonyms for the imagination.

The Beauty Imagined in the Text

Philosophy possesses an existential dimension. It cannot be completely objective, but must also be grounded in the particulars of human experience. To phrase this somewhat differently, humans can only think with the contents of their imagination, their memories, and their experiences. We can only apprehend that which exists without form by means of form, the incorporeal through the corporeal. In this section, I argue that the initiatory tale functions as a type of meditation manual, providing a sequence of events or places that are not only highly structured but also function to structure the experiences of the reader. These tales construct a spatial journey by means of which the reader can connect and compare the text to his or her own experiences. It is primarily this use of images and the imagination that helps explain the highly visual nature of medieval Neoplatonism, which culminates in the intellectual vision of spiritual or incorporeal forms. Here it is important to keep in mind that the medievals conceived of the memory as a physical structure in which the individual places images that the imagination locates at a later date.[121] I want to suggest here that the *Ḥayy ibn Yaqẓān* cycle represents the textualization of this process.

According to Aristotle, memory belongs to the same part of the soul as does the imagination.[122] Both are intimately connected to the formation of mental images or pictures that, in turn, order and categorize our interactions with sense data. This process is subsequently responsible for further thinking. In her discussion of the use of memory in the medieval Christian monastic tradition, Mary Carruthers argues that

> The art of meditation is fundamentally an art of thinking with a well-furnished memory. Though the goal of spiritual life is the unmediated vision of God, divine *theoria*, one can only get there by traveling through one's memory. A person's entire memory is a composition among whose places, routes, and pathways one must move whenever one thinks about anything.[123]

Within this context, the *Ḥayy ibn Yaqẓān* cycle embodies a synergy between imagination/memory, an imaginative journey through a structured, textual space, and a distinct theory of aesthetics. Although this cycle's relationship to aesthetics is the subject of chapter 5, let me begin to articulate here how it plays out in terms of these other two features. Each tale produces both a repeated and repeatable sequential journey that functions as a structured background through which the imagination moves. Reading these tales enables the individual to develop the craft of meditation by means of which one becomes self-conscious and self-reflexive of making an inner journey among various places, situated on a vertical hierarchy. These tales, consequently, are compositions that guide the individual to a specific and pre-stated goal. It is, of course, up to the individual reader to develop the wherewithal to proceed on this journey.

It is at this point that aesthetics become so important. Influenced by Plotinus's discussion "On Intellectual Beauty,"[124] the medieval Islamic and Jewish Neoplatonists argued that physical beauty is an image that issues ontically from a non-physical source and is not a mere shadow or pale imitation as it was for Plato. Explicit in this discussion is the claim that the arts both contain and convey knowledge of the intelligible world. In experiencing tangible beauty, the individual is presented with a corporeal or physical form by which he or she can contemplate and observe proportion, integrity, and clarity.[125] This, in turn, allows him or her to recognize those principles in his or her own soul that are also reflective of the harmony within the universe.[126] Physical beauty, then, like the imagination, represents the presencing of absence, the cloaking of the incorporeal within corporeal form. Aesthetic theory, then, was based on the notion that one encounters in physical objects an unmediated reflection of the divine. It is thus important not to circumscribe aesthetics to the domain of "literature" by claiming that "philosophy," by nature, is devoid of artistic or emotive expression. Explicit in this is the awareness that literature, unlike philosophy, has the ability to address the particular concerns of human beings by addressing such concerns in their totality and in all their possibilities.[127] Within this context, aesthetics bridges the gap between philosophy and literature because its focus is on the universal significances of particular objects or forms of contemplation (e.g., harmony, balance, order). This discipline of aesthetics, as developed by the medieval Neoplatonists, was inseparable from broader ontological and metaphysical concerns. These philosophers were not interested in artistic and literary creativity *per se;* rather, they investigated how this creativity related to a specific noetic development.[128] Consequently, they made explicit, as Deborah Black has demonstrated, the interconnections between mimesis and the faculty of the imagination.[129]

In his *Risāla fī al-ᶜishq*, for example, Avicenna argues that both the rational and the animal souls "invariably love what has beauty of order (*ḥusn al-niẓām*), composition (*al-taᵓlīf*), and harmony (*al-iᶜtidāl*).[130] For Avicenna, both the animal and the rational souls are attracted to beautiful objects that are defined by their order, composition, and harmony. The goal is that the individual will be able to align his or her imagination with his or her rational soul in such a manner that the former will resemble the latter.[131]

Beauty was not something based on mere artistic sentiment. On the contrary, it is an intelligible principle founded upon the ontology of emanation.[132] By encountering and recognizing the way in which images reveal a certain moment or manifestation of the divine, the individual is able to relate the order, composition, and harmony of the contemplated object to its universal significance. Plotinus, as the harbinger of medieval aesthetics, argued that beautiful objects and images create a tranquility in the soul that enables it to perceive a transcendent beauty otherwise inaccessible to the senses.[133] In encountering artistic beauty, the individual intuits and apprehends immaterial truth.[134] This encounter, in effect, enables the individual to reverse the emanative process by translating the particular image and relating it back to its ontic source.

Significantly, Avicenna wrote not just one, but two commentaries to Aristotle's *Poetics*.[135] He wrote the first, found in his *Kitāb al-majmuᶜ* and entitled *al-ḥikma al-ᶜarūdiyya fī maᶜānī kitāb al-shiᶜr*, fairly early in his career. The other is found in the logical section of his magnum opus, *al-Shifāᵓ*. Two things become clear from this. First, as was typical of the Alexandrian commentators, the Islamic philosophers included the *Poetics* as part of Aristotle's *Organon*.[136] Second, the fact that he wrote two commentaries to this work shows that Avicenna, as one of the few Islamic philosophers who wrote allegories and poetry,[137] was intimately concerned with the nature of the logical relationship between literature and philosophy.

The starting point for Avicenna's interest in poetry and literature, as for Aristotle before him, is that humans possess a universal instinct for both engaging in mimetic activity and for taking pleasure in observing its representations. He writes in the commentary from *al-Shifāʾ:*

> What is delightful is not the form itself nor what is portrayed but its being a precise imitation of something else. For this reason, learning is pleasant not to philosophers alone but to common people due to the imitation that is in it, and because learning consists of a certain representation of a thing in the "seat" of the soul. Men, therefore, find great delight in portrayed forms if they can well relate these to their originals.[138]

Mimetic representations, according to this passage, evoke an active participation on the part of the individual. This, in turn, throws into relief the importance of the imaginative faculty in the acquisition of knowledge. For the individual—as a listener, reader, or viewer—must effectively use the imagination in the service of the intellect in order to draw comparisons either between particulars or between particulars and universals. It is through the contemplation of the subsequent configuration or juxtaposition that we take pleasure. There thus exists within the mimetic arts an important aesthetic quality that is in the service of reason. This pleasure that comes from the tranquility of the soul leads to the subsequent acquisition of knowledge.

Since he inherited the *Poetics* as part of the *Organon,* Avicenna spends a great deal of time analyzing the formal structures behind the poetic syllogism. For Avicenna, both demonstrative and poetic utterances share a similar logical structure. Although the poetic utterance, unlike its demonstrative counterpart, is ultimately unconcerned with the truth or falsity of a statement, it nevertheless requires an assent (*taṣdīq*) that is based on the pleasure (*ladhdha*) and awe (*taᶜajjub*) we experience in it.[139]

Like Alfarabi before him,[140] Avicenna divides syllogisms into different types: demonstrative, dialectical, rhetorical, and poetic. Each type of syllogism implies, respectively, a different degree of conviction: certitude, strong opinion, persuasion, and imaginative assent.[141] The last one is not conviction properly speaking because it is based on wonder (*taᶜajjub*) as opposed to strict analytical assent. In his later commentary, Avicenna writes:

> Both imaginative assent and conviction are [kinds of] compliance. Imaginative assent, however, is a compliance due to the wonder and pleasure that are caused by the utterance itself, while conviction is a

> compliance due to the realization that the thing is what it is said to be. Imaginative assent results from the utterance itself, conviction from what is spoken of, i.e., the focus is on the matter being conveyed.[142]

Despite this statement, Avicenna does see a similar structure in poetic and demonstrative syllogisms. Only the former is contingent on its ability to affect the imaginative faculty. Poetic syllogisms occupy a position far below that of the other forms of syllogistic reasoning. Nevertheless, conclusions still follow formally from a poetic syllogism. Thus when we read a poem or another piece of literature, we are essentially reading imprecise or non-traditional philosophical conclusions, to which we must intuit the minor and major premises.

Let me now relate this discussion specifically to the *Ḥayy ibn Yaqẓān* cycle. These tales represent the creative synthesis of poetry and philosophy, something that was well-suited to medieval Neoplatonism. To interpret these tales solely as poetry or simply as philosophical treatises misses the mark. Indeed, our authors' philosophical expression cannot be separated from their loyalties to poetics, literature, and aesthetics. Metaphors, allegories, and myths—as I argued in the last chapter—become more than simple literary devices: they are important keys that unlock the unfolding structure of the universe. These devices—because they point beyond themselves and are more than what they appear—are what allow an individual to glimpse a reality that is otherwise unknowable or ungraspable. This is precisely what these initiatory tales do: they provide an account or map of reality, and its structures, in spatial and corporeal terms.

The central plot of the *Ḥayy ibn Yaqẓān* cycle is the human soul's attainment of perfection. This is based on the ontological unfolding of the universe from a single source and the subsequent return of the perfected human soul to its point of origin. Within this context, the ontological system of Neoplatonism is all about hierarchies, one above the sphere of the moon and one below it. The former concerns the emanation of the celestial spheres, intellects, and planets from the One; the latter concerns mineral, plants, animals, and culminates in humans. Significantly, humans, in particular human souls, are essentially the only entity that is afforded a certain mobility within these hierarchies. If one purifies the soul, it can ascend the celestial world until it reaches its source. The imagination plays an important role in this process since it is the faculty that makes the absent present and, as a result, is ultimately responsible for producing or translating images to help the rational soul transcend particulars.

The *Ḥayy ibn Yaqẓān* cycle represents a non-factual presentation, expressing, without fully capturing, that which is inherently ungraspable.

In other words, because the universe discloses itself in a manner that is distinctly non-objective, it cannot be grounded in objective explanations.[143] Sense phenomena are necessary conditions for our knowledge of both the transcendence of the world and what is transcendent to the world. From the embodied human perspective, Neoplatonic articulations are layered in such a manner that the higher are founded on the lower, and in such a way that this foundation can always be brought to light. Images, then, are what allow a finite individual, composed of form and matter, to gain access to that which exists without matter. As a result, the supralunar world cannot be explained discursively or objectively, since we have never experienced it in such ways. It is at this point that literature is of the utmost importance. For literature acts upon us in such a way that it clears a space and subsequently discloses the universe intuitively and in such a way that things present themselves to us.[144]

Our three authors present their tales as works of literature in both this aesthetic and phenomenological sense, thereby providing a particular insight that recognizes our inability to grasp the nature of the supralunar world objectively. In so doing, these tales present the structure of the ideal journey through which the individual soul ideally moves. It is precisely for this reason that the imagination becomes so important, since it is the faculty responsible for the creation of images of incorporeal and spiritual beings. These tales encourage the reader to form the correct images and also provide the spaces or loci in which they should be located. Through linguistic devices such as metaphor and allegory, the imagination is drawn to the aesthetic dimension of particulars, thereby focusing the soul's gaze upon the truth/universal behind the particular.

To illustrate this point, let me provide a series of examples from our three authors. In the following section of Avicenna's tale, Ḥayy informs the unnamed protagonist of a specific cosmographical region, near the king (*malik*),

> [He] who succeeds in leaving this clime enters the clime of the angels (*malāʾika*), among which the one that marches with the earth (*al-arḍ*) is a clime in which the terrestrial angels (*al-malāʾika al-arḍiyyun*) dwell. These angels form two groups. One occupies the right, and they are the angels who know and order. Opposite them, a group occupies the left side: they are the angels who obey and act.[145]

On one level, this is a description of the theoretical and practical intellects of the individual.[146] Having subsumed the faculties of the animal soul (including the imagination) into the rational faculty, such an individual is able to think with the theoretical intellect and put this knowledge into praxis with the practical intellect. However, such a passage is more than just an allegory. In effect, it intimates non-discursively and non-objectively a situation or a process that is unknowable without images. By using images to produce a coherent picture of the rational soul, this portrait is more effective than an analytical account. Avicenna graphically and effectively portrays the nature of the rational soul and its division into theoretical and practical components. Significantly, though, this portrayal can only be fully understood by means of the imagination. In the section immediately following, Avicenna describes what the aforementioned state can lead to:

> a certain road leading out of this clime and he who is able to accomplish this emigration will find an exit to what is beyond the celestial spheres. Then he will see (*raʾā*) the heavens (*samāʾ*) of the primordial creation (*al-khalq al-aqdam*), over whom rules a King (*malik*) who is obeyed (*muṭaᶜ*). There, the first border is inhabited by servants (*khadam*) of their sublime King, they pursue the work that brings them near to their king. They are a pure people (*umma*), who respond to no solicitations of greed, lust, iniquity, or laziness. They attend to the edifice of the empire where they live. They live in a metropolis (*ḥāḍira*), dwelling in lofty castles and magnificent buildings, whose clay (*ṭīna*) was mixed with such care that it does not resemble the clay of your clime.[147]

In this passage we essentially have an allegorical description of the standard Avicennian notion of the soul's fate after the death of the body.[148] Here the account is much more descriptive and vivid than the one we encounter in his more analytical treatises.[149] Since we have no objective or discursive knowledge of what this fate is about, what better way is there to describe it? Again, the sight that the soul sees cannot be described without recourse to familiar images. These particular images—which appeal to the imagination—provide an understanding of what the fate of the soul *is like.* The imagination, therefore, translates this knowledge into the intellect in such a way that the force of the images is not lost. Because this fate is beyond all particular descriptions, a proper account of it should not pretend to be purely descriptive. Such a configuration allows the imagination, which is connected to the lived experiences of the individual, to grasp intuitively the intentionality behind this presentation. Here, I concur with Heath, who argues that

> Philosophical discourse could represent, indeed was the best representational mode for, the first and greater part of Avicenna's philosophical program: logic and most of metaphysics. But it could not adequately portray the crucial climax of his program, *maᶜād* [afterlife], as understood not in terms of conventional Muslim eschatology, but in the specific Plotinian sense of "journey of the alone to the alone."[150]

Initiatory tales thus provided Avicenna with a vehicle in which he could push beyond the accounts we witness in his standard, more analytical presentations. His *Ḥayy ibn Yaqẓān* provides a non-transferable inspiration to the imagination, which is grounded in the existential concerns of the embodied individual. The transparency of this tale, its non-referential use of language, is consistent with limitations of human corporeality. Implicit in this is the notion that it is impossible, on any level, to escape this use of mythic or allegorical language precisely because such language speaks to individuals as humans, as composites of soul and body. Although there exists an ontological gap forever separating human from divine, the language of the initiatory tale tries to overcome this separation by pointing beyond the here and now of this world.

I certainly have no desire here to replace Avicenna's philosophical *oeuvre* with a vague sort of mysticism. On the contrary, I only draw attention to the role of the imagination within his *oeuvre*. Equally, this is not an imposition since there exists ample evidence in his own writings, most notably his *Kitāb al-ishārāt wa al-tanbīhāt*. By only focusing on Avicenna's scientific and discursive treatises, however, we tend to overlook his other forms of understanding and engagement with the world. Although no one would argue that the analytical tradition is paramount for the pursuit of knowledge, we also have to acknowledge, as Avicenna himself did, that the analytical tradition is unable to traverse beyond a certain point because it runs into the limits of human finitude. In contrast, imaginative representation—its ability to bring form to the formless and corporeality to the incorporeal—attempts to overcome such limits by addressing the various dimensions and experiences of the individual.

Ḥay ben Meqitz, like *Ḥayy ibn Yaqẓān*, is a literary-aesthetic work that attempts to describe that which is ultimately beyond description. For example, the unnamed protagonist explains to the reader the nature of the element of air:

> He made me cross these lakes
> He brought me to a large boundary.
> I saw winds and gusts
> Exhaling
> Fluttering.
> Storms, horrors, tremors
> Dismantling mountains, laying bare rocks.
> Their lightning bolts appear
> Thunder roars.
> Clouds screen
> Showers pour down.[151]

Here we are presented with an account of air as it exists on its own, unmixed with the other elements. This, however, is certainly anything but an abstract discussion. On the contrary, we have a very vivid description, in which this element, imperceptible to the senses on its own, is described by means of imagery associated with the natural world. Ibn Ezra essentially uses our experiences of air in storms (i.e., winds, gusts) to enable us to understand the destructive capacity of this element. The description is much more forceful and experiential than an abstract account. For instance, the verse "clouds screen" invokes Lamentations 3:44, wherein God's anger ("You have screened Yourself off . . . ") is described as a cloud preventing the accessibility of prayers. Paradoxically, in using such images to describe air, the reader apprehends its nature without being able literally to perceive it.

Another example that illustrates the importance of image in these novels occurs when Ḥay first speaks to the unnamed protagonist:

> In words he answered me
> Full of stones and gems.
> In words arranged
> Like *thummim* and *urim*.
> . . .
> "Ḥay ben Meqitz is my name
> The Holy City is my home.
> My work is what you see
> I toil and do not grow weary.
> I wander throughout cities and states
> Searching every nook and cranny.
> My father guides me in the way of wisdom
> He teaches me understanding and counsel.
> I am with Him as a confidant
> In Baal Hamon.
> In the coolness of his shade
> I delight to sit.
> I will not leave Him
> For His fruit is sweet to my mouth."[152]

In this passage, Ḥay essentially explains who he is and describes his activities. This is an allegorical way of alluding to the fact that he represents the Active Intellect, or the principle by which knowledge is imparted to individuals. To show that this is no ordinary conversation, ibn Ezra compares it to the *thummim* and *urim* that, according to Exodus 28:30, were placed inside the high priests' breastplate in order to designate some kind of oracle. In many ways *thummim* and *urim* symbolize the narrative, since the conversation between these two individuals is not so much discursive as it is allusive or oracular.

When Ḥay describes his occupation of wandering throughout the earth, he alludes to the fact that his occupation is that of a philosopher (e.g., a "peripatetic").[153] The ultimate source of the wisdom that arises from these wanderings, however, is God, who has taught Ḥay both theoretical and practical wisdom ("understanding and foresight"). Significantly, the terminus of this knowledge blends both philosophical and mystical terms, and biblical and Sufi images. This knowledge, conjuring up Solomon's vineyard in Song 8:11, is described in luscious and graphic terms. It is described as a tasting (Ar. *dhawq;* Heb. *ta^cam*)[154] that is pleasant to the senses.

Probably the best example of the way in which his tale intimates at the unknowable occurs when the protagonist glimpses God:

> I said to him, "Can I see everything with my eyes?
> Is there anything I cannot perceive with my pupils?"
> He replied
> . . .
> "From an abundance of greatness
> His knowledge is hidden from men.
> From the greatness of His appearance
> Seeing Him is prevented.
> Since the sun is hidden by its light
> We cannot know it.
> When it rises at dawn
> We barely visualize it.
> In this way souls are unable to know Him
> Hearts unable to perceive Him.
> He has neither shape nor likeness
> He has no image by which one can compare Him."[155]

In this passage, Ḥay tells the protagonist that God is essentially unknowable. Despite this, the protagonist speaks of his vision of God. This vision, however, does not seem to have come from the vision of the eyes, but through the vision of the imagination. Although he can never perceive the actual structure of the divine world he is, nonetheless, provided with images that describe what it is like. These images, as I have suggested throughout this chapter, bridge the gap between the incorporeal and the corporeal, the invisible and the visible, by giving form to a transcendental truth. By ascending the various celestial realms, the protagonist's soul (re)ascends the ontological hierarchy. Just as Ḥay reveals to the protagonist the geometric and spatial structure of the universe, we, too, as readers, apprehend this journey and experience.

Likewise in his *Ḥayy ibn Yaqẓān,* ibn Ṭufayl employs a series of literary devices, symbols, imaginative accounts, and aesthetics to push the reader to gain access to truth for himself or herself. These meanings, according to Salim Kemal, "are cumulative, and the sense gained from a complex of terms is unlikely to be preserved if we try to translate the complex into a series of simple meanings."[156] The goal of his narrative, as ibn Ṭufayl constantly reminds us in his prologue, is to push the reader to "a state so wonderful that the tongue cannot describe it, for it belongs to a different order of being, a different world."[157]

The entire narrative is an attempt to bring a certain form to the otherwise unknowable or unapprehendable experience that the individual attains at the epitome of his or her journey. This is a stage, as I showed earlier, that ibn Ṭufayl conceived of as greater than that which the philosophers of his day could acquire. It is a stage that he describes in the following way:

> Passing through a deep trance to the complete death-of-self (*fanāʾ*) and real contact (*wuṣūl*) with divine, he saw (*shāhada*) a being corresponding to the highest sphere, beyond which there is no body (*lā jism lahu*), a subject free of matter, and neither identical with the truth (*al-ḥaqq*) and the One nor with the sphere itself, nor distinct from them. Just as the form of the sun appearing in a polished mirror is neither sun nor mirror, and yet distinct from neither. The splendor, perfection, and beauty he saw in the essence of that sphere were too magnificent to be described and too delicate to be clothed in written or spoken words. But he saw it to be the pinnacle of joy, delight, and rapture, in blissful vision of the being of the truth, glorious be His majesty.[158]

This account is replete with highly sensual and imaginative descriptions. This state, which the narrator describes as the "pinnacle of joy," is one of vision.[159] It is a seeing into the divine. Such a seeing or vision, however, cannot simply be one of the sense of sight. On the contrary, it is an internal seeing, which, as I have argued, occurs internally through the faculty of the imagination. Ibn Ṭufayl's *Ḥayy ibn Yaqẓān,* then, is essentially a road map through which the ideal reader ascends through the structure of the text, which reflects the divine cosmology. Indeed, the entire narrative is an attempt, as ibn Ṭufayl himself readily admits, to help "restore the sight" of those who truly love God and yearn to apprehend Him.

Conclusions

The subject of this chapter is what I consider to be one of the great paradoxes of Western philosophy: the imagination. The paradox turns on the fact that, in theory, we are truly ourselves only when we employ our intellects or engage in intellectual activity. Despite this, every philosopher from Plato onwards realized that images and the faculty in which they are produced are absolutely necessary for cognitive activity. This paradox has resulted in the traditional formulation that although the philosophers need the imagination for certain activities, they are quick to constrain and delimit its activity. This delimitation takes its most extreme form in the Platonic criticism of mimesis. Yet already in Plato's student, Aristotle, we see this criticism begin to wither: Aristotle realized that humans are mimetic creatures and that certain types of mimetic activity are essential to our ability to function as humans. The medieval Neoplatonists inherited these contradictory theories of the imagination, not to mention the highly enigmatic comments found in Plotinus's *Theology,* which was circulated under the name of Aristotle.

I have attempted to provide an in-depth historical and phenomenological analysis of the imagination as it relates specifically to the initiatory tale. The former has allowed me to try and reconstruct the imagination as the medievals conceived it. Where, for example, is it located? And how does it relate to the intellect, on the one hand, and to the body and the senses, on the other? The phenomenological, by contrast, allows us a glimpse into why, despite their initial hesitance regarding this faculty, all three of our authors ultimately fall back on the ocular model that the imagination provides. They do this, I have argued, because they realized that the imagination has the ability to produce images that are necessary for both the conceptualization and the visualization of incorporeal and spiritual forms. These images, in turn, are symbols that allow the spiritual and the incorporeal to appear in human consciousness. Even though the philosophers realized that God is without form and cannot be contained by matter, they nonetheless concede that form and corporeality are essential to the Neoplatonic vision.

The imagination is, then, primarily hermeneutical. It presents the absent, it makes the incorporeal corporeal, and it gives the formless form. Rather than regard the imagination as a passive faculty, I have argued that these three authors acknowledge that it is active and responsible for the creation of appropriate symbols. The imagination becomes crucial for understanding transcendent truth, since it is what ultimately mediates between the invisible and the visible. It is at this juncture that I argued that the initiatory tale becomes so important. For these tales presuppose a way of uncovering the world that is fundamentally different from more analytical presentations. These tales are the textual counterpart of the imagination and are well suited to the activity of this faculty and its quest to apprehend the divine. To use Heidegger's language, these tales open up a "clearing" wherein the individual gains access to and apprehends Being. However, this is not to make the claim that the tales conjure up some form of vague or enigmatic "Oriental Wisdom." On the contrary, I have stressed that even if the knowledge that these tales impart is not necessarily and qualitatively different from analytical works, they nevertheless proceed in a fundamentally different manner. This difference is contingent on the fact that the authors recognized the limitations of the embodied human to grasp that which is essentially immaterial. In so doing, these tales disclose a coherent picture of the universe that is connected to the way in which humans, as composites of body and soul, interact experientially with the world around them. By providing the supralunar world with spatial and geometric extension, these tales allow the individual to experience the transcendent world in terms of the particular images of this world of lived experience.

Chapter 4 builds on the present one by suggesting and examining various ways in which the initiatory tale affects and transforms the reader. I contend that these tales are so effective because they force the reader's imagination, much like the actual textual protagonist, to undergo a form of symbolic ritual activity. This activity is what is ultimately responsible for inscribing specific truths, whether cultural or intellectual, onto the individual. It is at this point that we witness the initiation of the philosopher.

4

The Initiation of the Philosopher: Ritual Poetics and the Quest for Meaning

In a classic definition, Clifford Geertz argues that religion constitutes a complex system of symbols, offering both a context and an order for various moods and motivations.[1] Religion provides an interlocking set of codes by which a community, and the individuals within that community, formulate an "order of the world which will account for, and even celebrate, the perceived ambiguities, puzzles, and paradoxes of human experience."[2] Religious symbols and their semantics not only reflect particular social situations, but they also reshape such situations in the light of the problems of meaning that arise in real human experiences.

Ritual activity is an essential component within this construction of meaning. In ritual, according to Geertz, "the world as lived and the world as imagined, fused under the agency of a single set of symbolic forms, turn out to be the same world."[3] Rituals function in at least two ways. On the one hand, they give bodily activity and motion cosmic significance. On the other, they provide an awareness, a form of consciousness, that is central to the formation of meaning.[4] Ritual activity is, thus, interpretive. Such activity provides a focusing lens through which the individual perceives and reflects upon his or her own situation in the light of an ideal.[5]

The present chapter explores key features of ritual activity in order to illumine the *Ḥayy ibn Yaqẓān* cycle from another dimension. Whereas other chapters in this study have examined or will examine the literary, aesthetic, and psychological facets of these tales, the focus now switches to their sensual and kinesthetic apparati to show how these generate meaning. For even a cursory reading of these texts reveals a fullness of ritual vocabulary and a conceptual framework in which it is expressed. In each of these three narratives, we encounter for example the relinquishing of one's home and family, and the motion toward a certain goal. This journey, in turn, is informed by ritual activity: the protagonist becomes an initiate who must undergo baptisms in springs, encounters with eternal fires, and ascents up sacred mountains. The goal here is to show that these features are not arbitrary, but are crucial to unlocking the hermeneutical secrets of these works.

Since ritual activity is a complex religious and social medium, it plays a variety of roles and communicates a density of meanings.[6] Although there exists no unified theory of ritual, the work of van Gennep and Turner looms large.[7] In what follows, I adopt and adapt parts of their theories in order to shed light on these tales. In doing this, my intention is not to put a rigid or artificial framework on these tales, making them conform to a modern theory that stresses the tripartite dimension of ritual. On the contrary, my goal is to use ritual theory as a light with which to illumine some of the inner dimensions of these narratives. Sometimes there exists a very close fit between the theory and the tale (especially in ibn Ezra's account); other times the fit is less evident. Despite this, however, I persist in the attempt to take particular aspects of ritual theory to show how it aids our understanding of the telos that we encounter in all three of these tales: the initiation of the philosopher.

However, a problem immediately presents itself. A rite is a performance and we have no evidence that these tales were ever performed. There is, then, a certain hermeneutical gap between a textual or symbolic account of ritual activity on the one hand, and an actual performance of it on the other.[8] But this gap need not be prohibitive, since, as I stated at the outset, these texts reflect broader cultural and intellectual concerns. In particular, how is it possible to apprehend the divine? Under what circumstances can this occur? It is in response to such questions that we need to contextualize these tales. According to Eliade, the rite of passage provides the vehicle by which the initiate can potentially attain religious perfection.[9] I wish to elaborate on his insight by arguing that the *Ḥayy ibn Yaqẓān* cycle provides the dynamics by which the initiate achieves intellectual perfection, which in medieval philosophical parlance was tantamount to religious perfection.

These tales are ritualistic in both form and function. However, the protagonists of these tales are not the only ones undergoing the transformative aspect of ritual. The second part of this chapter suggests that there exists an increasing identification between the protagonist and the reader. By employing a series of textual strategies, these tales invite the reader into the narrative, encouraging his or her active participation. This is in keeping with the authors' commitment to Neoplatonism, which envisaged philosophy as a spiritual progression, not an analytical system based on propositional logic. To this end, these tales are intimately concerned with the positive transformation of the individual.

Establishing the Ritual Pattern

Common to each of these tales is a tripartite structure. This structure is neither coincidental nor part of an arbitrary description of the universe. On the contrary, it provides an important ritual pattern that is related to the initiation of both the protagonist and the reader.[10] I keep my definition of "ritual" intentionally inclusive: a set of symbolic communications that consists of a fixed sequence of words and acts.[11] More important than giving a watertight definition at this stage of the analysis is the necessity to provide an appreciation that ritual attempts to alleviate some of the dissonance associated with the human condition. Of particular importance is that between a desire to live in a fully meaningful and comprehensible world, on the one hand, and our seeming inability to do so, on the other.

Ritual, much like the initiatory tale, turns on mimesis, imbuing the actor's movement with cultural, religious, and social meaning. Such activity has the potential to be liberating and transformative, becoming a medium by which an individual discovers that he or she is connected to broader social, intellectual, and cosmic rhythms. Here I seek to establish a correspondence between ritual, broadly defined, and the Neoplatonic texts, by arguing that both attempt to foster within the individual an experiential and non-discursive way of knowing.[12] Within this context, both ritual and Neoplatonic texts use a symbolic vocabulary to force the initiate's movement into a new way of being in the world. However, there exists an important difference between the two. Whereas the Neoplatonic text forces the individual to employ his or her imagination in tandem with the intellect, ritual focuses on the nexus between imagination and body. Foundational to both types of activities, however, is the imaginative faculty.

Arnold van Gennep is one of a long list of theorists who claim that the ontological gap between the sacred and the profane is so great that one can only cross it by entering an intermediate stage.[13] In order to move from one state to another, van Gennep argues that the individual or the group must undergo rites of passage, "rites which accompany every change of place, state, social position and age."[14] Moreover, for van Gennep all rites of passage consist of a tripartite structure: that of separation ("preliminal"), marginalization ("liminal"), and aggregation ("postliminal").[15] The first phase consists of an individual's or group's detachment from normal social stability and the cultural conditions that create it. This departure coincides with the entrance into a marginal or "liminal" state, wherein the individual or group is characterized by ambiguity, or what Victor Turner calls the moment of being "betwixt and between."[16] The third phase represents the completion of the passage as the individual or group re-enters a state of stability. It is in the last phase, according to Turner, that

> The ritual subject, individual or corporate, is in a relatively stable state once more and, by virtue of this, has rights and obligations vis-à-vis others of a clearly defined and "structural" type; he is expected to behave in accordance with certain customary norms and ethical standards binding on incumbents of social position in a system of such positions.[17]

Other theorists are especially concerned with, and greatly elaborate upon, the importance of the liminal phase of this process. Of particular importance is the aforementioned Turner, who argues that in this phase the initiate's behavior

> is normally passive or humble; they must obey their instructors implicitly, and accept arbitrary punishment without complaint. It is as though they are being reduced or ground down to a uniform condition to be fashioned anew and endowed with additional powers to enable them to cope with their new station in life.[18]

This tripartite structure of the rite of passage can help us clarify and, in the process, shed new insight into the structure of the initiatory tale. Like ritual activity, these initiatory tales concern themselves with the problematics that are of the utmost human concern: pollution and purification, death and rebirth, ignorance and gnosis, mortality and immortality. Just like the initiate in a rite of passage, the protagonist/reader must effectively negotiate the ontological gap or threshold separating the profane and the sacred. This can only be done by means of entering an interstitial phase, wherein the individual receives the wherewithal to complete the journey in order to return to the stability he or she has left and to which he or she subsequently returns as a new person. The rite of passage paradigm thus enables us to understand more fully the significance behind the protagonist's departure and separation from his companions, his lengthy journey (either alone or with Ḥayy), and his subsequent return as a changed individual.

Suzanne Stetkevych argues that a key feature in Arabic poetry is the recurring juxtaposition between nature and culture, immortality and mortality.[19] For instance, it is in the world of nature that the protagonist ultimately discovers the secret of his or her own immortality. The tension between nature and culture, however, is not unique to the Islamic ode (*qaṣīda*); rather, it is central to the way in which ritual generates meaning. Within this context, ritual activity is part of the broader cultural activity that, in the words of Lévi-Strauss, takes the "raw" inevitabilities of the natural world and subsequently "cooks" and re-presents them as cultural regularities.[20] This, in turn, is related to the recognition that the world of nature, although symbolizing immortality, is potentially *other*, dangerous. Nature is something upon which the categories and codes of a culture must be placed in order to make sense of it.

This motif is apparent in each one of the initiatory tales. In all three, the protagonist must leave his home in order to undergo a series of adventures in the unknown wilderness of the universe. Each tale culminates in the acquisition of a special gnosis and the subsequent return to one's home. In the first section of this chapter, I examine each tale, showing how the ritual paradigm helps us better understand these narratives.

The Quest of the Initiate

At the beginning of ibn Ezra's *Ḥay ben Meqitz*, the protagonist separates himself from the sterility and mortality of culture, here symbolized by the presence of his so-called friends.[21] Narratively, this represents the initial phase of separation as the protagonist, having departed the regular socio-cultural rhythms, must now begin the lengthy task of searching for the seeds of immortality. This entails the separation from previous habits of acting, thinking, and feeling; in so doing, it signals that the initiate is now cut off from his customary way of apprehending and engaging the world. It is for this reason that the rest of the narrative essentially takes place against the backdrop of the rich and variegated natural world, the locus of immortality.

Away from the city, but still in the company of his friends, the potential initiate begins a conversation with the enigmatic Ḥay, who subsequently informs him that his companions are anything but friendly.[22] On the contrary, they are secretly responsible for his entanglement with the world of matter. Unknown to the protagonist, they are a synecdoche for death. On the narrative level, the phase of separation is complete once the protagonist becomes aware of the true identity of these friends. He no longer perceives them as traveling companions, but as a threat not only to his own psychological stability but also to his ability to carry out the journey successfully. Only upon the separation from these individuals can he undergo the heroic quest, which coincides with the narrative in the long middle section describing the intermediate world (*ha-olam ha-emṣaᶜi*).

According to theorists such as van Gennep and Turner, there must be a physical ritual act that marks the individual's successful separation from society and subsequent motion toward the critical phase of liminality. We witness this narratively in lines 213–218, when Ḥay brings the protagonist to a spring that

> calls out
> Announcing its voice from afar.
> Its streams are as wide as rivers
> Its waters gush forth.
> They cure every wound and ailment
> Providing remedy and recovery.

After an immersion in, and drinking from, the waters of the spring, the protagonist is subsequently able to proceed to the next stage of the journey. The initiate describes the process in the following poetic manner:

> I drank from the water of life
> The water that gives life to souls.
> My pains and my afflictions left me.
> My loyal yet bad companions
> They became like a balsam
> Healing my fractures, soothing my limbs.
> I drank enough
> My sickness was cured.
> He reached out his hand and grabbed me
> Lifting me from the depth of the spring.[23]

This ritual brings to a culmination the protagonist's separation, both physically and symbolically, from his previous surroundings.[24] Like all rites of separation, it has the effect of purifying the initiate, allowing entrance into that which is otherwise forbidden or dangerous. Such rites, according to Bell, remove impersonal forms of contagion that can afflict an individual, such as being in a group or crowd of other individuals.[25]

It is the ritual immersion in the spring that subsequently enables the protagonist to undertake the second, or liminal, phase of the journey. The water's fluidity brings about a metamorphosis, offering the initiate the potential for immortality. Liminality, to reiterate, is synonymous with the initiate entering a marginal state, a universe in which

> all attributes that distinguish categories and groups in the structured social order are here in abeyance; the neophytes are merely entities in transition, as yet without place or position. . . . The neophyte in liminality

> must be a *tabula rasa,* a blank slate, on which is inscribed the knowledge and wisdom of the group.[26]

In other words, the liminal phase is what allows the initiate to return to society as a new person. Before this can occur, however, the initiate must undergo a journey, either literally or metaphorically. In the textual setting that ibn Ezra provides, the protagonist experiences a downward journey into the domains of the four elements (lines 308–390), out of which everything in the sublunar world is composed. Understanding this structure is what will subsequently enable him to gain access into the world of the heavenly spheres, whose motion is responsible for the combination of these elements. Since ritual activity is concerned primarily with boundaries and their successful negotiation, it should come as no surprise that the initiate must undergo a further rite that makes an upward journey, from the sublunar to the supralunar world, possible. This involves the encounter with the all-consuming fire occupying the middle part of the narrative. Ibn Ezra initially describes it in the following terms:

> After this boundary there is a consuming fire
> To the heavens it reaches.
> Coals burn
> Sparks rage.
> Its blades are like swords
> Its sparks like stars.
> Rains do not extinguish it
> Rivers are unable to flood it.
> Rocks are molted by its fire
> Boulders melt from its flame.[27]

This description is especially rich in its invocation of Jewish motifs, especially those associated with the early mystical tradition. The encounter with fire and subsequent purification of the initiate, for instance, is a leitmotif that runs throughout the early Merkabah and Hekhalot texts.[28] If we examine these texts through a history of religions prism, we notice that the all-encompassing, purifying fire strips anything with which it comes into contact down to nothing or its component parts. For encounter with fire, like that with water, offers the potential for immortality.[29] But ibn Ezra does not dwell for long on the level of universal symbol; rather, he is much more concerned with grounding this initiation within the context of the Jewish tradition. It is in a chariot of fire drawn by horses of fire, for example, that Elijah was carried into heaven (2 Kings 2:11). In like manner, he uses the Song of Songs in such a way that the original context that described the inextinguishable passion of the lover for the Beloved (8:6–7) is now used to account for the inextinguishable nature of the fire's powerful flames.

In his encounter with this fire, the protagonist is metaphorically ground down to prime matter, only to emerge at the end of this rite as someone upon whom knowledge and gnosis will be impressed. The protagonist describes his encounter with the all-consuming flame in the following manner:

> My hands were weak
> My knees trembled.
> My eyes smoked over from fear
> I fell onto my face.
> I was unable to stand
> My whole being was stricken with terror.
> He came to me
> Set me upon my feet.
> He said, "Do not be afraid,
> do not lose heart.
> When you walk through fire, you will not be burned
> Though a flame, it will not burn you."
> He passed before me and said
> "Come in, O blessed of the Lord."
> He took me swiftly from there
> Moving me into the flame.
> I saw the fires touch in front of him
> The sparks surrounding him burned.
> The flashes encircled us
> Although surrounded
> We were not consumed.[30]

Ibn Ezra again draws on the rich vocabulary of post-biblical Jewish literature in order to imbue this encounter with a pathos drawn from his own tradition.[31] The protagonist subsequently emerges from the fire both untouched and as a new person, someone now able to experience the fullness of the phase of liminality (*ha-olam ha-emṣa^{c}i*). For it is in the intermediate world that the protagonist must pass through a phase that, according to Turner, "has few or none of the attributes of the past or coming state."[32] Unlike the previous encounter with the spring, the protagonist now becomes the actor, as opposed to the victim, of separation. The ritual of immersion in the spring had been associated with a motion downwards, in which the protagonist experienced the natural world. After the contact with the fire, however, he undertakes a quest that leads him in the opposite direction, upwards to the planets and, eventually, toward the Ineffable.

In encountering each of the planets within their heavenly spheres, the protagonist, in the company of Ḥay, enters into a world he has seen from afar but has never experienced. It is a world whose characteristics are juxtaposed against the world he has just left. It is characterized by immortality and, because of this, danger. As a result, the protagonist must effectively negotiate and maneuver the various boundaries of this world if he is to emerge as a transformed individual at the narrative's end. The intermediate world, which I am here equating with the liminal phase of initiation, functions as a test in which the protagonist must overcome the fear of his own mortality and subsequent death. The encounter with the various inhabitants of the spheres, here personified according to each planet's astrological attributes, is potentially misleading. For although the liminal phase is traditionally associated with ambiguity and wilderness, here the protagonist encounters various heavenly "civilizations" or "social groups." These various groups further increase the message of human mortality because in them the initiate encounters the specter of death in a way that would have been impossible for him had he remained in the lower world and in the unhealthy company of his so-called "friendly" companions. Although in the intermediate world the protagonist glances at the ultimate source of earthly traits and characteristics, he nonetheless experiences these in a way that is unlike anything he has encountered before.

Textually, the protagonist approaches the terminus of the liminal phase at line 648 ("It happened that when we came to its borders"). Not surprisingly, this is the textual setting of another threshold (*zebul*), that between the outermost edge of the planetary spheres and the beginning of the uppermost world (*ha-olam ha-eliyon*). Looking toward this world, with his glance fixed firmly above at what is still to come, the protagonist proclaims:

> It happened that when we came to its borders
> We approached to cross it.
> I saw wonderful forms
> Awesome visions.
> Angels stood guard
> They were mighty ones.
> Cherubim
> Enormous and many.
> Seraphim standing
> Praising and announcing His unity.
> Angels and ofanim
> Lauding and singing.
> Souls
> Consecrating.
> Spirits
> Glorifying.[33]

At this point, the protagonist becomes fully conscious of both his mortality and his potential for immortality. According to the basic ritual paradigm, the period of liminality must ultimately give way to one of aggregation or incorporation. This is the goal of the quest, from which the individual gradually re-emerges into a state of stability as a new person. The way in which ibn Ezra presents this stage of the journey occurs at the moment in which Ḥay informs the protagonist that he is able to know God and apprehend (*laḥazot*) Him:

> I said, "Please, my Lord, listen to my plea for mercy
> To you I turn my eyes.
> Upon you I cast my troubles
> To your hand I entrust my spirit.
> Tell me with what shall I approach Him?
> How shall I know Him?
> I have truly longed to know Him
> I yearn to see Him."
> He replied, "Uphold my words
> Keep my teaching.
> Walk in my path, and do not depart from me.
> You will know your spirit
> As is fitting to your ability and your strength.
> Then you will be able to know Him
> To apprehend Him."[34]

Interestingly, this "knowing" and "seeing" occur immediately after Ḥay informs the protagonist that God has neither image nor countenance. As I argued in chapter 3, this knowing and seeing refer neither to an intellectual nor a sensual activity; rather, they refer to the internal processes that are ultimately the responsibility of the imaginative faculty. The narrative, however, does not elucidate this aspect at any length. Indeed, as I argued in previous chapters, there are important epistemological reasons for this.

The last section of ibn Ezra's tale involves two types of incorporation. Primarily, the text here reports the soul's return to its home in the divine. No longer trapped in the matter of this world, the soul has undergone a lengthy, arduous, and often dangerous journey, the primary goal of which was the re-absorption of the individual soul back into the universal soul (*nishmat ha-kol*). But this is only part of the phase of incorporation. The other part involves the return to where the narrative first began: firmly in this world of generation and corruption. Since the soul has not yet departed the body fully (a feature that can occur only at corporeal death), it has no option but to return to this world. These two incorporations are, however, intimately related: although the soul returns to this world, its newfound awareness of its true home is what permits the individual to live here appropriately. Ritually, these two returns are symbolized by the single activity of basking in the divine presence. This basking represents the textual setting of the rite of incorporation, whereby the protagonist can subsequently re-emerge from the journey as a new person, someone who has been re-incorporated into society:

> I said to him
> "May you be forever blessed.
> You have brought me thus far
> To enter and come out again in peace.
> Happy are you
> And happy are your friends.
> Those who uphold your religion
> And pay heed to your wise words.
> Praised be the Lord your God
> Who made you governor of His World
> Who put you in charge of His people.
> He who brought me to you.
> Who made me listen to your words.
> He is above all majesty and greatness
> Exalted above every blessing and praise.
> He alone does great things
> His steadfast love is eternal."[35]

At the end of the tale, the protagonist speaks from the same position in which he began. He is presumably back in his city, re-acquainted with his various relations. Only now, he sees this world for what it really is. He is, in typical philosophical fashion, both in the world and separate from it.[36] Since he began the tale with the verbs in the past tense, the entire journey has been recounted solely for the reader's benefit, so that he or she may also undergo the initiation. No longer in the company of his "friendly" companions, the ephemeral and abandoned house of section one has given way to the initiate's willingness to re-enter society. In typical Jewish fashion, he realizes that he must now put the theoretical knowledge that he has acquired on his journey into praxis. It is not sufficient that the protagonist has received this knowledge; he must now return to society and work for its improvement.

This ritual pattern is also apparent in Avicenna's initiatory tale, *Ḥayy ibn Yaqẓān*. Avicenna, like ibn Ezra, begins his account on the outskirts of a city, in which the protagonist and his companions see, in the distance, an enigmatic yet beautiful stranger. Moving toward the stranger, the protagonist (and his companions) departs the city, again functioning as a symbol for the various cultural, social, economic, and religious transactions that have the potential to make one forget one's true identity.

As they approach Ḥayy, we become aware of a stark juxtaposition between Ḥayy and the protagonist. Whereas the protagonist is in a group, Ḥayy is alone; whereas the protagonist is from a terrestrial, though unspecified, city, Ḥayy is the inhabitant of a holy abode (*al-bayt al-muqaddus*); whereas the protagonist's gaze is horizontal, Ḥayy looks heavenward, his "face is turned toward [his] father."[37]

The motion of the protagonist and his companions toward the mysterious and beautiful stranger once again signals the initial stage of the ritual phase of separation. Here the initiate leaves behind his social identity and well-being. As was the case in ibn Ezra's tale, this culminates in the section in which Ḥayy informs the protagonist of the true identities of his various traveling companions:

> When he described these companions to me, I suddenly found myself willing to consent (*taṣdīq*) to what he had taught me. I subjected them to the test and practical experience (*al-mukhtibar*) confirmed the report about them. I am [now] in pursuit (*muzāwala*) of them and am [trying to] temper them. Sometimes I have the upper hand, and sometimes they do. May God grant me the grace to live with these companions until separation [from them].[38]

Whereas ibn Ezra's protagonist was successful in separating himself from his companions, Avicenna argues that, as long as one is alive, complete separation is impossible. The best that one can hope for is intermittent periods of separation. This is in keeping with the crucial difference between these two tales: whereas ibn Ezra recounts the actual journey that the protagonist has already undergone, Avicenna claims that this journey is epistemologically and ontologically impossible so long as one possesses a body. Despite this, even though Avicenna's protagonist is unable to divorce himself completely from his companions, he nonetheless comes to the crucial realization of their true identities. And it is this realization that enables the protagonist to progress further on the journey. Moreover, it is this realization that signals the first threshold (*barzakh*) that the initiate must cross, symbolizing the motion from the phase of separation to that of liminality.

As we would expect, this motion across the threshold coincides with ritual activity. This occurs as Ḥayy and the initiate venture toward "a flowing spring near the tranquil Spring of Life" (*ᶜayn kharāra fī jiwār ᶜayn al-ḥayawān al-rākida*):

> [Ḥayy] leads (*hadā*) the pilgrim to it, as [the pilgrim] cleanses himself (*taṭahhara*) in [this Spring] and drinks from its sweet waters, a vigor is

> created in his limbs (*jawāriḥ*). This increases his power to cross vast deserts, and he does not sink in the surrounding waters (*al-baḥr al-muḥīṭ*). He climbs Mount Qāf, and the wicked angels (*al-zabāniyya*) cannot fling him down into hell (*al-hāwiyya*).[39]

After the protagonist immerses himself in the vivifying spring, drinking its healing water, he is ritually purified and thus able to enter the liminal phase of his journey. This phase, as Ḥayy informs him, involves crossing vast deserts, walking on water, and an ascent up a sacred mountain. The spring represents the threshold or barrier (*barzakh*) through which the protagonist must pass in order to attain the level of "one of the two boundaries intersecting [the world] (*aḥad al-ḥaddayni al-munqaṭi*ᶜ ᶜ*anhumā*)."[40]

On the liminal phase of his journey, the protagonist imaginatively apprehends the composition of the physical universe, including prime matter and the elements from which all material phenomena are created. Just as in ibn Ezra's tale, the protagonist experiences a feeling of no identity or affiliation: he has effectively left behind his old world, including all of its social obligations, in order to undergo a series of ordeals. These ordeals, in turn, are what will enable him both to experience his true home in the divine world and subsequently to reemerge as a new person, upon whom has been inscribed the requisite philosophical gnosis of the universe's structure.

As the protagonist moves through the various celestial spheres, they do not receive nearly the same treatment as they did in ibn Ezra's account.[41] Despite this, however, the protagonist describes in much greater detail the confrontation with his own soul. At one point, for instance, the protagonist is introduced to the various "demons" (*qarnāni al-shayṭān*) that threaten to corrupt even the healthiest of souls. Most insidious in this regard is a group that

> leads one to deny what he does not see or form sensually (lit., in his own presence: *ladaihi*). [All that exists is accordingly] physical beauty and human production. [They also succeed in] blackening the heart of humans by denying the existence of the hereafter, consequences of bad and good [actions] and God in Heaven.[42]

Even near the climax of the journey there still exists the omnipresent threat that the soul will abandon its quest, for there are many malevolent forces that would be all too happy to expedite such a failure. Once Ḥayy successfully maneuvers the protagonist through this section, he is able to progress beyond such malevolent forces and pass into the realm of benevolence, wherein he encounters, in ascending order, *jinn* and *hinn*, terrestrial angels (*al-malā*ʾ*ika al-arḍiyyun*), and angels that guide the various spheres. The further one progresses up this chain, the closer one gets to God, here described as the King (*al-malik*).

The encounter with the King represents the telos of the protagonist's long journey. Avicenna describes this stage of the journey in the following manner:

> He who withholds his allegiance (*al-wafāʾ*) in his praise is delirious. [The King] is not subject to [any type of] qualification in His description. He possesses no resemblances (*al-amthāl*). . . . His beauty is the veil (*ḥijāb*) of His beauty, His manifestation (*ẓuhūr*) is the cause of His concealment (*buṭūn*), and His revelation (*tajallin*) the cause of His hiddeness (*khafāʾ*).[43]

Returning to the rite-of-passage paradigm, this description signals the end of liminality and the beginning of the postliminal phase. We would expect at this point for the protagonist to return as a new person to the city whence he came. However, Avicenna only hints at the final stage of aggregation:

> Sometimes solitary individuals (*afrād*) migrate toward Him and He receives them from His surplus (*fawāḍil*). He does not afflict them and He causes them to grasp intuitively (*shaᶜarahum*) the wretchedness of the delights of this world (*iḥtiqār matāᶜ al-iqlīmikum*). They are transformed from being in His presence.[44]

However, this should not be cause for alarm: the ritual paradigm does not break down because of it. On the contrary, it only reinforces the point already made, namely, because Avicenna argues that the journey is only hypothetical, certain problems arise in the map of the cosmos that he subsequently presents. Even though the protagonist, unlike ibn Ezra's and ibn Ṭufayl's, does not return to his point of origin, Ḥayy nonetheless intimates, as the last quotation shows, that individuals do indeed return from basking in the divine presence. As a result, the person who is able to undergo such a journey will return to the world that he has left behind. And, upon his return, he will be a new person, able to put his mystical and intellectual gnosis into praxis.

Ibn Ṭufayl's tale reveals a similar tripartite structure.[45] His *Ḥayy ibn Yaqẓān*, as mentioned consistently throughout this study, is considerably more complex and dramatic than the previous two. This results in significant departures from the ritual paradigm already presented. Of immediate interest is the fact that the main protagonist, as opposed to a celestial or heavenly guide, is called Ḥayy, who now undergoes similar rites of passage as the unnamed protagonists in the other tales.

Whereas ibn Ezra and Avicenna begin their tales with an adult initiate departing from his native city, ibn Ṭufayl introduces his tale with a birth narrative. In the introduction, ibn Ṭufayl informs the reader that there exist two possible accounts of Ḥayy's birth. According to the first account, Ḥayy was born, without father and mother, on a temperate equatorial island (*jazīra*) off the coast of India. Because of a host of geoclimatic conditions, this island receives just the correct amount of heat and light so that various existent beings come to be generated spontaneously.[46]

The other account records that Ḥayy was born secretly to the sister of a jealous king, who refuses to let her marry before he himself has found an appropriate mate.[47] However, she secretly takes a lover by the name of Yaqẓān and gives birth to Ḥayy. Uncertain as to what will become of him if she makes his birth public, she sets the infant adrift in a small ark (*tābūt*) one evening.[48] A powerful current subsequently brings the ark to the aforementioned island, whereupon Ḥayy is nourished and adopted by a doe. Although ibn Ṭufayl relates both of these accounts and leaves it to the reader to choose the one that he or she prefers, he seems to hint later in the narrative that the second of the two accounts is most plausible, as he describes how the doe would warm the infant Ḥayy with the feathers from his ark.[49]

The second account of Ḥayy's birth, according to Hillel Fradkin, is not arbitrary; rather, it tells us that Ḥayy's situation is originally social.[50] Try as one might, one cannot escape either one's social origins or social conditioning. Even though Ḥayy's noetic and imaginative progression requires the solitude that the island offers him, such solitude is not natural to humans. In this way, ibn Ṭufayl departs from his predecessors, Avicenna and ibn Ezra, both of whom were not nearly as concerned with the political and social aspects of the journey. Indeed, the entire third part (i.e., the postliminal phase) of ibn Ṭufayl's *Ḥayy ibn Yaqẓān* is primarily concerned with Ḥayy's encounter with neighboring islanders. This concern with the political aspects is in keeping with the fact that ibn Ṭufayl, like so many Muslim Andalusian thinkers, was preoccupied with the problematics of political philosophy.[51]

To return to the ritual paradigm, ibn Ṭufayl's preference for the social account of Ḥayy's birth nicely fits with the separation stage. Unlike the accounts of Avicenna and ibn Ezra, ibn Ṭufayl's Ḥayy does not remove himself as soon as he begins to realize the illusory nature of the physical world. Rather, an external agent, his mother, physically removes him before he can realize his own predicament. Ibn Ṭufayl's Ḥayy thus grows up and develops outside the customary familial and social structures.[52]

Ḥayy gradually matures on the island thanks, in large part, to the kindness and sustenance of his adopted mother. The relationship between Ḥayy and the doe is a very close one and is described with considerable pathos. So long as the doe is alive, Ḥayy does not really question either his existence or his identity, social or otherwise. The seminal moment occurs in a moving passage where the narrator describes the subsequent death of the doe. At this point, Ḥayy gradually awakens to the fact that he is not like the other animals around him. Following the death of the doe, now referred to as his mother (*umm*),[53] Ḥayy decides to dissect her in order to ascertain the cause of death. This is a significant moment in the narrative:

> The [mother's] body now seemed something low and worthless compared to the being he was convinced had lived in it for a time and then departed. Ḥayy turned his thoughts on that being. What was it? What was its manner of existence? What connected it to the body? Where had it gone and how had it gotten out? What drove it away if it was forced to leave; or, if it left of its own free choice, what made it so loathe the body? His mind was filled with these questions. He soon dropped the body and thought no more of it, knowing that the mother who had nursed him and showed him so much kindness could only be that being which had departed.[54]

Ḥayy will essentially spend the rest of the journey trying to ascertain the answers to these various questions. In Avicenna's and ibn Ezra's tales, the movement from the phase of separation to that of liminality coincides with the realization of the true identities of the traveling companions. Here, however, it is marked by the death of the mother and Ḥayy's concomitant understanding that there exists a fundamental division between the soul and the body. Following the transition from the phase of separation to that of liminality, Ḥayy undergoes the long journey wherein he slowly learns the answers to the various questions he posed. This stage of the journey is structurally similar to those found in both Avicenna's and ibn Ezra's accounts. All these accounts involve the noetic development of the individual, which gradually gives way to an experiential and imaginative apprehension of the divine. This is a steady progression by which Ḥayy moves from the various physical and biological sciences (e.g., the distinction between form and matter), to the science of psychology (e.g., the existence of a soul, the various faculties of the soul). Gradually he casts his gaze heavenward so that he becomes aware of the stars and the heavenly spheres. Eventually he comes to the realization that the heavens must have an incorporeal cause.[55]

The culmination of the phase of liminality is symbolized by the mystical union (*ittiṣāl*) that Ḥayy has with the divine. This primarily involves various ritual activities that Ḥayy himself develops in order to mimic the activities and motions of the celestial bodies.[56] In particular, he makes sure that his own appearance is clean, fragrant, and fresh in order to symbolize the vitality that he apprehends in the celestial bodies.

> In addition, Ḥayy prescribed himself circular motions of various kinds. Sometimes he would circle the island, skirting along the beach and roving in the inlets. Sometimes he would march around his house or certain large rocks a set number of times. Or at times he would spin around in circles until he got dizzy. . . . [He would also] fix his mind on the Necessary Existent Being, cut away the bonds of all objects of the sense—shut his eyes, stop his ears, use all the force at his command to restrain the play of the imagination—and try with all his might to think only of Him. Often he would aid himself by spinning around faster and faster.[57]

Ḥayy here employs a variety of ritual activities to focus the mind upon its divine source. Although these rituals are similar to those practiced by the Sufis, he intimates that such activities are natural, arising from the observance of the rhythms of the universe. Moreover, rather than have his imagination get the better of him, he perceives that ritual activity forces this faculty to work in the service of his intellect.[58] Together these two faculties are, ideally, able to expel all inappropriate thoughts that might arise. After such a concentrated effort, Ḥayy is able to apprehend the divine. This stage, as the narrator himself proclaims, is indescribable.

> Still I shall not leave you without hints (*ishārāt*) as to the wonders Ḥayy saw (*shāhada*) from this height, not by pounding on the gates of truth, but by coining symbols (*mithāl*), for there is no way of finding out what truly occurs at this plateau of experience besides reaching (*wuṣūl*) it [yourself].[59]

It is at this point that Ḥayy's self is extinguished into the Self of the divine. This state, in Arabic known as *fanāʾ*, culminates in the blurring of the distinction between God and self. Ḥayy, however, is reminded by God that this is not the case as he apprehends that there does exist a line separating God from all else. The state of *fanāʾ*, then, gives way to one of contact (*ittiṣāl*):

> Passing through a deep trance to the complete death-of-self (*fanāʾ*) and real contact (*wuṣūl*) with divine, he saw (*shāhada*) a being corresponding to the highest sphere, beyond which there is no body (*lā jism lahu*), a subject free of matter, and neither identical with the truth and the One nor with the sphere itself, nor distinct from them. Just as the form of the sun appearing in a polished mirror is neither sun nor mirror, and yet distinct from neither. The splendor, perfection, and beauty he saw in the essence of that sphere were too magnificent to be described and too delicate to be clothed in written or spoken words. But he saw it to be the

> pinnacle of joy, delight, and rapture, in blissful vision of the being of the truth, glorious be His majesty.[60]

After this vision, Ḥayy gradually returns to the sensual world. On his way down this ontological ladder, he apprehends the immaterial images associated with the lower spheres, the images of those righteous and privileged souls who had made the journey before him and, finally, the torment in which the souls of the wicked ultimately find themselves. Much like the tales of both ibn Ezra and Avicenna, the concluding section of ibn Ṭufayl's narrative witnesses Ḥayy firmly back in the sensual world and back in the society that he had originally departed. This corresponds to the third part of the ritual paradigm, that of aggregation, in which the initiate returns to society as a changed individual, prepared to work for social betterment.[61] As we shall see, however, ibn Ṭufayl's tale presents this portion not only in considerably greater detail than in the other two accounts, but also with significant and surprising differences.

The circumstances that lead to the political dimensions of Ḥayy's career occur in his association with a neighboring island, whose inhabitants possess a divinely revealed law (*sharīᶜa*).[62] On this island, the narrator informs us, live two upstanding and principled young men, Absāl and Salāmān. The former is interested in the inner dimension (*al-bāṭin*) and is inclined toward allegorical interpretation (*al-taʾwīl*), whereas the latter is more interested in the outer dimension (*al-ẓāhir*) of the law.[63] One day, Absāl visits Ḥayy's island to seek instruction in the deeper meanings of his own religious teaching. After a tense first encounter, Ḥayy and Absāl gradually befriend one another and Ḥayy learns to speak the language of Absāl. Absāl then informs Ḥayy of the law on his island and Ḥayy is intrigued, thinking that it corresponds to the truths that he has experienced personally. Ḥayy, however, is unclear as to why the law is concerned with symbols and metaphors, as opposed to the reality behind them. Ḥayy agrees to accompany Absāl back to his island in order to teach society about the truths that are behind their religious symbols.

Unlike ibn Ezra's and Avicenna's narratives, we actually witness the fate of the initiate in society. In Ḥayy's case, it is not pleasant. As soon as Ḥayy begins to teach the inhabitants about the truths to which he has immediate access, they recoil in horror. They are content to know God in simple and human terms, for their religion is based on fear of punishment as opposed to intellectual and imaginative apprehension. Ḥayy concludes

> That most men are no better than unreasoning animals, and realized that all wisdom (*ḥikma*) and guidance (*hidāya*), all that could possibly help

> them was contained already in the words of the prophets (*rusul*) and the religious law. None of this could be different. There was nothing to be added.[64]

Following this realization, Ḥayy decides that he cannot be a part of this society.[65] As a result, he and Absāl return to Ḥayy's island. There they spend the rest of their days in contemplation of the divine, until "man's certain fate overtook them."

Although the ritual paradigm offered by the likes of van Gennep and Turner culminates in the initiate's return to society, ibn Ṭufayl here argues that the philosophical initiate's role in society is a potentially precarious one. This stems, it seems to me, from the fact that the initiate in all three of these tales receives a gnosis that, although theoretically open to all, is only actualized by a select few. The tripartite model proposed by van Gennep, by contrast, is concerned primarily with initiation into the various secrets of a specific social group.

But these differences should not trouble us. My goal has not been to find a perfect fit between these tales and the various theories on the rite of passage. On the contrary, I have found it useful to employ the latter as a point of departure to illumine the former. This section has argued that the conclusions reached by van Gennep and Turner concerning the structure and function of the rite of passage are *mutatis mutandis* applicable to these tales penned by medieval Islamic and Jewish philosophers. For these three narratives share with the rite-of-passage paradigm presented here a tripartite structure (separation, liminality, and incorporation). As far as the *Ḥayy ibn Yaqẓān* cycle is concerned, I have suggested that the structure is not arbitrary, but intimately related to their form and function. The tripartite structure of the rite of passage should alert us to the narrative initiations of these protagonists. This initiation, whether in ritual theory or in the initiatory tale, is tantamount to the radical transformation of the way in which the initiate apprehends, engages, and exists within the world. In the following section, I tease out the implications that this structure has on the reader of these tales.

Text as Meditation Manual

As I argued in chapter 2, the reader is not simply the passive recipient of the text's message. On the contrary, he or she is actively encouraged to join the quest with the narrative's protagonist in order to experience imaginatively the same initiation into the secrets of the cosmos. Within this context, the telos of these tales, regardless of the author or the author's religious commitment, is the guidance of the reader toward a certain mental attitude, bringing about the transformation of the individual and his or her being-in-the-world. In the present section, I return to the tales to show how they contribute, ideally, to the reader's symbolic initiation into philosophical gnosis.

Within this context, it is important to recall that medieval Neoplatonism was not simply about theory. On the contrary, as I argued in chapter 2, it was a "way of life," a practical guide by which one could live well and practically on a daily basis. For the ancient and medieval Neoplatonists, the true aim of philosophy was not an encyclopedic knowledge of the universe simply for its own sake, but only insofar as this knowledge served as a prolegomena to the purification of the soul so as to enable it to return to its true celestial home. The *Ḥayy ibn Yaqẓān* cycle represents an imaginative blueprint for undergoing this process. The goal of these texts, then, is nothing other than the metamorphosis of the reader—and the authors employ all means at their disposal to accomplish this.

Of central concern to the Neoplatonists is the soul, which requires purification. This proves difficult, due to the corporeal casing in which it finds itself.[66] To begin to extricate itself from its mortal coil, the soul needs various intellectual and imaginative exercises. Such an extrication, as all of our authors remind us, cannot happen completely as long as the soul remains in the body. However, the soul can prepare itself for the coming rupture with the body. It is precisely within this context that we must situate the initiatory tale.

Sara Rappe argues that the Neoplatonic philosophical text functions as a type of "meditation manual." In particular, she claims that the works of Plotinus and those Neoplatonists who came after him conceived of the writing of philosophy in significantly different ways than we do today. Agreeing with the likes of Pierre Hadot, she emphasizes the non-discursive elements of ancient Neoplatonic texts, stressing the manner in which they force the reader to use and ultimately to discard them:

> The *Enneads* and the texts that follow in its train represent a disciplined attempt to foster, to awaken, or at least to acknowledge what the Neoplatonists conceived to be a sometime dormant capacity in human beings, for *theoria* or vision, for insight and self-awakening.[67]

These texts encourage the reader to enter into and subsequently contemplate their contents. The reader does not just passively read these texts, but he or she assimilates them, making them part of his or her own life.[68] According to Rappe, "this training in concentration is part of the non-discursive methodology that complements the textual side of the tradition."[69] It is precisely this that we see at work in the initiatory tales of our authors. In effect, they provide an imaginary geography of the cosmos by which the reader measures or gauges his or her own inner journey. In ibn Ezra's and Avicenna's tales, Ḥayy guides not only the unnamed protagonist, but also the reader toward a specified and pre-determined goal.

This is why these tales are written in a particular manner. They do not recount or retell the story of a protagonist who lived some time in the distant past. Rather, they relate the story that each reader ideally undergoes during the readerly activity. By employing a particular mode of language—replete with poetic, aural, and rhythmic significances—these authors try to transform the reader, to call out to every aspect of his or her being (e.g., the sensual, the imaginative, the intellectual). For ancient and medieval philosophers, the written work is nothing but a reflection of broader "pedagogic, psychagogic, and methodological preoccupations."[70]

But how exactly does this affect the reader? It is within this context that we need to situate the medieval discussion of mimesis. Mimesis (*muḥākā*), according to Avicenna, "is natural to man, giving the likeness of a thing and not the thing itself."[71] Of all the animals, humans are the most capable of imitation and, for the medieval philosophers, it is in this activity that we derive great pleasure (*ladhdha*):

> What is delightful is not that form itself nor what is portrayed but its being a precise imitation of something else. For this reason, learning is pleasant not to philosophers alone but to common people due to the imitation that is in it, and because learning consists of a certain representation (*taṣwīr*) of a thing in the "seat" of the soul (*ruqᶜa al-nafs*). Men, therefore, find great delight in portrayed forms if they can well relate these to their originals.[72]

Mimesis is responsible for moving the soul of the reader from passivity to activity. This activity, unlike pure ratiocination, turns on the imagination: it involves images and an ability to relate them to a non-corporeal reality. Mimesis thus encourages the reader to experience pleasure in encountering an imaginative representation of something. This is accomplished, according to Avicenna who here follows Aristotle, by means of poetry or poetic utterances. For this reason, Avicenna argues:

> Poetry aims at imaginative representation, not the statement of opinions. . . . Poetry, therefore, has come to be more akin to philosophy than the other kinds of speech, because it has a greater grasp of the existent and a more precise execution of universal judgment.[73]

It is precisely through the prism of mimesis that I want to examine each of the three initiatory tales. Through their complex and dynamic use of language, each tale in its own way encourages the reader to identify with the protagonist, to apprehend the world through the protagonist's eyes, and ultimately to discard both the protagonist and the narrative. These tales are rich imaginative accounts that invite the reader into their textual universes so that he or she may identify imaginatively, on a mimetic level, with the protagonist.

At the beginning of ibn Ezra's *Ḥay ben Meqitz*, for example, the protagonist declares that his story is not unique. Explicit here is that if it were unique, the story would not be worth recounting. On the contrary, what the protagonist has experienced is offered as the true fulfillment of every individual, something open to anyone with appropriate intentionality and proper training. In essence, he asks readers to imagine themselves in his position:

> Listen, O wise men, to my words
> Those versed in knowledge pay heed.
> Men, young and old, understand
> Ignoramuses and youth listen up.
> Truth will my mouth pronounce
> Uprightness will issue from my lips.[74]

The protagonist here signals that what follows will be the communication of a specific type of intellectual and existential experience. Lest this message be lost on the reader, ibn Ezra uses language that echoes the call narratives of the prophetic and wisdom literature associated with the Hebrew Bible.[75] Moreover, as in the later Apocalyptic literature, the subsequent ascent of the soul can only take place in the presence of a guide, for one can only reach the highest level of being in a person-to-person relationship. The protagonist becomes to the reader what Ḥay is to the protagonist: a guide who instructs the initiate into the secrets of the philosophical journey. The text that the reader confronts is more than just words on a page; it represents the contours of an ideal relationship between two individuals on a personal level. The text attempts to create in the reader a lived experience or an "awakening," not one that is simply theoretical.

As the protagonist undergoes his various initiations, he encourages the reader to experience the journey through his or her own eyes. A transference throughout the novel exists as the reader gradually begins to identify with, and is subsequently subsumed into, the protagonist. For example, when Ḥay first addresses the protagonist, he speaks to the reader as well:

> While we were talking
> his words opened up.
> Extended to *those who desire to understand*
> *the true nature of things and to searchers of the straight path.*[76]

What is to follow is not a specific chance encounter; rather, it is universal, open to anyone who reads the text with the proper "desire to understand." For the protagonist is not the only one who has companions that prevent him from achieving his full promise. This is why the protagonist receives no name: he is, in effect, every reader of the text. To provide him with a name would be to limit him; he is everyone, yet no one. This transference between the protagonist and the reader occurs throughout the narrative, until finally it culminates in the following exchange:

> "Tell me with what shall I approach Him?
> How shall I know Him?
> I have truly longed to know Him
> I yearn to see Him."
> He replied, "Uphold my words
> Keep my teaching.
> Walk in my path, and do not depart from me.
> You will know your spirit
> As is fitting to your ability and your strength.
> Then you will be able to know Him
> To apprehend Him."[77]

The teaching that Ḥay refers to is essentially the narrative that the reader has in front of him- or herself. The line separating the word and the world blur to such an extent that, in typical Neoplatonic fashion, they possess an organic and interlocking relationship. To apprehend God involves understanding such relationships, plus having the equally important knowledge of the self. This knowledge, however, can only be obtained in the presence of a guide or a text to point out the direction and to help negotiate the initiate through the various pitfalls that arise on the journey.

A similar situation exists in Avicenna's *Ḥayy ibn Yaqẓān*. He begins the tale with a brief prologue, wherein he states that despite his initial resistance, he has agreed to record the adventures of Ḥayy. With this, Avicenna not only signals a departure from his other more Peripatetic works that lack such a tension between public and private discourse; he also intimates that what follows will not be an ordinary or straightforward philosophical treatise.

Interestingly, Avicenna speaks in the first person in the prologue and continues to use the first person when he begins the narrative. This first-person account intimates that what is to follow will be autobiographical or semi-autobiographical. This need not surprise us because Avicenna is one of the few medieval Islamic or Jewish philosophers who composed an autobiography. Accordingly, the following questions emerge: What is the nature of the relationship between the autobiography and *Ḥayy ibn Yaqẓān*? Is the personal development that Avicenna relates in his autobiography reflected in the intellectual development of the unnamed protagonist?

Despite the autobiographical nature of the tale, Avicenna did write his *Ḥayy ibn Yaqẓān* in an impersonal manner. For in it, there exist no specific or identifiable places, persons, or relationships. The unnamed protagonist, as mentioned above, is everyone yet no one. Born in an unnamed city, with unnamed friends, he progresses through an unfamiliar universe in search of intellectual perfection. Avicenna maps out a similar progression in his autobiography, but now he mentions specifics. He tells us that he was born in a small village named Afshanah in Bukhārā. Moreover, he also provides both a survey and the order of the specific sciences that he has mastered. He writes that after he had learnt the logical sciences,

> I devoted myself to studying the texts—the original and the commentaries—in the natural sciences and metaphysics, and the gates of knowledge began opening for me. Next I sought to know medicine, and so I read the books written about it. Medicine is not one of the difficult sciences, and therefore I excelled in it in a very short time, to the point that distinguished physicians began to read the science of medicine under me.[78]

While mastering the various sciences, Avicenna informs us that this mastery did not come about only by natural means:

> And because of those problems which used to baffle me, not being able to solve the middle term of the syllogism, I used to visit the mosque frequently and worship, praying humbly to the All-Creating, until he opened the mystery of it to me and made the difficult seem easy. At night I would return home, set out a lamp before me, and devote myself to reading and writing. Whenever sleep overcame me or I became conscious of weakening, I would turn aside to drink a cup of wine, so that my strength would return to me. Then I would return to reading. And whenever sleep seized me I would see those very problems in my dream; and many questions became clear to me in my sleep. . . . Thus I mastered the logical, natural, and mathematical sciences, and I now reached the science of metaphysics.[79]

The emphases that Avicenna here puts on both the progression through the various sciences and the importance of the imaginative apprehension of them are precisely what he allegorizes in *Ḥayy ibn Yaqẓān*. In addition, mixed in with Avicenna's discussion of his mastery of the various sciences is the recurring motif of travel. Like the unnamed protagonist in *Ḥayy ibn Yaqẓān,* Avicenna traveled and moved about frequently, with each new place associated with a new intellectual adventure. In Bukhārā, for instance, Avicenna tends to the ailing sultan, Nūḥ ibn Manṣūr, and is able to gain access into the court library, where

> I saw books whose names had not reached very many people and which I had not seen before that time, nor have I seen since. I read these books and mastered what was useful in them and discovered the status of each man in his science.[80]

After this, he moved to Gurgānj, where he worked in the court of the Amīr, ᶜAli ibn Maᵓmūn. Following his employment there, Avicenna traveled to Nasā, Bāward, Ṭūs, Samanqān, Jājarm, and Jurjān. During all of these travels, he was involved in a number of political intrigues, was banished from states, and imprisoned in the castle Fardajān in Hamadhān (where, according to his biographer, al-Jūzjānī, he wrote *Ḥayy ibn Yaqẓān*), and was threatened with execution.

Despite such activity, which is reminiscent of the unnamed protagonist's busy life before he began his journey with Ḥayy, Avicenna was intellectually prolific. It is for this reason, it seems to me, that Avicenna is much more cautious in his *Ḥayy ibn Yaqẓān* than both ibn Ezra and ibn Ṭufayl were in his claim that the best one can hope for in this life is intermittent glimpses of the divine. It is for reasons such as these that I contend Avicenna creates *Ḥayy ibn Yaqẓān* as a highly stylized, impersonal account of his own intellectual development. In so doing, he recounts in highly poetic fashion the intimate relationship that develops between a solitary individual and the various philosophical disciplines. This returns us to a point originally made with ibn Ezra: as soon as one personalizes a narrative, it becomes unique and potentially unrepeatable. Thus, the universal aspects of the narrative become marginalized. The more general that one can keep a narrative, the more universal its significances. Furthermore, by presenting a stripped-down, impersonal account of his own imaginative account of the universe, Avicenna encourages his readers to undertake a similar journey. What he presents as a text, then, is nothing other than the traces and signposts of his own journey.

Avicenna invites the reader to join him on a pilgrimage similar to his own. Thus while the textual initiate has undergone the journey in the company of the enigmatic Ḥayy, Avicenna here presents his text as the guide to the prospective reader. The encounter with Ḥayy, though stylized, is not supernatural. As in ibn Ezra's account, it is theoretically open to every reader. As soon as the textual initiate sees Ḥayy in the distance,[81] Ḥayy is welcoming, ready to address us in "a pleasant manner of speaking (*ᶜan lahja maqbūla*)."[82] Ḥayy's words, then, are not addressed solely to the protagonist, but also to every potential initiate.

Avicenna also engages in a clever transference in which he, the protagonist, and the reader become metonyms for one another. When Ḥayy looks into the protagonist's face, for example, the physiognomical prognostication is so general that it refers to everyone:

> Physiognomy (*ᶜilm al-firāsa*) reveals in you a surplus of moral characteristics and a mixture of clay and inanimate matter. If you choose the side of reform and order, it will bring you perfection; but if a seducer deceives you onto the road of baseness, you will be turned and he will convert you.[83]

This description, though addressed directly to the protagonist, is inclusive as opposed to exclusive. Thus begins the lengthy process by which the reader slowly identifies with the unnamed protagonist. In a subsequent section, Ḥayy speaks not only to the protagonist, but to everyone who resembles the protagonist:

> And he said *you and he who is on a path similar to yours,* my journey is impossible and its path closed to *you and him* until you have the good fortune to separate yourself [from your companions].[84]

Finally, at the telos, the culmination of the imaginative journey, Ḥayy speaks not to the protagonist in the second person, but in the much more impersonal third-person plural:

> Sometimes solitary individuals migrate toward Him and He receives them from His surplus. He does not afflict them and He causes them to grasp intuitively the wretchedness of the delights of this world. They are transformed from being in His presence.[85]

With this passage, and the employment of personal pronouns, the identification between the reader and the protagonist is complete. In the next passage, the conclusion of the tale, Ḥayy issues an invitation—"Now if you will, follow me, come with me toward Him"—that is directed as much to the reader as it is to the protagonist. In contrast to the beginning of the novel, where Avicenna clearly differentiates between the *I* of the tale and the *you* or *he* of the reader, by the end of the tale they are essentially one and the same.

Similar strategies are at work in ibn Ṭufayl's novel. In his prologue, ibn Ṭufayl informs his reader that he too has composed his tale in response to a disciple's inquiry; only now his purpose is to provide an answer about the true nature of Avicenna's enigmatic "Oriental Wisdom" (*al-ḥikma al-mashriqiyya*).[86] Such an answer, he subsequently informs the reader, will be neither discursive nor straightforward. On the contrary, it will be cryptic, experiential, and not open to everyone.[87] Ibn Ṭufayl presents his *Ḥayy ibn Yaqẓān* not as a written lecture to be read passively by the reader, but as a gateway through which the reader can enter into a drama that involves the individual soul and its struggle toward philosophical enlightenment.

Unlike Avicenna, ibn Ṭufayl does not present this drama in the first person. His narrator, instead, is omniscient, recounting the tale, for the most part, in the third person. In the prologue, ibn Ṭufayl, presumably speaking in his own voice, informs his reader that the state to which he refers is that of love:

> But to those who reach love, God grants what I purely metaphorically call another faculty. This corresponds to the restoration of sight. And sometimes, rarely, there comes a man whose eyes, as it were, are always open, whose glance is always piercing, who does not need to search.[88]

Ibn Ṭufayl endeavors to awaken in his reader a faculty that is metaphorically akin to sight. He subsequently argues that the actual content of this sight is only the true provenance of the individual who undergoes it, and that the contents cannot be put down in writing. All that he can do, in other words, is point the reader in the correct direction:

> To give you a brief glimpse of the road that lies ahead, let me tell you the story of *Ḥayy ibn Yaqẓān,* Absāl, and Salāmān, who were given their names by Avicenna himself. For the tale points a moral for all with heart to understand, "a reminder for anyone with a heart or ears to listen and to hear."[89]

The story that follows provides the intellectual, moral, and spiritual progression of Ḥayy ibn Yaqẓān. Again, we witness the transference between the main character of the narrative and the reader. Just as Ḥayy progresses from being an infant at the whim of the natural world who gradually develops his rational and mystical faculties to transcend this world, so too is the reader invited to experience this journey through Ḥayy's own textual movements. Ibn Ṭufayl thus creates a text in which the reader must essentially mimic the journey that Ḥayy makes. In this regard, Ḥayy's goal, like that of all medieval (and ancient) philosophers, was to understand the workings and principles of the universe. Is there, for example, order behind the seeming randomness of the natural world? What is the nature of the relationship between this world of form and matter and the celestial world? What happens to humans when they pass away?

The majority of ibn Ṭufayl's tale, as I mentioned above, is the story of ascending the *scala naturae*, finding various repeating patterns in the natural world.[90] For example, Ḥayy originally surveys the natural world and sees nothing but chaos and a plethora of animals. Gradually, however, he comes to the realization of genera and species. The journey then, is essentially one of taxonomy, showing the movement from seeing things in their multiplicity to apprehending the unity behind everything. Such a journey is neither solitary nor a figment of the mythic past. On the contrary, it is one that every reader of the tale undergoes, symbolizing the freedom from randomness and multiplicity:

> By this time it was plain to him that each animal, although many in respect of its parts, its various senses and types of motion, was nonetheless one in terms of that spirit which stems from a single fixed place and diffuses there to all the organs.[91]

This is no simple teaching. On the contrary, it is a symbolic initiatory progression that recounts philosophical principles in a highly literary way. This is not a cold, analytic description; rather, it is a highly dynamic narrative that ultimately draws on experiences and cultural categories already familiar to the reader. The reader must take his or her own traditional and customary ways of looking at the world and transform them in order to apprehend the world in a new way.[92] The result is transformative, as both Ḥayy and the reader are initiated into the imaginative wonders of philosophy. Each piece of the ontological puzzle falls into place and builds upon what went before it. Eventually Ḥayy comes to the realization that

> The only way to apprehend Him, then, must be by some non-physical means, something which is neither a bodily faculty nor in any way bound up with body—neither inside nor outside, neither in contact with it nor disjointed from it.[93]

Gradually Ḥayy and the reader move from knowledge of the physical world to the divine source behind this knowledge. This path, in turn, leads to knowledge of the Necessarily Existing Being (*al-mawjūd al-wājib al-wujūd*), and the subsequent desire of the initiate to model his own behavior on the celestial spheres.[94] After his meeting with Absāl and their subsequent return to the solitude that the island grants them, the narrator provides the reader with an epilogue:

> And this—may God give you spirit to strengthen you—is the story of Ḥayy ibn Yaqẓān, Absāl, and Salāmān. It takes up a line of discourse not found in a book or heard in the usual sort of speeches. It belongs to a concealed science (*al-ᶜilm al-maknūn*) received only by those with gnosis of God (*ahl al-maᶜrifa bi-allah*) and unknown except to those with a high rank with God (*ahl al-ᶜizza bi-allah*).[95]

As the reader approaches the end of the tale, his or her identity gradually takes on the characteristics of Ḥayy's personality, and the reader becomes like him, an initiate into the esoteric dimensions of philosophical knowledge. The reader began the narrative as an infant, someone to whom the secrets of the universe were closed; by the end of the tale, the ideal reader has imaginatively experienced Ḥayy's journey and emerges from this experience, much like Ḥayy himself, as a transformed individual. Only the reader who properly understands can penetrate behind the veils (*ḥujub*) that guard the secrets of the narrative.

As should now be apparent, all three of these narratives serve as invitations, gateways, or thresholds rather than as propositional or discursive texts. The reader, like the textual protagonist, finds himself or herself on a threshold that leads, under ideal circumstances, to a transformative experience. In the context of this chapter, I have argued that this transformation is in many ways reminiscent of an initiatory experience. Initiation, as the theorists I have here cited inform us, occurs at particular moments of social disjunction or tension. The rite is one way that the individual or society can attempt, but not always successfully, to ameliorate such moments. Although I have for the most part kept the tripartite model, my claim is not that these tales rigidly or artificially fit into it, but that these tales, at the level of both the text and the reader, represent the symbolic initiation of the philosopher into a deeper gnosis that cannot be deduced intellectually. By using this tripartite model as a segue into the initiatory tale, this chapter has argued that the meaning that one derives from these texts is not straightforward, but non-discursive, imaginative, and experiential. And that the reader, like the protagonist, takes on the characteristics of an initiate who must successfully pass through the narrative's threshold in order to imagine the divine.

Conclusions

Reading in both antiquity and the Middle Ages was not a solitary activity.[96] On the contrary, as Hadot expresses it, "reading customarily meant reading aloud, emphasizing the rhythm of the phrase and the sounds of the words, which the author himself had already experienced when he dictated his work."[97] It is thus important not to impose a utilitarian straightjacket on these tales. Just as I have argued in previous chapters that we must not lose sight of their literary and imaginative components, in this chapter I contend that we must not marginalize the ritualizing and initiatory components of these narratives.

Moreover, as I will show in chapter 5, it is important to contextualize these initiatory tales within the poetic and aesthetic world of medieval Islamicate civilization. The recitation of such poetry was a collective as opposed to a solitary activity that drew upon the sensory experiences of its audience. If the vocabulary and the language employed were so far removed from the cultural and intellectual concerns of the audience, the tales would surely fall on deaf ears. The significance of these tales is that they employ, and use for philosophical purposes, the rich literary traditions that were an intimate part of medieval Islamicate civilization.

In all three of the narratives, we encounter the quest of an individual to move beyond the inherited way of apprehending the world. Although this is a motif that dates at least to the time of Socrates, the way in which each of our authors has drawn on the themes and tropes of his own literary, poetic, and religious tradition is significant. All three authors attempt to harmonize the philosophical and the monotheistic paradigms. In this chapter I have argued that one of the ways in which they could do this was through the initiatory dimensions of Neoplatonic texts. For this reason, we must be sensitive to the ways in which these tales employ media such as songs, verbal formulae, and rhythmic patterning in an attempt to heighten communication.[98]

We also must not lose sight of the mimetic dimensions of these tales. The stories are composed in such a manner that the reader is invited to enter into the character of the protagonist to undergo his experiences. There thus exists an intimate relationship between the protagonist and the reader. The Neoplatonic system—with employment of artistic and narrative dimensions—enables these three authors to create narratives that encourage the reader to be more than just a passive observer of their words. On the contrary, the reader ideally uses these texts ultimately to move beyond them.

These tales are far from trivial or ludic compositions, whose primary intentionality is to educate the philosophically uninformed. Rather, they succeed precisely because they carve out a ritual space in which various media of communication—for example, the sensory, the aural, the visual—are employed to enhance and improve the reader's engagement with the world. This has the effect of pulling the reader, both emotionally and cognitively, into the narrative. The goal is not to impart new information, but to encourage the reader to experience the world in newfound ways. In short, the reader is transformed and emerges as a different person when he or she finishes the tale.

This is primarily accomplished by means of the rich, sensual descriptions of the natural world that these tales offer. These are not descriptions meant to be propositional or analytical; their goal is not to appeal solely to the intellect. On the contrary, they are rich, sensual, and imaginative descriptions that appeal to the entire individual. This is certainly not to deny that there exists a doctrinal component to these texts. My concern in this chapter has been to analyze these texts from the discipline of religious studies, specifically from the perspective of the rite of passage. In the following chapter, I will examine the doctrinal components of these tales in order to show that they are philosophically significant. I will again reiterate my argument that they are not simple texts meant for the masses. This analysis will involve examining more closely the aesthetic component of the tales, for this aspect is intimately connected to their philosophical content.

5

"God Is Beautiful and Loves Beauty": The Role of Aesthetics in Medieval Islamic and Jewish Philosophy

THE RICH INTERPLAY BETWEEN ISLAMICATE CULTURE ON THE ONE HAND, AND Arabic and Hebrew poetics on the other, has been well documented.[1] Rather than attempt to retell this relationship here, the aim of the present chapter is to establish the important place of aesthetics within medieval Islamicate philosophy. In so doing, I attempt to demarcate a distinct theory of beauty and show how this theory found practical expression in the initiatory tale. Using the three authors as a case study, I argue that the medieval Islamic and Jewish philosophers—in much the same manner as their precursors Plato, Aristotle, and Plotinus—speculated on beauty in ways that we would today call distinctly functional.[2] These individuals worked within a symbolic universe in which beauty was one of the defining characteristics of the intelligible world. Within this context, the beautiful objects in our world, the world of form and matter, participated in this intelligible beauty. Consequently it is to the intelligible world that the soul is naturally drawn when it observes and contemplates physical beauty. The subsequent result was the elucidation of an ontological relationship between intelligible and sensible beauty in which the latter becomes essential for the apprehension of the former. Aesthetics was more than an appreciation of art for art's sake; rather, it was an important subdiscipline of medieval philosophy. The philosophical importance of beauty resided in its centrality to the noetic development of the individual.

The various medieval Islamic and Jewish thinkers worked, as I argued in chapter 2, within the parameters of an eclectic and interdisciplinary philosophical system that we today call "Neoplatonism." Although there exist many problems in applying this term to diverse thinkers, they nonetheless shared a common set of ontological, existential, and psychological assumptions. According to the standard Neoplatonic ontology, the One—existing outside of time and space and thus unclassifiable—makes itself known through emanation.[3] This process is, from a phenomenological perspective, predicated on the notion that the transcendental is not ontically different from the phenomenality by which it shows itself. To use the language of Heidegger, Being exists only in its manifestations:

> "Behind" the phenomena of phenomenology there is essentially nothing else; on the other hand, what is to become a phenomenon can be hidden. And just because the phenomena are proximally and for the most part *not* given, there is need for phenomenology. Covered-up-ness is the counter-concept to "phenomenon."[4]

To translate this into Neoplatonic thought, the One—or the concept of a transcendent, unmediated truth—is inseparable from the images by which it appears. Even though the One can show itself in many ways that are dependent upon the different modes of access we have to it, it can nevertheless be hidden by the various ways in which it appears. It is for this reason, as I suggested in chapter 3, that the role of hermeneutical activity becomes central to both the presentation and recovery of truth.[5] One must interpret the transcendental within the phenomenal. Hermeneutics thus presents us with the mechanism that enables us to recognize the One as it reveals itself in this world.

Within the world of Neoplatonism, it is crucial to remember that emanation, from the embodied human perspective, is what allows the individual to apprehend the unknown from the perspective of the known. Within this context, images issue ontically from a non-material source, thereby providing the conditions for our knowledge of that which does not exist corporeally or spatially. From the perspective of our world, these images provide the prolegomena to the higher articulations of the universe in such a manner that the latter cannot exist without the former. Images, then, are what allow finite individuals, composed of form and matter, to have access to that which exists without matter.

Embodied individuals require the modalities and categories of everyday sensual experience to apprehend the One and the spiritual world. Without such modalities and categories, humans are simply incapable of grasping the intelligible. As Wolfson persuasively argues, we should not assume that the sensual is simply appealed to *post factum* in order to attempt to explain or translate what is otherwise ineffable.[6] Rather than play no part in the actual experience, the sensual becomes the quiddity of the actual experience, presenting the terms of reference through which spiritual forms appear to human consciousness. As a consequence, language, metaphor, and mythopoesis become more than simple literary tropes: they, in effect, become the conceptual apparati that aid in comprehending reality. Language and vision therefore become important features of medieval aesthetics and the various theories of artistic representation.

Even though the One cannot be reduced to or exhausted by the many, there nonetheless exists an intimate relationship between them. And it is precisely this interrelationship that the medieval Neoplatonists were so interested in exploring and delineating. Their approaches ultimately translated into an aesthetics, whereby the medieval philosophers argued that material images embodying a certain geometric proportion, harmony, and balance pointed beyond themselves to a celestial, non-material and intellectual beauty. Appreciation of this relationship enabled these thinkers to conceptualize concrete images as important vehicles by which the individual could re-ascend the ontological hierarchy. Physical objects and images do not exist in a vacuum; on the contrary, they are related to the principle of emanation in which the One manifests itself in the many. The One is thus inaccessible without images, for it is only by means of the latter that humans have access to the former. This leads to an intimate connection between the material and immaterial worlds, between image and truth, and between imagination and reason. It is precisely these connections that this chapter examines. Although this will be done primarily within the context of the initiatory tale, the subsequent conclusions will provide important insights into a much-neglected aspect of medieval philosophy.

Historians of medieval Islamic and Jewish philosophy rarely focus on concepts such as aesthetics, poetics, or rhetoric.[7] Instead, their overwhelming tendency is to gravitate toward traditional topics such as metaphysics, ontology, and psychology—all of which focus on the nature of the intelligible world, and how and where humans are located within this structure. Such an approach, however, often overlooks the artistic and creative aspects of medieval philosophy by marginalizing phenomena such as language, metaphor, and the importance of vision. This chapter attempts to address such phenomena in order to examine how medieval philosophers struggled with the finitude of human existence. Questions that are of concern include the following: Why were so many of the Islamic and Jewish Neoplatonists also poets? How and why did these poet-philosophers employ metaphors and other linguistic devices? How do the form and style, in which the content is described, work within the philosophical enterprise of these thinkers?

My main concern here is how the sensible, material world provides the primary vehicle by which the embodied individual ascends the ontological hierarchy. So, rather than start from the customary vantage point of the way in which the One manifests Itself, I prefer to start from the other direction, at the bottom of the ontological hierarchy looking up. My point of departure concerns the various perspectives through which the philosophers conceptualize this manifestation. This change of direction provides a fresh focus that will enable us to understand the importance of aesthetics, much like the imagination, as the mediator between sensual and intelligible. Physical beauty is not simply an end in itself that occupies a position near the bottom of the great chain of being; rather, it functions as a means that enables the finite and embodied individual to transcend his or her particularity. The result has been the creation and development of a distinct philosophical vocabulary that attempts both to use and transcend beauty at one and the same time.

The first part of this chapter examines the philosophical antecedents of Muslim and Jewish speculation on beauty. I will look briefly at the theories of beauty found in Plato, Aristotle, Plotinus, and the Neoplatonists of late antiquity. In the second part, I focus on the important role of aesthetics among medieval Islamic and Jewish philosophers, showing how they not only inherited the discourse from the ancients, but in the process redefined it because they were forced to address distinct monotheistic concerns. The third and final part of this chapter attempts to answer the central question of this study: Why would Avicenna, ibn Ezra, and ibn Ṭufayl—all important philosophers in their respective traditions—choose to write philosophical treatises in a highly literary style?

Denying the Visual: The "Absence" of Aesthetics

Before proceeding, it is worthwhile to nuance the common assumption that both Islam and Judaism are mistrustful of images and therefore devoid of aesthetics and artistic sentiment. This assumption turns on the paradox that in order to protect God's omnipotence and omniscience, which is the hallmark of monotheism, He must be incorporeal and transcendent. Yet the flipside of this is that God cannot be wholly transcendent and aloof; He must also be intimately involved and concerned with human affairs.[8] This paradox resides at the heart of monotheism and historically has led many to attempt to visualize or imagine the divine. For instance, although both Islam and Judaism are, for the most part, regarded as aniconic religions, there is ample evidence that both traditions did employ figurative representations in their religious art.[9] Imagination and aesthetics, as I have suggested throughout this study, are intimately connected with the appearance and apprehension of the divine. Yet, not coincidentally, both are often marginalized in studies devoted to medieval epistemology.

Many contemporary scholars are categorical in their denial that the medievals created a distinct theory of aesthetics. In Platonic fashion, this world is deemed impermanent and thus of no value to the supreme goal of philosophical speculation; namely, to attain permanence. This denial of aesthetics is predicated on two assumptions: one romantic and the other religious. The former is the most difficult to contend with because the medievals operated within a distinctly different orbit than we do when it came to aesthetics. Today we tend to regard aesthetics as a distinctly individual phenomenon, as something that arises from the deep pathos and emotion of the artist, and as something that concomitantly awakens a positive response in the viewer, reader, or listener.[10] Artwork accordingly is regarded as a highly original and highly personal creation of the artist. Medieval artists did not regard beauty as an individual response to an object or an image; rather, it was meant to be universal, something grounded in preconceived and well-articulated notions of harmony, proportion, and structure. Furthermore, medieval Islamicate literary expression was not based on the romantic assumption of creating a work *ex nihilo,* but upon the recycling and subsequent elaboration of well-known motifs (*maᶜānī*).[11]

The religious assumption derives from the prohibition against iconism that is inscribed into Judaism in the form of the second commandment:

> You will not make for yourself a sculptured image, or any likeness of what is in the heavens above, or on the earth below, or in the waters under the earth.[12]

This prohibition would, at least on the surface, certainly seem to curtail either art or aesthetics in Jewish thought. Indeed, the late Steven Schwarzschild, for example, writes that historically not only were there few Jewish artists, but there has never been a distinctly Jewish aesthetics:

> it has been noted that, however creative Jews have been in such fields as religion, law, literature, science, and economics until recent times—no Jewish art was produced, nor were there Jewish artists of any great

> significance. There can thus be no surprise that there has never been any body of Jewish literature on art or aesthetics. How then Jewish aesthetics—that is, a Jewish theory of Art?[13]

In a similar pronouncement, Ze'ev Levy argues that Jewish thought was under the spell of Platonism and thus hostile to the human representation of the divine.[14] Although Jews may have been interested in beautiful objects, Levy claims that they never engaged in aesthetic speculation.[15] Yet the evidence belies such claims. For instance, archeological remains from synagogues of late antiquity not only document the expressions of art, but also the figurative representation of God.[16] Furthermore, the rich illuminated manuscript tradition in medieval Judaism also reveals a rich treatment of the parts of God's body (e.g., an outstretched arm) in order to give artistic expansion to a particular biblical narrative.[17]

Despite the fact that Islam lacks the equivalent of a second commandment, the overwhelming assumption is that it too is vehemently opposed to artistic, especially figurative, representation. Indeed, Islam is often regarded as the aniconic tradition par excellence.[18] Nevertheless, we do know that in its earliest context, figural representation was regarded as entirely appropriate.[19] Yet, in his formulation of the medieval Islamic discussion of art, aesthetics, and beauty, S. Kahwaji argues that Arabic civilization has traditionally lacked both the vocabulary and the concepts associated with aesthetics. For instance, he claims that

> A general theory on what is known as *ᶜilm al-djamāl* [i.e., aesthetics] and precise definitions of the terms used in this field are lacking in the history of Arabic civilization.[20]

This has led to the oft-repeated formulation that Islamic art is by nature devoid of representation; that it is essentially based on geometric and symbolic patterning or arabesques. The result is that images have played a marginalized role in treatments not only of Jewish art, but also Islamic. But are we to conclude from such statements that both Muslims and Jews have historically lacked the critical apparatus to enjoy, describe, and take pleasure in images? Is the corollary of the second commandment that whenever one contemplates an image, one becomes an idolator?[21] Are images by their very nature hostile to both the religious life and the philosophical pursuit of wisdom? Are images so subversive that they have little or no bearing on the cognitive development of the individual?

A somewhat different approach to the myth of aniconism, but one that strikes me as equally misguided is that medieval Islamicate aesthetics becomes the precursor to our modern discourse. Recently Behrens-Abouseif has argued that

> Medieval European and Islamic philosophical thought have many similarities and common traditions. However, a major difference that struck me has prompted the writing of this book [*Beauty in Arabic Culture*]: the separation between the good and the beautiful in Arabic culture, and the appreciation of beauty in poetry and the visual arts for its own sake, without commitment to religious or moral criteria, an attitude uncommon in medieval Europe but one that anticipates modernity.[22]

This approach fails to contextualize Arab conceptions of beauty within its autochthonous cultural milieu. Whereas modern aesthetics, as I mentioned above, is based on subjective criteria of both the artist and the viewer, such qualities are utterly lacking in the formal parameters of medieval Arabic poetry. The primary vehicle of expression, the *qaṣīda* (ode), was highly formal and stylistic. A good poet did not create a work from nothing, but by manipulating the standard repertoire of tropes and images.[23] In like manner, the Islamicate philosophers, whom I will discuss shortly, considered without exception that the sole function of art and beauty was to help the individual transcend his or her materiality. For these philosophers contended that aesthetics was intimately connected to religious concerns. Of course, what they meant by "religious" was somewhat different from mainstream contemporaneous theological discussions of this topic; for the philosophers, religion was predicated on the abstraction of intellectuals and the ability to conform to the good life.

Kalman Bland has recently challenged this myth of aniconism. He situates the myth of Jewish aniconism against the backdrop of nineteenth-century German antisemitism, and its subsequent absorption by Jewish reformers.[24] Often based on essentialist stereotypes such as Jewish auralism versus Greek visualism,[25] many individuals—both Jews and non-Jews—have used this stereotype to perpetuate a fundamental disconnect between Jews and European Christian culture. Bland contends that German-Jewish thinkers, under the influence of Kantian and Hegelian categories, stressed the spiritual virtuosity of Judaism by denying the existence of any sort of authentic Jewish art.[26] In other words, these Jewish thinkers used Kant's and Hegel's critique of Judaism in such a way that they could paradoxically argue for its superiority.

Yet the view of Jewish aniconism, contrary to much evidence, has stubbornly persisted as "common wisdom" into the twenty-first century. Although there has yet to be a full-scale treatment dealing with the various political and ideological factors that have contributed to the denial of the visual in Islamic art, it is most likely related to the similar essentialist Semitic category that marks Jewish aniconism. In other words, both Islam and Judaism, due to some reified Semitic spirit or consciousness, were perceived to advance the cause of aniconism. For this reason, the art *par excellence* in Islam is generally if not universally considered to be poetry, which is verbal as opposed to visual. The novelty of Bland's thesis, however, is that once we acknowledge that the concept of Semitic aniconism is of a distinctly modern provenance, and once we re-introduce aesthetics into the discussion, aesthetics "suggests a fresh understanding of medieval Jewish [and Islamic] philosophy."[27]

What follows is devoted to showing—contrary to the aforementioned claims—that medieval Islamic and Jewish philosophers speculated on beauty and, in the process, conceived of an intimate relationship between it and access to truth. It is high time to review the evidence in order to ascertain how medieval philosophers, both Jewish and Muslim, thought about beauty and where precisely they situated beauty in the cognitive development of the individual. It is in the light of this discussion that we need to situate the initiatory tale.

Beauty in the Eye of the Neoplatonic Beholder

Lying just beneath the surface of medieval philosophical aesthetics resides the thought of Plato, Aristotle, and Plotinus. Although these individuals defined the nature of the relationship between the material and the immaterial worlds in different terms, they nonetheless agreed that the true end of the individual involved transcending the impermanence of matter by grasping that which is permanent, universal, and transcendent. Despite this, none of these individuals, no matter how hard they might try, could fully dispense with either the body or the concept of embodiedness. For the body is inseparable from human nature: because humans possess bodies they are firmly rooted in the world of material and sensible particulars. If one is to move beyond such particulars, the key to such motion must reside in the nature of particularity.

This notion of embodiedness plays out in the various ways that these philosophers comprehend beauty. For the Neoplatonists, this world is not a pale imitation of a transcendent truth, but the locus where our emotions, our feelings, our perceptions, and our imaginations are activated.[28] One is unable to apprehend the suprasensible or intelligible world without first coming to terms with the sensible or corporeal one. There thus exists an ontological connection between the One and that which proceeds from it. Within this context, the finite individual—as a composite of form and matter, soul and body—is noetically unable to grasp or apprehend either the One or the celestial world. The only way that this comprehension is possible is to recognize that concrete particulars or images are specific contexts by which the immaterial world displays itself.

One of the threads that weaves throughout medieval aesthetics is that there is an ontological gulf, but one that is not necessarily unbridgeable, between this world and the superlunar world. From the top looking down, the divine, through the process of emanation, becomes increasingly corporealized as it reaches this world of form and matter. From the bottom looking up, however, sense phenomena are all we possess to grasp the transcendental. From the embodied human perspective, Neoplatonic articulations are layered in such a manner that the individual can only experience the spiritual world through the phenomena of this world. In other words, the apprehension of the spiritual world does not come at the expense of denying this world. Similarly, the spiritual cannot negate the physical because the finite individual can only conceive of the former through the latter. The human and the divine, the material and the immaterial, thus coincide at the level of the image. As far as aesthetics is concerned, although the divine or spiritual world may be the ideal locus of beauty, the only way to gain access to it is by means of specific, sensual objects that ontologically participate in it.

This sounds an important theme that is the hallmark of medieval aesthetics. In effect, aesthetic experience is not simply a passive mode of sensory perception on the part of the reader or viewer. On the contrary, the reader or viewer must become an active participant in the construction of meaning. As a result, the work of art invites the individual into its interpretive universe in such a manner that he or she must reconcile the world of the artwork with his or her own experiences. This leads to a transformative experience: the individual must integrate his or her own experiences with that of the text or object, thereby producing meaning.[29] As the individual does this, his or her imagination begins to desist from its usual activity. And the imagination, in tandem with the intellect, begins to move beyond the text and up the ontological hierarchy.

Underpinning the medieval philosophical discourse on aesthetics is the Platonic notion of vision and cognition. In his discussion of beauty in the *Phaedo,* Plato claims that

> If someone tells me that the reason why a given object is beautiful is that it has a gorgeous color or shape or any other such attribute, I disregard

> all these other explanations—I find them all confusing—and I cling simply and straightforwardly and no doubt foolishly to the explanation that the one thing that makes that object beautiful is the presence in it or association with it, in whatever way the relation comes about, of absolute beauty. I do not go so far as to insist upon the precise details—only upon the fact that it is by beauty that beautiful things are beautiful.[30]

For Plato, a beautiful object in this world participates in the eternal, unchanging paradigm of beauty. Despite this correspondence, Plato is ultimately mistrustful of ephemeral beauty precisely because it is changing and accordingly is ultimately unreliable. For instance, if one confines one's attention solely to that which is beautiful in this world, one will overlook the fact that the only reason things here and now are beautiful is because they participate in an eternal principle. Plato deems this dangerous because such an oversight could easily result in the misconception that this world is all that exists. Such materialism, for him, would contribute to the cultivation of the vices (e.g., incontinence). According to Plato, the lover of physical beauty is to Beauty what the Sophist is to philosophy: both claim knowledge but without recourse to first principles. To conceive of ephemeral beauty as true beauty is tantamount to making the mistake that the essence of the individual resides in the body as opposed to the soul. In the *Republic,* for example, Plato claims that

> the lovers of sounds and sights . . . delight in beautiful tones and colors and shapes and in everything that art fashions out of these, but their thought is incapable of apprehending and taking delight in the nature of the beautiful in itself.[31]

These "lovers of sights and sounds" live their lives as if in a dream, mistaking resemblance for truth. Such individuals are mired in impermanence, whereas the philosophical quest is to search for permanence. Although Plato is critical of the incontinent aesthete who mistakes the material world for reality, he nevertheless acknowledges that there exists an intimate relationship between physical and metaphysical beauty. The individual who understands and is able to distinguish this relationship is able to get at that which exists beyond sensible beautiful objects. Plato's epistemology reinforces this modified aesthetics that is based on metaphysical participation. Once again, he argues in the *Republic:*

> The man whose mind is truly fixed on eternal realities has no leisure to turn his eyes downward upon the petty affairs of men, and so engaging in strife with them to be filled with envy and hate, but he fixes his gaze upon the things of the eternal and unchanging order, and seeing that

> they neither wrong nor are wronged by one another, but all abide in harmony as reason bids, he will endeavor to imitate them and, as far as may be, to fashion himself in their likeness and assimilate himself to them.[32]

Plato here intimates that when an individual contemplates the divine world, he or she participates in it and in the process becomes god-like. Or, to use his own words, "the lover of wisdom associating with the divine order will himself become orderly and divine in the measure permitted to man."[33] When the soul contemplates an object, a symmetry is created between the knower and the object known, with the consequence that the former begins to resemble the latter. Since one cannot know the immaterial world on its own terms, embodied humans must ultimately contemplate this world in order to transcend it. As a result, particulars are crucial in establishing this movement. Like many of the philosophers who will follow him, Plato believes that to think about beauty—which often results from seeing a beautiful object—is to become beautiful oneself.[34]

The other feature of Platonic discourse that will be picked up by Plotinus and, subsequently, the medieval Muslim and Jewish Neoplatonists, is a specific mode of writing. Although Plato is highly critical of artists whom, he claims, distort and manipulate for the sake of rhetorical effect,[35] he himself nevertheless is a formidable artist who frequently appeals to mythopoesis. In the *Gorgias,* for example, Plato writes:

> Listen, then, as they say to a very fine account (*logou*) which you, I suppose, will consider a story (*mythos*) but which I treat as the actual truth (*logon*). For what I am going to tell you I offer to you as truth.[36]

In this passage, Plato hints that what seems like a "myth" to the average person can actually be *logos* to the person with proper understanding. As a result, the poetic and mythic presentation of the truth/*logos* becomes extremely important to Platonic and Neoplatonic articulations. Such mythopoesis is necessary precisely because of the gap that exists between the material and the immaterial: the primary way to access the latter is to appeal to the former. However, in so doing, one must use language that is "double-edged." For this reason, Plato uses myths, metaphors, and other tropes so that the ideal reader will be able to move beyond such language.[37]

In his definition of beauty, Aristotle focuses more specifically on the various attributes that are responsible for contributing to the quiddity of a beautiful object. In Book 8 of the *Metaphysics,* he claims that

> The chief forms of beauty are order and symmetry and definiteness, which the mathematical sciences demonstrate in a special degree. And

> since these are obviously causes of many things, evidently these sciences must treat this sort of cause also in some sense of a cause.[38]

In other words, central to Aristotle's aesthetics are the formal criteria of form, order, and proportion.[39] In the *Poetics,* Aristotle further clarifies this:

> To be beautiful, a living creature, and every whole made up of parts, must not only present a certain order in its arrangement of parts, but also be of a certain definite magnitude. Beauty is a matter of size and order and therefore impossible either in a very minute creature, since our perception becomes indistinct as it approaches instantaneity; or in a creature of vast size—one, say, 1000 miles long—as in that case, instead of the object being seen all at once, the unity and wholeness of it is lost to the beholder.[40]

Aristotle argues that beauty is what gives significance to the form of a natural object.[41] This teleological approach to art enables Aristotle to connect artistic sentiment to the universal first principles of philosophy. When one appreciates beauty, one is able to take pleasure in the object. Consequently, Aristotle acknowledges an important interplay between the senses, the emotions, the imagination, and the intellect. This interaction, as he claims in the *Poetics,* proves indispensable to our ability to interact with the world and, subsequently, to form knowledge about it.

Plotinus is the thinker at the background of virtually all trends within both medieval philosophy and mysticism. Paradoxically, however, none of the medieval thinkers would have known his name. Instead, when they read what was in fact selections from his *Enneads,* they thought that they were reading the culmination of Aristotle's *ouevre,* the *Theology* (Ar. *uthūlūjiyya*).[42] The *Theology,* unknown in Greek, is actually a collection of *Enneads* 4–6.[43] It was in the "name" of Aristotle, then, that the medievals received the aesthetic component of plotinianism.

For Plotinus, beauty is used not only to describe the intelligible world, but also analogously to describe the One.[44] Furthermore, beauty is the principle responsible for creating a delight within the soul of the individual whenever he or she contemplates intelligibles.[45] The principle of beauty, however, is not confined solely to the immaterial and intelligible world: beauty also exists in sensible bodies that are accessible to the various sense faculties. Although physical and immaterial beauty are ontically related to each other, the latter is superior to the former because of its proximity to the paradigm of beauty.[46] This ontological relationship between the material and the immaterial holds the key to the noetic development of the individual. Once someone recognizes and falls in love with a sensible object that is beautiful, he or she ideally recognizes it for the image that it is and subsequently transfers this love felt for the sensible onto the real thing. Consequently, beauty is responsible for awakening the human soul and allowing it to recognize its relationship to the immaterial world.[47] Although Plotinus is generally less critical of artistic representation than Plato, he nevertheless warns against finding satisfaction in sensibles.[48] One must recognize the image for what it is: a springboard that enables the individual to move into the intelligible world.

For Plotinus, this translates into a distinct theory of beauty in which physical beauty functions as a symbol for a higher reality. In her insightful and refreshing study of Neoplatonism, Rappe argues that such symbols function "as crossroads, as junctures that allow the soul to trace its path back to its origins."[49] In other words, there exists an intimate relationship between the human soul and the divine world. Moreover, this relationship revolves around the symbol and the image. Provided that one does not mistake the image or the symbol for the reality, Plotinus argues that such images double back on themselves. These images and symbols, then, are negative in the sense that they are not the One (i.e., they have emanated from it), yet also positive because they allow the embodied individual to re-ascend the ontological hierarchy.

Beauty, therefore, is not something based merely on artistic sentiment. On the contrary, it functions as an intelligible principle founded upon the ontology of emanation. By encountering and recognizing the way in which images reveal a certain moment or manifestation of ultimate reality, the individual is able to relate the order, composition, and harmony of the contemplated object to its universal paradigm. In so doing, Plotinus argues, beautiful objects and images create a tranquility in the soul that enables it to perceive a transcendent beauty that is otherwise inaccessible to the senses.[50] In encountering artistic beauty, the individual intuits and apprehends immaterial truth.[51] This encounter enables the individual to reverse the emanative process by translating the particular image and relating it back to its source.

Following the lead of Plotinus, later Neoplatonists envisaged the various levels of being within the universe as corresponding to the various levels of knowledge. Crucial for many of these individuals was the role of myth and poetry, both of which aid in the ability to ascend and descend the various ontological levels. One of the key figures in this exposition was Proclus (ca. 410–485), an important conduit in the transmission of ideas from late antiquity to the Middle Ages.[52] In his discussion of the *Iliad* and the *Odyssey*, Proclus argues that the surface of the narrative simultaneously reveals and conceals truths in such a manner that each reader must actively participate in the creation of meaning.[53] The work of art thus possesses a similar polysemous structure to the world it mirrors.[54] Just as the universe is composed of material and immaterial parts, with the former participating in and pointing to the latter, so does the work of art function in a similar way. In his *Commentary on the Republic*, for example, Proclus claims that

> in each order, stretching from the gods to the lowest members and pervading all classes of being, the last members of the series can be seen having attributes that the myths assign to the gods, attributes that instantiate and refer to events by means of which the poets clothe their secret vision of the first principles.[55]

There exists an intimate ontological connection between the physicality of this world and the intelligibility of the celestial world. Events and objects in this world mask within themselves and subsequently mirror the divine world. It is precisely this relationship that art and literature imitate. This is also the reason why the hermeneutical act is so important to philosophy, since it forces the individual to get at the form behind matter.

Explicit in the preceding discussion is the claim that the arts both contain and convey knowledge of the intelligible world. In experiencing tangible beauty, the individual is able to contemplate and observe its proportion, integrity, and clarity. This allows the individual to recognize these same principles in his or her own soul. This, in turn, reinforces the microcosmic–macrocosmic relationship that is at the heart of Neoplatonism. Art is ultimately what allows the individual to acknowledge within himself or herself the same harmony that is ultimately at work in the universe.[56] Medieval philosophical aesthetics, then, is ultimately based on the premise that one encounters in physical objects an unmediated reflection of a metaphysical reality.

This theory of aesthetics turns on the assumption that although the human mind is distinct from the world and that it is capable of grasping reality by means of abstract principles, it nevertheless requires images to re-ascend the ontological hierarchy. Art works so effectively because it bridges the ontological gap between the material and the immaterial. Aesthetics is grounded in a specific ontology that in turn makes epistemology possible. Images provide the individual with a vehicle by which he or she can access the transcendent world that is beyond the ken of human experience. Significantly, though, the only way one can reach the transcendent is by means of the embodied categories of the mundane. Images are not only crucial to the individual's ascension, but they also become the currency of the imagination, allowing the individual to experience that which exists without corporeal extension.

Medieval Discussions of Beauty

Medieval Islamic and Jewish philosophical conceptions of beauty derive primarily from the thought of Plotinus. Despite this inheritance, they were forced to integrate his theory of aesthetics into their monotheistic heritage. In so doing, these individuals did not simply recycle this discourse;[57] rather, they absorbed it and, in the process, adopted and adapted certain of its trajectories to fit their own concerns. In particular, they were most interested in when, how, and why the formal structures of speech, melodies, and visual objects influence and affect the soul of the individual.[58] God now became associated with the realm of beauty. The result was a theory of aesthetics that focused primarily on the various ways in which the individual soul could ascend from this world to the celestial world in order to contemplate and apprehend the divine.

At the center of their discourse on aesthetics are three principles: composition (Ar. *taʾlīf*), harmony (Ar. *iʿtidāl*), and order (Ar. *niẓām*). These three principles were regarded as responsible for enabling the individual to apprehend divine beauty by means of concrete particulars. The cognizance of these three principles in particulars ideally enables the individual to recognize that such particulars ultimately participate in a celestial prototype. Without the apprehension of such principles in this world of form and matter, the individual would be unable to recognize that such principles operate on a higher level.

From a theoretical point of view, the medieval Islamic and Jewish philosophers did not enjoy art in and of itself. The notion of *l'art pour l'art* would have been entirely foreign to them.[59] For these individuals, the only justifiable purpose for artistic enjoyment resided in the fulfillment of some basic psychological or noetic need that in turn could enable the individual to fulfill his or her true telos. As a result, the medieval philosophical conception of beauty was rarely treated as a distinct subject of philosophical inquiry. Rather, it was often subsumed within other discussions, particularly those relating to ontology, epistemology, metaphysics, and ethics. The majority of medieval philosophical discourse devoted to aesthetics was interested primarily in excavating, nuancing, and clarifying the relationship between sensual beauty and its relationship to divine beauty as a side issue relating to the unfolding structure of the universe. Despite this, however, and despite the fact that the philosophers' main concern was divine beauty, this did not, as is commonly argued, necessarily result in the denigration of the physical or the sensual. On the contrary, the philosophers realized that it was only through the physical that the metaphysical could be adequately grasped or apprehended.

Although Muslim and Jewish philosophers approached aesthetics from what we would today call a number of different disciplinary perspectives, common to all is the role and function of beauty in the noetic development of the individual. This involves, as we have already seen, a process whereby an individual encounters a beautiful object, resulting in a subsequent correspondence between the soul of the knower and the object known. This correspondence in turn allows the individual to recognize the beauty of the intelligible world. The actual discussions of this correspondence are extremely diverse and wide-ranging in the various medieval Muslim and Jewish philosophers. For instance, the *Ikhwān al-Ṣafāʾ* are primarily interested in exploring this relationship within the context of musical harmony, whereas Alfarabi's fullest treatment of beauty occurs in his discussion of the ideal political state. Avicenna, by contrast, exposes his main discussion of aesthetics in a treatise devoted to love. Love becomes, for him, the principle that sustains the universe and defines the relationship between Creator and created. Ibn Ezra, in turn, is most interested in the relationship between legitimate and idolatrous images, especially as this relates to the infamous episode of the Israelites and the Golden Calf. And finally, Maimonides is concerned with the soothing effects that sculpture and cloth have on the soul of the philosopher. Although the *Ikhwān,* Alfarabi, Avicenna, ibn Ezra, and Maimonides are concerned with what we today consider to be distinct disciplines, their respective discussions are ultimately predicated on the same assumption of what beauty is and how it functions in the individual's intellectual life.

How do the medieval philosophers define beauty? All agree that beauty is one of the main attributes of God. When one contemplates a beautiful object, one is drawn to its principles and ideally the subsequent realization that physical objects of beauty derive their essence from a non-material source. Based on medieval epistemology, which equates the knower with the known, the individual takes on the qualities of the beauty of the object.[60] Because beautiful objects participate in the beauty of the immaterial world, the individual also participates in that world. The result is that the individual who observes and contemplates beautiful objects, and subsequently recognizes beautiful objects for what they are, apprehends the divine.

The majority of aesthetic speculation resides in elucidating the relationship between the macrocosm and the microcosm, which is one of the defining features of medieval Neoplatonism. In their discussion of music, for instance, the Brethren of Purity (*Ikhwān al-Ṣafāʾ*)[61] argue that there exists an intimate correspondence between the musical harmony that the motion of the spheres produces and those of earthly harmonies produced by instruments. Although the latter is but a pale imitation of the former, it nonetheless produces various effects on the soul of the listener. Musical harmony thus has the potential to move the listener in a particular way, making him or her either more or less susceptible to philosophical inquiry, depending upon the harmony. In a section entitled "The Rhythm of the Movement of the Spheres Resembles the Rhythms of Lutes" (*ḥarakāt al-aflāk naghamāt ka-naghamāt al-ʿīdān*) from their *Epistle on Music,* they write that

> The movements of the spheres and heavenly bodies produce rhythms (*naghamāt*) and melodies (*alḥān*) that are sweet and rejoice the souls of their inhabitants. These rhythms and melodies remind non-composite souls (*al-nufūs al-basīṭa*) inhabiting the world of spirits (*ʿālam al-arwāḥ*) which is above the spheres and whose substances are more noble than those of the world of the spheres. This is the world of souls (*ʿālam al-nufūs*) and the dwelling place whose delight is entirely repose and perfume in the various degrees of paradise as God most high has pronounced in the Qurʾān.[62]

Musical harmonies, in other words, reflect the order, harmony, and proportion that are found in the unchanging nature of the superlunar world. As such, the inner harmony produced in the soul by musical harmonies produced on instruments or through prosody is akin to and ultimately reflects this celestial harmony. Although harmony is ultimately based on mathematical principles, it cannot simply be reduced to the latter. For this reason, the Brethren contend that music does not appeal simply to the intellect; on the contrary, its harmony, rhyme, rhythm, and cadence have the composite effect of touching and ultimately influencing the entire soul of the individual. The Brethren in typical Neoplatonic fashion recognize the embodied quality of human existence. Musical harmony is so effective because it allows the listener to appreciate and subsequently move beyond the specific and the concrete. As a result, music becomes an important feature of intellectual activity: it becomes a mechanism that moves the entire individual, not just the intellect, from potentiality to actuality.

In the introduction to their *Epistle on Music,* the Brethren claim that "musical melodies (*alḥān al-mūsīqā*) which are composed of notes (*aṣwāt*) and rhythms (*naghamāt*) leave an impression on the soul similar to that made by the artisan's work (*ṣināᶜa*) on the material which is the substratum (*al-hayūliyāt al-mawḍūᶜa*) of his art."[63] Although the Brethren recognize that discordant sounds can have a negative effect on the soul of the listener, concordant harmonies create an equilibrium in the soul that in turn is a prerequisite for all subsequent philosophical activity.[64] Musical harmony is essential for enabling the individual to realize that there exists a world above the material one. Upon listening to a particular harmony, observing and delighting in its tone and rhythms, one is reminded that the soul, unlike the body, is not of this world. In a chapter entitled "Aphorisms of the Philosophers on Music" (*nawādir al-falāsifa fī al-mūsīqā*) from the same treatise, one of the discussants argues as follows:

> When the traces of the beauty (*al-ḥisān*) of sensory things are imprinted on the individual soul (*al-nafs al-juzʾiyya*), it conforms to the universal Soul (*al-nafs al-kulliyya*), attunes itself to it, aspires to it and seeks to join it. Now, when the soul will have left its corporeal residence, it will mount towards the kingdom of heaven and rejoin the world of intelligible substances.[65]

We witness a similar discussion albeit with slightly different emphases in the writings of the great Islamic political philosopher, Alfarabi (870–950). In his *Mabādiʾ ārāʾ ahl al-madīna al-fāḍila* (*Views of the Citizens of the Best State*), he defines beauty (*jamāl*) as that which "is in its most excellent state of existence and that has attained its ultimate perfection."[66] Following the basic Neoplatonic schema, Alfarabi argues that the One's beauty surpasses all other types of beauty, which ultimately derive their own beauty from It:

> But since the First is in the most excellent state of existence, its beauty (*jamāl*) surpasses the beauty of every other beautiful existent, and the same applies to its splendor (*zīna*) and its brilliance (*bahāᶜ*). Further, it has all of these in its substance (*jawhar*) and essence (*dhāt*) by itself and by thinking its essence. But we have beauty and splendor and brilliance as a result of accidental qualities, and of what our bodies have in them and because of exterior things, but they are not in our substance. The beautiful (*al-jamīl*) and the beauty (*al-jamāl*) in the First are nothing but one essence, and the same applies to the other things predicated of it.[67]

According to Alfarabi, the beauty of the First Principle contains absolute perfection within itself. All other types of beauty are ultimately derivative because they participate in this beauty. When humans perceive sensible objects that are beautiful, they envisage only a perspective or appearance of beauty, one that is contingent upon the arrangement of a particular object's constituent parts. When we observe a concrete beautiful object, the pleasure we take in it is reminiscent of the pleasure that the One takes in Itself. Only the pleasure and self-enjoyment that the One takes from self-contemplation is beyond the human ken of understanding. Nevertheless, the pleasure and enjoyment that we take in the contemplation of beautiful objects and melodies, despite its fleeting and impermanent duration, approximates the self-knowledge of the One insofar as material creatures can approximate the One's immateriality.[68]

It is within this context that Alfarabi discusses the attributes of the perfect city-state (*al-madīna al-fāḍila*). Alfarabi uses an organic metaphor and compares the perfect state to a perfect and healthy body (*al-badan al-nāmm al-ṣaḥīḥ*), whose limbs and organs cooperate harmoniously with one another.[69] Like everything that is perfect and healthy, the ideal city is one that embodies proportion, order, and harmony. For Alfarabi, such a state mirrors the same principles of proportion, order, and harmony that exist within the celestial world. He claims for example that

> the relations of the First Cause to the other existents is like the relation of the king of the excellent city to its other parts. For the ranks of the immaterial existents are close to the First. Beneath them are the heavenly bodies, and beneath the heavenly bodies are the material bodies. All these existents act in conformity with the First Cause, follow it, take it as their guide and imitate it; but each existent does that according to its capacity, choosing its aim precisely on the strength of its established rank in the universe: that is to say the last follows the aim of that which is slightly above it in rank, and in the same way the third existent has an aim which is above it. Eventually existents are reached which are linked with the First Cause. Those which are from the very outset provided with all the essentials of their existence are made to imitate the First and its aims from the very outset, and hence enjoy eternal bliss and hold the highest ranks; but those that are not provided from the outset with all the essentials of their existence, are provided with a faculty by which they move towards the expected attainment of those essentials and will then be able to follow the aim of the First. The excellent city ought to be arranged in the same way: all its parts ought to imitate in their actions the aim of the first ruler according to their rank.[70]

In this passage, Alfarabi argues that everything that is composed of order, harmony, and proportion reflects the same principles that exist essentially in the One, and which are found to a lesser degree in the celestial intelligences. Consequently, the cosmic order becomes the model not only for human life and behavior but also for any kind of creative or artistic activity.[71] The appreciation of this beauty then is not *ad hoc,* but is tantamount to a philosophical interpretation of reality. Just as the perfect state is composed of a proper hierarchy with the ruler (*raʾīs*) at the top and followed by a descending order imitating the emanative ontology of the universe, the work of art is composed of a similar imitative structure: it possesses a harmonious and balanced relationship between its various parts. For Alfarabi, the various types of ignorant states lack these principles in such a manner that their citizens miss the proper environment to realize their full human potential.[72]

Alfarabi contends that one needs to live in the best state in order to fulfill one's potential as a human.[73] The best state is a beautiful state; the soul of the individual in such a state is equally beautiful; and therefore one is afforded the opportunity in which to cultivate and appreciate beauty. Alfarabi argues that the happy soul is one that is able to transcend the material and that the activity of the highest happiness is that of intellection.[74] Such activities can only occur in an environment in which one is able to contemplate various physical imitations of beauty that facilitate the upward motion of the soul. An individual therefore needs the beauty and harmony that perfection embodies in order to attain his or her proper functioning as a human.

Avicenna's discussion, as we have seen throughout this study, is dependent upon earlier Neoplatonic discussions. Following people like the *Ikhwān* and Alfarabi, his discourse on aesthetics is contingent upon the interpenetrating relationship between the macrocosmic and the microcosmic. His main discussions of beauty occur when he examines the One and its perfection. In his *Kitāb al-najāt,* for instance, Avicenna argues that

> It is impossible for there to be beauty (*jamāl*) or splendor (*bahāʾ*) above pure intellectual essence or pure benevolence. [Beauty and splendor] do not exist in deficient things, since they form a complete unity. The Necessary Being (*al-wājib al-wujūd*) possesses beauty and pure splendor. It is the origin of every harmony (*kull iʿtidāl*) because every harmony exists either in multiplicity or as a composite, and thus [divine beauty] creates unity in multiplicity. The beauty and splendor of every thing is imposed upon it. . . . Every appropriate beautiful thing (*kull jamāl mulāʾim*) and every rational good (*khayr mudrik*) is desirable and loved (*maḥbūb wa-maʿshūq*) and is the origin of its apprehension (*mabdaʾ idrākihi*). This is true be it the faculty of sense, that of the imagination, that of estimation, that of opinion, and the intellect.[75]

Avicenna picks up and elaborates on this discussion of beauty and love in his *Risāla fī al-ʿishq* (Treatise on love). Here Avicenna argues that both the rational and the animal souls within the individual

> invariably love what has beauty of order (*ḥusn al-niẓām*), composition (*al-taʾlīf*), and harmony (*al-iʿtidāl*), as for example harmonious sounds, harmoniously blended tastes of well-prepared dishes and suchlike. . . .

> It recognizes that the closer a thing is to the first object of love, the more steadfast is it in its order, and the more beautiful in its harmony, and that what follows it immediately attains a greater degree of unity.[76]

In other words, Avicenna here claims that both the animal and the rational souls are attracted to beautiful objects that are defined by their order, composition, and harmony. Every thing from a harmonious melody to a finely embroidered garment to a well-prepared meal possesses a similar structure. The individual should ideally realize "the unity behind the multiplicity" and that all of these phenomena represent particular loci wherein the transcendental shows itself. The important feature for Avicenna, like the other individuals we have already encountered, is not to mistake the beauty or harmony of a particular object as *sui generis;* rather, all reflect a higher reality. The soul of the philosopher knows this and is thus able to move from sensible to intelligible, with the aid of the imaginative faculty.

Unlike Alfarabi who is seemingly quite critical of the imaginative faculty,[77] Avicenna contends that the goal is that the individual will be able to align his imagination with his rational soul in such a manner that the former will resemble the latter.[78] Indeed, because the soul is trapped within a body, access to intellectual beauty occurs only through the sensual beauty of particulars:

> But whenever he loves a pleasing form with an intellectual consideration... then this is to be considered as an approximation to nobility and an increase in goodness. For he covets something whereby he will come nearer to the influence of that which is the first source of influence and the pure object of love, and more similar to the exalted and noble beings.... For this reason one will never find the wise... to be free from having their hearts occupied with a beautiful human form.[79]

In this passage, Avicenna argues that physical beauty is necessary if one is to grasp intellectual beauty. Moreover, the faculty that bridges not only these two types of beauty, but also the animal and the rational souls, is the imagination. So long as one realizes that the sensible object is not beautiful in and of itself, but is based on Beauty in which it ontically participates, one should take pleasure in such objects.

The other two authors who are the subject of this study, ibn Ezra and ibn Ṭufayl, did not explicitly engage the theme of aesthetics. Ibn Ezra does, however, offer a fairly extended discussion of images, and their relationship to the celestial world, especially as they relate to idolatry. Apropos for our purposes are his comments concerning the infamous affair of the Israelites and the Golden Calf in Exodus 32.

Before examining this, it is worthwhile to examine his comments to the second commandment. Ibn Ezra is not critical of artistic representation. Indeed, in keeping with his interest in astrology,[80] he argues that there exists an intimate relationship between planets and various peoples, on the one hand, and their religions, on the other.[81] He argues that both natural and created images have the ability to act as a conduit for a people or a religion in order to bring down heavenly powers.[82] In his short Commentary to Exodus 20:5, for instance, he argues that there exist "crafters of forms (*baᶜalei ha-ṣurot*) who think that they are able to bring down the power of the uppermost world (*koaḥ ha-eliyonim*) to this world."[83] Ibn Ezra realizes that images or statues serve a purpose that is more than simply artistic. Images and other artistic representations have the potential to create an intimate relationship between this world and the divine world, with the images essentially mediating this relationship.

One of ibn Ezra's prerequisites for artistic representation is that such representations must correspond to reality. In his comments to Exodus 20:4, he maintains that

> You are forbidden regardless of the craft to make an image (*temunah*) that is in heaven, for there are only forty-eight forms. As for skilled theurgists (*hakhmei ha-ṣurot*) who make things that do not exist [in reality], their deeds approximate idolatry.

In this passage, ibn Ezra objects to any attempt to represent the spiritual forms literally. He does not, however, object to the creation of certain images that exist in reality and that can function as magical devices or talismans to bring astral powers down to the human level.[84] In Bland's opinion, ibn Ezra was not opposed to "the theurgic goals themselves," even though he was critical of some of the theurgists.[85] It is within this context that ibn Ezra argues for the theurgical efficacy of certain Jewish practices and symbols.[86] Even though ibn Ezra contends that it is forbidden to make the shape of a heavenly body, this does not lead him to deny that one can create certain images in order to harness the powers of the heavenly bodies.[87] It is within this context, as I show shortly, that he interpreted the Golden Calf. For ibn Ezra, certain properties of the Jewish tradition (e.g., the Land of Israel) and certain structures of Jewish religious praxis (e.g., sacrifice, the tabernacle) can function as symbolic images of the structure of the universe.[88] In particular, he acknowledges that some images represent and, thus, participate in the divine world, and that these images are responsible for drawing down the divine power. Bland argues that ibn Ezra's discussion here turns on the notion of intentionality: "even the most accurate depiction of a natural figure would amount to idolatry if the artifact was not understood to be a gesture of honor addressed to the utterly transcendent, unmediated, and solitary power of God."[89]

It is crucial that the individual not mistake an image or a statue or any other sort of harmonious "construction" for the reality behind it. The key to ibn Ezra's argument resides in the basic Neoplatonic aesthetic that one must not focus on the beauty of this world; rather, one must appreciate it for what it is: a conduit to the apprehension of the divine. Here we have to understand ibn Ezra's comments on the Golden Calf. Whereas rabbinical tradition holds that the Israelites, led by Aaron, committed a major sin at the foot of Sinai, ibn Ezra chooses to read these events in the light of his astrological theory. For him, the Israelites were fearful that Moses, after being on the Mountain for forty days and nights, had perished and, consequently, looked to Aaron to help them in their hour of need.[90] According to ibn Ezra's reading, neither Aaron nor the overwhelming majority of the Israelites sinned; rather, the Golden Calf represented a vessel to bring down the higher powers in the perceived absence of Moses. In his short commentary to Exodus, ibn Ezra neatly, if vaguely, summarizes these events as follows:

> There are some in India who believe that the form of the image (*ha-ṣurah*) receives a higher power (*koaḥ eliyon*). This is what [the Israelites] think about Moses. I will now reveal to you the secret of the Calf by means of hints. I have already explained to you concerning the verse "you will be God to him [i.e., Pharoah] (Ex. 7:1)...."[91] They thought that Moses was dead because he had not returned, so Aaron built an altar to God and they raised offerings to Him. The problem is that it was not done in a proper manner, and without the proper sanctification. There are some who think that this was idolatry... But he who understands the secrets of the heavens knows why it was in the form of a Calf.[92]

In his longer commentary to this verse, ibn Ezra claims that when this episode occurred, the majority of astrologers believed that the large conjunction of the planets occurred in the constellation of the Bull. He disagrees and maintains that the constellation was Aquarius (i.e., the sign or *mazal* of Israel). But as Bland notes, this explanation does not really help us to understand how the issue relates to the Calf; ultimately, the episode of the Golden Calf "remains an open question."[93]

Ibn Ezra's argument seems to revolve around an important, if somewhat vaguely stated, difference between improper and proper images.[94] Only the latter function as a proper vessel for receiving heavenly forces. Yet unfortunately he never defines clearly what constitutes a proper image and how it would differ from an improper one. Is it that the latter, as he suggests in his comments to Exodus 20:4, do not resemble anything that exists in reality? Whereas, do "proper" images adequately reflect, symbolize, or portray a divine reality to which they ultimately point? Or is it that the propriety has nothing to do with the image, but instead refers to the intentionality with which individuals approach that image? In other words, is a proper image one that is appreciated as a medium as opposed to the divine itself?

Although ibn Ezra does not clarify this, it seems safe to assume that he is not opposed to images that reflect reality and that are appreciated as pointing beyond themselves. This is difficult to translate into a distinct theory of aesthetics. Nevertheless, it does seem that ibn Ezra, and we will see this play out in his *Ḥay ben Meqitz,* acknowledges that humans require images to help them apprehend the divine.

Maimonides, the most famous of the Jewish philosophers, was also interested in the merits and inner proportions of beauty. In his *Mishneh Torah,* he argues that "it is forbidden to make images for [the sake of beauty] even though they are not to be used for idolatry."[95] Maimonides' discussion, however, is not as simple as this. He subsequently argues that one can make images providing they are not of the human form and are not found on reliefs.[96] He claims that "if the form is sunken or of a medium like that of images on panels or tablets or those woven in fabric, it is permitted."[97]

His most sustained treatment of this issue is in his introduction to *Pirqei Avot,* known as *Shemonah Peraqim* (Eight chapters).[98] According to Maimonides, the individual has a psychological need for beautiful objects. Art is not something to be appreciated on its own merit, but is something that aids the individual in a pursuit of intellectual knowledge.[99] Physical objects that are deemed beautiful are so important for Maimonides because they have the potential to uplift the human soul.[100] They do this because they enable the individual to exercise naturally all of the various senses. In chapter 5, Maimonides argues as follows:

> someone who adheres to this goal will not be moved to decorate walls with gold or to put a gold border on his garment—unless he intends thereby to give delight to his soul for the sake of its health and to drive sickness from it, so that it will be clear and pure to receive the sciences.[101]

The perception of beauty is thus propaedeutic not only to mental well-being, but also to philosophical activity. The individual who does not take the time to contemplate and observe beautiful objects fails to realize his or her full potential as a human. This is tied to the concept that our senses, intimately tied to our bodies, provide the gateway to philosophical activity.[102] Humans have a basic need for aesthetic experience, provided, of course, that one does not mistake the means with the end.

The appreciation of beautiful objects, according to Maimonides, is one of the primary ways that the philosopher can calm the soul after continuous philosophical activity. Maimonides' argument here revolves around the nature of our embodiedness. Since humans are composed of form and matter, soul and body, they are unable to engage in constant intellectual activity. As a result, they need beautiful objects around them to soothe their souls. If one's soul is tired or lacking equilibrium, one is unable to engage in theoretical activity. Maimonides argues that

> the soul becomes weary and the mind dull by continuous reflection upon difficult matters, just as the body becomes exhausted from undertaking toilsome occupations until it relaxes and rests and then returns to equilibrium. In a similar manner, the soul needs to rest and to do what relaxes the senses, such as looking at beautiful decorations and objects, so that weariness be removed from it. . . . Now it is doubtful that when done for this purpose, these are bad or futile, I mean, decorating and adorning buildings, vessels, and garments.[103]

If one ignores one's body, emotions, and imagination, one is unable to progress in the acquisition of theoretical knowledge. Bland argues that Maimonides here acknowledges that each of the senses must be used in such a manner that its full potential is actualized.[104] For example, the eye should gaze upon beautiful paintings and statues, the ear should hear mellifluous tones, and the nose should smell the blossoming of flowers in a garden. These activities create an emotional and somatic stability in the individual—both of which are essential for engaging in philosophical activity.[105]

The goal of this section was to offer a non-exhaustive survey showing that the medieval Islamic and Jewish philosophers did conceive of beauty and, as a consequence, succeeded in creating a distinct theory of aesthetics. Although this plays out differently in virtually all of the philosophers concerned, there nonetheless exists a common Neoplatonic thread linking them. Their theory of aesthetics is predicated on the notion that there exists an intimate relationship between this world and the heavenly world. The latter, because it exists without matter, cannot be comprehended by the embodied human who exists in matter. But this does not result in the assumption that one can never access the intelligible world. On the contrary, it leads to the conception that the embodied individual can apprehend the divine by means of appropriate images that function as particular instantiations of that world. Images, then, become the locus whereby the ideal individual, one who possesses the appropriate philosophical training, can gain access to the realm of intelligibility or incorporeality. In other words, the image becomes diaphanous, allowing for the sensory (re)presentation of that which ultimately exists without matter. Although one cannot experience Beauty as it exists in and of itself, one can apprehend beautiful objects that are presentations of it.

Initiatory Tales

It is now time to begin to connect this theory of aesthetics to the genre of the initiatory tale. My contention, to reiterate, is that the initiatory tale represents both the practical application and the literary expression of this theory of aesthetics. The key to unlocking these tales is to envisage them as exploring the nature of the relationship between this world of form and matter and the world that exists without matter. Since our world and the phenomena within it are ontically related to the intelligible world, these tales focus poetically on this world and attempt to show how the beauty within it relates to the divine world. Just as the only way we can access the concept of an intelligible beauty is through beautiful particulars, so, too, the only way we apprehend the unseen is through the seen (either through the eye or the imagination) or the supratextual through the textual. It is at this juncture, as I have argued throughout this study, that imagination becomes crucial to the philosophical enterprise, since the imagination is the faculty that is ultimately responsible for bridging the gap between the phenomenal and the transcendental.

On a structural level, both the literary and philosophical dimensions of these tales are meant to mirror the order, balance, and harmony that conform to the intuited structure of reality. All of them, for instance, begin firmly in this world of form and matter and move to the intelligible world. This lower world is surprisingly not described as the ugly world of generation and corruption; rather, it is a world that holds the key to unlocking the secrets of the universe. Avicenna describes this state in the following manner:

> One who confronts that Darkness and does not recoil from it, reaches a vast and unlimited space (*faḍāʾ*), boundless and filled with light. The first thing that one sees is a living spring whose waters spread like a river

> over the *barzakh.* Whoever ritually bathes (*ightasala*) in it becomes so light that he can walk on water without sinking, and can climb the highest peaks without weariness, until finally he comes to one of the two borders (*aḥad al-ḥaddayni*) that intersects [the universe].[106]

In other words, the region that Avicenna describes as "darkness," presumably a metaphor for this world of form and matter, becomes the region or space that the individual must ultimately confront if he or she is to move beyond it. This region of darkness paradoxically becomes the gateway to that of "light," a metaphor for the intelligible world. To phrase this differently: the only way that human consciousness can apprehend an immaterial reality is by perceiving it in the particulars of materiality. This is certainly in keeping with Avicenna's theory of aesthetics that, as I characterized in the previous section, is contingent upon the fact that the philosopher grasps the intelligible principle of beauty through beautiful particulars, something often done imaginatively.

We see a similar description at work in ibn Ezra's *Ḥay ben Meqitz.* Sharing Avicenna's basic Neoplatonic cosmology, he also contends that the physical is the prolegomena to the metaphysical. When the unnamed protagonist first encounters Ḥay, the latter informs him about a large part of Ḥay's toil: "I wander throughout cities and states / Searching every nook and cranny."[107] Even though philosophical inquiry ultimately culminates in the divine vision—again something that takes place through the ocular model—the only way to achieve such a telos is by means of the modalities of this world. In subsequent sections, ibn Ezra gives extremely rich and detailed accounts, with imagery and vocabulary drawn almost exclusively from the biblical narrative. In the passages where he describes the four elements of this world, for instance, he resorts to elaborate sensual accounts. The following is his description of the element of air, here described spatially as a geographical area on a vertical journey:

> He made me cross these lakes
> He brought me to a large boundary.
> I saw winds and gusts
> Exhaling
> Fluttering.
> Storms, horrors, tremors
> Dismantling mountains, laying bare rocks.
> Their lightning bolts appear
> Thunder roars.
> Clouds screen
> Showers pour down.
> Rains (*revivim*), showers (*resisim*), dew

The last rains, showers, all types of liquid.
There are hail stones in the vault
Put away for a time of adversity
For a day of war and battle.[108]

In this description, ibn Ezra uses many words and phrases from the Bible to situate his description within specific terms of reference. For instance, the term "rains" (*revivim*) is used infrequently in the biblical text, and in Jeremiah 3:3 and 14:22 it is primarily associated with God's ability to bring sustenance and fruition to the earth. In like manner, the term "showers" (*resisim*) is also used rarely and in the context of water is found only in Song 5:2, where it describes the sweet dampness of night (*resisei leila*) that envelops the lover's brow. This passage thus paints a rich portrait of the sensual world. It is not a world that is profane, the locus of corruption; on the contrary it is the world where one encounters the divine, a world imbued with a rich texture that ultimately derives from the sacred language of the biblical text. In the section immediately following this one, the protagonist and Ḥay prepare to enter the geographical boundary separating the material and intelligible worlds. Ibn Ezra describes it as a "consuming fire" (*esh okelah*), invoking the Burning Bush in Exodus 3:2–3,[109] that melts and consumes everything in its path. The point is that one can only get to this realm, the opaque line separating the sub- and superlunar worlds, by immersing oneself in the sensual world. The thick descriptions that ibn Ezra provides are not meant to denigrate this world. Rather, they focus on it by employing sacred imagery and vocabulary to highlight its connection to the non-sensual world.

A similar attitude is witnessed in ibn Ṭufayl's *Ḥayy ibn Yaqẓān*, another treatise that shares the basic Neoplatonic worldview that defines the other two tales. Ibn Ṭufayl's text, however, differs considerably from the other two since his Ḥayy makes a solitary journey, whereas Avicenna's and ibn Ezra's protagonists journey in the company of Ḥayy. Ibn Ṭufayl's Ḥayy is firmly stuck in the sensual world and must, by means of his own intellectual endeavors, raise himself to the level of the intelligible world. Indeed, roughly the first third of his tale (following the prologue) is devoted to charting Ḥayy's ability to move from the potentially chaotic organization of this world to creating a taxonomy that allows him to transcend the material world:

> He found that if hc molded clay into some shape, for example into a ball, it had length, width and depth in a certain ration; if he then took this ball and worked it into a cube or egg shape, its length, width and depth took on different proportions. But it was still the same clay; and, no matter what the ration, it could not be divested of length, breadth, and depth. The fact that

one proportion could replace another made it apparent to him that the dimensions were a factor in their own right, distinct from the clay itself.[110]

This culminates in Ḥayy's realization that all corporeal entities are a composite of form and matter, and subsequently that every composite thing must by its nature have a cause. By means of his own intellectual ability, Ḥayy moves from the sensual phenomena of this world to the notion of an intelligible cause that is ultimately responsible for the existence of everything in this world. This leads Ḥayy to the following conclusion:

> Now Ḥayy knew by necessity (*bi al-ḍarūra*) that all that comes into being must have a cause (*ḥāditha*).... One by one he went over the forms (*al-ṣūr*) he had known before and saw that all of them had come to be and all must have a cause.... Ḥayy realized that the same would be true of all forms. Clearly the acts emerging from forms did not really arise in them, but all the actions attributed to them were brought about through them by another Being.[111]

Ḥayy makes the connection that the sensual world is not an *ad hoc* collection of unrelated forms.[112] Rather, it is all intimately related to the First Principle that sustains the universe. According to ibn Ṭufayl, so long as the sensual world is properly understood, one is able to move almost naturally and effortlessly beyond it to the intelligible world. However, one is only able to make this movement precisely by means of the sensual world. By grasping the order and harmony of this world, one intuitively grasps the principles of order and harmony that inform it.

The subsequent unfolding of these tales represents both the literal and existential journey of a protagonist through the cosmos. This is a hierarchical process: one must begin firmly in the phenomenal world and, as one progresses in the various sciences, one gradually moves through the various heavenly spheres. Reflecting this, all of the initiates begin firmly in this world of sense and experience, move toward the search for universal principles, and subsequently end their journey with an ocular or imaginative gaze into the divine. This telos is an interesting amalgam of ecstasy, mysticism, and intellectual gnosis. These tales are primarily concerned with the embodied human perspective in which the only way to understand the upper emanations that sustain the celestial world is to conceptualize the lower emanations that ultimately derive from it. Even though according to Neoplatonic ontology the lower comes from the higher, the only way to conceive of the latter is through the former.

Within this framework, one is unable to progress on the philosophical journey unless one has a basic understanding of the ontological connection between this world, which is composed of form and matter, and the celestial world, which is not. For it is, to reiterate, only such a realization that makes epistemology possible. As the individual ascends, he or she encounters the interconnectedness of the universe: each level and each image gives way to the next. These tales document every stage of the progression, providing an imaginative account of the individual ascent. These tales are not mystical treatises; rather, they represent the philosophical journey that leads from logic to the physical sciences all the way up to metaphysics. The denouement of the journey, however, culminates in the wondrous and beatific vision that occurs once the soul has reached its true home. The telos occurs when the initiate has experienced the transcendent beauty that the natural world has both presented and participated in.

Moreover, this ontological-epistemological journey occurs within a framework of beauty. The language used to describe each level is often elaborate, thereby imbuing its contents with a rich and multi-hued narrative. This world of form and matter is not simply documented and catalogued; on the contrary, the reader is invited into the narrative to experience the multiple states of being that the narrative unfolds. These tales do not simply describe the universe and what is found in it; rather, they provide rich descriptions that appeal to the senses with the understanding that the senses are the gateway to both the imagination and the intellect.

A good example of this type of sensual description is demonstrated by how these various tales treat the physical world. If, from the top of the Neoplatonic hierarchy, this world is the lowest part of the cosmos, from the embodied perspectives of these tales, the physical world becomes the starting point for the philosophical journey. In Avicenna's description of the mineral and plant worlds, for example, we read:

> And you will come across a region wherein you will encounter mighty mountains, rivers, blowing winds and clouds heavy with rain. There you will find gold, silver, and all genie and species of precious and lowly substances. But there is neither growth nor germination there. Crossing from here you will come to a region loaded with what we mentioned above: all types of vegetation springing forth and fruit-bearing and other types of non–fruit-bearing trees and seeds.[113]

This description occurs as Ḥayy and the protagonist begin their journey eastward along the horizontal axis. On the surface, it is an allegorical description of the various forms and species of this world.

According to the standard philosophical account, these forms exist without matter and the only way to comprehend them is intellectually as opposed to through the various senses. Yet Avicenna's description is anything but a dry and discursive account. On the contrary, it is replete with a rich use of language that ultimately stems from and appeals to one's experience within the sensual world. It is a world of "mighty mountains" (*jibāl rāsiyya*), of gold and silver, and of "all types of vegetation springing forth and fruit-bearing and other types of non–fruit-bearing trees and seeds." Once again, Avicenna takes the position that the only access we have to the formal, incorporeal, and intelligible world is by means of concrete sensual particulars.

We see a similar description in ibn Ezra's account of the plant world, which he describes in the following manner:

> He took me down to an orchard
> In it was every fruit tree and meadow.
> There, birds of the sky dwell
> Singing among the foliage.
> Springs gush forth
> Plants sprout.
> Its vineyards are ripe
> The ground tilled and cleared of stones.
> Roots are watered by a stream
> Rivulets of water cause its shoots to flower.
> On a carrying frame its gleanings are carried
> Upon a shoulder its clusters borne.
> Its skies concealed by clouds
> Furrows saturated by showers.
> Branches drip a medicinal sap.
> Its canopy oozes pleasant fragrances.
> In its streams the pomegranates are in bloom
> Roses radiate in flower beds.
> At its door are fruits
> New and freshly picked.
> Date palms give forth their fruit
> Green figs form on the trees.
> The vine is ripe
> Mandrakes yield their fragrances.[114]

In this description, we experience the rich and verdant pleasures associated with the world of vegetation. The description is full of the language and imagery of the biblical narrative, especially the Song and the Psalms. The first line of this quotation, for instance, invokes the lover's descent to his garden to see and appreciate it in full bloom (Song 6:11). Much of the imagery in the last verses of this quotation—the discussion of the pomegranates, the figs, and the mandrakes—is again taken directly from the Song. The effect here is that ibn Ezra uses some of the most sensual imagery in the biblical narrative, something that would not be lost on his medieval reader.[115] He describes the plant world with a lushness that would not be foreign to his reader's worldview, either narratively by employing the Song or literally by reflecting the rich garden culture of al-Andalus.[116] The only way to apprehend the abstract concept of various plant species is by means of their particular, sensual manifestations.

Much of the middle section of this passage invokes the language of the Psalms. The second line ("In it was every fruit tree and meadow"), for example, comes from Psalm 148:9, where in its original context all of creation is commanded to sing praise to its Creator, from whom all things ultimately derive their source and strength. Once again, ibn Ezra easily places this verse into a Neoplatonic framework. The original context of the third and fourth lines ("There, birds . . . singing among the foliage") is from Psalm 104:12. This verse strengthens the previous one, since it also is devoted to praising the Creator by means of the beauty of this world:

> Bless the Lord, O my soul;
> O Lord, my God, You are very great;
> You are clothed in glory and majesty;
> Wrapped in a robe of light;
> You spread the heaven like a tent cloth. . . .
>
> You make springs gush forth in torrents;
> They make their way between the hills;
> Giving drink to all the wild beasts;
> The wild asses slake their thirst.
> *The birds of the sky dwell beside them*
> *And sing among the foliage;*
> You water the mountains from Your lofts;
> The earth is sated from the fruit of Your work. (Psalm 104:1–13; my italics)

Ibn Ezra essentially reaffirms the main tenor of the Psalms—that the only way to apprehend the Creator is to apprehend the beauty of his creation—and puts this meaning within the ontology of Neoplatonic emanation. To use another example, the eighth line ("The ground tilled and cleared of stones") comes from Isaiah 5:2, whose original context is a song that a lover sings for his beloved. Once again ibn Ezra invokes biblical language whose original setting speaks to the beauty of creation in order to use this beauty as the key by which to understand God or, in Neoplatonic language, the concept of celestial beauty and harmony.

These rich descriptions are more than simple constructions based on the cultural and social norms of our authors. Rather, we witness in them the description of the phenomenal world in which aesthetic speculation dovetails with the literary-poetic ideals of *adab*. These descriptions in turn are a far cry from an analytical or scientific description. Rather, one narratively enters the world of vegetation in order to experience its full sensual beauty. For it is only by experiencing, and not just by understanding, each cosmological level that one can proceed up the ontological hierarchy.

In his description of the animal kingdom, ibn Ṭufayl uses similar imagery drawn from the world of the senses. The sensual world, according to the following description, holds the key to unlocking the intelligible world:

> Then Ḥayy turned his attention to all the species of animals (*anwā*ᶜ *al-ḥayawān*) together. He saw that they were alike in having sensation, nutrition, and voluntary motion in whichever direction they pleased. These activities, he had learned already, were characteristic of the animal spirit (*al-ruḥ al-ḥayawānī*); whereas the respects in which they differed, were not particularly essential to the animal spirit. These reflections made it apparent to him that the animal spirit in all animal genera (*jins al-ḥayawān*) is in reality one, despite the slight differences that differentiate one species from another. Just as water from a single source may be divided into different bowls, and may be cooler in some than in others, so the animal spirit is one; its specific differentia are like the different temperatures of the water, while the animal itself is like the water, which remains one even though it happens to be divided. By thinking in this way Ḥayy was able to see the whole animal kingdom as one.[117]

This reference again fits nicely with the leitmotif that runs throughout ibn Ṭufayl's tale; namely, the need to bring some sort of order to the sensual world and the notion that this order, once discovered, allows the individual to apprehend its divine source.[118] Ḥayy can penetrate this divine source only after he observes and makes various connections between the phenomena of this world. After his realization of the unity behind the multiplicity of species that make up the animal world and the rest of the world of form and matter, he is able to proceed up the ontological hierarchy. Comprehension of the physical world thus leads to an understanding of the metaphysical world. Although this world at first blush may seem chaotic and disjointed, it is actually arranged according to a divine plan of harmony and beauty. The key for the individual is to ascertain this and project it back on the intelligible universe. After grasping the harmony and beauty of this world, Ḥayy subsequently looks for something that keeps it all together and brings order to the whole:

> Regarding all bodies, living and non-living in the same light, Ḥayy saw that the being of each of them was made up in the same way of corporeality plus some factor or factors. Before him loomed the forms of physical things in all their diversity. This was his first glimpse of the spiritual world (*al-ᶜālam al-rūḥāniyya*). For these forms cannot be apprehended by the senses, but only by reasoning (*al-naẓar al-aqalī*).[119]

Up to this point in the narrative, the only world that Ḥayy knows is the natural one. From this point forward, he grasps its overall structure before proceeding to the intelligible world. On the boundary between these two worlds, he searches for an entity that provides form to the matter of this world. Without such form, the world would be nothing other than a mass of undifferentiated prime matter. As he casts his glance heavenward, he sees that the heavens (including the stars and the planets) cannot be infinite because they are composed of bodies. Based on his experiences in the sensual world, Ḥayy realizes that the heavens cannot be infinite because all things that have a body must by nature be finite. Accordingly, they too must have a cause. This realization leads him to search for a cause existing beyond the heavenly world:

> When first reflecting on the world of generation and corruption (*ᶜālam al-kawn wa al-fasād*), Ḥayy had become aware that the substantiality of any material thing rests in its form, that is its propensity for certain types of motion. Its being, on its material side, is defective at best, and in itself scarcely conceivable. If so, the being of the whole universe (*wujūd al-ᶜālam kullihi*) is ultimately no more than its capacity to be moved by a Great Mover (*al-muḥarrik al-barīʾ*), who is free of matter and all its attributes and transcends all that sense can perceive or imagination approach.[120]

Again Ḥayy's ability to grasp and apprehend the intelligible world occurs primarily, almost solely, by means of the principles that he has already observed in the sensual world. One can, in other words, only understand the transcendental by means of its manifestations. Or to phrase this in terms of Neoplatonic aesthetics, absolute beauty can only be reached by means of the beautiful objects of the sensual world.

This becomes even more evident in the three tales when one examines their denouements that, as I have already shown, culminate in an ocular moment that is heavily dependent upon the powers of the imaginative faculty. Aesthetics also plays a crucial role in this ultimate visionary moment. As Avicenna's Ḥayy informs the unnamed protagonist of the cosmological map that awaits him, he speaks of a people who are situated just below the One, referred to as the King (*al-malik*). These people engage in eternal contemplation of the King and act as His intimates. All of the individuals that make up this community are described as perfect (*al-ḥusn*) since they receive "a beauty that keeps the beholder trembling with admiration, a stature that has attained its perfection."[121] This group of people mirrors and reflects the Beauty that is essential to the King. In other words, all who contemplate the One ultimately receive a part of Its beauty.

At the end of his tale, Avicenna gives a description of the One. It is a description that is not meant to be taken literally, but one that ultimately reveals as it conceals:

> His beauty (*ḥusn*) obliterates the vestiges of all other beauty. His generosity debases the worth of all other generosity. When one of those who surround His immensity undertakes to meditate on Him, his eye blinks with stupor and he comes away dazzled. Indeed his eyes are almost ravished even before he turns them upon Him. His beauty (*ḥusn*) is the veil (*ḥijāb*) of His beauty, His manifestation (*ẓuhūr*) is the cause of His occultation (*buṭūn*), His revelation (*tajallin*) is the cause of His hiddeness (*khafāʾ*).... In truth, the King manifests His beauty on the horizon of those who are His; towards them He does not spare His vision.... Whoever perceives (*shāhada*) a trace of His beauty (*jamāl*) halts before it in contemplation (*laḥẓa*), and does not turn their gaze from Him, even for a second.[122]

In this passage, there are several nuances to the term "beauty." First, as in keeping with his comments in *R. al-ᶜishq*, Avicenna claims that the beauty of the One (i.e., the concept of celestial beauty) is superior to all other types of beauty. No sensual beautiful object can either approach or compete with God's beauty. Despite this, the only way that one can apprehend God's beauty is, paradoxically, by means of sensual and tangible objects that are beautiful. Second, the phrase "His beauty is the veil of His beauty" is telling in that it intimates the paradox around which Neoplatonism, in general, and Neoplatonic aesthetics, in particular, revolve. Although God is defined in part by beauty, it is an attribute that cannot be grasped by finite humans. No matter how hard an individual may try, there will ultimately always be a gap between physical and metaphysical beauty.

Finally, in this passage Avicenna argues that the individual who apprehends "a trace of His beauty" fixes his or her contemplation upon God forever. Implicit here once again is the concept that a finite individual can never apprehend intelligible beauty on its own; one simply lacks the noetic ability to do so. However, one does have tangible and symbolic beauty in this world to contemplate, and the initiate is someone who knows how to make the appropriate connection between the visible and spiritual worlds. For, to reiterate, the conditions and modalities of the former are the only way into the latter.

The denouement of ibn Ezra's tale is remarkably similar to that of Avicenna's. In particular, ibn Ezra emphasizes both the visual and the beautiful components of the initiate's philosophical telos. The following important passage, which I already cited in chapter 3, indicates the importance of the visual at the uppermost stages of the Neoplatonic hierarchy:

> I was afraid and said
> "How awesome is this place that I see."
> He replied: "From your feet
> Remove the sandals.
> From the matter of your corpse
> Lift your soul.
> Forsake your thoughts
> Relax your eyelids!
> See by the eyes of your interior
> The pupils of your heart."[123]

In this passage, ibn Ezra emphasizes the visual and the ocular. He argues that the key to the philosophical initiation is one in which the initiate must no longer apprehend the world through the physical eye, but through the interior eye, the eye of the imagination. Ibn Ezra again uses biblical language to emphasize his point. The line "How awesome is this place that I see" is especially telling since these are the exact words that Jacob utters in Genesis 28:16 after he awakens from a dream. In this dream he perceives a ladder upon which angels are ascending and descending; this is also the dream in which God renews His covenant with the Jewish people. Furthermore, Ḥay's immediate response about removing the sandals is a quotation of the exact words that God uttered to Moses through the Burning Bush in Exodus 3:5. Both of these biblical prooftexts attest to the visual nature of the protagonist's experience. For both of these biblical events attest to experiences of the transcendental through the phenomenality of this world.

Subsequent to this, the unnamed protagonist inquires into exactly what it is that he sees. Ḥay's response reiterates the ineffability of the divine:

> He replied, "He is one, none is second to Him
> He has neither son nor brother.
> Places are unable to contain Him

Time cannot predate Him.
Hearts grow weary from enumerating His greatness
Tongues rejoice in recounting His praise.
He has glory and magnificence
Eternity and glory.
Strength
Splendor.
Kingship
Greatness. . . ."[124]

In this passage, we again encounter the beauty of God. This is a beauty that is ultimately responsible for the governance and sustenance of the rest of the cosmos. Returning to the theme of aesthetics, it is a beauty that the protagonist experiences in terms of tangible and symbolic forms. We also see this at play in ibn Ṭufayl's *Ḥayy ibn Yaqẓān.* After Ḥayy has discovered the order and harmony of the sensible world and has begun to understand the way in which it relates to the intelligible order, he apprehends the telos of the Neoplatonic system, self-knowledge:

> The only way to apprehend Him, then, must be by some non-physical means, something which is neither a bodily faculty nor in any way bound up with a body—neither inside nor outside, neither in contact with it nor disjoined from it. Ḥayy had also realized that what had brought him his awareness of the being would be his true self.[125]

The discovery of this faculty coincides with, as ibn Ṭufayl himself mentioned in his prologue, a vision (*mushāhada*) and a taste (*dhawq*) of the divine.[126] This vision, as we subsequently learn, is that of beauty:

> He saw the perfection (*al-kamāl*), the splendor (*al-bahāʾ*), and the beauty (*al-ḥusn*) in the essence of that sphere. They were too magnificent to be described and too delicate to be clothed in written or spoken words. But he saw it to be at the pinnacle of joy, delight, and rapture, in blissful vision (*mushāhada*) of the being of the Truth (*al-ḥaqq*), glorious be His Majesty.[127]

Ḥayy's noetic perfection, like that of the unnamed protagonists in both Avicenna's and ibn Ezra's tales, culminates in a vision of celestial beauty, order, and harmony. All three protagonists achieve spiritual illumination by means of observing the beauty, harmony, and order of the world around them. These principles point beyond themselves, thereby reflecting similar principles in the celestial world. Significantly, none of the three protagonists requires Scripture to attain such knowledge or gnosis. Physical beauty as witnessed through the various senses appears to be sufficient to enable the individual to experience the divine world. Such experiences culminate in an ecstatic vision of God and are achieved primarily by means of the senses and their encounter with the physical objects of this world. Ibn Ṭufayl juxtaposes this experience with that of divine legislation. When Ḥayy visits the island whose inhabitants possess Scripture he realizes that they completely de-emphasize the relationship between the structure of this world and the intelligible world.[128] He quickly becomes disappointed and ultimately leaves that island to return to his life of solitude.

It is for precisely these reasons that aesthetics and the imagination are intimately connected not only in these tales, but in Neoplatonism as a whole. For the beauty that the initiate apprehends is ultimately based upon his or her sense experience. However, the actual vision cannot be simply reduced to the sensible realm of everyday experience. Nor is it simply a translation of an otherwise ineffable experience. Rather, the initiate sees the various forms that sensory experience provides and "whose phenomenality is characterized by a tangibility appropriate to sense data."[129] This is why the imaginative faculty is so important: it functions as the vehicle whereby transcendent reality, otherwise unknowable and imperceptible, is apprehended as it exists in sensual, concrete particulars. Beauty is central here because of both the Platonic and Neoplatonic notion that the One is characterized by beauty, yet the only way to reach it is by means of the tangible beauty.

This chapter has argued that the medieval Islamicate philosophers possessed a distinct theory of beauty. Although this theory was ultimately based upon Greek precedents, it nonetheless was adopted and adapted in such a manner that it could address distinctly monotheistic concerns. This is in keeping with the broader theme of combining the rich images of both Neoplatonism and one's own scriptural heritage to explore and nuance the soul's relationship to God. Moreover, it was an aesthetics that revolved around a distinct ontological hierarchy, grounded in the theory that this world of form and matter is the primary locus wherein one encounters the intelligible world. It is within this context that we need to situate the *Ḥayy ibn Yaqẓān* cycle, for its primary concern is the phenomenality of this world and how this ultimately aids in the apprehension of the spiritual world.

It is also important to locate medieval philosophical aesthetics in general, and the initiatory tale in particular, within the interplay between poetry and philosophy. Whereas philosophy was concerned with elucidating the form, structure, and relationship between particulars and their participation in a super-sensible abstract beauty, poetry was interested in mining the metaphoric expression of beautiful images. At the heart of this interplay resides the desire to apprehend the divine. And such an apprehension can only take place within the context of the tangible and the corporeal. Aesthetics thus becomes a crucial part of medieval philosophy since it is the discipline that ultimately enables the individual to experience universals in a particular way. Since humans are noetically limited by their embodiedness, artistic representations provide a way of confronting and transcending one's particularity. It is for this reason that aesthetics became so important for the authors under discussion here, since beauty is that which allows us to recognize truth.

Aesthetics is neither absent from nor a marginal component within medieval Islamicate philosophy. In this chapter I hope to have made the case that by re-introducing aesthetics into our understanding of medieval Islamic and Jewish philosophy, we are able to examine some of its features in a new light. This world no longer becomes simply that of generation and corruption, but also becomes the locus that provides us with the conceptual apparati to apprehend the eternal world. Although mainstream opinion has it that the goal of philosophy is for the individual to leave this world in order to become like one of the divine Intellects, this chapter has argued that such a goal is unattainable without the initiate first encountering the sensible realm of everyday experience. For as long as the individual remains embodied, this realm can never be jettisoned.

The imagination is thus central to medieval Islamic and Jewish Neoplatonism. In particular, aesthetics is inextricably linked to the imaginative faculty because both are concerned with the phenomenal world and how this world reveals the structure of the divine. Without aesthetics or the imagination, we are left without images; and without images we are unable to gain knowledge of that which exists without matter. Beautiful particulars are crucial in this regard because they focus the imaginative gaze upward to the heavens as opposed to downward and the generation and corruption of matter. The imagination then is naturally drawn toward beauty. Nevertheless, it uses beauty not as an end in itself, but as a vehicle with which to engage in creative hermeneutics.

Conclusion

This study has explored the intertwining of imagination and aesthetics in medieval Neoplatonism. To do this I focused on a distinct genre within the Jewish and Islamic philosophical sources, what I have called the "initiatory tale." In particular, I examined what is probably its most famous manifestation: the *Ḥayy ibn Yaqẓān* cycle as composed by Avicenna, ibn Ezra, and ibn Ṭufayl. These individuals are three key names in the history of Islamic and Jewish philosophy. This should immediately alert us to the fact that these tales have a distinct philosophical component. However, since all three individuals wrote within the highly literary and interdisciplinary world of Neoplatonism, it is also necessary to emphasize the artistic and poetic dimensions of their work. Yet rather than see these two trajectories—the philosophical and the literary—as unrelated, I have put them into conversation with each other. The goal in doing this is to show how they interact and, ultimately, how they cross-pollinate.

I have chosen to emphasize the problem of the visual and the act of visualization within the philosophical enterprise associated with medieval Neoplatonism. This feature of visualization, which turns on the role of the imagination, is often marginalized in the secondary literature. The imagination is regarded as untrustworthy, the faculty that obstructs the proper functioning of the intellect. Despite this, the imagination is the faculty that grasps the incorporeal and the spiritual that resides behind the corporeal and the physical, thereby permitting the individual to experience the divine world in terms of familiar categories. This creates many potential problems, however, as both Jewish and Islamic thinkers were forced to undertake their speculation in what were essentially perceived to be aniconic traditions. The key for them was to use and combine the traditional imagery associated with prophecy in their own traditions with the speculative blueprint afforded by Neoplatonism. In effect, they fused these two aspects together in such a manner that the authors rarely strayed from the aniconic parameters as defined by theological orthodoxy. But even if they did not overstep what was, in effect, a line drawn in the sand, we must not marginalize, as has traditionally been done, the visual and the role of visualization in both medieval Jewish and Islamic thought.

Within these tales (or, indeed, within Jewish and Islamic Neoplatonism as a whole), aesthetics is to imagination what poetry is to philosophy. In other words, aesthetics and poetry become the currency whereby the imagination and philosophy are able to tease out and subsequently map the various relationships between the physical and the metaphysical. It is precisely this set of relationships between the concrete and the spiritual that is at the heart of medieval Jewish and Islamic Neoplatonism. Poetry and literature, not to mention more analytical treatises, are all concerned, in one way or another, with the contours of this relationship. It is precisely for this reason that I have tried in this study to introduce the body, the visual, and the imaginative into the contemporary discussion of Jewish and Islamic philosophy. The initiatory tale, as I have argued, is the ideal point of departure for this enterprise. But the discussion need not stop here. Indeed, we are able to see similar features at work in virtually all of the treatises associated with medieval Jewish and Islamic Neoplatonism.

The key to understanding these tales resides in situating them against medieval Neoplatonic aesthetics. This goes a long way in avoiding the traditional maximalist and minimalist approaches that have traditionally been employed to examine these treatises. According to my reading, these tales are neither part of some larger, inchoate "Oriental Wisdom" nor unimportant treatises meant for the non-philosopher. On the contrary, they become the concrete expression of a distinct aesthetical worldview, one that recognizes in the particular a diaphanous screen through which the individual encounters the divine. The particular, therefore, allows the individual access into a world that is otherwise closed and forbidden. The realm of the particular presents the abstract as the concrete, thereby enabling the individual to see the incorporeal divine as cloaked in the specificity of the corporeal. Both the imagination and aesthetics thus enable one to encounter and apprehend the divine as something, but not as it is in itself (which is, after all, impossible). This is in keeping with the philosophical dictum that one can never know or grasp God's essence.

The use of poetry, metaphor, and other such devices is not somehow antirational or aphilosophical, but a convenient way in which to explore the nature of the relationship between this world and the intelligible world. Rather than work on the assumption that if a philosopher turns to the literary or the poetic he or she must be uncertain or is just reworking an analytical statement in poetic garb, we need to begin to be sensitive to such modes of expression. Indeed, such modes of expression represent a valid form of intellectual speculation. Rather than attempt to translate it simply and woodenly into "analytical prose," it is worthwhile for us to examine it phenomenologically.

These tales are representative of an important genre whereby medieval Islamic and Jewish philosophers could articulate the structure and meaning of tangible and concrete beauty. These tales thus attempt to contextualize the incorporeal beauty of the divine world. This contextualization revolves around the pivot of the image. Much like the imagination, these tales move back and forth between the material and immaterial worlds, allowing the initiate or reader to experience the immaterial through the modalities of the material. This is in keeping with Neoplatonic cosmology that stresses the ontic relationship between the sensible and the material. In this framework, the initiate can only have access to the transcendent by means of the experiences of everyday existence.

Since such tales provide ontological maps of the Neoplatonic universe, they encourage the participation of the reader. This participation culminates in a form of noetic and psychic transformation as the reader finds himself or herself within, and subsequently transcending, the cartography of the text. The reader, as I have argued throughout, is invited to experience the same journey as the protagonist. Since the beauty of the intelligible world consists in the art of seeing, there is a fundamental correspondence between the beauty seen in this world and the imaginative gaze of the soul in the transcendent world. This is where the imagination becomes so important. The imagination's gaze enables the individual to "see" the intelligible world based on the formal criteria of the corporeal world. In order to accomplish this, one must direct one's imagination from physical objects that are beautiful accidentally to the essential beauty of the immaterial world. It is precisely this motion toward that these initiatory tales not only document but also actively recreate.

Appendix

In what follows I provide the first complete English translation of ibn Ezra's *Ḥay ben Meqitz*. I base my translation on the critical edition of the Hebrew text as provided by Levin.[1]

Keeping with my main argument of this study—namely, that these tales were composed in a certain form for particular philosophical purposes—I have tried to avoid producing a literal and wooden translation of what is a very vibrant original. In like manner, I have refused to translate what is a very poetical text into a prose narrative. My rendition, therefore, attempts to present the essential meaning of every line but in a way that recreates, in English, the aesthetic dimension of the original.

My translation attempts both to retain the tenor of the original Hebrew images or metaphors and to present them in ways that communicate the brevity and force of the original language. However, there is no way of recreating the rhyme and rhythm of the original in English without resorting to the most awkward and artificial constructions. In fact, I have had to emend the Hebrew into readable English in just about every line. A consultation of the original Hebrew text, however, will make this readily apparent.

Similarly, I have also avoided "translating" the poem into scientific prose. This would, once again, go against my phenomenological reading of the work. Rather than taking every section of the poem and saying that it corresponds to a particular feature of ibn Ezra's larger corpus, I have kept my comments in the notes to the translation to a minimum. My main concern in these notes is to point out the biblical matrix[2] from which ibn Ezra's poem derives its potency.

Ḥay ben Meqitz
An Initiatory Tale by Abraham ibn Ezra

Listen, O wise men, to my words
Those versed in knowledge pay heed.[3]
Men, young and old, understand

Ignoramuses and youth listen up.
Truth will my mouth pronounce
Uprightness will issue from my lips.[4]
I have abandoned my house
Walked away from my possessions.[5]
I left my home
My birthplace, my people.
The sons of my mother put me in charge
But they did not let me attend to my vineyard.[6]
I arose to travel
In search of tranquility.
My spirit[7] called out for relaxation
My soul[8] demanded peace
I was in need of seclusion.[9]
With me were my friends
Fellow companions on life's journey.
An old man was walking in the field[10]
Praising God, giving thanks.
His appearance was like that of kings
An aura surrounding him, shining like the angels.
Seasons had not changed him
Years seemed not to pass him.
His eyes shone like those of a dove[11]
His brow gleamed as a slice of pomegranate.[12]
Neither distortion in his height
Nor weakness in his strength.
Neither darkness in his eyes
Nor was his vigor unabated.[13]
His fragrance was wondrous
Like that of spikeman.[14]
His mouth was delicious,
All of him was delightful.[15]
I called out to him: Your physical state prospers
You will never perish.
Whose son are you, what is your name?
What is your occupation?
Is this place your home?
In words he answered me[16]
Full of stones and gems.[17]
In words arranged
Like *thummim* and *urim*.[18]
He said to me: "May God enrich your name[19]

May your prosperity be like a river.[20]
May He always be your trust
Preventing your feet from slipping.[21]
Ḥay ben Meqitz is my name
The Holy City is my home.
My work is what you see
I toil and do not grow weary.
I wander throughout cities and states
Searching every nook and cranny.
My father guides me in the way of wisdom[22]
He teaches me understanding and counsel.[23]
I am with Him as a confidant[24]
In Baal Hamon.[25]
In the coolness of his shade
I delight to sit.[26]
I will not leave Him
For His fruit is sweet to my mouth."[27]
While we were talking
his words opened up.
Extended to those who desire to understand
the true nature of things and to searchers of the
straight path.
He said, "The countenance of your face speaks
Your form attests to your sincerity
Your ears are open to receive admonitions.
Your soul[28] has the ability
To acquire wisdom and understanding.
This is the art which I examine and research
It never lies nor cheats.
It is to the truth like scales
Like the eyes are to vision
He who relinquishes it will grope at noon.[29]
These friends
Who rule over you
They are not companions
They are rebellious.
They are not friends
They are evildoers.
They are not lovers
But rather enemies.
They hunt and destroy
Spreading their snares and traps.[30]

They arrest and torture
The heroic and the mighty.
Blessed is the man who is rescued from them
Happy is the sinner trapped by them.[31]
He who is snared in their nets does not escape
He who is seized by their nets is not let go.
My son, turn away from their abodes!
Do not face them, ignore their words
Their feet run after evil![32]
The one who walks before you
He always lies, disregarding the truth.
The companion on your right
He subdues you, captures you.
In every season he is angry
He is always furious.
Every day he roars
He is forever angry.
His swords strike his relatives
Its sparks consume everything that is around him.
His wrath breaks forth like a fire[33]
His fury is like a blade that rampages.
In everything he sins and makes a mockery
He turns from every truth, ridiculing it in the process.[34]
He is likened to a lion that likes to devour[35]
Like a cub sitting secretly, waiting to pounce.
As for the companion on your left
He makes you fail and ultimately destroys you.
He is forever hoping and expecting
Always coveting and desiring.
Even if you pound the fool in a mortar
His folly will not leave him.[36]
Even if you hit him with a hammer
You will not stop his foolishness.
He loves all foods
He is not sated from wanting more.
He who is with them
He neither understands nor can he become wise.
He will say nothing and he will utter nonsense
He will make fun of justice and righteousness,
  confusing the truth.[37]
There are distortions in his heart[38]
In bed he plots mischief.[39]

His eyes do not have the strength to see
His ears are unable to hear.[40]
You desire to follow them[41]
Your heart lusts after them.
You do not understand that he who walks in
their company
Fails to survive their corruptible influences.[42]
Can a man rake embers into his own bosom
Without burning his clothes?
Can a man walk on coals
Without scorching his feet?[43]
This is the lot of he who is swayed by the
sweetness of their mouths.
To the one who is tempted
By the pleasantness of their words.
My son, do not walk in this path with them
Keep your feet from their path.[44]
They have struck dead many
They subdued the mighty and the powerful.[45]
Their way is the way to hell[46]
Their road is the road toward death.
Rule over them!
Master them!
Subdue the fool with the use of desire and use
desire against the fool!
Judge them with justice
Do not deviate from judgment!
As for he who speaks nonsense
Do not assent or give heed to him.[47]
Though he be fair-spoken
Do not trust him for seven abominations
are in his heart.[48]
Do this, my son, and extricate yourself![49]
Before the day blows gently and the shadow flees![50]
Heed my words! Do not forget them
Never abandon them!
Always keep them close to you
Inscribe them upon your heart's tablet.[51]
They will be yours alone
Others having no part with you.[52]
Let them be as a graceful wreath upon your head
A necklace about your throat.[53]

You will spend your days in happiness
Your years in delight."[54]
When I had heard his words
They were more precious than pearls.[55]
I knew what the fate would be for one
Who deviates from his morals.
One who changes his words
Who throws away even one of his words.
Such a person corrupts his soul[56] and destroys it[57]
Offends his rational soul and kills it.
But he who holds them[58] and does not let go
He will live forever and will not perish.
Since they are life to him who finds them,
Healing for his whole body.[59]
I said to him, "Let me follow you. Let us run.
I will delight in you and rejoice.
In your love I will celebrate
From your elixir I will drink spiced wine."[60]
He replied, "You are unable to run in my presence[61]
You cannot fly with me.
Your wings are broken
You have not the limbs for it."
I said, "Would that I had the wings of a dove!
I would fly away and find rest![62]
My Lord
Do not be cruel to me.
I lay down my case before you[63]
I cast my burden upon you, sustain me.
In you are my hopes and my nourishment
Cure my illness and bind my wounds."
He took me to a nearby road
leading to a land, long and wide.[64]
It was divided into three parts
deep and distant.
The beginning of the first was in water
its end in the heavens.
The other two
are the main ones.
The one has its border in the East
The other has its beginning in the West.
The former sheds its light upon the latter
The latter clothes the former in its majesty.

Among these the land is apportioned as shares[65]
Dating back to the beginning.
It is impossible to walk in the high parts
Except for a man who is full of God's spirit.[66]
At the edge of this land a spring calls out
Announcing its voice from afar.
Its streams are as wide as rivers
Its waters gush forth.
They cure every wound and ailment
Providing remedy and recovery.[67]
We approached the spring
And stood bcsidc it.
He undressed me, my clothes he cast aside
He led me naked toward it.
He said, "Drink the water from its source
The fluids flowing from its well![68]
In it your fractures will be healed
Your limbs will be dressed.
You will have wings
To fly in the heavens."
I drank from the water of life
The water that gives life to souls.
My pains and my afflictions left me.
My loyal yet bad companions
They became like a balsam
Healing my fractures, soothing my limbs.
I drank enough
My sickness was cured.
He reached out his hand and grabbed me
Lifting me from the depth of the spring.
He took me to a city
Ancient and old.
It kills its lovers
Consumes its inhabitants.[69]
In it were tents
Dark and lightless.
The sun is far away from them
The moon does not shine upon them.
Behind the abodes is a hot spring
Into which the sun sets.
Its source is not blocked
It changes like clay under a seal.[70]

In this city are men
Poor, without possessions.
Their days are few and evil
They spend them building and planting.
They see their buildings ruined
Their seed trampled.
Palaces are destroyed
Trees are uprooted.
Everything falls into a trap
No one demands, no one asks.[71]
How do they remain?
Why are they not separated?
They are gathered and grouped
Protected from their enemies and opponents.
Yet they have neither peace nor tranquility
Neither satisfaction nor joy.
Good is mixed with evil
Happiness with pain.
Joy
With groans.
Rejoicing
With sighs.
Merriment
With disaster.
Those who know do not find favor in their knowledge.
The light do not chase their lightheartedness.
Men of strength will not be saved by their strength
The time of mischance comes to all.[72]
There the horns of Satan are high and lofty
By them he gores people and entire nations.
One moves around the earth
The other circles in the heavens.
Darkness is not extinguished by them
The sun shines between them.
The horn that wanders bifurcates into two spirits
One that flies into ten families.
Five external senses which scout
Five intermediaries which receive from them.
From the former to the latter, things arrive
The latter hear from and oversee the former.
They bring things to their king
He understands them and becomes wise.

The two spirits are noisy
Constantly interacting with one another.
One is wrathful like a lion
The other craves and desires like a pig.
One is quick to anger
The other craves to eat and devour.
Above them guards a wise and poor man
Who prepares their need
And ensures their way.
Remove stones from their paths
Pave their circuits.
From the grave and death he removes them
In peace and life he joins them.
From sin and crime he stops them
To righteousness and truth he leads them.
On the border are men
Armed with all types of animals.
Doves, birds
Crows and turtle doves.
Sheep, oxen[73]
Carnivorous lion cubs.
Mules, horses
Roebucks and plump geese.[74]
Foxes, goats
She-asses and camels.[75]
Sand lizards, mice and turtles
Jackals, cobras and scorpions.
Frogs and fish
All the other living creatures in the sea.
He took me down to an orchard[76]
In it was every fruit tree and meadow.[77]
There, birds of the sky dwell
Singing among the foliage.[78]
Springs gush forth[79]
Plants sprout.
Its vineyards are ripe
The ground tilled and cleared of stones.[80]
Roots are watered by a stream[81]
Rivulets of water cause its shoots to flower.[82]
On a carrying frame its gleanings are carried[83]
Upon a shoulder its clusters borne.
Its skies concealed by clouds

Furrows saturated by showers.[84]
Branches drip a medicinal sap
Its canopy oozes pleasant fragrances.
In its streams the pomegranates are in bloom[85]
Roses radiate in flower beds.
At its door are fruits
New and freshly picked.[86]
Date palms give forth their fruit
Green figs form on the trees.[87]
The vine is ripe
Mandrakes yield their fragrances.[88]
He raised me from the gardens
To jagged mountains.[89]
There was the gold of Ophir[90]
Precious onyx and sapphire.[91]
Bronze and copper[92]
Fitdah and vareqet.[93]
Tin and lead[94]
Topaz and emerald.
Beryl[95] and crystal[96]
sulfur and salt[97]
Every zaphenath and paneaḥ.[98]
Under the mountains
Aforementioned.
There exists a broad land[99]
Whose circumference is encircled by water.
In it there are broken boulders
Gushing fountains.
Hills
And valleys.
Waves
And brooks.
Wilderness
And rivers.
Lakes
And seas.
Their waves hum
Their waters foam.[100]
They storm mountains with their high tide
Yet they do not cross their allotted boundaries.[101]
He made me cross these lakes
He brought me to a large boundary.

I saw winds and gusts
Exhaling
Fluttering.
Storms, horrors, tremors
Dismantling mountains, laying bare rocks.
Their lightning bolts appear
Thunder roars.
Clouds screen
Showers pour down.
Rains, showers, dew
The last rains, showers, all types of liquid.
There are hail stones in the vault[102]
Put away for a time of adversity
For a day of war and battle.[103]
After this boundary there is a consuming fire[104]
To the heavens it reaches.
Coals burn[105]
Sparks rage.[106]
Its blades are like swords[107]
Its sparks like stars.
Rains do not extinguish it
Rivers are unable to flood it.[108]
Rocks are molted by its fire[109]
Boulders melt from its flame.[110]
I envisioned it
Staring into its likeness.
My hands were weak
My knees trembled.[111]
My eyes smoked over from fear[112]
I fell onto my face.[113]
I was unable to stand
My whole being was stricken with terror.[114]
He came to me
Set me upon my feet.[115]
He said, "Do not be afraid,
do not lose heart.[116]
When you walk through fire, you will not be burned
Though a flame, it will not burn you."[117]
He passed before me and said
"Come in, O blessed of the Lord."[118]
He took me swiftly from there
Moving me into the flame.

I saw the fires touch in front of him
The sparks surrounding him burned.
The flashes encircled us
Although surrounded
We were not consumed.
And when we came out from those areas
We survived their heat.
I saw next to the city
Eight kingdoms.
They had spheres
Enormous and large.
Forceful and strong
Like a mirror of cast metal.[119]
One by one their gardens drew near
Not even a breath could enter them.[120]
One is linked to the other
They are united and do not come apart.
Their customs neither vanish nor change
Their hosts are neither numbered nor countable.
All of them sing praise
In unison they lavish acclaim.[121]
They always stand still
Constantly worshipping their Maker.[122]
They preserve their regular course[123]
Holding fast to their covenant.[124]
Harm does not befall them
Disease does not touch their tents.[125]
Their motion is that of those who strive
Their worship[126] that of those who yearn.
Their forms crave
Their souls[127] desire.
Upon them a light shines forth[128]
From the pure abode.[129]
A garden spring
A well of fresh water.[130]
In the first kingdom there are many men
Saintly, pure and fresh, clean.
Their bodies are young and small
Their faces pure and white.
Running they do not grow tired
Walking they do not become weary.
Their officer is second to the king

From the aura of his glory, he derives benefit.
He is afraid of his anger
Fearful of [the king's] terror.
If he approaches he is overpowered
From his light, he is held back.
His body is jailed
His vision is beyond us.
If he strays away he radiates
Like a lightning bolt he shines.
His form is full
To every eye he is perceptible and revealed.
In the second kingdom there are men noble
Wise and illustrious.
Wise and loyal in their worship[131]
Swift workers in their craft.
Writers of epistles
Those who engage in contemplation.[132]
Mixers of spices[133]
Those who persuade by elaboration.[134]
Among them people
Who are miracle workers and magicians.
Heroes, ministers, lieutenants
Governors, officers, barons.
They advise
They advocate.
They admonish
With the appropriate words.
Each one in his craft is master and father
Like Bezalel and Oholiab.[135]
Above them is a ruler
Swift like a gazelle, he does not stumble.
The scribe of the king and his servant
Who knows when he comes, whence he goes
Whither he travels and when he encamps.
From his presence he does not emerge
From his vision he does not depart.
In the third kingdom there are pleasant women
Singing and playing.
They play lutes and flutes
They sing songs.[136]
They are drummers and dancers
Playing cymbals and harps.

Leaping and whirling[137]
They dance and sing.
Above them a queen
Delightful and tender.
Her face like the sun when it rises[138]
Like the moon in its fullness.
Her eyes are like swords
Her teeth like a flock of sheep.[139]
They are all equal
Perfect and none are missing.
Her lips are like a crimson thread[140]
Her locks like the color of a raven.[141]
Through her veil[142]
Her brow gleams like a slice of pomegranate.[143]
Her navel is like a round goblet[144]
She is the form of the sun.
Her light shines, creating a shadow
The one who sees her is astounded and frightened.
In the fourth kingdom there are strong men
The mighty ones
Upon everything they shed light.
Among them the king wanders
With his deputy he consults.
From his own glory he clothes him
Wrapping him with his light.
He is like a groom coming from his chamber[145]
Like a hero eager to run[146] his course.
Nothing is hidden from his brightness
Nothing escapes his heat.[147]
A man is unable to look straight at him
One cannot recognize his face.
Like a shepherd he pastures his flock[148]
From the path he never strays.[149]
By wisdom he guides them
With reason he leads them.
In the fifth kingdom there are red men
Spillers of blood.[150]
Destroyers
Hypocrites.
Robbers
Plotters.
Battle is their craft

War their art.
They take bribes
And murder souls.
They throw down the dead
Consuming the plunder.
They are lovers of wickedness and deceit
Haters of knowledge and counsel.[151]
Their ruler is a man of war
His temper hot.
Polishing his swords
Gnawing his teeth.
His spears are ready, his lances prepared
His arrows sharpened, his bows drawn.[152]
His horses' hoofs are like flint
His chariot wheels swift like the whirlwind.[153]
He kills the innocent
Robs the poor.
Wickedness is his work
Misery his toil.
He does not shy away from deceit
Nor does he refrain from trickery.
In the sixth kingdom are righteous men
Adhering to purity.
Their paths clear
Their deeds just.
They wash their hands of bribery[154]
Looking upon evil their eyes are shut.[155]
They practice righteousness
Despising profit.[156]
They dwell in tents[157]
They are teachers and judges.
Magistrates and officials
Judges and companions.
Prophets
Princes.
Priests
Academy heads.
Above them is a commander
Righteous and pious.
He judges his nations truthfully
Treating his friends justly.
Corruption and villainy are not found in him

His royal sceptre is a sceptre of equity.[158]
In the seventh kingdom reside the masters of
prudence and counsel
Understanding and craftiness.
Cautious in their deeds
Tarrying as they walk.
They protect and preserve loving-kindness
They avenge and guard against sin.
Unafraid of misfortune
From anger they do not turn back.
Yet slow to strife and contention[159]
They refuse easy reconciliation or appeasement.
Among their number is a righteous one,
broken and crushed
Also an evil one, wicked and boastful.[160]
Magnate and counselor, captain of fifty
Skilled artisan and expert enchanter.[161]
Butcher, baker
Healer and doctor.
Trader, shopkeeper
Painter and money-changer.
A truthful one and a deceiver
A generous person and a miser.
Lord to those below him
Tyrant over them.
A man strong in his wisdom
Singular in intelligence.
Above him is glory
Pomp and magnificence.[162]
He boasts of his understanding
Adorns himself with the crow of wisdom.
In the eighth kingdom are peoples
Nations
Great and mighty.
Innumerable and uncountable
Save to He who created and fashioned them.
In the midst of these soldiers
There stand twelve towers.
In them they dwell
These abodes they call home.
To one side they walk
To one corner they are dragged.

Those at the end
Unable to overtake those at the beginning.
These travel and the others stop behind them.
Their faces shine
The gleam of amber.[163]
They are seen to collapse
Like swords they shine.[164]
After these kingdoms there is a boundary
Its foundation unformed and void.[165]
Long and wide its land
Like the desert and barren prairie.[166]
Empty of inhabitant or dweller
In it neither occupant nor resident.
Its circumference is immeasurable
The size of its stature unknown.[167]
Everything within is structured
Arranged and perfect.
From an abundance of strength it subdues the others
By the greatness of its power it drives them.
From it derive appointed times, seasons, time
Divisions, hours, days, years.
It happened that when we came to its borders
We approached to cross it.
I saw wonderful forms
Awesome visions.[168]
Angels stood guard
They were mighty ones.
Cherubim
Enormous and many.
Seraphim standing
Praising and announcing His unity.
Angels and ofanim[169]
Lauding and singing.
Souls
Consecrating.
Spirits
Glorifying.[170]
I was afraid and said
"How awesome is this place that I see."[171]
He replied: "From your feet
Remove the sandals.[172]
From the matter of your corpse

Lift your soul.
Forsake your thoughts
Relax your eyelids!
See by the eyes of your interior
The pupils of your heart."
I said to him, "Can I see everything with my eyes?
Is there anything I cannot perceive with my pupils?"
He replied, "He is one, none is second to Him
He has neither son nor brother.[173]
Places are unable to contain Him[174]
Time cannot predate Him.
Hearts grow weary from enumerating His greatness
Tongues rejoice in recounting His praise.
He has glory and magnificence
Eternity and glory.
Strength
Splendor.
Kingship
Greatness.[175]
There is no God save Him
No Creator except Him.[176]
There is no limit to His knowledge
No bound to His wisdom.
His possessions cannot be enumerated
His contents cannot be known.
From an abundance of greatness
His knowledge is hidden from men.
From the greatness of His appearance
Seeing Him is prevented.
Since the sun is hidden by its light
We cannot know it.
When it rises at dawn
We barely visualize it.
In this way souls are unable to know Him
Hearts unable to perceive Him.
He has neither shape nor likeness[177]
He has no image[178] by which one can compare Him.
The fountain of wisdom and its source
He is the abode of reason and its foundation.
He knows the concealed as if revealed[179]
The hidden as if visible.
He searches hearts

Probes minds.[180]
Righteousness and justice[181] are His laws
Loving-kindness and truth[182] His disposition.
Equity is His path
Righteousness His deeds.
There is no perfection outside of His perfection
No dignity without His dignity
No peace save His peace."
I said, "Please, my Lord, listen to my plea for mercy[183]
To you I turn my eyes.[184]
Upon you I cast my troubles
To your hand I entrust my spirit.[185]
Tell me with what shall I approach Him?[186]
How shall I know Him?
I have truly longed to know Him[187]
I yearn to see Him."
He replied, "Uphold my words
Keep my teaching.
Walk in my path, and do not depart from me.
You will know your spirit
As is fitting to your ability and your strength.
Then you will be able to know Him
To apprehend Him."
I said to him
"May you be forever blessed.[188]
You have brought me thus far[189]
To enter and come out again in peace.[190]
Happy are you
And happy are your friends.
Those who uphold your religion
And pay heed to your wise words.
Praised be the Lord your God
Who made you governor of His World
Who put you in charge of His people.
He who brought me to you.
Who made me listen to your words.
He is above all majesty and greatness
Exalted above every blessing and praise.[191]
He alone does great things
His steadfast love is eternal."[192]

Notes

Introduction

Citations of sources are abbreviated, giving only the author's surname and the main title of the work. For full facts of publication of primary and secondary sources, please refer to the bibliography.

1. When dealing with all three narratives together I refer to them by the Arabic *Ḥayy ibn Yaqẓān* even though ibn Ezra translated his version literally into Hebrew as *Ḥay ben Meqitz*. When I refer to ibn Ezra's treatise alone I use his Hebrew designation.

2. A fourth is by the Persian philosopher Suhrawardī (d. ca. 1191). Although Suhrawardī is clearly an important Islamic philosopher, I have chosen not to discuss him at any length. He did, nevertheless, compose a very short treatise (three pages) by the name of *Ḥayy ibn Yaqẓān*. Even though this text is certainly worth scholarly attention, I have decided to remain in the western Islamicate world (viz., al-Andalus or Muslim Spain), thereby confining my analysis to ibn Ezra's and ibn Ṭufayl's narratives and their various points of contact with the work of Avicenna. I have, however, discussed Suhrawardī's use of this genre elsewhere. See my "Reading Islamic Philosophy." Also see the review article of Landolt, "Suhrawardī's 'Tales of Initiation.'"

3. For the Arabic texts, I have used Amīn, ed., *Ḥayy ibn Yaqẓān li ibn Sīnā wa ibn Ṭufayl wa al-Suhrawardī*. In addition, I have consulted the English translation of Avicenna's *Ḥayy ibn Yaqẓān* found in Corbin, *Avicenna and the Visionary Recital*, pp. 137–150. For an excellent English translation of ibn Ṭufayl's text, see Goodman, *Ibn Tufayl's Hayy ibn Yaqzan: A Philosophical Tale*. For the most part, I use Goodman's translation, but modify it accordingly and supply the requisite Arabic terms.

4. Abraham ibn Ezra, *Ḥay ben Meqitz*. I have provided a full English translation of this work in the appendix.

5. Synopses of these three texts, along with biographies of their authors, may be found in chapter 1 below.

6. In using the term "Islamicate," I follow the lead of the great historian of Islam, Marshall Hodgson. He writes that this term refers "not directly to the religion, Islam, itself, but to the social and cultural complex historically associated with Islam and the Muslims, both among Muslims themselves and even when found among non-Muslims." See Hodgson, *The Venture of Islam*, vol. 1,

p. 59. In this manner, although ibn Ezra was certainly not an "Islamic" philosopher, we could refer to him as an "Islamicate" philosopher. Even though he was deeply committed to Judaism, Jewish values, and Jewish sources, he nevertheless expressed himself in terms of the vocabulary and categories of Arabo-Islamic civilization. In what follows I tend to use "Islamic and Jewish" philosophy and "Islamicate" philosophy interchangeably.

7. Ibn Ṭufayl, *Ḥayy ibn Yaqẓān,* p. 89 (Goodman, p. 131).

8. Faur, *Homo Mysticus,* p. 62. He subsequently claims matter-of-factly: "Imagination is the source of pagan civilization" (p. 66).

9. E.g., *Republic* 476, 479; *Symposium* 210b–211e; *Phaedo* 65, 75d, 78de; *Phaedrus* 249c–250b.

10. See the discussion in Corbin, *Le Paradoxe du monotheisme.*

11. Hughes, "Imagining the Divine," pp. 33–36.

12. E.g., Seeskin, *Searching for a Distant God,* esp. pp. 23–39.

13. E.g., Auerbach, "Odysseus's Scar," in *Mimesis,* pp. 3–23; Ong, *The Presence of the Word,* pp. 2ff.

14. This has been well documented in the history of Judaism in Bland, *The Artless Jew,* pp. 13–36.

15. Wolfson, *Through a Speculum that Shines,* pp. 60–61.

16. In many ways this is related to the "perennial philosophy" school of mysticism that states all experiences, regardless of the religious tradition, are the same. The only difference, then, is in how the individual translates the experience. See, e.g., Huxley, *The Perennial Philosophy;* Schuon, *Islam and Perennial Philosophy.* For a harsh indictment of this approach, see Zaehner, *Mysticism Sacred and Profane,* pp. 198ff. My own take on this resembles the work of Stephen Katz, who argues that there cannot be a pure, unmediated experience because the individual always brings a "pre-mystical consciousness" to it. See Katz, "Language, Epistemology, and Mysticism." For an excellent overview of the various debates with the academic study of mysticism, see McGinn, *The Foundations of Mysticism,* pp. 265–343.

17. For the basic details of this, see Watt, *A History of Islamic Spain,* pp. 13–26. For a much more complete picture, however, see Collins, *The Arab Conquest of Spain;* Simón, "The Itinerary of the Muslim Conquest of al-Andalus in the Light of a New Source," pp. 1–12.

18. Chejne, *Muslim Spain,* pp. 31–38. For a detailed account of Abd al-Raḥman's political strategy, see Kennedy, *Muslim Spain: A Political History of al-Andalus,* pp. 83–99.

19. Chejne, *Muslim Spain,* p. 35; on Abd al-Raḥman's contribution to the development of the arts and sciences in al-Andalus, see Imamuddin, *Muslim Spain, 711–1492 A.D.,* pp. 137–145, 163–185.

20. This resulted in the period known as the *mulūk al-ṭawāʾif* ("the party-kings"); cf. Chejne, *Muslim Spain,* pp. 50–68; Kennedy, *Muslim Spain: A Political History of al-Andalus,* pp. 124–153.

21. Hodgson, *The Venture of Islam,* vol. 1, p. 309. The best history of this period is Solomon Katz, *The Jews in the Visigothic and Frankish Kingdoms of Spain and Gaul.* The Jews of Spain supposedly welcomed the Muslim armies with open arms. Indeed, there exist many legends to the effect that the Jews even helped the invading armies against their Christian oppressors. See Ashtor, *The Jews of Moslem Spain,* vol. 1, pp. 15–22; Wasserstein, "The Muslims and the Golden Age of the Jews in al-Andalus," pp. 179–181.

22. Bonebakker, "Adab and the Concept of Belles-Lettres," p. 24. Also, see Franz Rosenthal, *Knowledge Triumphant,* pp. 12–18, 35–40.

23. Kraemer, *Humanism and the Renaissance of Islam,* pp. 1–30.

24. Brann, *The Compunctious Poet,* pp. 23ff.

25. Scheindlin, *Wine, Women, and Death,* p. 5. Brann calls Jewish Andalusi society "an adaptive subculture." See his *Compunctious Poet,* p. 24. Although marginal, the Jews within the orbit of Islam fared much better, both legally and culturally, than they did in Christian Europe. For an excellent comparison, see Cohen, *Under Crescent and Cross.*

26. Cf. Berlin, *Biblical Poetry through Medieval Jewish Eyes,* pp. 16–29.

27. Brann, *The Compunctious Poet,* p. 14.

28. Pagis, "The Poet as Prophet in Medieval Hebrew Literature," p. 141.

29. Tanenbaum, *The Contemplative Soul.*

30. In asking these questions, I am influenced by the discussion found in Brann, "The Arabized Jews," pp. 438–439.

31. This is the approach, e.g., of Halkin, "Judeo-Arabic Literature," pp. 121–154.

32. E.g., Ratzaby, "Arabic Poetry Written by Andalusian Jews," pp. 329–350.

33. See, e.g., Brann, *The Compunctious Poet,* pp. 23ff.

34. Brann, "Power in the Portrayal," pp. 1–22. For an extended study of the trope of "representation," see his *Power in the Portrayal.*

35. Gerber, *The Jews of Muslim Spain,* p. 80.

36. Some, however, fled to North Africa; the most famous example of this is the Maimon family, which settled in Fez.

1. Reading the Divine

1. Ibn Ezra's reliance on Avicenna has been intimated at by many scholars, although due to the nature of ibn Ezra's exposition, this relationship is notoriously difficult to map with any certainty. See, e.g., Harvey, "The First Commandment and the God of History," p. 208; Ravitzky, "The Anthropological Doctrine of Miracles in Medieval Jewish Philosophy," pp. 32ff.; Idel, "Hitbodedut as Concentration in Jewish Philosophy," esp. p. 44.

2. See Conrad, "Introduction," in Conrad, ed., *The World of ibn Ṭufayl,* pp. 6–7.

3. E.g., Smith, "In Comparison a Magic Dwells," in his *Imagining Religion,* pp. 20–22.

4. Smith, *Drudgery Divine,* pp. 43–51.

5. See my comments in chapter 2.

6. Hadot, *Philosophy as a Way of Life;* for the Islamicate context, see the brief comments in Hamīd, "The Philosophical Significance of Ibn Ṭufail's *Ḥaiy Ibn Yaqẓān,*" p. 66.

7. Pococke gave the treatise the following rather cumbersome title: *Philosophus autodidactus, sive epistola Abi Jaafar, Ebn Tophail de Hai Ebn Yokdhan. In qua Ostenditur, quomodo ex Inferiorum contemplatione ad Superioirum notiam Ratio humana ascendere possit.* On the popularity and influence of this translation on late seventeenth- and eighteenth-century literature, see Kruk, "An Eighteenth-Century Descendant of Ḥayy Ibn Yaqẓān and Robinson Crusoe."

8. E.g., Goodman, *Ibn Tufayl's Hayy ibn Yaqzan: A Philosophical Tale.*

9. Hawi, *Islamic Naturalism and Mysticism.*

10. E.g., Gauthier, ed., *Hayy ben Yaqdhān, roman philosophique d'Ibn Thofail;* Bürgel, "Symbols and Hints."

11. Corbin, *Avicenna and the Visionary Recital.*

12. E.g., Gutas, *Avicenna and the Aristotelian Tradition,* pp. 299–307; Walbridge, *The Leaven of the Ancients,* pp. 97–105.

13. See, in particular, her collection of essays in *Love's Knowledge.* And, of course, the genre of the initiatory tale is by no means unique to Islamicate civilization. Famous examples from late antiquity include Apuleius's *Golden Ass* (2nd century C.E.). On the role of the novel in this period, see Holzberg, *The Ancient Novel;* Sandy, *The Greek World of Apuleius;* Schmeling, ed., *The Novel in the Ancient World.*

14. Nussbaum, "Transcending Humanity," in *Love's Knowledge,* p. 385.

15. See the discussion in Lakoff and Johnson, *Philosophy in the Flesh,* pp. 4–5.

16. Nussbaum, "Transcending Humanity," in *Love's Knowledge,* p. 385. In this context, she cites Plato, who claims that the gods do not need to engage in philosophy because they are already wise (*Symposium* 204a).

17. On the seductive power of philosophy, see Nussbaum, "Reading for Life," in *Love's Knowledge,* p. 238.

18. See the comments in Bürgel, "Symbols and Hints," pp. 114–132.

19. Here I follow Bürgel, who refers to these tales as "initiational." Significantly, he begins his discussion by referring to them as "philosophical novels" (p. 132), but he ultimately changes his mind.

20. Initiation, as I will show below, was an important aspect of medieval Islamicate thought. There is no evidence, however, that the readers or potential readers of these texts underwent a literal, physical initiation. Accordingly, I prefer to think of these narratives as symbolic initiations involving the transferal of intellectual gnosis or secrets.

21. This tripartite structure is the subject matter of chapter 4 below.

22. Cf. Lane. *An Arabic-English Lexicon,* vol. 7, p. 2528.

23. Lane, *An Arabic-English Lexicon,* vol. 3, p. 1084.

24. The Arabic text with facing English translation may be found in Gohlman, *The Life of Ibn Sīnā.* My goal in the next few paragraphs is only to give the briefest outline of Avicenna's life, since, of the three thinkers who are the subject of this study, we know the most about his life and career. I attempt to provide fuller biographies of ibn Ezra and ibn Ṭufayl. There exist many excellent biographies of Avicenna: Afnan, *Avicenna: His Life and Works;* Nasr, *Three Muslim Sages: Avicenna, Suhrawardī, Ibn ᶜArabī;* Goodman, *Avicenna,* pp. 1–48.

25. Gohlman, *The Life of ibn Sīnā,* p. 37.

26. See, e.g., Siraisi, *Avicenna in Renaissance Italy.*

27. Avicenna, *Ḥayy ibn Yaqẓān,* p. 40 (Corbin, p. 137).

28. On the importance of the term *rūḥāniyya* in medieval Islamicate thought, especially its relationship to theurgy and the occult sciences, see Pines, "On the Term *Ruḥaniyyot* and Its Origin and on Judah Halevi's Doctrine."

29. Avicenna, *Ḥayy ibn Yaqẓān,* p. 45 (Corbin, p. 145).

30. Ibn Ẓaddik and ibn Ezra not only knew each other personally, but also corresponded and sent each other poems. See Levin, *Abraham ibn Ezra: His Life and Poetry,* p. 14.

31. According to some legends, Abraham ibn Ezra married Judah Halevi's daughter. For this and other legends, see Alexander, "Hagiography and Biography," pp. 11–16. Also, Fleischer, "Judah Halevi: Remarks Concerning His Life and Poetical Oeuvre," pp. 264–270. It is, however, likely that Judah Halevi left Spain in 1140 with ibn Ezra's son, Isaac. On this, see al-Ḥarizi, *Taḥkemoni,* p. 45. Isaac, incidentally, became a student of the famed Abū al-Barakāt in Baghdad and, like his master, converted to Islam. It appears, however, that he later returned to the fold of Judaism. See Joseph Yahalom, "Judah Halevi: Records of a Visitor from Spain," pp. 133–134. Such public, high-profile "conversions," however, are surely worthy of further study.

32. See his *Sefer ha-Qabbalah,* Hebrew section p. 73.

33. See Moses ibn Ezra's comments about Abraham ibn Ezra in *Kitāb al-muḥāḍara wa al-mudhākara,* p. 78.

34. See the discussion in Greive, *Studien zum jüdischen Neuplatonismus,* pp. 35ff.; Bacher, *Abraham Ibn Esra als Grammatiker,* pp. 1–30. An attempt to piece together some of the fragments of the early part of ibn Ezra's life, with varying degrees of success, may be found in Silver, "New Light on Abraham Ibn Ezra [*sic*] Early Life from [*sic*] Analysis of His Exegesis and Other Prose Works," in Esteban, ed., *Abraham Ibn Ezra y Su Tiempo,* pp. 317–324.

35. Levin, *Abraham ibn Ezra,* p. 15. Although it is difficult to ascertain when ibn Ezra composed this treatise, it seems probable that he did so some time before 1160, the year in which he mostly likely left Spain for Western Europe.

36. For the controversy surrounding this date, see Fleischer, "When did R. Abraham Ibn Ezra leave Spain?"

37. Significantly, 1146–1147 was the time of the second Crusade in Europe.

38. He wrote commentaries to the Torah, Isaiah, the Twelve Minor Prophets, Psalms, Job, the Five Megillot, and Daniel. In addition, in a variety of places ibn Ezra tells us that he also wrote commentaries (which we do not now possess) to Joshua, Judges, Samuel, Jeremiah, Ezekiel, Proverbs, Ezra, and Nehemiah.

39. For his method of interpretation, see his introduction to the *Commentary to the Torah,* ed. Weiser, pp. 1–10. Also, see the comments in Sarna, "Abraham Ibn Ezra as an Exegete," in Twersky and Harris, eds., *Rabbi Abraham ibn Ezra,* pp. 1–27; and now Lancaster, *Deconstructing the Bible.*

40. See the list in Levy's introduction to Abraham ibn Ezra, *The Beginning of Wisdom,* pp. 14–15.

41. I disagree with this traditional claim, and will argue that we need to see his *Yesod Mora* and *Ḥay ben Meqitz* as philosophical treatises. True, these are not distinctly analytical treatises, but they are philosophical writings that were common to the school of Neoplatonism.

42. The most extreme example of this may be found in Graetz, *History of the Jews,* vol. 3, pp. 366ff. For a less extreme view, but one that nonetheless still adopts the same premise, see Guttmann, *Philosophies of Judaism,* p. 134; Husik, *A History of Medieval Jewish Philosophy,* pp. 187ff.

43. E.g., al-Qayrawānī, *Al-ᶜUmda fī mahāsin al-shiᶜr,* vol. 2, p. 280; Moses ibn Ezra, *Kitāb al-muḥāḍara wa al-mudhākara,* p. 174. See, in this regard, the discussion in Dana, *Poetics of Medieval Hebrew Literature according to Moses ibn Ezra,* pp. 18–37.

44. Conrad, "Introduction," in Conrad, ed., *The World of Ibn Ṭufayl,* pp. 5–6.

45. de Vaux, "Ibn Ṭufail," p. 957. On the importance of Ceuta, see Cornell, "The Way of the Axial Intellect."

46. Al-Marrākushī, *Al-Mu^{c}jib fī talkhīṣ akhbār al-maghrib,* pp. 174–175.

47. Al-Andalusī, *Al-Mughrib fī ḥulā al-maghrib,* vol. 2, p. 85.

48. Ibn al-Abbār, *Al-Muqtadab min kitāb tuḥfat al-qadīm,* p. 72.

49. Ibn Ṭufayl, *Ḥayy ibn Yaqẓān,* pp. 55–56 (Goodman, p. 99).

50. See the discussion in Conrad, "Introduction," in Conrad, ed., *The World of Ibn Ṭufayl,* pp. 9ff.

51. Conrad, "Introduction," in Conrad, ed., *The World of Ibn Ṭufayl,* pp. 12–13.

52. Cornell, "Ḥayy in the Land of Absāl," p. 163.

53. Cornell, "Ḥayy in the Land of Absāl," pp. 135–136.

54. For an important though understudied attempt to make sense of ibn Ṭufayl's narrative within a Jewish context, see the commentary of Moses Narboni (d. ca. 1362), which currently exists only in manuscript.

55. See, e.g., the collection of essays in Athanassiadi and Frede, eds., *Pagan Monotheism in Late Antiquity;* Valantasis, ed., *Religions of Late Antiquity in Practice.* In like manner, Avicenna's other initiatory tale, *The Story of Salāmān and Absāl,* had its origin in Hellenistic literature and was subsequently translated into Arabic by Ḥunayn ibn Isḥāq (d. 873). See, e.g., the comments in Corbin, *Avicenna and the Visionary Recital,* p. 294. Also, much of the Gnostic literature deals in a narrative format with the problem of the soul in this world and its fate after death. Probably one of the best examples of this is *The Hymn of the Pearl,* translated in Layton, ed. and trans., *The Gnostic Scriptures,* pp. 366–375. Corbin identifies this relationship, but he draws a far too explicit connection between Avicenna and the Gnostics. For Corbin, they both share the same archetypal gnostic worldview; in addition, he hints at some form of "causal historical filiation," or, at least, "we see arising between them the continuity of 'hierophanic time.'" See Corbin, *Avicenna and the Visionary Recital,* p. 17. It is, of course, virtually impossible to draw a direct line between the Islamicate initiatory tales and their precursors from late antiquity.

56. Pines, "On the term *Ruḥaniyyot* and Its Origin and on Judah Halevi's Doctrine," p. 534.

57. My goal here is not to ascertain the historical connections between this Ismā^{c}īlī literature and the *Ḥayy ibn Yaqẓān* cycle; rather, it is to bring out certain phenomenological comparisons. Others (cf. n. 79) have already shown how Islamic and Jewish thinkers used Ismā^{c}īlī terminology. Within this context, it is worth restating H. A. Wolfson's comments that often "concepts ride on the back of terms." See the comments in Lobel, *Between Mysticism and Philosophy,* p. 6. This section owes much to the helpful comments of Steven M. Wasserstrom.

58. For general background and historical trends, see Stern, *Studies in Early Ismā^{c}īlism;* Daftary, *The Ismā^{c}īlīs: Their History and Doctrines.*

59. On Ismā^{c}īlī cosmology, see Halm, "The Cosmology of the pre-Fatimid Ismā^{c}īliyya."

60. See Stern, "The 'Book of the Highest Initiation' and Other Anti-Ismā^{c}īlī Travesties," in his *Studies in Early Ismā^{c}īlism,* pp. 56–83.

61. Halm, "The Isma^{c}ili Oath of Allegiance (*^{c}ahd*) and the 'Sessions of Wisdom' (*majālis al-ḥikma*) in Fatimid Times."

62. For a dissenting opinion, see Netton, *Muslim Neoplatonists,* pp. 95–104.

63. Netton, *Muslim Neoplatonists,* p. 3; Nasr, *An Introduction to Islamic Cosmological Doctrines,* p. 30.

64. *Rasāʾil Ikhwān al-Ṣafāʾ*, vol. 4, p. 168.

65. Netton, *Muslim Neoplatonists,* p. 3.

66. *Rasāʾil,* vol. 4, pp. 411–412. Quoted in Netton, *Muslim Neoplatonists,* p. 6.

67. See the discussion in Halm, "The Ismaʿili Oath of Allegiance," pp. 94–104.

68. Ikhwān al-Ṣafāʾ, *Rasāʾil Ikhwān al-Ṣafāʾ*, epistle 21. There is an English translation entitled *The Case of the Animals Versus the Men before the King of the Jinn: A Tenth-Century Ecological Parable by the Pure Brethren of Basra,* trans. Lenn E. Goodman. Also, see the medieval Hebrew translation of this work by Qalonymos ben Qalonymos, *Iggeret baʿalei ha-Ḥayyim.*

69. The form of this dialogue was, in turn, appropriated into Judaism by Yehudah ben Nissim ibn Malka in his *Uns al-gharib,* in ibn Malka, *The Hebrew Version of K. Uns al-gharib and the Commentary to the Sefer Yetsirah by Rabbi Yehudah ben Nisim ibn Malka.* On the influence of the Ismāʿīlīs on his thought, see Vajda, *Juda ben Nissim ibn Malka,* esp. pp. 5ff.; Wasserstrom, *Between Muslim and Jew,* p. 131.

70. Al-Yaman, *The Master and the Disciple,* pp. 92–93.

71. *The Master and the Disciple,* pp. 94–95.

72. *The Master and the Disciple,* p. 79.

73. See the remarks in Pouzet, "Remarques sur l'autobiographie dans le monde arabo-musulman au Moyen-Āge." It is probably no coincidence that the two most famous autobiographies of medieval Islam—those of Avicenna and Ghazali—were written in environments that were heavily influenced by Ismāʿīlism.

74. Naṣīr al-Dīn al-Ṭūsī, *Contemplation and Action,* p. 30.

75. E.g., al-Ṭūsī, p. 44.

76. This was also a genre that Islamicate civilization inherited from the world of late antiquity. See the discussion in Grignaschi, "Le Roman épistolaire classique conservé dans la version arabe de Sālim Abū al-ʿAlā."

77. Both of these thinkers also, and probably not coincidentally, share the theme of the *philosophus autodidactus.* Whereas for ibn Ṭufayl this is expressed through the character of Ḥayy ibn Yaqẓān, for Maimonides it is the patriarch Abraham. See, in this context, Jones, "From Abraham to Andrenio."

78. Maimonides, *Guide of the Perplexed,* vol. 1, pp. 3–4.

79. Although there do exist several Ismāʿīlī elements in the thought of Maimonides. See, e.g., Ivry, "Neoplatonic Currents in Maimonides' Thought."

80. The best known examples are ʿAttar's *Conference of the Birds* and Rūmī's *Māthnawī.*

81. Stroumsa, "Avicenna's Philosophical Stories," p. 186. One possible exception is the Tabula of Cebes, a first-century C.E. allegory that was rendered into Arabic by an unknown translator around the tenth century. Cf. Rosenthal, "The Symbolism of the Tabula Cebitis according to Abū l-Faraj Ibn al-Tayyib." Concerning the foreign influences on Avicenna, see Pines, "The Origin of the Tale of Salāmān and Absāl."

82. Not without significance, these are also the names of the two individuals who, in ibn Ṭufayl's tale, occupy the neighboring island to Ḥayy ibn Yaqẓān.

83. See the comments in Corbin, *Avicenna and the Visionary Recital,* pp. 204–207. An English translation of this text may be found in the same volume, pp. 224–226.

84. Cf. ibn Ṭufayl, *Ḥayy ibn Yaqẓān,* p. 66 (Goodman, p. 109).

85. An English translation may be found in Corbin, *Avicenna and the Visionary Recital,* pp. 186–192.

86. Ivry, "The Utilization of Allegory in Islamic Philosophy," p. 164.

87. Corbin, *Avicenna and the Visionary Recital,* p. 187.

88. See the remarks in Stroumsa, "Avicenna's Philosophical Stories," pp. 188–189.

89. Corbin has translated al-Jūzjānī's Persian commentary into English in *Avicenna and the Visionary Recital,* pp. 282–380.

90. In this regard, see Iser, "The Reading Process: A Phenomenological Approach," pp. 50–69.

91. Quoted, with modification, in Gutas, *Avicenna and the Aristotelian Tradition,* pp. 52–53.

92. Quoted, with modification, in Gutas, *Avicenna and the Aristotelian Tradition,* p. 45.

93. Cf. the critical comments in Gutas, *Avicenna and the Aristotelian Tradition,* p. 130, n. 28.

94. Ibn Ṭufayl, *Ḥayy ibn Yaqẓān,* p. 52 (Goodman, p. 95); cf. pp. 57–58 (Goodman, pp. 100–101).

95. For a criticism of this strategy, see the comments in Gutas, "Ibn Ṭufayl on Ibn Sīnā's Eastern Philosophy."

96. See my "Reading Islamic Philosophy," pp. 19–20.

97. See the comments in Izutsu, "Ishrāqīyah," pp. 296–301.

98. See Adams, "The Hermeneutics of Henry Corbin," p. 143.

99. Corbin, *En Islam iranien,* vol. 1, p. xxvii. Significantly, by "practitioner" Corbin does not mean the average Muslim, but the great mystics and philosophers of (predominantly Iranian) Islam.

100. "Le phénoménologue herméneute doit toujours être là (*da-sein*), parce qu'il n'y a jamais rien pour lui de passé ou de dépasse. C'est en faisant lui-même acte de présence, qu'il fait se manifester ce qui est occulté sous le phénomène apparent." See Corbin, "De Heidegger à Sohravardi," p. 26. Some of Corbin's students, most notably Seyyed Hossein Nasr, seem to replace the Heideggerian concept of being for the more obscure *sophia perennis.* See, e.g., his *Introduction to Islamic Cosmological Doctrines,* pp. 32ff.

101. Landolt, "Henry Corbin," p. 484. Landolt's article is one of the few essays devoted to Corbin that stresses his relationship with Heidegger. The article by Adams (above n. 98), while stressing Corbin's phenomenology, makes no mention of Heidegger. This is unfortunate as it leads to a fundamental misunderstanding of Corbin's larger philosophical agenda.

102. Writing of Suhrawardi, he claims: "Simplement il *est là:* il fait acte de présence. La passé du vieil Iran zoroastrien, il le prend en charge, il le met ainsi au présent." See Corbin, "De Heidegger à Sohravardi," p. 29 (his italics). See the important study of Wasserstrom, *Religion after Religion,* pp. 148ff.

103. Corbin, *The Concept of Comparative Philosophy,* p. 3. Also, see Landolt, "Henry Corbin," p. 484.

104. See Wasserstrom, *Religion after Religion,* pp. 29–30.

105. Landolt, "Henry Corbin," p. 486.

106. Corbin, *The Concept of Comparative Philosophy,* pp. 13–15; idem, *Mundus Imaginalis,* pp. 8–9.

107. Corbin often talks about two distinct modes of cognition: "il y a une connaissance formelle (^{c}*ilm sūrī*) qui est la connaissance de forme courante; elle se produit par l'intermédiare d'une *re-présentation*, d'une *species*, actualisée dans l'âme. Et il y a une connaissance qu'ils désignent comme connaissance présentielle (^{c}*ilm hozūrī*) laquelle ne passe pas par l'intermédiare d'une re*présentation*, d'une *species*, mais est présence immédiate, celle par laquelle l'acte de présence de l'âme suscite elle-même la présence des choses et se rend présentes à elles-même, non plus des objets, mais des présences." Corbin, "De Heidegger à Sohravardi," p. 31 (his italics).

108. Corbin, *Avicenna and the Visionary Recital*, p. 4.

109. Gutas, *Avicenna and the Aristotelian Tradition*, p. 127.

110. Shlomo Pines, "'Philosophie Orientale' d'Avicenne et sa polémique contre les Bagdadiens."

111. Gutas, *Avicenna and the Aristotelian Tradition*, p. 3.

112. Gutas, *Avicenna and the Aristotelian Tradition*, p. 306.

113. Gutas, *Avicenna and the Aristotelian Tradition*, p. 306. Also, see the comments in Saliba, "Philosophical Symbolism and the Use of Myth among Arab Philosophers."

114. Gutas, *Avicenna and the Aristotelian Tradition*, p. 302.

115. Gutas, "Avicenna V: Mysticism," p. 80 (my italics).

116. For a sustained critique, see Marmura, "Plotting the Course of Avicenna's Thought."

117. See, in particular, my discussion in chapter 3 below.

118. Frye, "Allegory," p. 12.

119. E.g., Whitman, *Allegory*, pp. 1ff.; Clifford, *The Transformations of Allegory*, pp. 3ff.

120. Greenblatt, "Preface," in Greenblatt, ed., *Allegory and Representation*, p. vii.

121. Whitman, p. 13.

122. The classic study of this remains Strauss, *Persecution and the Art of Writing*, pp. 22–37.

123. See the comments in Fineman, "The Structure of Allegorical Desire," in Greenblatt, ed., *Allegory and Representation*, pp. 26–60.

124. Heath, *Allegory and Philosophy in Avicenna*, p. 194.

125. See the discussion in Lamberton, *Homer the Theologian*, p. 186.

126. Nussbaum, "Transcending Humanity," in *Love's Knowledge*, pp. 385ff.

127. See the discussion, and subsequent attempts to rehabilitate the genre of allegory, in Honig, *Dark Conceit*, esp. pp. 39–54.

128. Heath, *Allegory and Philosophy in Avicenna*, p. 3. This paragraph relies heavily on Heath's discussion on pp. 3–7.

129. Heath, *Allegory and Philosophy in Avicenna*, p. 7.

130. David Stern, e.g., has argued that these assumptions render allegory unhelpful when one attempts to understand the rabbinic *mashal*, or parable. See his *Parables in Midrash*, p. 11.

131. For a recent attempt to call attention to the negative treatment of allegory, see the edited volume by Russell, *Allegoresis*. As is typical with most works dealing with medieval literary criticism, however, none of the essays in this volume deals with the role of allegory in either its Arabic or Hebrew contexts.

132. One of the few scholars who has devoted any space to a literary analysis of Avicenna's tales is Peter Heath. He is sensitive to the emotive possibilities within these treatises.

133. Walbridge, *The Leaven of the Ancients,* pp. 97–105; idem, *The Wisdom of the Mystic East.* I would like to thank Prof. Walbridge for letting me see a version of the latter before its publication.

134. Walbridge, *The Leaven of the Ancients,* p. 102.

135. Walbridge, *The Leaven of the Ancients,* p. 102.

136. Walbridge, *The Leaven of the Ancients,* p. 103.

137. Walbridge, *The Leaven of the Ancients,* p. 102.

138. See, e.g., Frye, *Anatomy of Criticism,* p. 91.

139. Daniel Boyarin, "The Eye in the Torah," p. 47.

140. 17:1–3. All Qur$^{\circ}$ānic translations are based on those found in Arberry, *The Koran Interpreted.*

141. See, e.g., the selection of texts on this topic in Sells, *Early Islamic Mysticism,* pp. 47–56.

142. Quoted, with some modification, from Böwering, *The Mystical Vision of Existence in Classical Islam,* p. 213.

143. Böwering, *The Mystical Vision of Existence in Classical Islam,* pp. 231–261.

144. Quoted, with some modification, in Archer, *A Reader on Islam,* p. 634.

145. Sells, "Bewildered Tongue," pp. 87–124.

146. Sells, *Early Islamic Mysticism,* p. 47.

147. Wolfson, *Through a Speculum that Shines,* p. 21.

148. All biblical quotations come from *Tanakh: The Holy Scriptures* (Philadelphia: Jewish Publication Society, 1985).

149. For a distinct tension in the biblical narrative regarding this concept of vision, see, e.g., Exodus 33:20 wherein Moses is prevented from seeing the divine.

150. On the difficulties of defining this literature as a genre, see John J. Collins, "Introduction."

151. See Merkur, "The Visionary Practices of the Jewish Apocalyptists"; Rowland, "The Visions of God in Apocalyptic Literature."

152. Wolfson, *Through a Speculum that Shines,* p. 29.

153. Translated by F. I. Anderson in Charlesworth, ed., *The Old Testament Pseudepigrapha,* p. 136.

154. For an attempt to compare certain features of the Islamic and Jewish ascent narratives, see Halperin, "Hekhalot and Mi^{c}rāj," pp. 269–288.

155. On the tension between this goal and the prohibition against this, see Wolfson, *Through a Speculum that Shines,* pp. 87ff. This tension, as Wolfson points out, has led scholars to radically different views regarding the telos of this mystical system. Scholem, e.g., argued against the visualization of God. For example, *Major Trends in Jewish Mysticism,* p. 66. In this regard, also see Gruenwald, *Apocalyptic and Merkabah Mysticism,* p. 94. For the view that these mystics can perceive the divine, see Ira Chernus, "Visions of God in Merkabah Literature," pp. 146ff.; Wolfson, *Through a Speculum that Shines,* pp. 95ff.

156. Schäfer, ed., *Synopse zur Hekhalot-Literatur,* sec. 164 (quoted in Wolfson, *Through a Speculum that Shines,* p. 101).

157. One of the best articulations of this position is found in Davidson, "The Study of Philosophy as a Religious Obligation," pp. 53–68.

158. E.g., Alfarabi, *Risāla fī qawānīn ṣinā^{c}a al-sh^{c}ir,* pp. 149–158. For an English translation of this, see Arberry, "Fārābī's Canons of Poetry." Avicenna,

Kitāb al-majmu^{c}: al-ḥikma al-^{c}arūdiyya fī ma^{c}ānī kitāb al-shi^{c}r; idem, *al-Shifāʾ: Kitāb al-sh^{c}ir*, in A. Badawi, ed., *Arisṭūṭālīs fann al-sh^{c}ir*, pp. 159–198. For an English translation of the latter, see Dahiyat, ed. and trans., *Avicenna's Commentary on the Poetics of Aristotle.*

159. See Kemal, *The Poetics of Alfarabi and Avicenna,* pp. 141–200.

160. Nussbaum, "An Aristotelian Conception of Rationality," in *Love's Knowledge,* pp. 77–78.

161. Avicenna in Dahiyat, ed. and trans., *Avicenna's Commentary on the Poetics of Aristotle,* p. 71.

162. See the excellent discussion in Black, *Logic and Aristotle's Rhetoric and Poetics in Medieval Arabic Philosophy,* p. 181. In this regard, also see Kemal, *The Poetics of Alfarabi and Avicenna,* p. 149.

163. Avicenna, *Kitāb al-majmu^{c}: al-ḥikma al-^{c}arūdiyya fī ma^{c}ānī kitāb al-sh^{c}ir,* pp. 15–16.

164. This, according to Avicenna, is based on our "natural love of harmonious combination and melodies" (Dahiyat, *Avicenna's Commentary on the Poetics of Aristotle,* p. 79).

165. For a good descriptive and historical analysis of the internal senses, of which the faculties of imagination and representation are a part, see H. A. Wolfson, "The Internal Senses in Latin, Arabic, and Hebrew Philosophical Texts." For a specific discussion of the faculty of estimation in Avicenna, see Rahman, *Avicenna's Psychology,* pp. 79–83.

166. This, of course, goes back to Aristotle, who claimed that we are unable to think without images (*de Anima* 431a16). In this regard also see Alfarabi, *Al-Fārābī on the Perfect State,* chapter 10.1, section IV, pp. 165ff.

167. Hawi, *Islamic Naturalism and Mysticism,* p. 21.

2. Reading between the Lines

1. Nussbaum, "Introduction," in *Love's Knowledge,* p. 5.

2. Here, I am influenced by the thought of Cassirer. He claims: "True, we still remain in a world of 'images'—but these are not images which reproduce a self-subsistent world of 'things'; they are image-words whose principle and origin are to be sought in an autonomous creation of the spirit. Through them we see what we call 'reality,' and in them alone we possess it: for the highest objective truth that is accessible to the spirit is ultimately the form of its own activity." From Cassirer, *The Philosophy of Symbolic Forms,* vol. 1, pp. 110–111. See also, Casey, *Imagining,* pp. xff.

3. Heidegger, "The Origin of the Work of Art," in *Martin Heidegger: Basic Writings,* p. 198. Cf. the discussion in Biemel, "Poetry and Language in Heidegger," p. 77; Eiland, "The Way to Nearness," pp. 43–44.

4. Heidegger, "The Origin of the Work of Art," p. 165.

5. Heidegger, "The Origin of the Work of Art," p. 199.

6. Here I am indebted to the discussion found in Zemach, *Real Beauty,* pp. 200ff.

7. *Commentary to Genesis* 1:26.

8. Cf. Ricoeur, "The Hermeneutical Function of Distanciation," in *Hermeneutics and the Human Sciences,* pp. 131–144; idem, "Existence and

Hermeneutics," in *The Conflict of Interpretations,* pp. 3–24. See the comments in Tirosh-Samuelson, "Maimonides' View of Happiness," p. 206.

9. I have capitalized Truth here because, unlike contemporary philosophers, the ancients and medievals were convinced that there existed an essential Truth that was external to the thinking subject and that could be grasped by, potentially at least, any intellect.

10. See the helpful comments in Gatti, "Plotinus," pp. 22–27.

11. This, in turn, made its way into the Islamic world. See, e.g., Alfarabi, *Philosophy of Plato and Aristotle.*

12. Sorabji, "The Ancient Commentators on Aristotle," in Sorabji, ed., *Aristotle Transformed,* pp. 1–30.

13. This certainly is not to deny that Neoplatonists were not interested in disciplines such as logic. In this regard, see the helpful comments in Lloyd, *The Anatomy of Neoplatonism,* pp. 1–35.

14. See my comments in chapter 1.

15. Earlier scholars, writing at the end of the nineteenth and beginning of the twentieth centuries, were convinced that these unsavory elements of philosophy were the result of "Oriental" influences. One of the key figures they pointed to was the Syrian Iamblichus. See, in this context, Shaw, *Theurgy and the Soul,* p. 95. Interestingly, the term "Oriental" would have a considerable different valence for the likes of Corbin.

16. Recently, there have been a series of excellent analyses that have begun to examine the religious and performative aspects of Neoplatonism: Shaw, *Theurgy and the Soul,* pp. 1–17; Rappe, *Reading Neoplatonism,* pp. 1–21.

17. Shaw, *Theurgy and the Soul,* pp. 13–15.

18. Shaw, *Theurgy and the Soul,* p. 129.

19. The *locus classicus* of this emanative framework is found in Plotinus, *Enn.* III.8.10.

20. Armstrong argues that Plotinus's imprecise theory of emanation represents the uneasy, and ultimately unresolvable, tension between a Stoic theory of an organic universe centered on the sun and a Platonic hierarchy of reality. See A. H. Armstrong, "Emanation in Plotinus," in Armstrong, ed., *Plotinian and Christian Studies,* p. 66; idem, *The Architecture of the Intelligible Universe in the Philosophy of Plotinus,* pp. 52–53.

21. Gadamer, *Truth and Method,* p. 324.

22. Wolfson, *Through a Speculum that Shines,* p. 53.

23. Rappe, *Reading Neoplatonism,* pp. 18–19.

24. E.g., O'Daly, *Plotinus' Philosophy of Self,* pp. 7–19; Miles, *Plotinus on Body and Beauty,* pp. 142–161; Merlan, *Monopsychism Mysticism Metaconsciousness,* pp. 4–84; Rappe, *Reading Neoplatonism,* pp. 67–90.

25. *Enn.* VI.7.36–42. See also the comments in Rappe, *Reading Neoplatonism,* pp. 43ff.

26. *Enn.* II.1.9. Here my argument relies on that in Rappe, *Reading Neoplatonism,* pp. 73ff.

27. Austin's introduction in ibn al-Arabi, *The Bezels of Wisdom,* p. 48.

28. Rorty's goal, of course, is to move beyond this metaphor, to arrive at a "philosophy without mirrors." See his *Philosophy and the Mirror of Nature,* pp. 357–394.

29. Plotinus, *Enn.* I.4.10.

30. Avicenna, *Kitāb al-ishārāt wa al-tanbīhāt,* vol. 3, p. 231. Significantly, ibn Ṭufayl cites this passage verbatim in his *Ḥayy,* p. 54 (Goodman, p. 97).

31. *Sefer Yesod Mora ve Sod ha-Torah,* in *Yalkuth ibn Ezra,* X.2 (p. 337).

32. Ibn Ṭufayl, *Ḥayy ibn Yaqẓān,* p. 109 (Goodman, p. 152).

33. Ibn Ṭufayl, *Ḥayy ibn Yaqẓān,* p. 110 (Goodman, p. 152).

34. Ibn Ṭufayl, *Ḥayy ibn Yaqẓān,* p. 111 (Goodman, p. 153).

35. *Enn.* VI.7.12. Translation in Rappe, *Reading Neoplatonism,* p. 43.

36. Marinus, *Vita Procli,* quoted in Siorvanes, *Proclus,* p. 192.

37. This trope, of course, is also used by Maimonides in the preface to his maze-like *Guide of the Perplexed.* I think it is no coincidence that ibn Ṭufayl and Maimonides were near contemporaries in both Spain and later the Western Maghrib.

38. Ibn Ṭufayl *Ḥayy ibn Yaqẓān,* p. 52 (Goodman, p. 95).

39. See the comments in Fradkin, "Ibn Ṭufayl's *Ḥayy ibn Yaqẓān* on the Relationship of Mysticism, Prophecy, and Philosophy," pp. 69–76.

40. Ibn Ṭufayl, *Ḥayy ibn Yaqẓān,* p. 55 (Goodman, p. 98).

41. Ibn Ṭufayl, *Ḥayy ibn Yaqẓān,* p. 56 (Goodman, p. 99).

42. Ibn Ṭufayl, *Ḥayy ibn Yaqẓān,* p. 58 (Goodman, p. 101).

43. Avicenna, *Kitāb al-ishārāt wa al-tanbīhāt,* vol. 3, p. 231.

44. Avicenna, *Kitāb al-ishārāt wa al-tanbīhāt,* vol. 3, p. 229.

45. Avicenna, *Kitāb al-ishārāt wa al-tanbīhāt,* vol. 3, p. 228.

46. See above, chapter 1, n. 42.

47. Cf. ibn Ezra, *Ḥay ben Meqitz,* lines 20–35.

48. E.g., Gutas, *Avicenna and the Aristotelian Tradition,* pp. 299ff.

49. Corbin, *Avicenna and the Visionary Recital,* p. 21. In other passages, Corbin equates Ḥayy with the "Watchers" of the Book of Enoch (pp. 65–66), one of the cherubs in Genesis (p. 65), and the angel Gabriel (p. 152).

50. On the dangers of this type of approach to comparison, see Smith, *Imagining Religion,* esp. pp. 21–22.

51. In many ways, this is similar to the Apocalyptic literature of the inter-testamental period. However, this genre is less philosophical in terms of both its noetic content and the fact that it is a special gnosis that is unattainable by everyone.

52. This theory was often elaborated within the commentary tradition to Plato's *Phaedrus.* In this regard, see Bielmeier, *Die neuplatonische Phaidrosinterpretation,* pp. 60ff.

53. O'Meara, *Pythagoras Revived,* p. 39; Shaw, *Theurgy and the Soul,* pp. 196–198.

54. Hermias, *Commentary on the Phaedrus* 1.1–5, quoted in O'Meara, *Pythagoras Revived,* p. 125.

55. E.g., lines 410–418, 654–664.

56. See the comments in Fradkin, "Ibn Ṭufayl's *Ḥayy ibn Yaqẓān* on the Relationship of Mysticism, Prophecy, and Philosophy," pp. 102ff.

57. E.g., *Phaedrus* 246a–257b.

58. E.g., *Enn.* IV.8.

59. Cassirer, *The Philosophy of Symbolic Forms,* pp. 192ff.

60. Cf. the discussion in Dronke, *Fabula,* pp. 4ff.

61. Kingsley, *Ancient Philosophy, Mystery, and Magic,* p. 80.

62. Avicenna, *Ḥayy ibn Yaqẓān,* p. 40 (Corbin, p. 137); ibn Ezra, *Ḥay ben Meqitz,* lines1–19; ibn Ṭufayl, *Ḥayy ibn Yaqẓān,* p. 52 (Goodman, p. 95).

63. Proclus, *In Platonis Rem Publicam Commentarii,* 76.17–86.23.

64. See the discussion in Coulter, *The Literary Microcosm,* p. 49.

65. Coulter, *The Literary Microcosm,* p. 51.

66. E.g., *Phaedrus* 246a–247c; *Republic* 10: 614c–618b; *Timaeus* 89e–90d; *Phaedo* 80ff.

67. Heath shows how all three of Avicenna's initiatory tales must be read together because each one looks at only one specific aspect of what he calls "cosmic geography." *Ḥayy ibn Yaqẓān* deals with the longitudinal East–West aspect, *Risāla al-ṭayr* with the latitudinal; and *Salāmān and Absāl* with the earthly dimension. See Heath, *Allegory and Philosophy in Avicenna,* pp. 170–173.

68. Heath, *Allegory and Philosophy in Avicenna,* pp. 98–99. In this regard also see Stroumsa, "Avicenna's Philosophical Stories," p. 186.

69. Heath, *Allegory and Philosophy in Avicenna,* p. 99. On p. 163, Heath writes that "poetic utterance has the potential to fashion demonstrative intelligibles and ontological realities into representational scenes and embodied entities. To this extent it can provide for a philosopher so-motivated the tools to depict concretely an abstract spiritual cosmos that is invisible to the senses but is known by him or her to be more real than the physical world that surrounds us."

70. See, e.g., *Long Commentary to Exodus* 25:40; *Commentary to Deuteronomy* 11:22; *Yesod Mora* VII.5, VII.12. Also, see the comments in Vajda, *L'amour de Dieu dans la théologie juive du Moyen Age,* pp. 113–114.

71. He does, however, talk about the preparation that one must undertake. See *Yesod Mora* VII.12; also see Idel, "*Hitbodedut* as Concentration in Jewish Philosophy," pp. 41–44; idem, "*Hitbodedut* as Concentration in Ecstatic Kabbalah," pp. 103–107; Hughes, "Two Approaches to the Love of God in Medieval Jewish Thought," pp. 139–151.

72. Ibn Ezra, *Ḥay ben Meqitz,* lines 719–733.

73. Olympiodorus, *Commentary on the First Alcibiades;* quoted in Coulson, *The Literary Microcosm,* p. 95.

74. In phenomenological terms, however, all being is ultimately phenomenal, so that which is apprehended or imagined beyond the veil is not distinct from what is perceived or conceived of in front of the veil.

75. Coulter, *The Literary Microcosm,* p. 102.

76. Westerink, ed. and trans., *Anonymous Prolegomena to Platonic Philosophy,* sec. 15.1–7.

77. Dahiyat, *Avicenna's Commentary on the Poetics of Aristotle,* p. 62.

78. Ibn Ṭufayl, *Ḥayy ibn Yaqẓān,* p. 122 (Goodman, p. 166).

79. Cf. Heidegger, *Being and Time,* pp. 203–205.

80. Lakoff and Johnson, *Philosophy in the Flesh,* pp. 6–7; idem, *Metaphors We Live By,* pp. 3–13.

81. Quinn, "The Cultural Basis of Metaphor," pp. 56–93.

82. In *Rhetoric* 1405b3, Aristotle claims that "the metaphor especially has clarity and sweetness and strangeness, and its use cannot be learned from someone else." Similarly, in *Poetics* 59a6–10, he writes that the ability to create metaphors "is a sign of natural ability, and something one can never learn from another: for the successful use of metaphor entails the perception of similarities."

83. See the comments in Cantarino, *Arabic Poetics in the Golden Age,* p. 64.

84. Virtually all of the major Islamic philosophers—al-Kindī, Alfarabi, Avicenna, and ibn Rushd—wrote such commentaries. For requisite secondary

literature, see Black, *Logic and Aristotle's Rhetoric and Poetics in Medieval Arabic Philosophy,* pp. 1–16; Kemal, *The Poetics of Alfarabi and Avicenna,* pp. 165ff.

85. Alfarabi, *Risāla fī qawānīn ṣināᶜa al-shiᶜr.* I have consulted the Arabic text as found in Arberry, "Fārābī's Canons of Poetry," p. 272. Here it is important to remember that both Alfarabi and Avicenna considered the *Poetics* as a logical work, part of the *Organon* (the so-called "Context Theory"). In this regard, see Black, *Logic and Aristotle's Rhetoric and Poetics in Medieval Arabic Philosophy,* pp. 1–51.

86. According to Dahiyat, *Avicenna's Commentary on the Poetics of Aristotle,* p. 114, n. 1, *naql* is the literal rendition of the Greek *metaphora.*

87. Dahiyat, *Commentary to Aristotle's Poetics,* p. 114.

88. Heath, *Allegory and Philosophy in Avicenna,* p. 177.

89. Moses ibn Ezra, *Kitāb al-muḥāḍara wa al-mudhākara,* p. 224.

90. On the friction between the Andalusian Hebrew poets and the jurists that this discussion presupposes, cf. Ross Brann, *The Compunctious Poet,* pp. 78–81; Fenton, *Philosophie et exégèse dans le Jardin de la Métaphore de Moïse ibn Ezra,* pp. 299–301.

91. Moses ibn Ezra, *Kitāb al-muḥāḍara wa al-mudhākara,* p. 224.

92. Moses ibn Ezra, *Kitāb al-muḥāḍara wa al-mudhākara,* p. 228.

93. E.g., Ferwerda, *La signification des images et des metaphores dans la pensée de Plotin,* pp. 7ff.; Blumenthal, "Plotinus in the Light of Twenty Years' Scholarship, 1951–1971," p. 572.

94. Rappe, *Reading Neoplatonism,* p. 98.

95. Lakoff and Johnson, *Metaphors We Live By,* p. 18.

96. *Enn.* III.8.10 (MacKenna, p. 245).

97. Sells, *Mystical Languages of Unsaying,* p. 15.

98. Ferwerda, *La signification des images,* p. 7.

99. In this regard, see Lloyd, "Non-Discursive Thought," and the response to this in Sorabji, "Myths about Non-Propositional Thought."

100. *Enn.* V.2.1 (MacKenna, p. 361).

101. Ferwerda, *La signification des images,* p. 195.

102. *Enn.* III.8.10 (MacKenna, p. 245).

103. Rist, *Plotinus,* pp. 73–74.

104. E.g., Armstrong, "Plotinus," in *Plotinian and Christian Studies,* p. 223.

105. Ibn Gabirol was influenced by the *Ikhwān al-Ṣafāʾ* who were responsible for the popularization of the Neoplatonic worldview. Al-Kirmānī, thought by many to be responsible for introducing the *Rasāʾil* to Spain, lived in Saragossa at the same time as ibn Gabirol. See Schlanger, *La philosophie de Salomon Ibn Gabirol,* pp. 94–95; Loewe, "Ibn Gabirol's Treatment of the Sources in *Kether Malkuth,*" p. 183. Another important source for ibn Gabirol was Isaac Israeli (d. ca. 932). See Schlanger, *La philosophie de Salomon Ibn Gabirol,* pp. 97–101; Altmann and Stern, *Isaac Israeli,* e.g., pp. 150–155, 192–194. Although certainly not a poet-philosopher, Israeli nevertheless did posit the existence of a first form and a first matter that ibn Gabirol would expand upon in his *Meqor Ḥayyim.* In addition, Israeli is interested in the career of the soul, although he never describes this in the same detail as Plotinus or ibn Gabirol or later Jewish Neoplatonists.

106. For an in-depth analysis of some of the philosophical and poetic themes of the *Keter Malkut,* see Tanenbaum, *The Contemplative Soul,* pp. 57–83. For an examination of the relationship between the *Meqor Ḥayyim* and the *Keter*

Malkut, see Hayoun, *L'exégèse philosophique dans le judaisme médiéval,* pp. 98–115.

107. See the discussion in Greive, *Studien zum jüdischen Neuplatonismus,* pp. 123–128.

108. On the genre of the *maqāma,* see Nicholson, *A Literary History of the Arabs,* pp. 327–329. On ibn Gabirol's use of this, see Tanenbaum, *The Contemplative Soul,* pp. 58–61.

109. I have used the English translation of the *Keter Malkut* found in *Selected Poems of Solomon Ibn Gabirol,* trans. Peter Cole, p. 141.

110. *Keter Malkhut,* p. 172; see Tanenbaum, *The Contemplative Soul,* pp. 68–70.

111. Similar metaphors, although lacking the same poetic sensibility as ibn Gabirol's, can be found among other Jewish poet-philosophers of al-Andalus. See, e.g., the anonymous author of the *Kitāb ma^{c}ānī al-nafs,* in Goldziher, ed., "*Kitāb ma^{c}ānī al-nafs:* Buch vom Wesen der Seele," esp. pp. 31ff. Also, see ibn Ẓaddik, *Ha-Olam ha-Qatan,* p. 40.

112. Avicenna, *Ḥayy ibn Yaqẓān,* p. 40 (Corbin, p. 137).

113. Ibn Ezra, *Ḥay ben Meqitz,* lines 63–90.

114. Physiognomy formed an important part of the Merkabah mystical tradition and was used to learn everything about a person, from his moral qualities to his health and family to his future. See, in this regard, Scholem, "Ein Fragment zur Physiognomik und Chiromantik aus der Spätantiken jüdischen Esoterik," pp. 175ff. Goichon, however, claims that it was a science originating with Galen; see her *Le récit de Ḥayy ibn Yaqẓān,* p. 17.

115. Goichon, *Le récit de Ḥayy ibn Yaqẓān,* p. 46.

116. There exists one other companion—the imagination—that I will not discuss here, but in the context of the following chapter.

117. For an excellent discussion of this, see Nussbaum, "Transcending Humanity," in *Love's Knowledge,* pp. 286–388.

118. Ibn Ezra, *Ḥay ben Meqitz,* lines 130–168.

119. Ibn Ṭufayl, *Ḥayy ibn Yaqẓān,* pp. 120–121 (Goodman, p. 163).

120. Wolfson, *Through a Speculum that Shines,* p. 61.

3. Polishing a Dirty Mirror

1. In his general survey of the imagination in Western philosophy, Kearney claims that the medievals regarded the imagination solely in a negative light. See Kearney, *The Wake of the Imagination,* e.g., p. 33. In this regard, he too easily dismisses the Islamic philosophers from his discussion: "Discussion of the Arabic/Islamic sources ... would have meant extending our analysis beyond the *dominant mainstream* of medieval thought ... [which was] largely conditioned by the conflation of Graeco-Roman and Judaeo-Christian modes of thinking" (p. 419, n. 1; his italics). This is incorrect on two points. First, the Islamic philosophers were not peripheral; in fact, they represent one of the earliest prototypes of what Kearney calls the "Graeco-Roman" and "Judaeo-Christian" synthesis. Second, he chooses to discuss Maimonides (d. 1204), a Jewish philosopher, as if he were unconnected to the Islamic philosophical milieu.

2. Wolfson, *Through a Speculum that Shines,* p. 280.

3. Indeed the main treatments of the imagination in both medieval Islam and medieval Judaism adopt this approach. See, e.g., Corbin, *Mundus Imaginalis,* pp. 8–9; idem, "De Heidegger à Sohravardi," p. 26. It is not without significance that Corbin was the first person to translate the work of Heidegger into French. In particular see Martin Heidegger, *Qu'est-ce que la métaphysique?* trans. Henry Corbin. A perceptive article that draws out the implications of Heidegger on Corbin's thought may be found in Landolt, "Henry Corbin, 1903–1978." It is much more difficult to isolate specific references to Heidegger in the thought of Elliot Wolfson, yet see *Through a Speculum that Shines,* p. 68, n. 61; idem, *Along the Path,* p. xii.

4. Husserl, *Ideas,* sec. 23. Also, see the discussion in Kearney, *Poetics of Imagining,* pp. 14–18.

5. Wolfson, *Through a Speculum that Shines,* p. 68, n. 61.

6. E.g., *Being and Time,* p. 61.

7. *Being and Time,* p. 40.

8. *Being and Time,* p. 265.

9. *Being and Time,* p. 58.

10. E.g, Heidegger, "The Origin of the Work of Art," in *Martin Heidegger: Basic Writings,* pp. 198–199.

11. Gadamer, *Truth and Method,* p. 306.

12. See, e.g., Avicenna, *Aḥwāl al-nafs,* pp. 90–95; *Kitāb al-najāt,* p. 210; Rahman, *Avicenna's Psychology,* p. 41.

13. See the discussion in Wolfson, *Through a Speculum that Shines,* pp. 63ff.

14. See chapter 2, pp. 52ff.

15. Sells, *Mystical Languages of Unsaying,* pp. 6–10; also see Hatab, *Myth and Philosophy,* p. 236.

16. Eva Brann, *The World of the Imagination,* pp. 32–34.

17. Indeed, it seems that Plato does not acknowledge that the imagination is a proper faculty. See Brann, *The World of the Imagination,* p. 40; Stalley, "Plato's Arguments from the Division of the Reasoning and Appetitive Elements within the Soul"; Woods, "Plato's Division of the Soul," pp. 23–47.

18. *Timaeus* 71a–b. All translations are from *The Collected Dialogues of Plato,* ed. E. Hamilton and H. Cairns.

19. Moreover, Plato also chose to end his *Republic* with a myth, that of Er (614b–621d). On Plato's ambivalent use of myth, see Edelstein, "The Function of Myth in Plato's Philosophy," pp. 463–481.

20. E.g., *Meno* 99b–100c.

21. E.g, Plato *Seventh Letter,* esp. 338a–345c; cf. the discussion in Hatab, *Myth and Philosophy,* pp. 233ff.

22. *Philebus* 39b; cf. also *Sophist* 263d–264b.

23. *Philebus* 40a–d; *Theaetetus* 195d.

24. Schofield, "Aristotle on the Imagination," p. 103. Aristotle's discussion of the soul falls under the branch of Physics, whose subject matter is that which is "separate but not changeless." See the discussion in Wedin, *Mind and Imagination in Aristotle,* pp. 4–6.

25. Wedin, *Mind and Imagination in Aristotle,* p. 23.

26. Schofield, "Aristotle on the Imagination," p. 103; Brann, *The World of the Imagination,* pp. 40–41; D.W. Hamlyn, *Aristotle's De Anima, Books II and III with Certain Passages from Book I,* p. xiv.

27. *De Anima* III.3 (427b15). All translations, unless noted, are from *The Complete Works of Aristotle,* ed. Jonathan Barnes.

28. *De Anima* III.3 (428a1–2).

29. *De Anima* III.3 (428a16–18). The most important sense for the production of images is, according to Aristotle, sight. Based on this, he tries to derive the word "imagination" (*phantasia*) from the Greek word for light (*phaos*), see *De Anima* III.3 (429a3–4).

30. *De Anima* III.3 (428b10–16).

31. Significantly, Wedin argues that, for Aristotle, the imagination is not a faculty but a general representational capacity that subserves all the other cognitive faculties by presenting them with images. See his *Mind and Imagination in Aristotle,* pp. 23–63.

32. Cf. *De Memoria* I (450a1–14); *De Anima* III.7 (431a15–16); *De Anima* III.8 (432a6–14).

33. E.g., *On Dreams* II (461b6–10).

34. See the discussion in Halliwell, *Aristotle's Poetics,* pp. 21–22. Halliwell correctly notes, however, that we must be aware of simplifying Plato's treatment of the mimetic arts especially when we compare Plato's theory of mimesis in, e.g., *Republic* 595bff. with that found in, e.g., *Laws* 817b.

35. Rather significantly, Aristotle nowhere offers a definition of what he means by the term "mimesis." For a useful comparison of Plato's and Aristotle's views on mimesis, see Paul Woodruff, "Aristotle on Mimesis," esp. pp. 74–82.

36. *Poetics* IV (1448b5–23). For this work, I have consulted Halliwell, *The Poetics of Aristotle.*

37. E.g., *Rhetoric* 1371b4–11; *Metaphysics* 982b12–28. In this regard, see Halliwell, *Aristotle's Poetics,* pp. 74ff.

38. Blumenthal, *Aristotle and Neoplatonism in Late Antiquity,* p. 102. On the syncretistic dimension of Plotinus's thought, see Porphyry, *Life of Plotinus* 14:10–16.

39. *Enn.* I.4.10. Translation modified from the Mackenna edition, p. 40.

40. On the identification of the mirror with the imagination, see Blumenthal, *Plotinus' Psychology,* p. 92.

41. Cf. *Enn.* I.4.10.16–17.

42. I quote here from *Plotini Opera,* ed. Henry and Schwyzer, vol. 2, p. 71; this passage corresponds to *Theology* II.47. For the Greek text of the *Theology,* along with English translation, see *Plotini Opera,* vol. 2, pp. 69–77. For the Arabic text of the *Theology,* see Badawi, *Al-Aflāṭūniyya al-muḥdatha ᶜind al-ᶜarab.* We know for certain that Avicenna read the *Theology* since we possess fragments of his commentary to it. In this regard, see Vajda, "Les notes d'Avicenne sur la *Théologie d'Aristote.*"

43. *Enn.* IV.4.5.11–13; quoted in *Plotini Opera,* ed. Henry and Schwyzer, vol. 2, p. 75. This corresponds to *Theology* II.69.

44. E.g., *Enn.* I.4.10.17–19; IV.3.25; IV.3.27; IV.3.31; IV.4.3.1–12; IV.4.4.2–6, 10–11. Significantly the last three passages were available to the Islamic philosophers by dint of the *Theology of Aristotle.*

45. E.g., *Phaedrus* 249b–c; *Phaedo* 75; *Timaeus* 51c–d.

46. *Poetics* IX (1451b5–7).

47. E.g., Plato's argument for the soul's immortality is based on the complete separation between the soul and the body; the evil of the body can in no way affect the soul (cf. *Republic* X, 608d). According to Aristotle, however, the soul is dependent upon the body and requires it for all of its basic activities (cf. *De Anima* 412b–415a). See the discussion in Druart, "Imagination and the Soul-Body Problem in Arabic Philosophy," pp. 327–329.

48. E.g., Avicenna, *Aḥwāl al-nafs,* pp. 99–105; idem, *al-Shifāʾ: al-ṭabīᶜīyāt,* pp. 204ff.; idem, *Avicenna's de Anima,* pp. 230ff.; idem, *Kitāb al-najāt,* pp. 222–223; Rahman, *Avicenna's Psychology,* pp. 56–58; *Ḥayy,* p. 40 (Corbin, p. 137).

49. *Aḥwāl al-nafs,* p. 57. The same passage can be found, almost verbatim, in *al-Najāt,* p. 197; Rahman, *Avicenna's Psychology,* p. 25; also, see *Ḥayy,* p. 40 (Corbin, p. 137). Avicenna bases his argument for this on the fact that because the different faculties are affected by one another, the soul, as the substrate of all experience, must be one substance. Although the soul is a unitary substance, the reason that plants receive only the vegetative soul—and animals only the vegetative and animal souls—is because certain bodies, owing to their temperaments, are unable to receive the whole soul. See Rahman, *Avicenna's Psychology,* pp. 109–110. In this respect, Avicenna follows Aristotle, *De Anima* 411a24–411b30.

50. According to *al-Najāt,* p. 197, the soul is like a genus (*ka-jins*) that is divided into three species (*aqsām*).

51. *Aḥwāl al-nafs,* pp. 57–58; *al-Najāt,* p. 197; Rahman, *Avicenna's Psychology,* p. 25.

52. *Aḥwāl al-nafs,* p. 58; *al-Najāt,* p. 197; Rahman, *Avicenna's Psychology,* pp. 25–26.

53. *Aḥwāl al-nafs,* p. 58; *al-Najāt,* p. 197; Rahman, *Avicenna's Psychology,* pp. 25–26.

54. Heath, *Allegory and Philosophy in Avicenna,* p. 61.

55. *Aḥwāl al-nafs,* pp. 58–59; *al-Najāt,* pp. 197–198; Rahman, *Avicenna's Psychology,* p. 26; *Ḥayy,* p. 41 (Corbin, p. 139).

56. *Aḥwāl al-nafs,* p. 59; *al-Najāt,* pp. 198–200; Rahman, *Avicenna's Psychology,* pp. 26–29.

57. A general discussion of this subject may be found in H. A. Wolfson, "The Internal Senses in Latin, Arabic, and Hebrew Philosophic Texts." A convenient diagram of this breakdown may be found in Fakhry, *A History of Islamic Philosophy,* p. 140.

58. *Aḥwāl al-nafs,* p. 61; *al-Najāt,* p. 201. According to Rahman, "The localization of the internal senses in the brain is Galenic. According to Aristotle, the heart is the seat of *sensus communis* and therefore of imagination and memory" (*Avicenna's Psychology,* p. 79).

59. This is based on Aristotle's distinction between the sensual and rational imagination in *de Anima* 433b29 and *de Motu Animalarium* 702a19. In this regard, see Portelli, "The 'Myth' that Avicenna Reproduced Aristotle's 'Concept of the Imagination' in *De Anima,*" pp. 122–134.

60. *Aḥwāl al-nafs,* p. 61; *al-Najāt,* p. 201; Rahman, *Avicenna's Psychology,* p. 31; *Ḥayy,* p. 41 (Corbin, p. 139). I shall discuss this faculty in greater detail below.

61. It is for this reason that many medieval Neoplatonists, most notably Alfarabi and Maimonides, claim that the prophet must have a perfected imaginative faculty.

62. *Aḥwāl al-nafs,* p. 62; *al-Najāt,* p. 202; Rahman, *Avicenna's Psychology,* p. 31.

63. *Aḥwāl al-nafs,* p. 62; *al-Najāt,* p. 202; Rahman, *Avicenna's Psychology,* p. 31.

64. *Aḥwāl al-nafs,* p. 63; *al-Najāt,* p. 202; Rahman, *Avicenna's Psychology,* p. 32.

65. *Aḥwāl al-nafs,* p. 62; *al-Najāt,* pp. 202–203; Rahman, *Avicenna's Psychology,* p. 32.

66. *Al-Najāt,* p. 203; Rahman, *Avicenna's Psychology,* pp. 32–33; *Ḥayy,* pp. 41–42 (Corbin, p. 140).

67. *Al-Najāt,* pp. 209, 210–213; Rahman, *Avicenna's Psychology,* pp. 40–42; *Ḥayy,* p. 42 (Corbin, p. 140).

68. *Aḥwāl al-nafs,* pp. 90–95; *al-Najāt,* p. 210; Rahman, *Avicenna's Psychology,* p. 41.

69. It is for this reason that Avicenna assigns all of the internal senses a certain locus within the brain. See the discussion, in Druart, "Imagination and the Soul-Body Problem in Arabic Philosophy," pp. 330–335.

70. *Al-Najāt,* p. 217; Rahman, *Avicenna's Psychology,* p. 50.

71. Here, see the discussion in Davidson, *Alfarabi, Avicenna, and Averroes, on Intellect,* pp. 95ff.

72. *Al-Najāt,* p. 231; *Ḥayy,* p. 40 (Corbin, p. 137). Also, see Rahman's translation of this passage in *Avicenna's Psychology,* p. 68.

73. *Aḥwāl al-nafs,* pp. 87–88; *al-Shifāʾ,* pp. 511ff.; *de Anima,* p. 59; *al-Najāt,* pp. 220–221; *Ḥayy,* p. 42 (Corbin, pp. 140–141); Rahman, *Avicenna's Psychology,* p. 55.

74. *Al-Najāt,* p. 221; Rahman, *Avicenna's Psychology,* p. 55.

75. *Al-Najāt,* p. 221; Rahman, *Avicenna's Psychology,* p. 55.

76. *Al-Najāt,* p. 221; Rahman, *Avicenna's Psychology,* pp. 55–56.

77. *Al-Najāt,* p. 221; Rahman, *Avicenna's Psychology,* p. 55.

78. Gutas, as I argued in the previous chapter, completely deemphasizes these sections of *al-Ishārāt* and argues that the thought of Avicenna is far removed from any mystical or esoteric dimensions. See Gutas, "Avicenna V: Mysticism," pp. 79–83. For a critique of this view, see Marmura, "Plotting the Course of Avicenna's Thought," esp. pp. 341–342.

79. *Al-Ishārāt,* vol. 3, p. 229. In this respect, also see the tenth section of *al-Ishārāt,* entitled *fī asrār al-āyāt* (The secrets of signs), vol. 3, p. 248.

80. E.g., *al-Ishārāt,* vol. 3, p. 242.

81. Avicenna wrote a treatise on dream interpretation. An English translation of this may be found in Khan, "Kitabu ta'bit-ir-ruya of Abu 'Ali b. Sina." Khan also published the Arabic version of the text as "A Unique Treatise on the Interpretation of Dreams." In what follows, page numbers refer to the English translation.

82. Khan, "Kitabu ta'bit-ir-ruya," p. 44.

83. Although he never specifies this in detail, it seems that the imagination has contact with the Active Intellect. See Khan, "Kitabu ta'bit-ir-ruya," p. 47.

84. *Al-Ishārāt,* vol. 3, pp. 246–247.

85. *Al-Ishārāt,* vol. 3, p. 205.

86. *Al-Ishārāt,* vol. 3, p. 205. In this regard, see also his commentary to the *Theology of Aristotle.* A French translation of this may be found in Vajda, "Les notes d'Avicenne sur la *Théologie d'Aristote,*" esp. p. 376.

87. Cf. the comments in Kreisel, "On the Term *kol* in Abraham Ibn Ezra," pp. 30–32.

88. See the discussion in Kreisel, *Prophecy,* pp. 22–23.

89. For a list of ibn Ezra's Jewish sources, see Rosin, "Die Religionsphilosophie Abraham Ibn Esras," no. 42 (1898), pp. 27–33, 58–59.

90. See the discussion in Kreisel, "On the term *kol* in Abraham Ibn Ezra," p. 32.

91. As I mentioned above, however, my goal here is not to provide the history of an idea (i.e., the imagination). So rather than engage in a discussion of

ibn Ezra's sources, which has already been done (see above, n. 89), my goal is to engage how ibn Ezra configured the imagination.

92. See the insightful comments in D. Boyarin, "The Eye in the Torah," pp. 30–48.

93. I have already discussed ibn Ezra's basic psychological system in "Two Approaches to the Love of God in Medieval Jewish Thought," pp. 141–143.

94. Mention should here be made of the debate in the secondary literature, reflective of ibn Ezra's own ambiguities, regarding his use of the term *kol* ("all"). According to Elliot Wolfson, this term refers to the demiurge that includes within itself all things. See his "God, the Demiurge and the Intellect," e.g., p. 77. Kreisel, on the other hand, debates this usage of the term and argues that it refers to God himself. See his "On the Term *kol* in Abraham Ibn Ezra," pp. 31–32.

95. Ibn Ezra, *Ḥay ben Meqitz,* lines 425–663. On the ibn Ezra's different, and sometimes conflicting, presentation of this cosmology, especially the last two spheres, see the appendix in Kreisel, "On the Term *kol* in Abraham Ibn Ezra," pp. 61–66.

96. E.g., *Long Commentary to Exodus* 3:15. But, as Wolfson has argued, ibn Ezra can also use this term to refer to the incorporeal light of the intelligible realm. See, "God, the Demiurge, and the Intellect," p. 85.

97. E.g., *Comm. to Genesis* 18:21; *Short Comm. to Exodus* 33:12.

98. E.g., *Long Comm. to Exodus* 20:1.

99. E.g., *Short Comm. to Exodus* 23:20. Although, in typical fashion, ibn Ezra nowhere goes into the specific details regarding these souls. For example, he provides no treatment of the internal senses and the ways in which these inform modes of knowing.

100. Compare with his *Yesod Mora,* in *Yalkuth ibn Ezra,* VII.4 (p. 330); *Comm. to Deut.* 6:5; *Comm. to Daniel* 10:21; and *atah yeṣaretani shokhen ᶜaliya,* in *Religious Poems of Abraham Ibn Ezra,* vol. 2, p. 215.

101. *Comm. to Psalms* 16:8.

102. E.g., *Comm. to Deut.* 10:20, 11:22.

103. *Comm. to Deut.* 20:17.

104. In his poem entitled *bedat el edebeqa,* ibn Ezra writes:

> By the life that You give to me, I cleave to Your Torah
> I expect my reward to be given from God.
> In its Garden of Eden my will indulges in luxuries
> But when I search for Him, He is my river.
> It is You that I see in my imagination (*ᶜein ha-lev*) and later
> In Your Torah, You are majestic in Your strength.
> By my comprehension of the precepts of the straight path
> I praise You—and You increase my splendor.
> If mountains and valleys cannot confine
> Your glory—then how can my words.
> In You my soul seeks refuge ...
> By Your name I am elevated and by it my glory is increased.

See *The Religious Poems of Abraham Ibn Ezra,* vol. 1, p. 26. Wolfson, however, claims that the "inner eye" (*ᶜein ha-lev*) in ibn Ezra, contrary to Halevi, refers to the intellect which, in turn, is unrelated to the imagination. See Elliot Wolfson, "Merkavah Traditions in Philosophic Garb," p. 208, n. 90. I argue that it would seem to refer to the imaginative faculty. See my "The Three Worlds of Ibn Ezra's *Ḥay ben Meqitz,*" pp. 14–18.

105. I.e., the world of the disembodied angels.

106. *Short Comm. to Exodus* 23:20; see, further, his *Comm. to Psalm* 139:18.

107. E.g., *Comm. to Gen.* 1:26; *Comm. to Ex.* 3:15. See Wolfson, "God, the Demiurge and the Intellect," p. 85.

108. Ibn Ezra *Ḥay ben Meqitz,* lines 648–673.

109. Ibn Ṭufayl, *Ḥayy ibn Yaqẓān,* p. 52 (Goodman, p. 95).

110. Ibn Ṭufayl, *Ḥayy ibn Yaqẓān,* p. 53 (Goodman, pp. 95–96).

111. Ibn Ṭufayl, *Ḥayy ibn Yaqẓān,* pp. 53–54 (Goodman, p. 96). My italics.

112. It is here that Vincent Cornell's study is very suggestive. He essentially argues that we need to situate ibn Ṭufayl within the context of both the study and the practice of many of the diverse trajectories of twelfth-century Maghribī Sufism. See his "Ḥayy in the Land of Absāl," pp. 162–164.

113. See the discussion in Efros, *Studies in Medieval Jewish Philosophy,* pp. 141–154.

114. Ibn Ṭufayl, *Ḥayy ibn Yaqẓān,* p. 54 (Goodman, p. 97).

115. Ibn Ṭufayl, *Ḥayy ibn Yaqẓān,* pp. 54–55 (Goodman, p. 98).

116. Ibn Ṭufayl, *Ḥayy ibn Yaqẓān,* p. 89 (Goodman, p. 131); in this regard, also see p. 92 (Goodman, p. 135).

117. Ibn Ṭufayl, *Ḥayy ibn Yaqẓān,* p. 99 (Goodman, p. 142).

118. Ibn Ṭufayl, *Ḥayy ibn Yaqẓān,* p. 100 (Goodman, p. 143).

119. Ibn Ṭufayl, *Ḥayy ibn Yaqẓān,* p. 101 (Goodman, p. 143).

120. Ibn Ṭufayl, *Ḥayy ibn Yaqẓān,* p. 108 (Goodman, pp. 149–150). My italics.

121. Cf. Yates, *The Art of Memory,* pp. 3ff.; Carruthers, *The Craft of Thought,* pp. 10ff.

122. Aristotle, *De memoria et remiscintia* 449b31. For Avicenna's comments on the relationship between memory and imagination, see *Aḥwāl al-nafs,* p. 62; *al-Najāt,* p. 202; Rahman, *Avicenna's Psychology,* p. 31.

123. Carruthers, *The Craft of Thought,* p. 115.

124. *Enn.* V.8. This, in turn, corresponds to *Theology of Aristotle,* chapter 4.

125. Eco, *Art and Beauty in the Middle Ages,* p. 72. Although Eco primarily focuses on aesthetic theory in the Christian and scholastic Middle Ages, his analysis provides useful generalizations that are applicable to the non-Christian Middle Ages.

126. Rist, *Psyche and Eros,* p. 22.

127. Nussbaum, "Transcending Humanity," in *Love's Knowledge,* pp. 390–391.

128. Black, "Aesthetics in Islamic Philosophy," p. 75.

129. Black, "Aesthetics in Islamic Philosophy," p. 76.

130. Avicenna, *Risāla fī al-ᶜishq,* p. 14. I have consulted and slightly modified the English translation of Fackenheim, "A Treatise on Love by Ibn Sina," p. 220.

131. Avicenna, *Risāla fī al-ᶜishq,* p. 13 (Fackenheim, p. 219).

132. Eco, *Art and Beauty in the Middle Ages,* p. 43.

133. E.g., Plotinus, *Enn.* I.6.9.

134. E.g., Plotinus, *Enn.* I.6.4, I.6.8. Also, see the discussion in Eco, *Art and Beauty in the Middle Ages,* p. 15.

135. On the reception of the *Poetics* among the Arabs, see the comments in ibn al-Nadīm, *The Fihrist,* p. 602. For appropriate secondary literature, see

Peters, *Aristoteles Arabus,* pp. 28–30; Tkatsch, *Die arabische Übersetzung der Poetik des Aristoteles,* vol. I, pp. 126aff.

136. Walzer, "Zur Traditionsgeschichte der Aristotelische Poetik," in his *Greek into Arabic,* pp. 132–134. Also see Madkour, *L'organon d'Aristote dans le monde arabe,* pp. 13ff; and Moraux, *Les listes anciennes des ouvrages d'Aristote,* pp. 179ff.

137. On Avicenna's poetic activity, see Alavi, "Some Aspects of the Literary and Poetical Activity of Avicenna."

138. Dahiyat, *Avicenna's Commentary on the Poetics of Aristotle,* p. 78.

139. Dahiyat, *Avicenna's Commentary on the Poetics of Aristotle,* p. 63.

140. Schoeler, "Der poetische Syllogismus," esp. pp. 48–49.

141. Avicenna, *Kitāb al-Shifāʾ,* Vol. I: *al-Burhān,* pp. 51ff. Also, see the discussion in Dahiyat, *Avicenna's Commentary on the Poetics of Aristotle,* p. 31.

142. Dahiyat, *Avicenna's Commentary on the Poetics of Aristotle,* p. 63.

143. Cf. Heidegger, *Being and Time,* p. 59.

144. Heidegger, "The Origin of the Work of Art," pp. 160–161.

145. Avicenna, *Ḥayy ibn Yaqẓān,* p. 48 (Corbin, p. 148).

146. Cf. ibn Zayla's commentary as quoted in Corbin, *Avicenna and the Visionary Recital,* pp. 360–361.

147. Avicenna, *Ḥayy ibn Yaqẓān,* p. 48 (Corbin, p. 148).

148. Cf. ibn Zayla's commentary in Corbin, *Avicenna and the Visionary Recital,* pp. 365–371.

149. E.g., Rahman, *Avicenna's Psychology,* p. 58.

150. Heath, *Allegory and Philosophy in Avicenna,* p. 162.

151. Ibn Ezra, *Ḥay ben Meqitz,* lines 375–385.

152. Ibn Ezra, *Ḥay ben Meqitz,* lines 41–62.

153. For the motif of "wandering" and its relationship to philosophy, see, further, Shem Tov ben Joseph ibn Falaquera, *Sefer ha-mevaqqesh,* ed. and trans. by M. Herschel Levine. Interestingly, this thirteenth-century individual also wrote his treatise in rhymed prose.

154. On the use of this term in Sufism and its subsequent influence on Jewish thought, see Efros, *Studies in Medieval Jewish Philosophy,* p. 148.

155. Ibn Ezra, *Ḥay ben Meqitz,* lines 674–705.

156. Kemal, "Justification of Poetic Validity," p. 217.

157. Ibn Ṭufayl, *Ḥayy ibn Yaqẓān,* p. 52 (Goodman, p. 95).

158. Ibn Ṭufayl, *Ḥayy ibn Yaqẓān,* p. 109 (Goodman, p. 152).

159. See Hamīd, "The Philosophical Significance of Ibn Ṭufail's *Ḥaiy Ibn Yaqẓān,*" pp. 58–59.

4. The Initiation of the Philosopher

1. Geertz, *The Interpretation of Cultures,* p. 90. Although, for a critique of this definition, see Asad, *Genealogies of Religion,* pp. 27–54.
2. Geertz, *The Interpretation of Cultures,* p. 108.
3. Geertz, *The Interpretation of Cultures,* p. 122.
4. See the discussion in Grimes, *Deeply into the Bone,* pp. 71ff.
5. Smith, "The Bare Facts of Ritual," in his *Imagining Religion,* pp. 63–64.
6. Bell, *Ritual,* pp. 66ff.
7. Grimes, *Research in Ritual Studies,* pp. 1–7.
8. See the note of caution in Grimes, *Deeply into the Bone,* p. 116.

9. Eliade, *Rites and Symbols of Initiation,* pp. 3ff.

10. Here I am influenced by S. Stetkevych's rich study of the ritual structure of the pre-Islamic *qaṣīda* ("ode"). See S. Stetkevych, *The Mute Immortals Speak.*

11. See Grimes, *Beginnings in Ritual Studies,* pp. 53–68; Tambiah, "A Performative Approach to Ritual," pp. 128ff.

12. Grimes, *Beginnings in Ritual Studies,* p. 61.

13. van Gennep, *The Rites of Passage,* p. 1. For various classical accounts that elaborate on the difference between the sacred and the profane, see Durkheim, *Elementary Forms of the Religious Life,* pp. 52ff.; Durkheim and Mauss, *Primitive Classification;* Eliade, *The Sacred and the Profane.* For an important critique of the sacred–profane dichotomy, see Jonathan Z. Smith, "The Wobbling Pivot," in *Map Is Not Territory,* pp. 88–103.

14. Quoted in Turner, *The Ritual Process,* p. 94.

15. Van Gennep, *The Rites of Passage,* pp. 11ff.

16. Turner, *The Ritual Process,* pp. 91ff.

17. Turner, *The Ritual Process,* p. 95.

18. Turner, *The Ritual Process,* p. 95.

19. S. Stetkevych, *The Mute Immortals Speak,* pp. 21–22.

20. Lévi-Strauss, *The Raw and the Cooked.*

21. Ibn Ezra, *Ḥay ben Meqitz,* lines 1–19.

22. Ibn Ezra, *Ḥay ben Meqitz,* lines 36–168.

23. Ibn Ezra, *Ḥay ben Meqitz,* lines 229–238.

24. Van Gennep, *The Rites of Passage,* p. 20.

25. Bell, *Ritual: Perspectives and Dimensions,* p. 118.

26. Turner, *The Ritual Process,* p. 103.

27. Ibn Ezra, *Ḥay ben Meqitz,* lines 391–400.

28. E.g., *Sefer Yesirah,* trans. Knut Stenring, p. 18. For further discussion, see my "The Three Worlds of ibn Ezra's *Ḥay ben Meqitz,*" pp. 19–21.

29. Edsman, "Fire," pp. 340–346.

30. Ibn Ezra, *Ḥay ben Meqitz,* lines 403–423.

31. Cf. *The Apocalypse of Abraham* 10:1–6; *1Enoch* 14:24–25, 17:1–8; *2Enoch* 56:2; *3Enoch* 1:7, 42:1. For all of these texts, I have consulted Charlesworth, ed., *The Old Testament Pseudepigrapha,* vol. 1: *Apocalyptic Literature and Testaments.*

32. Turner, *The Ritual Process,* p. 94.

33. Ibn Ezra, *Ḥay ben Meqitz,* lines 648–663.

34. Ibn Ezra, *Ḥay ben Meqitz,* lines 719–733.

35. Ibn Ezra, *Ḥay ben Meqitz,* lines 734–750.

36. On this motif, see Rosenthal, "The Stranger in Medieval Islam"; Fierro, "Spiritual Alienation and Political Activism."

37. Avicenna, *Ḥayy ibn Yaqẓān,* p. 40 (Corbin, p. 138).

38. Avicenna, *Ḥayy ibn Yaqẓān,* p. 42 (Corbin, p. 140).

39. Avicenna, *Ḥayy ibn Yaqẓān,* p. 43 (Corbin, pp. 141–142).

40. Avicenna, *Ḥayy ibn Yaqẓān,* p. 43 (Corbin, p. 142).

41. The reasons behind this stem from ibn Ezra's overwhelming interest in the science of astrology, a science that Avicenna regarded as little more than a pseudo-science.

42. Avicenna, *Ḥayy ibn Yaqẓān,* p. 47 (Corbin, p. 147).

43. Avicenna, *Ḥayy ibn Yaqẓān,* p. 49 (Corbin, pp. 149–150).

44. Avicenna, *Ḥayy ibn Yaqẓān,* p. 49 (Corbin, p. 150).

45. Hawi, however, argues that there are four distinct parts to ibn Ṭufayl's *Ḥayy:* (1) the "methodical" introduction; (2) the two accounts of Ḥayy's birth, and his early development; (3) Ḥayy's pantheism and extinction (*fanāʾ*) in God; and (4) his encounter with Absāl and subsequent adventures with the inhabitants of Absāl's island. He claims part four interrupts the natural flow of the rest of the narrative and is most likely a later addition by ibn Ṭufayl. See Hawi, *Islamic Naturalism and Mysticism,* pp. 22–28, 46–47.

46. Ibn Ṭufayl, *Ḥayy ibn Yaqẓān,* pp. 60–61 (Goodman, pp. 103–105). On the motif of spontaneous generation in medieval Islamicate thought, see Kruk, "A Frothy Bubble."

47. Ibn Ṭufayl, *Ḥayy ibn Yaqẓān,* pp. 62–63 (Goodman, pp. 105–106).

48. Ibn Ṭufayl, *Ḥayy ibn Yaqẓān,* p. 62 (Goodman, p. 105). The imagery of the ark here is reminiscent of the Qurʾānic account of the birth narrative of Moses (20:35ff., 18:1–15).

49. Ibn Ṭufayl, *Ḥayy ibn Yaqẓān,* p. 66 (Goodman, p. 109). In this regard, see the account in Fradkin, "Ibn Ṭufayl's Ḥayy ibn Yaqẓān on the Relationship of Mysticism, Prophecy, and Philosophy," pp. 90–125.

50. Fradkin, p. 118.

51. E.g., Mahdi, *Alfarabi and the Foundation of Islamic Political Philosophy,* pp. 65ff.; Butterworth, ed., *The Political Aspects of Islamic Philosophy.* For requisite primary sources, see ibn Bājja, *Tadbīr al-mutawaḥḥid;* Averroes, *Commentary on Plato's Republic.*

52. See Malti-Douglas, "*Ḥayy ibn Yaqẓān* as Male Utopia," p. 59.

53. Malti-Douglas, "*Ḥayy ibn Yaqẓān* as Male Utopia," pp. 61–62.

54. Ibn Ṭufayl, *Ḥayy ibn Yaqẓān,* pp. 81–82 (Goodman, p. 114).

55. Ibn Ṭufayl, *Ḥayy ibn Yaqẓān,* p. 89 (Goodman, p. 131). Interestingly, the one phenomenon that Ḥayy cannot ascertain with his unaided intellect is whether or not the universe arose temporally or is eternal, a problem that was of perennial interest to both Muslim and Jewish philosophers. On p. 90 (Goodman, p. 133): "He was no longer troubled by the dilemma of creation versus eternity, for either way the existence of a non-corporeal Author of the universe remained unscathed, a Being neither in contact with matter nor cut off from it, neither within nor outside it—for all these terms, 'contact' and 'discontinuity,' 'inside' and 'outside' are merely predicates of the very physical things which He transcends."

56. See the discussion in Brague, "The Imitation of the Heavenly Bodies in ibn Ṭufayl's *Ḥayy Ibn Yaqẓān.*"

57. Ibn Ṭufayl, *Ḥayy ibn Yaqẓān,* pp. 104–105 (Goodman, pp. 146–147). On the role of circumabulation, see Fenton, "The Symbolism of Ritual Circumabulation in Judaism and Islam," pp. 345–369.

58. This is certainly something that a Sufi would not agree with, since the goal of the Sufi is to separate the imagination from the discursivity of the intellect. See my "Imagining the Divine," pp. 41–45.

59. Ibn Ṭufayl, *Ḥayy ibn Yaqẓān,* p. 107 (Goodman, p. 149).

60. Ibn Ṭufayl, *Ḥayy ibn Yaqẓān,* p. 109 (Goodman, p. 152).

61. This ritual paradigm that culminates in the state of aggregation avoids the conclusion of Hawi. He argues, unpersuasively in my opinion, that the final part of ibn Ṭufayl's *Ḥayy* is narratively awkward and, thus, a later addition. See Hawi, *Islamic Mysticism and Islamic Naturalism,* pp. 46ff.

62. Ibn Ṭufayl, *Ḥayy ibn Yaqẓān,* p. 113 (Goodman, p. 156).
63. Ibn Ṭufayl, *Ḥayy ibn Yaqẓān,* p. 114 (Goodman, p. 156).
64. Ibn Ṭufayl, *Ḥayy ibn Yaqẓān,* p. 121 (Goodman, p. 164).
65. Ibn Ṭufayl, *Ḥayy ibn Yaqẓān,* p. 122 (Goodman, p. 165). The tense relationship between the philosopher and the rest of society is a recurring trope not only in Western philosophy in general (e.g., the fate of Socrates), but in Islamic philosophy in particular. See, e.g., Alfarabi, *Mabādiʾ ārāʾ ahl al-madīna al-fāḍila;* ibn Bājja, *Tadbīr al-mutawaḥḥid.*
66. E.g., Plato, *Phaedrus,* 245c–248c; *Phaedo* 64c–67d, 79b–84b.
67. Rappe, *Reading Neoplatonism,* pp. 2–3.
68. Rappe, *Reading Neoplatonism,* pp. 17ff.
69. Rappe, *Reading Neoplatonism,* p. 18.
70. Hadot, *Philosophy as a Way of Life,* p. 105.
71. Dahiyat, *Commentary to the Poetics of Aristotle,* p. 71.
72. Dahiyat, *Commentary to the Poetics of Aristotle,* p. 78.
73. Dahiyat, *Commentary to the Poetics of Aristotle,* p. 100. For the Aristotelian reference, see *Poetics* 1451a36–1451b10. In this regard, also see the comments in Stephen Halliwell, *The Poetics of Aristotle,* pp. 105–112.
74. Ibn Ezra, *Ḥay ben Meqitz,* lines 1–6.
75. E.g., Psalm 8:7; Job 34:2; Jeremiah 12:7.
76. Ibn Ezra, *Ḥay ben Meqitz,* lines 63–66; my italics.
77. Ibn Ezra, *Ḥay ben Meqitz,* lines 723–733.
78. Gohlman, *The Life of Ibn Sīnā,* pp. 24–27.
79. Gohlman, *The Life of Ibn Sīnā,* pp. 28–33.
80. Gohlman, *The Life of Ibn Sīnā,* pp. 36–37.
81. Avicenna, *Ḥayy ibn Yaqẓān,* p. 40 (Corbin, p. 137).
82. Avicenna, *Ḥayy ibn Yaqẓān,* p. 40 (Corbin, p. 137).
83. Avicenna, *Ḥayy ibn Yaqẓān,* p. 41 (Corbin, p. 138).
84. Avicenna, *Ḥayy ibn Yaqẓān,* p. 42 (Corbin, p. 141); my italics.
85. Avicenna, *Ḥayy ibn Yaqẓān,* p. 49 (Corbin, p. 150).
86. Ibn Ṭufayl, *Ḥayy ibn Yaqẓān,* p. 52 (Goodman, p. 95).
87. Based on these comments, Fradkin, opting for a strong Straussian reading, distinguishes between a "private" and a "public" teaching in the text. See Fradkin, "Ibn Ṭufayl's *Ḥayy Ibn Yaqẓān* on the Relationship of Mysticism, Prophecy, and Philosophy," pp. 18ff.
88. Ibn Ṭufayl, *Ḥayy ibn Yaqẓān,* p. 55 (Goodman, pp. 97–98).
89. Ibn Ṭufayl, *Ḥayy ibn Yaqẓān,* p. 60 (Goodman, p. 103).
90. See the comments in Kruk, "Ibn Ṭufayl," pp. 76–80.
91. Ibn Ṭufayl, *Ḥayy ibn Yaqẓān,* p. 74 (Goodman, p. 117).
92. E.g., Gadamer, *Truth and Method,* p. 304.
93. Ibn Ṭufayl, *Ḥayy ibn Yaqẓān,* pp. 92–93 (Goodman, pp. 135–136).
94. Ibn Ṭufayl, *Ḥayy ibn Yaqẓān,* pp. 105–106 (Goodman, pp. 145–146).
95. Ibn Ṭufayl, *Ḥayy ibn Yaqẓān,* p. 122 (Goodman, p. 165).
96. E.g., LeClerq, *The Love of Learning and the Desire for God;* Carruthers, *The Book of Memory;* idem, *The Craft of Thought.* As a cross-cultural trope, see J. Boyarin, ed., *The Ethnography of Reading.*
97. Hadot, *Philosophy as a Way of Life,* p. 62.
98. See the comments in Tambiah, "A Performative Approach to Ritual," pp. 145ff.

5. "God Is Beautiful and Loves Beauty"

1. E.g., Monroe, "Hispano-Arabic Poetry During the Caliphate of Cordoba: Theory and Practice," pp. 125–154; Bonebakker, "Adab and the Concept of Belles-Lettres"; Pagis, *Secular Poetry and Poetic Theory: Moses Ibn Ezra and His Contemporaries;* idem, *Change and Tradition in Secular Poetry;* Schippers, *Arabic Tradition and Hebrew Innovation;* Scheindlin, *Wine, Women, and Death;* idem, *The Gazelle;* idem, "The Hebrew Qasida in Spain"; idem, "Rabbi Moshe Ibn Ezra on the Legitimacy of Poetry"; Brann, *The Compunctious Poet.*

2. For a distinction between medieval and modern senses of the terms art and aesthetics, I have found very useful the discussion in Belting, *Likeness and Presence,* pp. xxiff.

3. The *locus classicus* of this emanative framework is found in Plotinus, *Enn.* 3.8.10. For a good discussion of the problematics that this creates, see Hyman, "From What Is One and Simple Only What Is One and Simple Can Come to Be," pp. 111–135.

4. Heidegger, *Being and Time,* p. 60.

5. Heidegger, *Being and Time,* p. 62.

6. Wolfson, *Through a Speculum that Shines,* pp. 52–73. Wolfson's comments need to be situated within the ongoing debate, of which there is a virtual cottage industry, concerning the quiddity of religious experience. Within this context, experience is such a murky term precisely because its various modes—religious, visionary, mystical, spiritual—are thought by many to constitute the essence of religion. See, e.g., the critical discussion in Proudfoot, *Religious Experience,* esp. pp. 119–154. For an excellent overview that problematizes the discussion in a useful manner, see Scharf, "Experience." My own discussion attempts to avoid the tendency to reduce the *Ḥayy ibn Yaqẓān* cycle to some form of numinous experience, and instead appreciate these texts on their own terms by analyzing their various theoretical and rhetorical moves, both of which are grounded within a specific spatial and temporal context.

7. There are of course notable exceptions. Some pioneering studies in this may be found in Black, *Logic and Aristotle's Rhetoric and Poetics in Medieval Arabic Philosophy;* Kemal, *The Poetics of Alfarabi and Avicenna;* Fenton, *Philosophie et exégèse dans le jardin de la métaphore de Moïse ibn Ezra, philosophe et poète andalou du XIIe siècle.*

8. Cf. Wolfson, *Through a Speculum that Shines,* pp. 3–5; Freedberg, *The Power of Images,* pp. 60ff.

9. E.g., Gutmann, "The 'Second Commandment' and the Image in Judaism"; Mann, *Jewish Texts on the Visual Arts,* pp. 1–18; Allen, "Aniconism and Figural Representation in Islamic Art," pp. 18ff.

10. See, e.g., von Grunebaum, "The Concept of Plagiarism in Arabic Theory," p. 234. It is important, then, to contrast this discussion with that of the anxiety of influence in post-Romantic thought. For a discussion of the latter, see Bloom, *The Anxiety of Influence.*

11. See, e.g., the discussions in al-^{c}Askarī, *Kitāb al-ṣinā^{c}atayn,* pp. 147ff.; al-Qayrawānī, *Al-^{c}umda fī mahāsin al-shi^{c}r,* vol. 2, p. 280. For a similar discussion in Hebrew poetics, see Moses ibn Ezra, *Kitāb al-muḥāḍara,* p. 174.

12. Exodus 20:4; cf. also Deuteronomy 5:8.

13. Schwarzschild, "Aesthetics," p. 1.

14. Ze'ev Levy, "The Status of Aesthetics in Jewish Thought," p. 86. Cf. Frank, "Idolatry and the Love of Appearances: Maimonides and Plato on False Wisdom," pp. 155–168.

15. Ze'ev Levy, "The Status of Aesthetics in Jewish Thought," p. 88.

16. Cf. Schubert, "Jewish Pictorial Traditions in Early Christian Art"; Fine, "Art and the Liturgical Context of the Sepphoris Synagogue Mosaic."

17. Wolfson, *Through a Speculum that Shines,* p. 3.

18. A popular misconception is that Muslim antipathy to the arts influenced Christian iconoclasm. For a corrective to this see Grabar, "Islam and Iconoclasm."

19. Terry, "Aniconism and Figural Representation," pp. 18–19; Grabar, *The Formation of Islamic Art,* pp. 92–98. In an important discussion, Steven Humphreys argues that the reason behind the dearth of studies devoted to the visual arts in Islamic history says less about their actual absence than it does about the lacunae in the academic study of Islam and the training of graduates in the field. See his *Islamic History,* pp. 59–65.

20. Kahwaji, "ilm al-djamāl," p. 1134. In this regard, also see the comments in Isa, "Muslims and Taswir." A long overdue corrective to these approaches may be found in Puerta Vílchez, *Historia del pensamiento estético árabe, al-Andalus y la estética árabe clásica.* Also, see the discussion in Gonzalez, *Beauty and Islam,* pp. 5–25.

21. See the discussion in Dorff, "In Defense of Images," pp. 129–154.

22. Behrens-Abouseif, *Beauty in Arabic Culture,* pp. 7–8.

23. In addition to the citations in note 11 above, see S. Stetkevych, *Abū Tammām and the Poetics of the ^{c}Abbāsid Age,* pp. 5–37; idem, "Toward a Redefinition of *badī^{c}* Poetry," pp. 1–29; Losensky, "'The Allusive Field of Drunkenness,'" p. 227.

24. Bland, *The Artless Jew,* pp. 15–36; also see his "Anti-Semitism and Aniconism," pp. 41–66.

25. E.g., Auerbach, "Odysseus's Scar," in his *Mimesis,* pp. 3–23; Meschonnic, *Critique du rythme: anthropologie historique du language.*

26. Bland, *The Artless Jew,* p. 16.

27. Bland, *The Artless Jew,* p. 8.

28. On the history of this, see Nussbaum, *The Therapy of Desire,* pp. 3–12; idem, "Introduction: Form and Content, Philosophy and Literature," in her *Love's Knowledge,* esp. pp. 40–43; Sorabji, *Emotion and Peace of Mind;* Sihvola and Engberg-Pederson, eds., *The Emotions in Hellenistic Philosophy.*

29. See my discussion in chapter 3.

30. *Phaedo* 100d.

31. *Republic* 476b; cf. *Republic* 510a; *Timeaus* 29c.

32. *Republic* 500c.

33. *Republic* 500d.

34. *Republic* 500b–500d.

35. Plato deals most fully with the potential danger of the "imitative arts" in chapter 10 of the *Republic.*

36. *Gorgias* 523a.

37. On the rationale behind this use of language, see Plato's *Seventh Letter:* "I do not, however, think the attempt to tell mankind of these matters a good thing, except in the case of some few who are capable of discovering the truth for themselves with a little guidance. In the case of the rest to do so would

excite in some an unjustified contempt in a thoroughly offensive fashion, in others certain lofty and vain hopes, as if they had acquired some awesome lore" (341e–342a).

38. *Metaphysics* 1078a35–1078b5.

39. E.g., *Politics* 1326a34ff.; *Parts of Animals* 645a23–645a26; *de Anima* 416a ff.

40. *Poetics* 1450b34–1451a2.

41. Cf. the discussion in Halliwell, *The Poetics of Aristotle*, p. 99.

42. See the discussion in Zimmermann, "The Origins of the So-Called *Theology of Aristotle*."

43. The *Theology* was but one medieval pseudepigraphical work attributed to or associated with Aristotle in the *Corpus Aristotelicum Arabicum*. Other works included the *Mystery of Mysteries*, attributed to Aristotle's most famous supposed pupil, Alexander the Great; and an account of Aristotle's death in the *Book of the Apple*, which is loosely based on Socrates' death in the *Phaedo*.

44. On the centrality of aesthetics in the thought of Plotinus, see Halliwell, *The Aesthetics of Mimesis*, p. 314.

45. *Enn*. I.6.5.17–20.

46. Gerson, *Plotinus*, pp. 212–213.

47. *Enn*. I.6.2.7–11.

48. On this tension, see Halliwell, *The Aesthetics of Mimesis*, pp. 315–317.

49. Rappe, *Reading Neoplatonism*, p. 12.

50. E.g., *Enn*. I.6.9.

51. E.g., Plotinus, *Enn*. I.6.4, I.6.8. Also, see the discussion in Eco, *Art and Beauty in the Middle Ages*, p. 15.

52. For a survey of his life, times, and place in the history of philosophy, see Rosán, *The Philosophy of Proclus;* Wallis, *Neoplatonism*, chapter 5; Siorvanes, *Proclus: Neoplatonic Philosophy and Science*.

53. Lamberton, *Homer the Theologian*, pp. 186ff.; Rappe, *Reading Neoplatonism*, p. 175.

54. Lamberton, *Homer the Theologian*, p. 188.

55. I.78.1–10, quoted in Rappe, *Reading Neoplatonism*, p. 176.

56. Cf. Rist, *Psyche and Eros*, p. 22.

57. On the notion that the Islamic philosophers imitated the Greek paradigm when it came to art and aesthetics, see the collection of essays in Rosenthal, *Four Essays on Art and Literature in Islam*.

58. Cf. Mahdi, "Islamic Philosophy and the Fine Arts," pp. 21–22.

59. See the brief discussion in Harvey, "Ethics and Meta-Ethics, Aesthetics and Meta-Aesthetics in Maimonides," p. 135.

60. Here they build on the theory found in Aristotle, *De Anima* III.4 (429a15–429b26). For the various ways in which this plays out in Western thought, see Lindberg, *Theories of Vision from al-Kindi to Kepler.*

61. For requisite historical background on the *Ikhwān al-Ṣafā*ᵓ see Netton, *Muslim Neoplatonists*, pp. 1–8; Nasr, *An Introduction to Islamic Cosmological Doctrines*, pp. 25–43. On the arrival of their *Rasāᵓil* into Spain, see chapter 2, n. 105.

62. *Rasāᵓil Ikhwān al-Ṣafā*ᵓ, vol. 1, p. 207. An English translation of this may be found in Shiloah, *The Epistle on Music of the Ikhwan al-Safa*, p. 37.

63. *Rasāᵓil*, p. 183 (Shiloah, p. 12).

64. *Rasāᵓil*, p. 196 (Shiloah, p. 25).

65. *Rasāᵓil*, p. 237 (Shiloah, p. 69).

66. Alfarabi, *Mabādiʾ ārāʾ ahl al-madīna al-fāḍila,* pp. 83–85. Long regarded as the epitome of Alfarabi's work, Mahdi has recently questioned the centrality of this work within the Farabian corpus. See his discussion in *Alfarabi and the Foundations of Islamic Political Philosophy,* pp. 6–11.

67. Alfarabi, *Mabādiʾ ārāʾ ahl al-madīna al-fāḍila,* pp. 84–85.

68. Alfarabi, *Mabādiʾ ārāʾ ahl al-madīna al-fāḍila,* pp. 86–87.

69. Alfarabi, *Mabādiʾ ārāʾ ahl al-madīna al-fāḍila,* pp. 230–231.

70. Alfarabi, *Mabādiʾ ārāʾ ahl al-madīna al-fāḍila,* pp. 238–239.

71. Cf. Alfarabi, *Al-Siyāsa al-madaniyya,* pp. 72–73.

72. Alfarabi, *Mabādiʾ ārāʾ ahl al-madīna al-fāḍila,* pp. 287–315.

73. On the various definitions that he gives of happiness (*saᶜāda*), see Galston, "The Theoretical and Practical Dimension of Happiness as Portrayed in the Political Treatises of al-Fārābī," pp. 100–113.

74. See the discussion in Galston, *Politics and Excellence,* pp. 166–175. On the controversy concerning Alfarabi's purported change of opinion late in life, see Pines, "The Limitations of Human Knowledge according to Alfarabi, ibn Bajja, and Maimonides," pp. 82–109. Pines bases his argument, in part, on comments found in ibn Ṭufayl, *Ḥayy ibn Yaqẓān,* p. 58 (Goodman, p. 100).

75. Avicenna, *al-Najāt,* pp. 281–282.

76. Avicenna, *Risāla fī al-ᶜishq,* p. 14 (Fackenheim, p. 220). Also, see the discussion in Black, "Aesthetics in Islamic Philosophy," pp. 75–79.

77. See my comments in "Imagining the Divine," pp. 38–41.

78. *R. fī al-ᶜishq,* p. 13 (Fackenheim, p. 219).

79. *R. fī al-ᶜishq,* p. 15 (Fackenheim, p. 221).

80. On the various problematics associated with ibn Ezra's use of astrology, see the comments in Jospe, "The Torah and Astrology according to Abraham Ibn Ezra," pp. 17–24; Langermann, "Some Astrological Themes in the Thought of Abraham ibn Ezra"; Sela, *Astrology and Biblical Exegesis in Abraham ibn Ezra's Thought;* pp. 103–106; Hughes, "The Three Worlds of ibn Ezra's *Ḥay ben Meqitz,*" pp. 9–14.

81. Ibn Ezra, *The Beginning of Wisdom,* pp. 193–204. Also, see the discussion in Raphael Levy, *The Astrological Works of Abraham ibn Ezra,* pp. 11–19. This, in turn, plays out in the descriptions that ibn Ezra provides of the various planets in his *Ḥay ben Meqitz.* Likely sources for ibn Ezra would have been Ptolemy's *Tetrabiblos.* For a detailed examination of ibn Ezra's use of Ptolemy, see Sela, *Astrology and Biblical Exegesis in Abraham ibn Ezra's Thought,* pp. 35ff. Another probable source for ibn Ezra's treatment was ibn Gabirol's *Keter Malkut.* On the relationship between these two, see Greive, *Studien zum jüdischen Neuplatonismus,* pp. 123–198; Rosin, "Die Religionsphilosophie Abraham ibn Esras," no. 42 (1898), pp. 29–33.

82. E.g., his excursus to Exodus 33:23. In terms of Israel, ibn Ezra follows on the heels of the rabbinic discussion in the Talmud (Shabbat 156b) that states that as long as Israel follows the Torah, it has no star or sign (*mazal*). However, in other works (e.g., *Sefer ha-Olam*) he seems to imply that Aquarius is Israel's astrological sign. See the comments in Sela, *Astrology and Biblical Exegesis in Abraham ibn Ezra's Thought,* pp. 103–106.

83. See Schwartz, *Astral Magic in Medieval Jewish Thought,* pp. 63–68.

84. Langermann, "Some Astrological Themes in the Thought of Abraham ibn Ezra," p. 47.

85. Bland, *The Artless Jew,* p. 134.

86. Schwartz, *Astral Magic in Medieval Jewish Thought,* pp. 68–72.

87. Sela, *Astrology and Biblical Exegesis in Abraham ibn Ezra's Thought,* pp. 98–102; Schwartz, *Astral Magic in Medieval Jewish Thought,* pp. 70–71.

88. Cf. his excursus to Genesis 4:13 and his comments to Exodus 25:40; Deuteronomy 31:16; Psalm 87:5–6. In addition, see the discussion in Langermann, "Some Astrological Themes in the Thought of Abraham ibn Ezra," pp. 34ff.

89. Bland, *The Artless Jew,* p. 135.

90. *Commentary to Exodus* 32:1. See the comments in Goetschel, "The Sin of the Golden Calf in the Exegesis of Abraham ibn Ezra," pp. 137–144.

91. I.e., if Moses functions in a god-like way, then Aaron becomes a prophet. Ibn Ezra is arguing that if Aaron has such an important position in the community there is no way that he could or would commit such an egregious sin.

92. *Short Comm. to Exodus* 3:1.

93. Bland, *The Artless Jew,* p. 137.

94. Schwartz, *Astral Magic in Medieval Jewish Thought,* pp. 71–72.

95. Maimonides, *Avodat kokhavim ve-hukkoteihem* 3:10; quoted in Mann, *Jewish Texts on the Visual Arts,* p. 23.

96. Maimonides, *Avodat kokhavim ve-hukkoteihem* 3:10; quoted in Mann, *Jewish Texts on the Visual Arts,* p. 24.

97. Maimonides, *Avodat kokhavim ve-hukkoteihem* 3:10; quoted in Mann, *Jewish Texts on the Visual Arts,* p. 24.

98. On the place of this work within the Maimonidean corpus, see Weiss, *Maimonides' Ethics,* pp. 9–32.

99. See the comments in Harvey, "Ethics and Meta-Ethics, Aesthetics and Meta-Aesthetics in Maimonides," p. 134; Weiss, *Maimonides' Ethics,* p. 28; Kreisel, *Maimonides' Political Thought,* pp. 68–69.

100. On the relationship between Maimonides' theory of ethics as it relates to the Jewish tradition, see the discussion in Benor, *Worship of the Heart,* pp. 39–61.

101. I have used the translation of *Eight Chapters* found in *Ethical Writings of Maimonides,* p. 77.

102. As Ralph Lerner has recently argued, Maimonides was also interested in disseminating such ideas to the general public. Cf. his *Maimonides' Empire of Light,* pp. 3–13.

103. *Eight Chapters,* p. 77.

104. Bland, *The Artless Jew,* p. 78.

105. Bland, *The Artless Jew,* p. 78.

106. Avicenna, *Ḥayy ibn Yaqẓān,* p. 43 (Corbin, p. 142).

107. Ibn Ezra, *Ḥay ben Meqitz,* lines 53–54.

108. Ibn Ezra, *Ḥay ben Meqitz,* lines 375–390.

109. The concept of a "consuming fire" is a common one throughout the Bible. Cf. *inter alia,* Deuteronomy 9:3; Isaiah 30:30.

110. Ibn Ṭufayl, *Ḥayy ibn Yaqẓān,* p. 84 (Goodman, p. 126).

111. Ibn Ṭufayl, *Ḥayy ibn Yaqẓān,* p. 85 (Goodman, p. 127).

112. See, e.g., ibn Ṭufayl, *Ḥayy ibn Yaqẓān,* pp. 76–77 (Goodman, p. 119).

113. Avicenna, *Ḥayy ibn Yaqẓān,* p. 46 (Corbin, p. 145).

114. Ibn Ezra, *Ḥay ben Meqitz,* lines 322–345.

115. Cf. Brann, *The Compunctious Poet,* pp. 39ff.; Kozodoy, "Reading Medieval Hebrew Love Poetry"; Pagis, *Hebrew Poetry of the Middle Ages and Renaissance,*

p. 13. On ibn Ezra's commentary to the Song, see *Ibn Ezra's Commentary on the Song of Songs,* ed. and trans. Richard A. Bloch.

116. On the motif of the garden in Andalusī architecture, cf. Ruggles, *Gardens, Landscapes, and Vision in Islamic Spain,* pp. 9ff.; Petruccioli, ed., *Gardens in the Time of the Great Muslim Empires: Theory and Design;* Brookes, *Gardens of Paradise,* pp. 8–16.

117. Ibn Ṭufayl, *Ḥayy ibn Yaqẓān,* p. 78 (Goodman, p. 120).

118. E.g., ibn Ṭufayl, *Ḥayy ibn Yaqẓān,* p. 79 (Goodman, p. 122).

119. Ibn Ṭufayl, *Ḥayy ibn Yaqẓān,* p. 80 (Goodman, p. 123).

120. Ibn Ṭufayl, *Ḥayy ibn Yaqẓān,* p. 90 (Goodman, pp. 132–133).

121. Avicenna, *Ḥayy ibn Yaqẓān,* p. 48 (Corbin, p. 149).

122. Avicenna, *Ḥayy ibn Yaqẓān,* p. 49 (Corbin, p. 150).

123. Ibn Ezra, *Ḥay ben Meqitz,* lines 664–673.

124. Ibn Ezra, *Ḥay ben Meqitz,* lines 676–687.

125. Ibn Ṭufayl, *Ḥayy ibn Yaqẓān,* p. 93 (Goodman, p. 135).

126. Ibn Ṭufayl, *Ḥayy ibn Yaqẓān,* p. 53 (Goodman, p. 96).

127. Ibn Ṭufayl, *Ḥayy ibn Yaqẓān,* p. 109 (Goodman, p. 152).

128. Ibn Ṭufayl, *Ḥayy ibn Yaqẓān,* pp. 120–121 (Goodman, pp. 163–164).

129. Wolfson, *Through a Speculum that Shines,* p. 61.

Appendix

1. *Iggeret Ḥay ben Mekitz,* ed. I. Levin. On the manuscript tradition of this text, see esp. pp. 7–9. The numbering of the poem is my own and does not correspond to Levin's.

2. For the biblical references to *Ḥay* I have, again, relied primarily on the critical edition supplied by Levin.

3. Cf. Job 34:2.

4. Proverbs 8:7.

5. Jeremiah 12:7.

6. Cf. Song of Songs 1:6.

7. Heb. *ruaḥ.*

8. Heb. *nefesh.*

9. The self here refers, it would seem, to the "rational soul" or *neshamah.*

10. Cf. Genesis 24:65.

11. Cf. Song 4:1, 3.

12. Cf. Deuteronomy 34:7; Song 4:3.

13. Cf. Deuteronomy 34:7.

14. Cf. Song 1:3, 12.

15. Song 5:16.

16. Cf. Job 23:5.

17. Cf. Song 5:14.

18. The meaning of these two words are uncertain in the biblical Hebrew. They are, according to Exodus 28:30, placed inside the high priest's breastplate and designate a kind of oracle.

19. Cf. I Kings 1:47.

20. Cf. Isaiah 48:18.

21. Cf. Proverbs 3:6.

22. Proverbs 4:11.

23. Proverbs 1:4.
24. Proverbs 8:30.
25. Song 8:11.
26. Song 2:3.
27. Song 2:3.
28. Heb. *nafshekha.*
29. Deuteronomy 28:29.
30. Cf. Qoheleth 7:26.
31. Cf. Qoheleth 7:26.
32. Isaiah 59:7.
33. Cf. Jeremiah 4:4.
34 Cf. Qoheleth 7:9.
35. Cf. Psalm 10:9.
36. Proverbs 27:22.
37. Cf. Qoheleth 7:7.
38. Proverbs 23:33.
39. Psalm 36:5.
40. Qoheleth 1:8.
41. Cf. Genesis 41:40.
42. Cf. Lamentations 4:20.
43. Proverbs 6:27–28.
44. Proverbs 1:15. The verse in the original is referring to sinners.
45. Cf. Proverbs 7:26.
46. Cf. Proverbs 7:27.
47. Deuteronomy 13:9. The reference is to false prophets.
48. Proverbs 26:25.
49. Proverbs 26:25.
50. Song 2:17. The reference is to death.
51. Cf. Proverbs 3:3.
52. Proverbs 5:17.
53. Proverbs 1:9.
54. Job 36:11.
55. Proverbs 3:15.
56. Heb. *nafsho.*
57. Proverbs 8:36.
58. Cf. Exodus 9:2.
59. Proverbs 4:22.
60. Cf. Song 1:4, 8:2.
61. Cf. Proverbs 6:18.
62. Psalm 55:7.
63. Jeremiah 11:20.
64. Cf. Job 11:9.
65. Numbers 26:53.
66. Cf. Genesis 41:38.
67. Cf. Jeremiah 30:13.
68. Cf. Proverbs 5:15.
69. Cf. Numbers 13:32.
70. Job 38:14.
71. Cf. Ezekiel 34:6.
72. Qoheleth 9:11.

73. Psalm 8:8.
74. I Kings 5:3.
75. Genesis 12:11.
76. Cf. Song 6:11.
77. Psalm 148:9.
78. Psalm 104:12.
79. Proverbs 5:16.
80. Cf. Isaiah 5:2.
81. Cf. Jeremiah 17:8.
82. Cf. Psalm 80:12.
83. Cf. Numbers 13:23.
84. Cf. Psalm 65:11.
85. Cf. Song 6:11.
86. Song 7:14.
87. Song 2:13.
88. Song 7:14.
89. Psalm 68:17.
90. Isaiah 13:12; Job 28:16.
91. Job 28:16.
92. Cf. Deuteronomy 33:25. Here referring to the security and permanence associated with Asher.
93. Exodus 28:17, 39:10. Here referring to the stones found in the high priest's breastplate.
94. Cf. Ezekiel 22:18, 22:20, 27:12; Numbers 31:22.
95. Cf. Exodus 28:20, 39:13; Ezekiel 28:13. All of which describe the contents of the stones found in the high priest's breastplate. Also, in Ezekiel 1:16 and 10:9 this stone is used to describe the wheels of the chariot (*merkabah*).
96. In Genesis 2:12 this term is used to refer to one of the minerals found in the river "Pishon." And, in Numbers 11:7 this mineral is employed to describe the color of manna.
97. Cf. Deuteronomy 29:22.
98. Cf. Genesis 41:45. This term refers to all else that exists in the mineral world under the ground. The reference from Genesis refers to the name that Pharaoh gave to Joseph.
99. Isaiah 22:18.
100. Cf. Isaiah 16:4.
101. Cf. Job 26:10.
102. Joshua 10:11. The context of this term refers to the stones that God sent against the Amorite armies.
103. Job 38:22–23.
104. Deuteronomy 4:24.
105. Cf. 2 Samuel 22:9; Psalm 18:9.
106. Cf. Song 8:6.
107. Nahum 3:3.
108. Cf. Song 8:7.
109. Cf. Ezekiel 24:9; Isaiah 30:33.
110. Cf. Ezekiel 21:3; Job 15:30.
111. Cf. Psalm 109:24. This image is also associated with the ecstatic experiences associated with the Book of Daniel.
112. Cf. Psalm 6:8.

113. Cf. Daniel 8:17.
114. Cf. Psalm 6:4.
115. Cf. Ezekiel 2:2.
116. Isaiah 7:4.
117. Isaiah 43:2.
118. Genesis 24:31.
119. Job 37:18.
120. Job 41:8.
121. Cf. Job 38:7.
122. Lit., rock (*ṣur*); in this regard, cf. Psalm 78:35.
123. Lit., laws in the religious sense.
124. The Hebrew term that is used here is *berit.*
125. Psalm 91:10. Ibn Ezra has changed the biblical text to read "their" in place of "your."
126. Lit., service (*avodah*) in the cultic sense.
127. Heb. *nefshot.*
128. Cf. Isaiah 60:2.
129. Cf. Psalm 68:6.
130. Song 4:15.
131. Heb. *avodatam.*
132. Lit., "thinkers of thought"; i.e., philosophers.
133. I.e., poets.
134. I.e., rhetoricians.
135. Exodus 36:1. Both of these individuals were experts skilled in the administration of the sanctuary.
136. Cf. Isaiah 25:5.
137. Samuel 6:16.
138. Cf. Psalm 19:5–6.
139. Song 4:2.
140. Song 4:3.
141. Cf. Song 5:11.
142. Song 4:1.
143. Cf. Song 4:3.
144. Song 7:3.
145. Psalm 19:6.
146. Psalm 19:6.
147. Psalm 19:7.
148. Isaiah 40:11.
149. Cf. Isaiah 35:8.
150. Cf. Lamentations 4:13.
151. The Hebrew term *mezimah* denotes "calculation" in the negative sense of the term. I have here translated it as a positive term ("counsel"), something that the inhabitants of Mars avoid.
152. Isaiah 5:28.
153. Isaiah 5:28.
154. Cf. Isaiah 33:15.
155. Cf. Habbakuk 1:13.
156. Cf. Isaiah 33:15.
157. Cf. Genesis 25:27, where the mildness of Jacob who "dwells in a tent" is juxtaposed against the physical prowess of Esau.

158. Cf. Psalm 45:7.
159. Isaiah 58:4.
160. Cf. Psalm 37:35.
161. Isaiah 3:3.
162. Cf. Psalm 21:6, 96:6, 104:1, 111:3.
163. Ezekiel 1:4.
164. Cf. Genesis 3:24.
165. Genesis 1:2.
166. Cf., for example, Deuteronomy 1:1; Jeremiah 50:12.
167. Heb. *shiᶜur qomato;* a reference to the fact that the divine cannot be measured and, thus, probably a criticism of the movement and literature (*shiᶜur qoma*) that claimed, and provided, such measurements.
168. Cf. Daniel 10:7–8.
169. Cf. Ezekiel 1:16.
170. The Hebrew term, *menaṣeḥot,* refers to the temple liturgy. Cf., for example, Psalm 4:1, 5:1, 8:1.
171. Cf. Genesis 28:17.
172. Exodus 3:5.
173. Cf. Qoheleth 4:8.
174. Cf. I Kings 8:27.
175. Cf. 2 Chronicles 29:11.
176. Cf. Psalm 18:32.
177. Cf. Isaiah 44:13.
178. Cf. Isaiah 40:18.
179. Cf. Deuteronomy 29:28.
180. Cf. Jeremiah 17:10.
181. Psalm 89:15.
182. Proverbs 14:22.
183. Cf. Psalm 130:2.
184. Psalm 123:1.
185. Psalm 31:6.
186. Micah 6:6.
187. Cf. Psalm 119:174.
188. Cf. Deuteronomy 7:14.
189. Samuel 7:18.
190. Cf. the story of Rabbi Akiva and his three companions who enter Pardes (*Ḥagigah* 14b).
191. Nehemiah 9:5.
192. Psalm 136:4.

Bibliography

Primary Sources

Alfarabi (Al-Fārābī, Abū Naṣr). *Mabādiʾ ārāʾ al-madīna al-fāḍila*. Published as *Al-Fārābī on the Perfect State: Abū Naṣr al-Fārābī's Mabādiʾ ārāʾ al-madīna al-fāḍila*. A Revised Text with Introduction, Translation, and Commentary by Richard Walzer. Oxford: Oxford University Press, 1985.

———. *The Philosophy of Plato and Aristotle*. Translated by Muhsin Mahdi. Ithaca, N.Y.: Cornell University Press, 1962.

———. *Risāla fī qawānīn ṣināʿa al-shʿir*. Pp. 149–158 in *Arisṭūṭālīs fann al-shʿir*. 2nd ed. Edited by ʿAbd al-Raḥman Badawī. Cairo: Dār al-thaqāfa, 1973.

———. *Al-Siyāsa al-madaniyya*. Edited by Fauzi Najjar. Beirut: Imprimerie Catholique, 1964.

al-Andalusī, Ibn Saʿīd. *Al-Mughrib fī ḥulā al-maghrib*. Edited by Shawqī Dayf. Cairo: Al-Matbaʿa al maʿārif, 1953–1955.

Aristotle. *The Complete Works of Aristotle*. 2 vols. Edited by Jonathan Barnes. Princeton, N.J.: Princeton University Press, 1984.

al-ʿAskarī, Abū Hilāl al-Ḥasan. *Kitāb al-ṣināʿatayn*. 2nd ed. Edited by ʿAli Muḥammad Bijāwī and Muḥammad Abū al-Faḍl Ibrāhīm. Cairo: ʿĪsā al-bābī al-halabi, 1971.

Attar, Farid al-Din. *The Conference of the Birds*. Translated by Afkham Darbandi and Dick Davis. Harmondsworth: Penguin, 1984.

Badawī, ʿAbd al-Raḥman, ed. *Al-Aflāṭūniyya al-muḥdatha ʿind al-ʿarab*. Cairo, 1955.

Charlesworth, J. H., ed. *The Old Testament Pseudepigrapha*. Garden City, N.Y.: Doubleday, 1983.

Gohlman, William E., trans. *The Life of Ibn Sīnā: A Critical Edition and Annotated Translation*. Albany: State University of New York Press, 1974.

Goldziher, Ignaz, ed. *Kitāb maʿānī al-nafs (Buch von Wesen der Seele). Abhandlungen der könliglichen Gesellschaft der Wissenschaften zu Göttingen, phil.-hist. Kl.*, Neue Folge IX (1907).

Halevi, Judah. *Kitāb al-radd waʾl-dalīl fīʾl-dīn al-dhalīl (al-kitāb al-khazarī)*. Edited by D. H. Baneth and H. Ben-Shammai. Jerusalem: The Magnes Press, 1977.

———. *Sefer ha-kuzari*. Edited and translated by J. Even-Shmuel. Tel Aviv: Dvir, 1994.

al-Ḥarizi, Judah. *Taḥkemoni.* Edited by A. Kaminka. Warsaw: n.p., 1899.

Ibn al-Abbār. *Al-Muqtaḍab min kitāb tuḥfat al-qadīm.* Edited by Ibrāhīm al-Abyārī. Cairo: Al-Matbaᶜa al-amīriyya, 1957.

Ibn al-Arabi. *The Bezels of Wisdom.* Translated by R. W. J. Austin. Mahwah, N.J.: Paulist Press, 1980.

Ibn Bājja. "*Tadbīr al-mutawaḥḥid.*" In *Opera Metaphysica,* edited by Majid Fakhry. Beirut: Dār al-Nahar, 1968.

Ibn Daud, Abraham. *The Book of Tradition* (*Sefer ha-Qabbalah*). Edited, translated, and notes by Gerson D. Cohen. Philadelphia: Jewish Publication Society of America, 1967.

Ibn Ezra, Abraham. *The Beginning of Wisdom: An Astrological Treatise by Abraham ibn Ezra, an Edition of the Old French Version of 1273 and an English Translation of the Hebrew Original.* Edited by Raphael Levy. Baltimore: Johns Hopkins University Press, 1939.

———. *Commentary to the Tanakh.* Printed in *Miqraot Gedolot.*

———. *Commentary to the Torah.* 3 vols. Edited by Asher Weiser. Jerusalem: Mossad Harav Kook, 1976.

———. *Ibn Ezra's Commentary on the Song of Songs.* Translated by Richard A. Bloch. Cincinnati: Hebrew Union College Press, 1982.

———. *Iggeret Ḥay ben Mekitz.* Edited by Israel Levin. Tel Aviv: Tel Aviv University Press, 1983.

———. *The Religious Poems of Abraham Ibn Ezra.* 2 vols. Edited by Israel Levin. Jerusalem: Israel Academy of Sciences and Humanities, 1975–1980.

———. *Yalkuth Ibn Ezra.* Edited by Israel Levin. Tel Aviv: Tel Aviv University Press, 1985.

Ibn Ezra, Moses. *Kitāb al-muḥāḍara wa al-mudhākara (Sefer ha-ᶜiyyunim ve ha-diyyunim).* Edited and translated by A. S. Halkin. Jerusalem: Mekize Niramim, 1975.

Ibn Falaquera, Shem Tov ben Joseph. *The Book of the Seeker.* Edited and translated by M. Herschel Levine. New York: Yeshiva University Press, 1976.

Ibn Gabirol, Solomon b. Judah. *Keter Malkhut.* Edited by Y. A. Zeidman. Jerusalem: Mossad Harav Kook, 1950.

———. *Meqor Ḥayyim.* Translated by Jacob Blubstein. Edited by Abraham Zifroni. Jerusalem: n.p., 1926.

———. *Selected Poems of Solomon Ibn Gabirol.* Translated by Peter Cole. Princeton, N.J.: Princeton University Press, 2001.

Ibn Malka, Yehudah ben Nissim. *The Hebrew Version of K. Uns al-gharib and the Commentary to the Sefer Yetsirah by Rabbi Yehudah ben Nisim ibn Malka.* Edited by Georges Vajda. Ramat Gan: Bar Ilan University Press, 1974.

Ibn Rushd (Averroes). *Commentary on Plato's Republic.* Edited, introduction, and notes by E. I. J. Rosenthal. Cambridge: Cambridge University Press, 1966.

Ibn Sīnā, Abū ᶜAli al-Ḥusayn (Avicenna). *Avicenna's Commentary on the Poetics of Aristotle: A Critical Study with an Annotated Translation of the Text.* Edited and translated by I. Dahiyat. Leiden: E. J. Brill, 1974.

———. *Avicenna's De Anima (Arabic Text): Being the Psychological Part of Kitāb al-Shifāʾ*. Edited by Fazlur Rahman. London: Oxford University Press, 1959.

———. "Ḥayy ibn Yaqẓān." Pp. 40–49 in *Ḥayy ibn Yaqẓān li ibn Sīnā wa ibn Ṭufayl wa al-Suhrawardī,* edited by Aḥmad Amīn. Cairo: Dār al-maᶜarīf, 1959.

———. *Kitāb aḥwal al-nafs*. Edited by Aḥmad Fuʾād al-Ahwānī. Cairo: Dār Iḥyāʾ al-kutub al-ʿarabiyya, 1952.
———. *Kitāb al-Ishārāt wa al-tanbīhāt*. Edited by S. Dunya. Cairo: Dār al-maʿārif bi miṣr, 1960.
———. *Kitāb al-majmuʿ: al-ḥikma al-ʿarūdiyya fī maʿānī kitāb al-shiʿr*. Edited by M. Salīm Sālim. Cairo: Dār al kutub, 1969.
———. *Kitāb al-Najāt*. Edited by M. Fakhry. Beirut: n.p., 1986.
———. *Kitāb al-Shifāʾ*. Vol. 1: *al-Burhān*. Edited by A. E. Affifi. Revised edition by Ibrahim Madkour. Cairo: Organisme Général des Imprimeries Gouvernmentales, 1956.
———. *Kitāb al-Shifāʾ*: *Kitāb al-shʾir. Arisṭūṭālīs fann al-shʿir*, 2nd ed. Edited by A. Badawī. Cairo: Dār al-thaqāfa, 1973.
———. *Kitāb al-Shifāʾ*: *al-Ṭabīʾīyat*. Vol. 6: *al-Nafs*. Edited by G. C. Anawati and S. Zayed. Revised edition by Ibrahim Makour. Cairo: al-hai'a al-miṣriyya al-ʿāma li al-kitāb, 1975.
———. "Risāla fī al-ʿishq." Pp. 1–27 in *Traités mystiques d'Abou Ali al-Hosain b. Abdallah ibn Sina ou d'Avicenne*. IIIième fasc. Edited by M. A. F. Mehren. Leiden, 1894.
———. "A Treatise on Love by Ibn Sina." Translated by Emil L. Fackenheim. *Mediaeval Studies* 7 (1945): 208–228.

Ibn Ṭufayl, Abū Bakr. *Ḥayy ben Yaqdhān, roman philosophique d'Ibn Thofail*. Texte arabe publié d'après un nouveau manuscrit avec les varientes des anciens textes et traduction français. Edited and translated by Léon Gauthier. Algiers: P. Fontana, 1900.
———. "Ḥayy ibn Yaqẓān." Pp. 52–122 in *Ḥayy ibn Yaqẓān li ibn Sīnā wa ibn Ṭufayl wa al-Suhrawardī*, edited by Aḥmad Amīn. Cairo: Dār al-maʿarīf, 1959.
———. Ibn Tufayl's *Hayy ibn Yaqzan: A Philosophical Tale*. Translated by Lenn Goodman. Los Angeles: Gee Tee Bee, 1983.
———. *Philosophus autodidactus, sive epistola Abi Jaafar, Ebn Tophail de Hai Ebn Yokdhan. In qua Ostenditur, quomodo ex Inferiorum contemplatione ad Superioirum notiam Ratio humana ascendere possit*. Translated by Edwin Pococke. Oxford: H. Hall, 1671.

Ikhwān al-Ṣafāʾ. *The Case of the Animals Versus the Men Before the King of the Jinn: A Tenth-Century Ecological Parable by the Pure Brethren of Basra*. Translated by Lenn Goodman. Boston: Twayne, 1978.
———. *The Epistle on Music of the Ikhwan al-Safa*. Edited and translated by Amnon Shiloah. Tel Aviv: Tel Aviv University Press, 1978.
———. *Rasāʾil Ikhwān al-Ṣafāʾ*. 4 vols. Beirut: Dār Sādir, 1957.

Maimonides, Moses. *Dalālat al-ḥaʾirīn*. Edited by Salomon Munk. Jerusalem: n.p., 1929.
———. "Eight Chapters." Pp. 59–104 in *Ethical Writings of Maimonides*, edited and translated by Raymond L. Weiss and Charles E. Butterworth. New York: New York University Press, 1975.
———. *Guide of the Perplexed*. 2 vols. Translated by Shlomo Pines. Chicago: University of Chicago Press, 1963.
———. *Mishneh Torah*. Warsaw: n.p., 1881.
———. *Sefer Moreh ha-Nevukhim*. Translated by Joseph Qafiḥ. Jerusalem: Mossad Harav Kook, 1977.

———. *Shemonah Peraqim (Haqdamah le-masekhet Avot)*. Pp. 375–399 in *Haqdamot ha-Rambam la-Mishnah*, edited and translated by Yitzhaq Sheilat. Jerusalem: n.p., 1994.

al-Marrākushī. *Al-Muᶜjib fī talkhīṣ akhbār al-maghrib*. 2nd ed. Edited by R. P. A. Dozy. Leiden: E. J. Brill, 1881.

al-Nadīm, Abū al-Faraj Muḥammad ibn Isḥāq. *The Fihrist: A Tenth Century AD Survey of Islamic Culture*. Edited and translated by Bayard Dodge. Chicago: Kazi Publications, 1998.

Plato. *The Collected Dialogues of Plato*. Edited by Edith Hamilton and Huntington Cairns. New York: Pantheon, 1961.

Plotinus. *The Enneads*. 7 vols. Edited and translated by A. H. Armstrong. Cambridge, Mass.: Harvard University Press, 1966–1988.

———. *The Enneads*. Translated by Stephen MacKenna. Abridged by John Dillon. Harmondsworth: Penguin, 1991.

———. *Plotini Opera*. 2 vols. Edited by Paul Henry and Hans-Rudolf Schwyzer. Paris and Brussels: Desclée de Brouwer et L'Édition Universelle, 1959.

Proclus. *In Platonis Rem Publicam Commentarii*. Edited by L.G. Westerink. Amsterdam: n.p, 1899–1901; reprint 1965.

Ptolemy. *Tetrabiblos*. Edited and translated by F. E. Robbins. London and Cambridge, Mass.: Heinemann and Harvard University Press, 1940.

ben Qalonymos, Qalonymos. *Iggeret baᶜalei ha-ḥayyim*. Edited by Yisrael Toporovski. Jerusalem, 1956.

al-Qayrawānī, Ḥasan Ibn Rashīq. *Al-ᶜUmda fī mahāsin al-shiᶜr*. 5th ed. Edited by Muhyī al-Dīnᶜ Abd al-Ḥamīd. Beirut: Dār al-jīl, 1981.

Rūmī, Jalāl al-Dīn. *Māthnawī*. 8 vols. Edited and translated by R. A. Nicholson. Leiden: E. J. Brill, 1925–1940.

Stenring, Knut, trans. *Sefer Yesirah*. New York: Ktav, 1970.

Suhrawardī, Shihāb al-Dīn Yaḥya. "Ḥayy ibn Yaqẓān." Pp. 124–127 in *Ḥayy ibn Yaqẓān li ibn Sīnā wa ibn Ṭufayl wa al-Suhrawardī*, edited by Aḥmad Amīn. Cairo: Dār al-maᶜārīf, 1959.

Ṭūsī, Naṣīr al-Dīn. *Contemplation and Action: The Spiritual Autobiography of a Muslim Scholar*. Edited and translated by S. J. Badakhchani. London: I. B. Tauris, 1998.

Westerink, L. G., ed. *Anonymous Prolegomena to Platonic Philosophy*. Amsterdam: North Holland Publishing Co., 1962.

al-Yaman, Jaᶜfar ibn Manṣūr. *The Master and the Disciple: An Early Islamic Spiritual Dialogue*. Translated by James W. Morris. London: I. B. Tauris, 2001.

Ibn Ẓaddik, Joseph. *Sefer ha-olam ha-katan (Der Mikrokosmos des Josef Ibn Saddik)*. Edited and translated by S. Horovitz. Breslau: n.p., 1903.

Secondary Sources

Adams, Charles J. "The Hermeneutics of Henry Corbin." Pp. 129–150 in *Approaches to Islam in Religious Studies*, edited by Richard C. Martin. Tucson: University of Arizona Press, 1985.

Afnan, Soheil M. *Avicenna: His Life and Works.* London: George Allen and Unwin, 1958.

Alavi, Mohd. Badruddin. "Some Aspects of the Literary and Poetical Activity of Avicenna." Pp. 65–72 in *Avicenna Commemoration Volume.* Calcutta: Iran Society, 1956.

Alexander, Tamar. "Hagiography and Biography: Abraham Ibn Ezra as a Character in the Hebrew Folktale." Pp. 11–16 in *Abraham Ibn Ezra y Su Tiempo,* edited by F. Diaz Esteban. Madrid: Asociación Española de Orientalistas, 1990.

Allen, Terry. "Aniconism and Figural Representation in Islamic Art." Pp. 17–37 in *Five Essays on Islamic Art,* edited by Terry Allen. Sebastopol, Calif.: Solipsist, 1988.

Altmann, Alexander, and S. M. Stern, eds. *Isaac Israeli: A Neoplatonic Philosopher of the Early Tenth Century.* Oxford: Oxford University Press, 1958.

Arberry, A. J. "Fārābī's Canons of Poetry." *Rivista degli Studi Orientali* 17 (1938): 267–278.

———. *The Koran Interpreted.* New York: Touchstone, 1996.

Archer, Jeffrey, ed. *A Reader on Islam: Passages from Standard Arabic Writings.* The Hague: Mouton, 1962.

Arkoun, Mohammed. *Pour une critique de la raison islamique.* Paris: Éditions Maisonneuve et Larose, 1984.

Armstrong, Arthur Hilary. *The Architecture of the Intelligible Universe in the Philosophy of Plotinus.* Cambridge: Cambridge University Press, 1965.

———. *Plotinian and Christian Studies.* London: Variorum, 1979.

Asad, Talal. *Genealogies of Religion: Disciplines and Reasons of Power in Christianity and Islam.* Baltimore: Johns Hopkins University Press, 1993.

Ashtor, Eliayahu. *The Jews of Moslem Spain.* 2 vols. Philadelphia: Jewish Publication Society of America, 1973–1979.

Athanassiadi, Polymnia, and Michael Frede, eds. *Pagan Monotheism in Late Antiquity.* Oxford: Clarendon, 2001.

Auerbach, Erich. *Mimesis: The Representation of Reality in Western Literature.* Translated by Willard Trask. Princeton, N.J.: Princeton University Press, 1968.

Bacher, Wilhelm. *Abraham Ibn Esra als Grammatiker.* Budapest: Kön. Ung. Universitäts-Buchdruckerei, 1881.

Behrens-Abouseif, Doris. *Beauty in Arabic Culture.* Princeton, N.J.: Markus Wiener Publishers, 1999.

Bell, Catherine. *Ritual: Perspectives and Dimensions.* New York: Oxford University Press, 1997.

Belting, Hans. *Likeness and Presence: A History of the Image before the Era of Art.* Translated by Edmund Jepcott. Chicago: University of Chicago Press, 1994.

Benor, Ehud. *Worship of the Heart: A Study of Maimonides' Philosophy of Religion.* Albany: State University of New York Press, 1995.

Berlin, Adele. *Biblical Poetry through Medieval Jewish Eyes.* Bloomington: Indiana University Press, 1991.

Bielmeier, Amandus. *Die neuplatonische Phaidrosinterpretation: Ihr Werdegung und ihre Eigenart.* Paderborn: F. Schöningh, 1930.

Biemel, Walter. "Poetry and Language in Heidegger." Pp. 65–93 in *On Heidegger and Language,* edited by Joseph J. Kockelmans. Evanston, Ill.: Northwestern University Press, 1972.

Black, Deborah L. "Aesthetics in Islamic Philosophy." Pp. 75–79 in *Routledge Encyclopedia of Philosophy,* vol. 1. London and New York: Routledge, 1998.

———. *Logic and Aristotle's Rhetoric and Poetics in Medieval Arabic Philosophy.* Leiden: E. J. Brill, 1990.

Bland, Kalman P. "Anti-Semitism and Aniconism: The Germanophone Requiem for Jewish Visual Art." Pp. 41–66 in *Jewish Identity in Modern Art History,* edited by Catherine M. Soussloff. Berkeley: University of California Press, 1999.

———. *The Artless Jew: Medieval and Modern Affirmations and Denials of the Visual.* Princeton, N.J.: Princeton University Press, 2000.

Bloom, Harold. *The Anxiety of Influence: A Theory of Poetry.* New York: Oxford University Press, 1973.

Blumenthal, Henry J. *Aristotle and Neoplatonism in Late Antiquity: Interpretations of the De Anima.* Ithaca, N.Y.: Cornell University Press, 1996.

———. "Plotinus in the Light of Twenty Years' Scholarship, 1951–1971." *Aufsteig und Niedergang der römischen Welt* 36, no. 1 (1987): 528–570.

———. *Plotinus' Psychology: His Doctrine of the Embodied Soul.* The Hague: Martinus Nijhoff, 1971.

Bonebakker, Seeger A. "Adab and the Concept of Belles-Lettres." Pp. 16–30 in *The Cambridge History of Arabic Literature: ᶜAbbasid Belles-Lettres,* edited by J. Ashtiany et al. Cambridge: Cambridge University Press, 1990.

Böwering, Gerhard. *The Mystical Vision of Existence in Classical Islam: The Qurʾānic Hermeneutics of the Sufi Sahl at-Tustarī.* Berlin: Walter de Gruyter, 1980.

Boyarin, Daniel. "The Eye in the Torah: Ocular Desire in Midrashic Hermeneutics." Pp. 30–48 in *Ocular Desire: Yearbook for Religious Anthropology,* edited by A. R. E. Agus and J. Assmann. Berlin: Akademie Verlag, 1994.

Boyarin, Jonathan, ed. *The Ethnography of Reading.* Berkeley: University of California Press, 1993.

Brague, Rémi. "Cosmological Mysticism: The Imitation of the Heavenly Bodies in Ibn Ṭufayl's *Ḥayy ibn Yaqzan." Graduate Faculty Philosophy Journal* 19, no. 19.2–20.1 (1997): 91–102.

Brann, Eva T. H. *The World of the Imagination: Sum and Substance.* Lanham, Md.: Rowman and Littlefield, 1991.

Brann, Ross. "The Arabized Jew." Pp. 435–454 in *The Literature of al-Andalus,* edited by María Rosa Menocal, Raymond P. Scheindlin, and Michael Sells. Cambridge: Cambridge University Press, 2000.

———. *The Compunctious Poet: Cultural Ambiguity and Hebrew Poetry in Muslim Spain.* Baltimore: Johns Hopkins University Press, 1991.

———. *Power in the Portrayal: Representations of Jews and Muslims in Eleventh- and Twelfth-Century Islamic Spain.* Princeton, N.J.: Princeton University Press, 2002.

———. "Power in the Portrayal: Representations of Muslims and Jews in Judah al-Ḥarīzī's *Taḥkemoni." Princeton Papers in Near Eastern Studies* 1 (1992): 1–22.

Brookes, John. *Gardens of Paradise: The History and Design of the Great Islamic Gardens.* New York: New Amsterdam Books, 1987.

Bürgel, J. C. "Ibn Ṭufayl and His *Ḥayy ibn Yaqẓān:* A Turning Point in Arabic Philosophical Writing." Pp. 830–846 in *The Legacy of Muslim Spain,* edited by Salma Khadra Jayyusi. Leiden: E. J. Brill, 1992.

———. "Symbols and Hints: Some Considerations Concerning the Meaning of ibn Ṭufayl's *Ḥayy ibn Yaqẓān.*" Pp. 114–132 in *The World of Ibn Ṭufayl: Interdisciplinary Perspectives on Ḥayy ibn Yaqẓān,* edited by L. I. Conrad. Leiden: E. J. Brill, 1996.

Butterworth, Charles E., ed. *The Political Aspects of Islamic Philosophy.* Cambridge, Mass.: Center for Middle Eastern Studies, 1992.

Cantarino, Vicente. *Arabic Poetics in the Golden Age.* Leiden: E. J. Brill, 1975.

Carruthers, Mary. *The Book of Memory: A Study of Memory in Medieval Culture.* New York: Cambridge University Press, 1990.

———. *The Craft of Thought: Meditation, Rhetoric, and the Making of Images, 400–1200.* Cambridge: Cambridge University Press, 1998.

Casey, Edward S. *Imagining: A Phenomenological Study.* Bloomington: Indiana University Press, 1976.

Cassirer, Ernst. *Language and Myth.* Translated by Susanne K. Langer. New York: Harper and Brothers, 1946.

———. *The Philosophy of Symbolic Forms.* Vol. 1: *Language.* Translated by Ralph Manheim. New Haven: Yale University Press, 1953.

Chejne, Anwar G. *Muslim Spain.* Minneapolis: University of Minnesota Press, 1974.

Chernus, Ira. *Mysticism in Rabbinic Judaism.* Berlin: Walter de Gruyter, 1982.

Clifford, Gay. *The Transformations of Allegory.* London: Routledge and Kegan Paul, 1974.

Cohen, Mark R. *Under Crescent and Cross: The Jews in the Middle Ages.* Princeton, N.J.: Princeton University Press, 1994.

Collins, John J. "Introduction: Towards the Morphology of a Genre." *Semeia* 14 (1979): 1–20.

Collins, Roger. *The Arab Conquest of Spain.* Oxford: Basil Blackwell, 1989.

Conrad, Lawrence I., ed. *The World of Ibn Ṭufayl: Interdisciplinary Perspectives on Ḥayy ibn Yaqẓān.* Leiden: E. J. Brill, 1996.

Corbin, Henry. *Avicenna and the Visionary Recital.* Translated by Willard Trask. Princeton, N.J.: Bollingen, 1960.

———. *The Concept of Comparative Philosophy.* Translated by Peter Russell. Ipswich: Golgonooza Press, 1981.

———. *Creative Imagination in the Sufism of Ibn ᶜArabi.* Translated by Ralph Manheim. Princeton, N.J.: Princeton University Press, 1969.

———. "De Heidegger à Sohravardi." Pp. 23–37 in *Henry Corbin,* edited by Christian Jambet. Paris: Éditions de l'Herne, 1981.

———. *En Islam iranien: Aspects spirituels et philosophiques.* 4 vols. Paris: Editions Gallimard, 1971–1972.

———. *Mundus Imaginalis; or, The Imaginary and the Imaginal.* Translated by Ruth Horine. Ipswich: Golgonooza Press, 1976.

———. *Le paradoxe du monotheisme.* Paris: L'Herne, 1981.

Cornell, Vincent. "Ḥayy in the Land of Absāl: Ibn Ṭufayl and Ṣūfism in the Western Maghrib during the Muwaḥḥid Era." Pp. 133–164 in *The World of Ibn Ṭufayl: Interdisciplinary Perspectives on Ḥayy ibn Yaqẓān,* edited by L. I. Conrad. Leiden: E. J. Brill, 1996.

———. "The Way of the Axial Intellect: The Islamic Hermeticism of Ibn Sab^{c}in." *Journal of the Muhyiddin Ibn ^{c}Arabi Society* 22 (1997): 42–79.

Coulter, James A. *The Literary Microcosm: Theories of Interpretation of the Later Platonists.* Leiden: E. J. Brill, 1976.

Daftary, Farhad. *The Ismā^{c}īlīs: Their History and Doctrines.* Cambridge: Cambridge University Press, 1990.

Dana, Joseph. *Poetics of Medieval Hebrew Literature according to Moses Ibn Ezra* (in Hebrew). Jerusalem: Dvir, 1982.

Davidson, Herbert. *Alfarabi, Avicenna, and Averroes, on Intellect: Their Cosmologies, Theories of the Active Intellect, and Theories of Human Intellect.* New York: Oxford University Press, 1992.

———. "The Study of Philosophy as a Religious Obligation." Pp. 53–68 in *Religion in a Religious Age,* edited by S. D. Goitein. Cambridge, Mass.: Association for Jewish Studies, 1974.

Dorff, Elliot N. "In Defense of Images." Pp. 129–154 in *Studies in Judaism: Proceedings of the Academy for Jewish Philosophy,* edited by D. Novak and N. Samuelson. Lanham, Md.: University Press of America, 1990.

Dronke, Peter. *Fabula: Explorations into the Uses of Myth in Medieval Platonism.* Leiden: E. J. Brill, 1974.

Druart, Thérèse-Anne. "Imagination and the Soul-Body Problem in Arabic Philosophy." *Analecta Husserliana* 16 (1983): 327–342.

Durkheim, Emile. *Elementary Forms of the Religious Life.* Translated by J. W. Swain. New York: Free Press, 1915.

———, and Marcel Mauss. *Primitive Classification.* Translated by Rodney Needham. Chicago: University of Chicago Press, 1963.

Eco, Umberto. *Art and Beauty in the Middle Ages.* Translated by Hugh Brodin. New Haven: Yale University Press, 1986.

Edelstein, Ludwig. "The Function of Myth in Plato's Philosophy." *Journal of the History of Ideas* 10, no. 4 (1949): 463–481.

Edsman, Carl-Martin. "Fire." Pp. 340–346 in *Encyclopedia of Religion,* vol. 5, edited by Mircea Eliade. New York: Macmillan, 1987.

Efros, Israel. *Studies in Medieval Jewish Philosophy.* New York: Columbia University Press, 1974.

Eiland, Howard. "The Way to Nearness: Heidegger's Interpretation of Purpose." *Philosophy and Literature* 8 (1984): 43–54.

Eliade, Mircea. *Rites and Symbols of Initiation: The Mysteries of Birth and Rebirth.* New York: Harper and Torchbook, 1958.

———. *The Sacred and the Profane: The Significance of Religious Myth, Symbolism, and Ritual within Life and Culture.* Translated by Willard R. Trask. New York: Harvest Press, 1957.

Esteban, F. Diaz, ed. *Abraham Ibn Ezra y su tiempo.* Madrid: Asociación Española de Orientalistas, 1990.

Fakhry, Majid. *A History of Islamic Philosophy.* 2nd ed. New York: Columbia University Press, 1983.

Faur, José. *Homo Mysticus: A Guide to Maimonides' Guide for the Perplexed.* Syracuse: Syracuse University Press, 1999.

Fenton, Paul. *Philosophie et exégèse dans le Jardin de la Métaphore de Moïse ibn Ezra, philosophe et poète andalou du XIIe siècle.* Leiden: E. J. Brill, 1997.

———. "The Symbolism of Ritual Circumambulation in Judaism and Islam: A Comparative Study." *Journal of Jewish Thought and Philosophy* 6, no. 2 (1997): 345–369.

Ferwerda, R. *La signification des images et des métaphores dans la pensée de Plotin.* Groningen: J. B. Wolters, 1965.

Fierro, Maribel. "Spiritual Alienation and Political Activism: The Gurabāʾ in al-Andalus during the Sixth/Twelfth Century." *Arabica* 47, no. 2 (2000): 230–260.

Fine, Stephen. "Art and the Liturgical Context of the Sepphoris Synagogue Mosaic." Pp. 227–238 in *Galilee through the Centuries: Confluence of Cultures,* edited by Eric M. Myers. Winona Lake, Ind.: Eisenbrauns, 1999.

Fleischer, Ezra. "Judah Halevi: Remarks Concerning His Life and Poetical Oeuvre" (in Hebrew). Pp. 264–270 in *Israel Levin Jubilee Volume.* Tel Aviv: Tel Aviv University Press, 1994.

Fleischer, J. L. "When Did R. Abraham Ibn Ezra Die?" (in Hebrew). *East and West* 2 (1929): 245–256.

———. "When Did R. Abraham Ibn Ezra Leave Spain?" (in Hebrew). *East and West* 3 (1929): 325–335.

Fradkin, Hillel. "Ibn Ṭufayl's *Ḥayy ibn Yaqẓān* on the relationship of mysticism, prophecy, and philosophy." Ph.D. dissertation, University of Chicago, 1978.

Frank, Daniel H. "Idolatry and the Love of Appearances: Maimonides and Plato on False Wisdom." Pp. 155–168 in *Proceedings of the Academy for Jewish Philosophy,* edited by D. Novak and N. Samuelson. Lanham, Md.: University Press of America, 1990.

Freedberg, David. *The Power of Images: Studies in the History and Theory of Response.* Chicago: University of Chicago Press, 1989.

Friedlaender, Michael. *Essays on the Writings of Abraham Ibn Ezra.* London: Trübner and Co., 1877. Reprint, Jerusalem: Mitshaf, 1964.

Frye, Northrop. "Allegory." Pp. 12–15 in *Princeton Encyclopedia of Poetry and Poetics,* edited by Alex Preminger. Princeton, N.J.: Princeton University Press, 1974.

———. *Anatomy of Criticism: Four Essays.* Princeton, N.J.: Princeton University Press, 1957.

Gadamer, Hans-Georg. *Truth and Method.* 2nd rev. ed. Translated by Joel Weinseimer and Donald G. Marshall. New York: Continuum, 1994.

Galston, Miriam. *Politics and Excellence: The Political Philosophy of Alfarabi.* Princeton, N.J.: Princeton University Press, 1990.

———. "The Theoretical and Practical Dimension of Happiness as Portrayed in the Political Treatises of al-Fārābī." Pp. 95–151 in *The Political Aspects of Islamic Philosophy: Essays in Honor of Muhsin S. Mahdi,* edited by C. E. Butterworth. Cambridge, Mass.: Harvard University Press, 1992.

Gatti, Maria Luisa. "Plotinus: The Platonic Tradition and the Foundation of Neoplatonism." Pp. 22–29 in *The Cambridge Companion to Plotinus,* edited by Lloyd P. Gerson. Cambridge: Cambridge University Press, 1996.

Geertz, Clifford. *The Interpretation of Cultures.* New York: Basic Books, 1973.

Gennep, Arnold van. *The Rites of Passage.* Translated by Monika R. Vizedom and Gabrielle L. Caffee. Chicago: University of Chicago Press, 1960.

Gerber, Jane. *The Jews of Muslim Spain: A History of the Sephardic Experience.* New York: Free Press, 1994.

Gerson, Lloyd P. *Plotinus.* London: Routledge, 1994.

Goetschel, Roland. "The Sin of the Golden Calf in the Exegesis of Abraham ibn Ezra." Pp. 137–144 in *Abraham Ibn Ezra y su tiempo,* edited by F. Diaz Esteban. Madrid: Asociación Española de Orientalistas, 1990.

Goichon, Anne-Marie. *Le récite de Ḥayy ibn Yaqẓān commenté pars des textes d'Avicenne.* Paris: Desclée de Brouwer, 1959.

Gonzalez, Valérie. *Beauty and Islam: Aesthetics in Islamic Art and Architecture.* London: I. B. Tauris, 2001.

Goodman, Lenn E. *Avicenna.* London: Routledge, 1992.

Grabar, Oleg. *The Formation of Islamic Art.* Revised and enlarged edition. New Haven: Yale University Press, 1997.

———. "Islam and Iconoclasm." Pp. 45–52 in *Iconoclasm,* edited by Anthony Breyer and Judith Herrin. Birmingham: Centre for Byzantine Studies, 1977.

Graetz, Heinrich. *A History of the Jews.* Vol. 3. Philadelphia: Jewish Publication Society of America, 1956. Orig. publ. 1894.

Greenblatt, Stephen J., ed. *Allegory and Representation.* Baltimore: Johns Hopkins University Press, 1981.

Greive, Hermann. *Studien zum jüdischen Neuplatonismus: Die Religionsphilosophie des Abraham Ibn Ezra.* Berlin: Walter de Gruyter, 1973.

Grignaschi, M. "Le Roman épistolaire classique conservé dans la version arabe de Sālim Abū al-ᶜAlā." *Muséon* 80 (1967): 211–269.

Grimes, Ronald L. *Beginnings in Ritual Studies.* Lanham, Md.: University Press of America, 1982.

———. *Deeply into the Bone: Re-Inventing Rites of Passage.* Berkeley: University of California Press, 2000.

———. *Research in Ritual Studies: A Programmatic Essay and Bibliography.* Metuchen, N.J.: Scarecrow Press, 1985.

Gruenwald, Ithamar. *Apocalyptic and Merkavah Literature.* Leiden: E. J. Brill, 1980.

Gutas, Dimitri. *Avicenna and the Aristotelian Tradition: Introduction to Reading Avicenna's Philosophical Works.* Leiden: E. J. Brill, 1988.

———. "Avicenna V: Mysticism." Pp. 79–83 in *Encyclopaedia Iranica,* vol. 3, pt. 1.

———. "Ibn Ṭufayl on Ibn Sīnā's Eastern Philosophy." *Oriens* 34 (1994): 222–241.

Gutmann, Joseph. "The 'Second Commandment' and the Image in Judaism." *Hebrew Union College Annual* 32 (1961): 161–174.

Guttmann, Julius. *Philosophies of Judaism: A History of Jewish Philosophy from Biblical Times to Franz Rosenzweig.* Translated by David W. Silverman. New York: Schocken, 1964.

Halkin, A. S. "Judeo-Arabic Literature." Pp. 784–816 in *The Jews: Their History, Culture, and Religion,* edited by Louis Finkelstein. 4th edition by Philadelphia: Jewish Publication Society of America, 1949.

Halliwell, Stephen. *The Aesthetics of Mimesis: Ancient Texts, and Modern Problems.* Princeton, N.J.: Princeton University Press, 2002.

———. *Aristotle's Poetics.* Chicago: University of Chicago Press, 1986.

———. *The Poetics of Aristotle: Translation and Commentary.* London: Duckworth, 1987.

Halm, Heinz. "The Cosmology of the pre-Fatimid Ismāᶜīliyya." Pp. 75–83 in *Mediaeval Ismaᶜili History and Thought,* edited by Farhad Daftary. Cambridge: Cambridge University Press, 1996.

———. "The Isma^cili Oath of Allegiance (*^cahd*) and the 'Sessions of Wisdom' (*majālis al-ḥikma*) in Fatimid Times." Pp. 91–115 in *Mediaeval Isma^cili History and Thought*, edited by Farhad Daftary. Cambridge: Cambridge University Press, 1996.

Halperin, David J. "Hekhalot and Mi^crāj: Observations on the Heavenly Journey in Judaism and Islam." Pp. 269–288 in *Death, Ecstasy, and Other Worldly Journeys*, edited by John J. Collins and Michael Fishbane. Albany: State University of New York Press, 1995.

Ḥamīd, Khwāja ^cAbdul. "The Philosophical Significance of Ibn Ṭufails's *Ḥaiy Ibn Yaqẓān*." *Islamic Culture* 22 (1948): 50–69.

Hamlyn, D. W. *Aristotle's De Anima, Books II and III with Certain Passages from Book I*. Oxford: Clarendon Press, 1968.

Harvey, Warren Zev. "Ethics and Meta-Ethics, Aesthetics and Meta-Aesthetics in Maimonides." Pp. 131–138 in *Maimonides and Philosophy: Papers Presented at the Sixth Jerusalem Philosophical Encounter, May 1985*, edited by Shlomo Pines and Yirmiyahu Yovel. Dordrecht: Martinus Nijhoff, 1986.

———. "The First Commandment and the God of Israel: Ibn Ezra and Maimonides versus Halevi and Crescas" (in Hebrew). *Tarbiẓ* 57, no. 2 (1988): 203–216.

Hatab, Lawrence J. *Myth and Philosophy: A Contest of Truths*. La Salle, Ill.: Open Court, 1990.

Hawi, Sami S. *Islamic Naturalism and Mysticism: A Philosophical Study of Ibn Tufayl's Hayy ibn Yaqzan*. Leiden: E. J. Brill, 1974.

Hayoun, Maurice-Ruben. *L'Exégèse philosophique dans le Judaisme médiéval*. Tübingen: J.C.B. Mohr, 1992.

Heath, Peter. *Allegory and Philosophy in Avicenna: With a Translation of the Book of the Prophet Muḥammad's Ascent to Heaven*. Philadelphia: University of Pennsylvania Press, 1992.

Heidegger, Martin. *Basic Writings*, edited by David Farrell Krell. San Francisco: HarperCollins, 1993.

———. *Being and Time*. Translated by John Macquarrie and Edward Robinson. Oxford: Blackwell, 1962.

———. *Qu'est-ce que la métaphysique?* Translated by Henry Corbin. Paris: Gallimard, 1938.

Hodgson, Marshall G. S. *The Venture of Islam: Conscience and History in a World Civilization*. 3 vols. Chicago: University of Chicago Press, 1974.

Holzberg, Niklas. *The Ancient Novel: An Introduction*. Translated by Christine Jackson-Holzberg. London: Routledge, 1995.

Honig, Edwin. *Dark Conceit: The Making of Allegory*. Evanston, Ill.: Northwestern University Press, 1959.

Hourani, George F. "The Principal Subject of Ibn Ṭufayl's *Ḥayy ibn Yaqẓān*." *Journal of Near Eastern Studies* 15, no. 1 (1956): 40–46.

Hughes, Aaron. "Imagining the Divine: Ghazali on Imagination, Dreams, and Dreaming." *Journal of the American Academy of Religion* 70, no. 1 (2002): 33–53.

———. "Reading Islamic Philosophy: Recent Contributions in the Field of Suhrawardī Studies." *Religious Studies Review* 68, no. 1 (2002): 19–24.

———. "The Three Worlds of ibn Ezra's *Ḥay ben Meqitz*." *Journal of Jewish Thought and Philosophy* 11, no. 1 (2002): 1–24.

———. "Two Approaches to the Love of God in Medieval Jewish Thought: The Concept of *devequt* in the Works of Ibn Ezra and Judah Halevi." *Studies in Religion* 28, no. 2 (1999): 139–151.

Humphreys, R. Stephen. *Islamic History: A Framework for Further Inquiry,* rev. ed. Princeton, N.J.: Princeton University Press, 1991.

Husik, Issac. *A History of Medieval Jewish Philosophy.* New York: Macmillan, 1916.

Husserl, Edmund. *Ideas: General Introduction to Pure Phenomenology.* Translated by W. Gibson. New York: Collier, 1962.

Huxley, Aldous. *The Perennial Philosophy.* New York: Harper, 1945.

Hyman, Arthur. "From What Is One and Simple Only What Is One and Simple Can Come to Be." Pp. 111–135 in *Neoplatonism and Jewish Thought,* edited by L. E. Goodman. Albany: State University of New York Press, 1992.

Idel, Moshe. "*Hitbodedut* as Concentration in Ecstatic Kabbalah." Pp. 103–169 in *Studies in Ecstatic Kabbalah.* Albany: State University of New York Press, 1988.

———. "*Hitbodedut* as Concentration in Jewish Philosophy" (in Hebrew). *Jerusalem Studies on Jewish Thought* 7 (1988): 39–60.

Imamuddin, S. M. *Muslim Spain, 711–1492 A.D.: A Sociological Study.* Leiden: E. J. Brill, 1981.

Isa, Ahmad Muhammad. "Muslims and Taswir." *The Muslim World* 45 (1955): 250–268.

Iser, Wolfgang. "The Reading Process: A Phenomenological Approach." Pp. 50–69 in *Reader-Response Criticism: From Formalism to Post-Structuralism,* edited by Jane P. Tompkins. Baltimore: Johns Hopkins University Press, 1980.

Ivry, Alfred L. "Neoplatonic Currents in Maimonides' Thought." Pp. 115–140 in *Perspectives on Maimonides: Philosophical and Historical Studies,* edited by Joel L. Kraemer. Oxford: Oxford University Press for the Littman Library, 1991.

———. "The Utilization of Allegory in Islamic Philosophy." Pp. 154–180 in *Interpretation and Allegory: Antiquity to the Modern Period,* edited by Jon Whitman. Leiden: E. J. Brill, 2000.

Izutsu, Toshihiko. "Ishrāqīyah." Pp. 296–301 in *Encyclopedia of Religion,* vol. 7. Edited by Mircea Eliade. New York: Macmillan, 1987.

Jones, Joseph R. "From Abraham to Andrenio: Observations on the Evolution of the Abraham Legend, Its Diffusion in Spain, and Its Relationship to the Theme of the Self-Taught Philosopher." *Comparative Literature Studies* 6 (1969): 69–101.

Jospe, Raphael. "Early Philosophical Commentaries on the Sefer Yezirah: Some Comments." *Revue des études juives* 149 (1990): 369–415.

———. "The Torah and Astrology according to Abraham Ibn Ezra." Pp. 17–24 in *Proceedings of the Eleventh World Congress of Jewish Studies, Jerusalem 1993,* vol. 2: *Jewish Thought, Kabbalah, and Hasidism.* Jerusalem: World Union of Jewish Studies, 1994.

Kahwaji, S. "*Ilm al-djamāl.*" Pp. 1134–1135 in *Encyclopaedia of Islam,* new edition. Leiden: E. J. Brill, 1954–.

Katz, Solomon. *The Jews in the Visigothic and Frankish Kingdoms of Spain and Gaul.* Cambridge, Mass.: Harvard University Press, 1937.

Katz, Stephen T. "Language, Epistemology, and Mysticism." Pp. 22–74 in *Mysticism and Philosophical Analysis,* edited by Stephen T. Katz. New York: Oxford University Press, 1978.

Kearny, Richard. *Poetics of Imagining: Modern to Post-Modern.* New York: Fordham University Press, 1998.

———. *The Wake of the Imagination: Ideas of Creativity in Western Culture.* London: Hutchinson, 1988.

Kemal, Salim. "Justification of Poetic Validity: Ibn Ṭufayl's *Ḥayy ibn Yaqẓān* and ibn Sīnā's *Commentary on the Poetics of Aristotle.*" Pp. 195–228 in *The World of ibn Ṭufayl: Interdisciplinary Perspectives on Ḥayy ibn Yaqẓān,* edited by L. I. Conrad. Leiden: E. J. Brill, 1996.

———. *The Poetics of Alfarabi and Avicenna.* Leiden: E. J. Brill, 1991.

Kennedy, Hugh. *Muslim Spain: A Political History of al-Andalus.* London: Longman, 1996.

Keyser, Eugénie de. *La Signification de l'Art dans les Ennéades de Plotin.* Louvain: Publications Universitaires de Louvain, 1955.

Khan, M. ᶜA. Muid. "Kitabu taᵓbit-ir-ruya of Abuᶜ Ali b. Sina." *Indo-Iranica* 9, no. 4 (1956): 43–57.

———. "A Unique Treatise on the Interpretation of Dreams." Pp. 255–307 in *Avicenna Commemoration Volume.* Calcutta: Iran Society, 1956.

Kingsley, Peter. *Ancient Philosophy, Mystery, and Magic: Empedocles and Pythagorean Tradition.* Oxford: Clarendon, 1995.

Kochin, Michael S. "Weeds: Cultivating the Imagination in Medieval Arabic Political Philosophy." *Journal of the History of Ideas* 60, no. 3 (1999): 399–416.

Kockelmans, Joseph J., ed. *On Heidegger and Language.* Evanston, Ill.: Northwestern University Press, 1972.

Kozodoy, Neal. "Reading Medieval Hebrew Love Poetry." *AJS Review* 2 (1977): 111–129.

Kraemer, Joel L. *Humanism in the Renaissance of Islam: The Cultural Revival during the Buyid Age.* Leiden: E. J. Brill, 1986.

Kreisel, Howard H. *Maimonides' Political Thought: Studies in Ethics, Law, and the Human Ideal.* Albany: State University of New York Press, 1999.

———. "On the Term *kol* in Abraham Ibn Ezra: A Reapprasial." *Revue des études juives* 152 (1994): 29–66.

———. *Prophecy: The History of an Idea in Medieval Jewish Philosophy.* Dordrecht: Kluwer, 2001.

Kruk, Remke. "An 18th-Century Descendent of *Ḥayy ibn Yaqẓān* and Robinson Crusoe: Don Antonio de Trezzanio." *Arabica* 34 (1987): 357–365.

———. "A Frothy Bubble: Spontaneous Generation in the Medieval Islamic Tradition." *Journal of Semitic Studies* 35, no. 2 (1990): 265–282.

———. "Ibn Ṭufayl: A Medieval Scholar's Views on Nature." Pp. 69–89 in *The World of Ibn Ṭufayl: Interdisciplinary Perspectives on Ḥayy ibn Yaqẓān,* edited by Lawrence I. Conrad. Leiden: E. J. Brill, 1996.

Lakoff, George, and Mark Johnson. *Metaphors We Live By.* Chicago: University of Chicago Press, 1980.

———. *Philosophy in the Flesh: The Embodied Mind and Its Challenge to Western Thought.* New York: Basic Books, 1999.

Lamberton, Robert. *Homer the Theologian: Neoplatonist Allegorical Reading and the Growth of the Epic Tradition.* Berkeley: University of California Press, 1986.

Lancaster, Irene. *Deconstructing the Bible: Abraham ibn Ezra's Introduction to the Torah.* London: RoutledgeCurzon, 2003.

Landolt, Hermann. "Henry Corbin, 1903–1978: Between Philosophy and Orientalism." *Journal of the American Oriental Society* 119, no. 3 (1999): 484–490.

———. "Suhrawardī's 'Tales of Initiation.'" *Journal of the American Oriental Society* 107 (1987): 475–486.

Lane, Edward W. *An Arabic-English Lexicon.* Beirut: Librairie du Liban, 1968.

Langermann, Y. Tzvi. "Some Astrological Themes in the Thought of Abraham ibn Ezra." Pp. 28–85 in *Rabbi Abraham Ibn Ezra: Studies in the Writings of a Twelfth-Century Jewish Polymath,* edited by Jay Harris and Isadore Twersky. Cambridge, Mass.: Harvard University Press, 1993.

Layton, Bentley, ed. *The Gnostic Scriptures.* New York: Doubleday, 1987.

Lazarus-Yafeh, Hava. *Intertwined Worlds: Medieval Islam and Bible Criticism.* Princeton, N.J.: Princeton University Press, 1992.

LeClerq, Jacques. *The Love of Learning and the Desire for God: A Study of Monastic Culture.* Translated by Catharine Misrahi. New York: Fordham University Press, 1961.

Lerner, Ralph. *Maimonides' Empire of Light: Popular Enlightenment in an Age of Belief.* Chicago: University of Chicago Press, 2000.

Levin, Israel. *Abraham Ibn Ezra: His Life and Poetry* (in Hebrew). Tel Aviv: Hakibbutz Hameuchad, 1969.

———. *Abraham Ibn Ezra Reader* (in Hebrew). New York/Tel Aviv: Israel Matrz Hebrew Classics/Edward Kiev Library Foundation, 1986.

———. "Hold to the Ladder of Wisdom" (in Hebrew). *Teᶜuda* 8 (1992): 41–86.

Lévi-Strauss, Claude. *The Raw and the Cooked.* Translated by John and Doreen Weightman. New York: Harper and Row, 1969.

Levy, Raphael. *The Astrological Works of Abraham ibn Ezra: A Literary and Linguistic Study with Special Reference to the Old French Translation of Hagin.* Baltimore: Johns Hopkins University Press, 1927.

Levy, Ze'ev. "The Status of Aesthetics in Jewish Thought" (in Hebrew). Pp. 83–102 in *Judaism and Art,* edited by David Cassuto. Bar Ilan: Bar Ilan University Press, 1988.

Lewis, Bernard. *The Jews of Islam.* Princeton, N.J.: Princeton University Press, 1984.

Lindberg, David C. *Theories of Vision from al-Kindi to Kepler.* Chicago: University of Chicago Press, 1976.

Lloyd, A. C. *The Anatomy of Neoplatonism.* Oxford: Clarendon Press, 1990.

———. "Non-discursive Thought: An Enigma of Greek Philosophy." *Proceedings of the Aristotelian Society,* n.s. 70 (1969–1970): 261–274.

Lobel, Diana. *Between Mysticism and Philosophy: Sufi Language of Religious Experience in Judah Ha-Levi's Kuzari.* Albany: State University of New York Press, 2000.

Loewe, Raphael. "Ibn Gabirol's Treatment of Sources in the Kether Malkhuth." Pp. 183–194 in *Studies in Jewish Religious and Intellectual History Presented to*

Alexander Altmann, edited by S. Stein and R. Loewe. Tuscaloosa: University of Alabama Press, 1979.

Losensky, Paul E. "'The Allusive Field of Drunkenness': Three Safavid-Moghul Responses to a Lyric by Bābā Fighānī." Pp. 227–262 in *Reorientations/Arabic and Persian Poetry,* edited by S. P. Stetkevych. Bloomington: Indiana University Press, 1994.

Madkour, Ibrahim. *L'Oganon d'Aristote dans le monde arabe,* 2nd ed. Paris: Librairie Philosophique, J. Vrin, 1969.

Mahdi, Muhsin. *Alfarabi and the Foundation of Islamic Political Philosophy.* Chicago: University of Chicago Press, 2001.

———. "Islamic Philosophy and the Fine Arts." Pp. 21–25 in *Architecture and Community: Building the Islamic World Today.* New York: Aperture, 1983.

Mallet, Dominique. "Les livres de Ḥayy." *Arabica* 44 (1987): 1–34.

———. "Qui enseigne qui? (Lectures du Ḥayy b. Yaqẓān d'Ibn Ṭufayl)." *Arabic Sciences and Philosophy* 8.2 (1998): 195–211.

Malti-Douglas, Fedwa. "*Ḥayy ibn Yaqẓān* as Male Utopia." Pp. 52–68 in *The World of Ibn Ṭufayl: Interdisciplinary Perspectives on Ḥayy ibn Yaqẓān,* edited by Lawrence I. Conrad. Leiden: E. J. Brill, 1996.

Mann, Vivian B. *Jewish Texts on the Visual Arts.* Cambridge: Cambridge University Press, 2000.

Marmura, Michael E. "Plotting the Course of Avicenna's Thought." *Journal of the American Oriental Society* 111 (1991): 333–342.

McGinn, Bernard. *The Foundations of Mysticism: Origins to the Fifth Century.* New York: Crossroad, 1994.

Merkur, Dan. "The Visionary Practices of the Jewish Apocalyptists." *Psychoanalytic Study of Society* 14 (1989): 119–148.

Merlan, Philip. *Monopsychism Mysticism Metaconsciousness: Problems of the Soul in the Neoaristotelian and Neoplatonic Tradition.* The Hague: Martinus Nijhoff, 1963.

Meschonnic, Henri. *Critique du rythme: Anthropologie historique du langage.* Paris: Verdier, 1982.

Miles, Margaret R. *Plotinus on Body and Beauty: Society, Philosophy, and Religion in Third-Century Rome.* Oxford: Blackwell, 1999.

Monroe, James. "Hispano-Arabic Poetry during the Caliphate of Cordoba: Theory and Practice." Pp. 125–154 in *Arabic Poetry; Theory and Practice,* edited by G. von Grunebaum. Wiesbaden: Harrassowitz, 1973.

Moraux, Paul. *Les listes anciennes des ouvrages d'Aristote.* Louvain: Editions Universitaires de Louvain, 1951.

Nasr, Seyyed Hossein. *An Introduction to Islamic Cosmological Doctrines.* Rev. ed. Albany: State University of New York Press, 1993.

———. *Three Muslim Sages: Avicenna, Suhrawardī, Ibn ᶜArabi.* Cambridge, Mass.: Harvard University Press, 1964.

Netton, Ian R. *Muslim Neoplatonists: An Introduction to the Thought of the Brethren of Purity.* Edinburgh: Edinburgh University Press, 1991.

Nicholson, Reynold A. *A Literary History of the Arabs.* Cambridge: Cambridge University Press, 1930. Reprint, Surrey: Curzon Press, 1993.

Nussbaum, Martha C. *Love's Knowledge: Essays in Philosophy and Literature.* Oxford: Oxford University Press, 1990.

———. *The Therapy of Desire: Theory and Practice in Hellenistic Ethics.* Princeton, N.J.: Princeton University Press, 1994.

O'Daly, Gerard J. P. *Plotinus' Philosophy of Self.* Shannon: Irish University Press, 1973.

O'Meara, Dominic J. *Pythagoras Revived: Mathematics and Philosophy in Late Antiquity.* Oxford: Clarendon Press, 1989.

Ong, Walter J. *The Presence of the Word: Some Prolegomena for Cultural and Religious History.* Minneapolis: University of Minnesota Press, 1981.

Pagis, Dan. *Change and Tradition in Secular Poetry* (in Hebrew). Jerusalem: Keter Publishing House, 1970.

———. *Hebrew Poetry of the Middle Ages and Renaissance.* Berkeley: University of California Press, 1991.

———. "The Poet as Prophet in Medieval Hebrew Literature." Pp. 140–150 in *Poetry and Prophecy: The Beginnings of a Literary Tradition,* edited by J. Kugel. Ithaca, N.Y.: Cornell University Press, 1990.

———. *Secular Poetry and Poetic Theory: Moses Ibn Ezra and His Contemporaries* (in Hebrew). Jerusalem: Bialik Institute, 1970.

Perlmann, Moshe. "Medieval Polemics between Islam and Judaism." Pp. 103–138 in *Religion in a Religious Age,* ed. S. D. Goitein. Cambridge, Mass.: Harvard University Press, 1974.

Peters, Francis E. *Aristoteles Arabus: The Oriental Translations and Commentaries of the Aristotelian Corpus.* Leiden: E. J. Brill, 1968.

Petruccioli, Attilio, ed. *Gardens in the Time of the Great Muslim Empires: Theory and Design.* Leiden: E. J. Brill, 1997.

Pines, Shlomo. "The Limits of Human Knowledge according to al-Farabi, ibn Bajja, and Maimonides." Pp. 82–109 in *Studies in Medieval Jewish History and Literature,* edited by I. Twersky. Cambridge, Mass.: Harvard University Press, 1979.

———. "On the Term *Ruḥaniyyot* and Its Origin and on Judah Halevi's Doctrine" (in Hebrew). *Tarbiẓ* 57, no. 4 (1988): 511–540.

———. "The Origin of the Tale of Salāmān and Absāl: A Possible Indian Influence?" Pp. 343–353 in *Studies in the History of Arabic Philosophy.* Jerusalem: Magnes Press, 1996.

———. "'Philosophie Orientale' d'Avicenne et sa polémique contre les Bagdadiens." *Archives d'histoire doctrinale et littéraire de Moyen Âge* 27 (1952): 5–37.

———. "Shiᶜite Terms and Conceptions in Judah Halevi's *Kuzari.*" *Jerusalem Studies in Arabic and Islam* 2 (1980): 165–251.

Portelli, John P. "The 'Myth' that Avicenna Reproduced Aristotle's 'Concept of the Imagination' in *De Anima.*" *Scripta Mediterranea* 3 (1982): 122–134.

Pouzet, Louis. "Remarques sur l'autobiographie dans le monde arabo-musulman au Moyen-Âge." Pp. 91–107 in *Philosophy and Arts in the Islamic World,* edited by U. Vermeulen and D. de Smet. Leuven: Peeters, 1998.

Proudfoot, Wayne. *Religious Experience.* Berkeley: University of California Press, 1985.

Puerta Vílchez, José Miguel. *Historia del pensamiento estético árabe, al-Andalus y la estética árabe clásica.* Madrid: Ediciones Akal, 1997.

Quinn, Naomi. "The Cultural Basis of Metaphor." Pp. 56–93 in *Beyond Metaphor: The Theory of Tropes in Anthropology,* edited by James W. Fernandez. Stanford, Calif.: Stanford University Press, 1991.

Rahman, Fazlur. *Avicenna's Psychology: An English Translation of Kitāb al-najāt, Book II, Chapter VI with Historico-Philosophical Notes and Textual Improvements on the Cairo Edition.* London: Oxford University Press, 1952.

Rappe, Sara. *Reading Neoplatonism: Non-discursive Thinking in the Texts of Plotinus, Proclus, and Damascius.* Cambridge: Cambridge University Press, 2000.

Ratzaby, Yehuda. "Arabic Poetry Written by Andalusian Jews" (in Hebrew). Pp. 329–350 in *Israel Levin Jubilee Volume,* edited by Reuven Tsur and Tova Rosen. Tel Aviv: Tel Aviv University Press, 1994.

Ricoeur, Paul. *The Conflict of Interpretations.* Edited by Don Ihde. Evanston, Ill.: Northwestern University Press, 1974.

———. *Hermeneutics and the Human Sciences: Essays on Language, Action, and Interpretation.* Translated by John B. Thompson. Cambridge: Cambridge University Press, 1981.

Rist, John M. *Plotinus: The Road to Reality.* Cambridge: Cambridge University Press, 1967.

———. *Psyche and Eros: Studies in Plato, Plotinus, and Origen.* Toronto: University of Toronto Press, 1964.

Rorty, Richard. *Philosophy and the Mirror of Nature.* Princeton, N.J.: Princeton University Press, 1979.

Rosán, Laurence J. *The Philosophy of Proclus.* New York: Cosmos, 1949.

Rosenthal, Franz. *Four Essays on Art and Literature in Islam.* Leiden: E. J. Brill, 1971.

———. *Knowledge Triumphant: The Concept of Knowledge in Medieval Islam.* Leiden: E. J. Brill, 1970.

———. "The Stranger in Medieval Islam." *Arabica* 44, no. 1 (1997): 35–75.

———. "The Symbolism of the Tabula Cebitis according to Abū l-Faraj Ibn al-Ṭayyib." Pp. 273–283 in *Recherches d'islamologie: Recueil d'articles offert à G. Anawati et L. Gardet par leurs collègues et amis.* Louvain: Peeters, 1977.

Rosin, David. "Die Religionsphilosophie Abraham ibn Esras." *Monatsschrift für Geschichte und Wissenschaft des Judenthums* 42 (1898): 17–33, 58–73, 108–115, 154–161, 200–214, 305–315, 345–362, 394–407, 444–457, 481–505; 43 (1899): 22–31, 75–91, 124–133, 168–184, 231–240.

Rowland, Christopher. "The Visions of God in Apocalyptic Literature." *Journal for the Study of Judaism* 10 (1979): 137–154.

Ruggles, D. Fairchild. *Gardens, Landscapes, and Vision in Islamic Spain.* University Park: Pennsylvania State University Press, 2000.

Russell, Stephen. *Allegoresis: The Craft of Allegory in Medieval Literature.* New York: Garland Publishing, 1987.

Saliba, Djemil. "Philosophical Symbolism and the Use of Myth among Arab Philosophers." *Diogenes* 10 (1955): 66–79.

Sandy, Gerald N. *The Greek World of Apuleius: Apuleius and the Second Sophistic.* Leiden: E. J. Brill, 1997.

Schäfer, Peter. *The Hidden and Manifest God: Some Major Themes in Early Jewish Mysticism.* Translated by Aubrey Pomerance. Albany: State University of New York Press, 1992.

———, et al., eds. *Synopse zur Hekhalot-Literatur.* Tübingen: Mohr, 1981.

Scharf, Robert. "Experience." Pp. 70–93 in *Critical Terms for Religious Studies,* edited by Mark C. Taylor. Chicago: University of Chicago Press, 1999, 70–93.

Scheindlin, Raymond P. *The Gazelle: Medieval Hebrew Poems on God, Israel, and the Soul.* Philadelphia: Jewish Publication Society of America, 1991.

———. "The Hebrew Qasida in Spain." Pp. 121–135 in *Qasida Poetry in Islamic Asia and Africa,* vol. 1, edited by S. Sperl and C. Shackle. Leiden: E. J. Brill, 1996.

———. "Rabbi Moshe Ibn Ezra on the Legitimacy of Poetry." *Medievalia et Humanistica,* n.s. 7 (1976): 101–115.

———. *Wine, Women, and Death: Medieval Hebrew Poems on the Good Life.* Philadelphia: Jewish Publication Society of America, 1986.

Schippers, Arie. *Arabic Tradition and Hebrew Innovation: Arabic Themes in Hebrew Andalusian Poetry.* 2nd ed. Amsterdam: University of Amsterdam Press, 1988.

Schlanger, Jacques. *La Philosophie de Salomon Ibn Gabirol: étude d'un néoplatonisme.* Leiden: E. J. Brill, 1968.

Schmeling, Gareth, ed. *The Novel in the Ancient World.* Leiden: E. J. Brill, 1996.

Schoeler, Gregor. "Der poetische Syllogismus: Ein Bertrag zum Verständnis der 'logischen' Poetik der Araber." *Zeitschrift der deutschen Morgenländischen Gesellschaft* 133, no. 1 (1983): 43–92.

Schofield, Malcolm. "Aristotle on the Imagination." Pp. 103–132 in *Articles on Aristotle,* vol. 4: *Psychology,* edited by J. Barnes, M. Schofield, and R. Sorabji. London: Duckworth, 1978.

Scholem, Gershom G. "Ein Fragment zur Physiognomik und Chiromantik aus der Spätantiken jüdischen Esoterik." Pp. 175–193 in *Liber Amicorum: Studies in Honour of Prof. C.J. Bleeker.* Leiden: E. J. Brill, 1969.

———. *Major Trends in Jewish Mysticism.* New York: Schocken, 1946.

Schubert, Kurt. "Jewish Pictorial Traditions in Early Christian Art." Pp. 141–259 in *Jewish Historiography and Iconography in Early and Medieval Christianity,* edited by Heinz Schreckenberg and Kurt Schubert. Assen and Maastricht: Van Gorcum, 1992.

Schuon, Frithjof. *Islam and Perennial Philosophy.* London: World of Islam Festival Publishing Co., 1976.

Schwartz, Dov. *Astral Magic in Medieval Jewish Thought* (in Hebrew). Ramat Gan: Bar Ilan University Press, 1999.

Schwarzschild, Steven S. "Aesthetics." Pp. 1–6 in *Contemporary Jewish Religious Thought: Original Essays on Critical Concepts, Movements, and Beliefs,* edited by Arthur A. Cohen and Paul Mendes-Flohr. New York: Charles Scribner's Sons, 1987.

Seeskin, Kenneth. *Searching for a Distant God: The Legacy of Maimonides.* Oxford: Oxford University Press, 2000.

Sela, Shlomo. *Astrology and Biblical Exegesis in Abraham Ibn Ezra's Thought* (in Hebrew). Ramat Gan: Bar Ilan University Press, 1999.

Sells, Michael A. "Bewildered Tongue: The Semantics of Mystical Union in Islam." Pp. 87–124 in *Mystical Union and Monotheistic Faith: An Ecumenical Dialogue,* edited by Moshe Idel and Bernard McGinn. New York: Continuum, 1999.

———. *Early Islamic Mysticism: Sufi, Qur᾿ān, Mi῾raj, Poetic and Theological Writings.* New York: Paulist Press, 1996.

———. *Mystical Languages of Unsaying.* Chicago: University of Chicago Press, 1994.

Shaw, Gregory. *Theurgy and the Soul: The Neoplatonism of Iamblichus.* University Park: Pennsylvania State University Press, 1995.

Sihvola, Juha, and Troels Engberg-Pedersen, eds. *The Emotions in Hellenistic Philosophy.* Dordrecht: Kluwer, 1998.

Simón, Emilio de Santiago. "The Itinerary of the Muslim Conquest of al-Andalus in the Light of a New Source: Ibn Shabbāt." Pp. 1–12 in *The Formation of al-Andalus,* vol. 1, edited by Manuela Marín. Translated by Michael Kennedy. Aldershot, England: Ashgate, 1998.

Siorvanes, Lucas. *Proclus: Neo-Platonic Philosophy and Science.* New Haven: Yale University Press, 1996.

Siraisi, Nancy G. *Avicenna in Renaissance Italy: The Canon and Medical Training at Italian Universities after 1500.* Princeton, N.J.: Princeton University Press, 1987.

Sirat, Collete. *Les théories des visions surnaturelles dans la pensée juive du Moyen Âge.* Leiden: E. J. Brill, 1969.

Smith, Jonathan Z. *Drudgery Divine: On Comparison of Early Christianities and the Religions of Late Antiquity.* Chicago: University of Chicago Press, 1990.

———. *Imagining Religion: From Babylon to Jonestown.* Chicago: University of Chicago Press, 1982.

———. *Map Is Not Territory: Studies in the History of Religions.* Chicago: University of Chicago Press, 1993.

Sorabji, Richard, ed. *Aristotle Transformed: The Ancient Commentators and Their Influence.* Ithaca, N.Y.: Cornell University Press, 1990.

———. *Emotion and Peace of Mind: From Stoic Agitation to Christian Temptation.* Oxford: Oxford University Press, 2000.

———. "Myths About Non-propositional Thought." Pp. 205–314 in *Language and Logos: Studies in Ancient Philosophy Presented to G. E. L. Owen,* edited by M. Schofield and M. Nussbaum. New York: Cambridge University Press, 1982.

Stalley, R. F. "Plato's Arguments from the Division of the Reasoning and Appetitive Elements within the Soul." *Phronesis* 20 (1975): 110–128.

Steinschneider, Moritz. *Polemische und apolgetische Literatur in arabischer Sprāche zwischen Muslimen, Christen, und Juden.* Leipzig: n.p., 1877.

Stern, David. *Parables in Midrash: Narrative and Exegesis in Rabbinic Literature.* Cambridge, Mass.: Harvard University Press, 1991.

Stern, Samuel M. *Studies in Early Ismā῾īlism.* Jerusalem: Magnes Press, 1983.

Stetkevych, Suzanne Pinckney. *Abū Tammām and the Poetics of the ῾Abbasid Age.* Leiden: E. J. Brill, 1991.

———. *The Mute Immortals Speak: Pre-Islamic Poetry and the Poetics of Ritual.* Ithaca, N.Y.: Cornell University Press, 1993.

———. "Toward a Redefinition of *badī῾* Poetry." *Journal of Arabic Literature* 12 (1981): 1–29.

Strauss, Leo. *Persecution and the Art of Writing.* Chicago: University of Chicago Press, 1952.

Stroumsa, Sarah. "Avicenna's Philosophical Stories: Aristotle's Poetics Reinterpreted." *Arabica* 9 (1992): 183–206.

Tambiah, Stanley J. "A Performative Approach to Ritual." Pp. 123–166 in *Culture, Thought, and Social Action,* edited by S. J. Tambiah. Cambridge, Mass.: Harvard University Press, 1985.

Tanenbaum, Adena. *The Contemplative Soul: Hebrew Poetry and Philosophical Theory in Medieval Spain.* Leiden: E. J. Brill, 2002.

Tirosh-Samuelson, Hava. "Maimonides' View of Happiness: Philosophy, Myth and the Transcendence of History." Pp. 189–213 in *Jewish History and Jewish Memory: Essays in Honor of Yosef Hayim Yerushalmi,* edited by E. Carlebach, J. Efron, and D. Myers. Hanover, N.H.: Brandeis University Press, 1998.

Tkatsch, Jaroslaus. *Die arabische Übersetzung der Poetik des Aristoteles: und die Grundlage der Kritik des grieschischen Textes.* 2 vols. Vienna and Leipzig: Hölder-Pichler-Tempsky, 1928–1932.

Turner, Victor. *The Ritual Process: Structure and Anti-Structure.* Ithaca, N.Y.: Cornell University Press, 1969.

Twersky, Isadore, and Jay Harris, eds. *Rabbi Abraham Ibn Ezra: Studies in the Writings of a Twelfth-Century Jewish Polymath.* Cambridge, Mass.: Harvard University Press, 1993.

Vajda, Georges. *L'Amour de dieu dans la théologie juive du Moyen Âge.* Paris: J. Vrin, 1957.

———. *Juda ben Nissim ibn Malka: Philosophe juif marocain.* Paris: Larose, 1954.

———. "Les notes d'Avicenne sur la *Théologie d'Aristote,*" *Revue Thomiste* 51, no. 2 (1951): 346–406.

———. "D'Une attestation peu connue du thème du 'philosophie autodidacte.'" *Al-Andalus* 31 (1966): 379–382.

Valantasis, Richard, ed. *Religions of Late Antiquity in Practice.* Princeton, N.J.: Princeton University Press, 2000.

de Vaux, Carra. "Ibn Ṭufail." Pp. 424–425 in *Encyclopaedia of Islam,* first edition. Leiden: E. J. Brill, 1987 (reprint).

Von Grunebaum, Gustav E. "The Concept of Plagiarism in Arabic Theory." *Journal of Near Eastern Studies* 3 (1944): 234–253.

Walbridge, John. *The Leaven of the Ancients: Suhrawardī and the Heritage of the Greeks.* Albany: State University of New York Press, 2000.

———. *"The Wisdom of the Mystic East": Suhrawardī and Platonic Orientalism.* Albany: State University of New York Press, 2001.

Wallis, R. T. *Neoplatonism.* London: Duckworth, 1972.

Walzer, Richard. *Greek into Arabic: Essays on Islamic Philosophy.* Oxford: Cassirer, 1962.

Wasserstein, David J. "The Muslims and the Golden Age of the Jews in al-Andalus." Pp. 179–196 in *Dhimmis and Others: Jews, Christians and the World of Classical Islam,* edited by Uri Rubin and D. J. Wasserstein. *Israel Oriental Studies* 17 (1997).

Wasserstrom, Steven M. *Between Muslim and Jew: The Problem of Symbiosis under Early Islam.* Princeton, N.J.: Princeton University Press, 1995.

———. *Religion after Religion: Gershom Scholem, Mircea Eliade, and Henry Corbin at Eranos.* Princeton, N.J.: Princeton University Press, 1999.

Watt, W. Montgomery. *A History of Islamic Spain.* Edinburgh: Edinburgh University Press, 1965.

Wedin, Michael V. *Mind and Imagination in Aristotle.* New Haven: Yale University Press, 1988.

Weiss, Raymond L. *Maimonides' Ethics: The Encounter of Philosophic and Religious Morality.* Chicago: University of Chicago Press, 1991.

Whitman, Jon. *Allegory: The Dynamics of an Ancient and Medieval Technique.* Cambridge, Mass.: Harvard University Press, 1987.

Wolfson, Elliot R. *Along the Path: Studies in Kabbalistic Myth, Symbolism, and Hermeneutics.* Albany: State University of New York Press, 1995.

———. "God, the Demiurge and the Intellect: On the Usage of the Word Kol in Abraham Ibn Ezra." *Revue des études juives* 149 (1990): 77–111.

———. "Merkavah Traditions in Philosophic Garb: Judah Halevi Reconsidered." *Proceedings for the American Academy of Jewish Research* 57 (1990/1991): 179–242.

———. "The Theosophy of Shabbetai Donnolo, with Special Emphasis on the Doctrine of *Sefirot* in his *Sefer Hakhmoni.*" *Jewish History* 6 (1992): 281–316.

———. *Through a Speculum that Shines: Vision and Imagination in Medieval Jewish Mysticism.* Princeton, N.J.: Princeton University Press, 1994.

Wolfson, Harry A. "The Classification of the Sciences in Medieval Jewish Philosophy." *Hebrew Union College Jubilee Volume* (1925): 275–278.

———. "The Internal Senses in Latin, Arabic and Hebrew Philosophical Texts." *Harvard Theological Review* 28 (1935): 69–133.

Woodruff, Paul. "Aristotle on Mimesis." Pp. 73–95 in *Essays on Aristotle's Poetics,* edited by Amélie Oksenberg Rorty. Princeton, N.J.: Princeton University Press, 1992.

Woods, M. J. "Plato's Division of the Soul." *Proceedings of the British Academy* 73 (1987): 23–47.

Wright, M. R. *Cosmology in Antiquity.* London: Routledge, 1995.

Yahalom, Joseph. "Judah Halevi: Records of a Visitor from Spain." Pp. 123–135 in *The Cambridge Genizah Collections: Their Contents and Significance,* edited by Stefan C. Reif. Cambridge: Cambridge University Press, 2002.

———. *The Poetic Language of the Ancient Palestinian Piyyut* (in Hebrew). Jerusalem: Magnes Press, 1985.

Yates, Frances A. *The Art of Memory.* Chicago: University of Chicago Press, 1966.

Zaehner, R. C. *Mysticism Sacred and Profane: An Inquiry into Some Praeternatural Experience.* New York: Oxford University Press, 1961.

Zemach, Eddy M. *Real Beauty.* University Park: Pennsylvania State University Press, 1997.

Zimmermann, Fritz W. "The Origins of the So-Called *Theology of Aristotle.*" Pp. 110–240 in *Pseudo-Aristotle in the Middle Ages: The "Theology" and Other Texts,* edited by J. Kraye et al. London: Warburg Institute, 1986.

Index

adab (polite ideal of cultured living), 10–12, 15–16, 178
aesthetics, 4, 11, 60–61, 103, 146–184, 185–187; Alfarabi's theory of, 163–165; Aristotle's theory of, 156–157; Avicenna's theory of, 165–166; denial of, Islam and Judaism, 5, 149–153; as distinct sub-field of medieval Islamicate philosophy, 9, 146–149; and *Ḥayy ibn Yaqẓān* cycle, 171–183; ibn Ezra's theory of, 166–169; *Ikhwān al-Ṣafā*ʾ's theory of, 162–163; and imagination, 3–5, 153–187; in initiatory tales, 171–183; Maimonides' theory of, 169–170; and ontology, 49–51, 159–160; Plato's theory of, 4, 154–156; Plotinus's theory of, 157–160; traditionally marginalized in secondary studies of medieval philosophy, 3, 148–149
ᶜ*ahd* (oath of allegiance), 26, 27
al-ᶜālam al-mithāl. See mundus imaginalis
Alfarabi, 24, 161, 163–165, 220n11
al-alḥān (musical harmony), 59; and *Ikhwān al-Ṣafā*ʾ, 162–163
allegoresis, 36–37, 132
allegory, 35–40; Arabic terms for, 37; definition of, 35–37; *Ḥayy ibn Yaqẓān* as, 17; Neoplatonic interest in, 68–70; polysemous nature of, 36; romantic assumptions of, 38
al-Andalus (Muslim Spain), 21, 23, 45, 75; brief history of, 10–11; concept of *adab* in, 10; downfall of Umayyad caliphate, 12; Jewish presence in, 11–12
aniconism, 5, 149–152
Anonymous Prolegomena to Platonic Philosophy, 69
Arabic: competition with Hebrew, 2, 11–12, 14–15, 23; poetics and relationship to Greek poetics, 64–65, 71–72; used by Jews, 11
ᶜ*ārif* (knower; gnostic), 35, 94
Aristotle, 8, 13, 45, 52, 54, 102, 105, 146, 153; Arab commentaries on, 71–72; *Poetics*, 45–46; theory of aesthetics, 156–157; theory of imagination, 88–89; union of knower and known, 54
Avicenna, 2, 9, 12, 14, 20, 24, 29–30, 30–35, 46–47, 54, 60, 63, 66, 72, 78, 97, 135, 161, 182; autobiography, 20, 138–139, 212n24; *Commentary to Aristotle's Poetics (al-Shifā*ʾ), 69–70, 105–106; *Ḥayy ibn Yaqẓān*, 20–21, 66–67, 77, 107–109, 125–128, 137–140,

171–172, 173–176, 179–181; *Kitāb al-ishārāt wa al-tanbīhāt*, 24, 35, 55, 59, 94–95, 96, 109; *Kitāb al-majmu*ᶜ, 46, 104–105; *Kitāb al-najāt*, 165; *Mantiq al-mashriqiyyīn*, 31, 33; and medieval poetics, 46, 71–72; and mysticism, 35, 94–95; and oriental wisdom (*al-ḥikma al-mashriqiyya*), 30–35, 58–59, 141 (*see also* Corbin, Henry; oriental wisdom); as poet, 104; prologue to *al-Shifā*ᵓ, 31, 33; *Risāla fī al-*ᶜ*ishq*, 104, 165–166, 180; *Risāla Salāmān wa Absal*, 29; *Risāla al-ṭayr*, 29–30; theory of aesthetics, 165–166; theory of the soul, 91–95

barzakh (threshold), 126, 127, 171–172
bāṭin (inner dimension), 26; *bāṭin al-bāṭin*, 27; initiation into, 25–30; versus *ẓāhir*, 132
beauty, 9, 146; as an attribute of God, 161–171; found in texts, 51–61, 102–106; and imagination, 103; Neoplatonic conceptions of, 153–160. *See also* aesthetics
Behrens-Abouseif, Doris, 152
Bell, Catherine, 120
Bland, Kalman, 152–153, 167–168, 170
body: duality, 46, 51, 76–77, 80, 87, 89–90, 91–93, 97–99, 100, 134–136, 155, 163; and embodiedness, 47, 50, 54, 62, 80, 148, 153–154; ephemeral nature of, 31; and imagination, 5–6, 87, 88, 94–95, 97–99, 100–103, 109, 112, 113–114, 117, 142; and importance for philosophy, 7, 55, 166, 186; and metaphor, 7, 54, 76; problem for philosophy, 7, 18, 130, 170; relationship to aesthetics, 50; and ritual, 117, 124–125, 126, 130, 134–136
Boyarin, Daniel, 40
Brann, Ross, 12

Carruthers, Mary, 103
Cassirer, Ernst, 219n2
celestial guide, 39, 61–64, 77; Ḥayy ibn Yaqẓān as, 63–64; in Neoplatonic literature, 62–63
Corbin, Henry, 32–34, 61–62, 216nn100–102
Cordoba, 10
Coulter, James, 68

devequt (cleaving), 56, 67, 95, 97. *See also ittiṣāl*
dhawq (taste), 19, 32, 58, 59, 92, 100, 111, 182
divine throne, 43–45, 56

Eliade, Mircea, 116
emanation, 52–53, 73–76, 86, 89, 104, 106, 147–149, 153–154, 158, 174, 177, 178
Enoch, 44, 45
esotericism. *See bāṭin*

*fanā*ᵓ (extinction; annihilation), 25, 112, 131
Fradkin, Hillel, 129

Gadamer, Hans-Georg, 53–54, 84–85
Geertz, Clifford, 115
van Gennep, Arnold, 9, 116, 117, 120, 133
al-Ghaiti, 42
al-Ghazali, Abū Ḥāmid, 24
al-Ghazali, Aḥmad ibn Muḥammad, 24
God, 25, 26, 31, 43, 50, 80, 94, 98, 111, 112, 128, 131, 132, 141, 160, 161, 168, 173, 178, 180, 181, 182; imaginative apprehension of, 1, 2, 6, 39, 40, 41–45, 58, 67, 99, 101, 103, 124, 137, 183 (*see also devequt; ittiṣāl*); literature as a way to speculate about, 1, 18; portrayed in art, 151; seen in text, 96; tension between absence and presence, 149–151;

transcendence of, 75, 82–83, 97, 113, 186. *See also* beauty; *fanā*ʾ
Grimes, Ronald, 9
Gutas, Dimitri, 34–35, 40

Hadot, Pierre, 52, 134, 143
Halevi, Judah, 21, 22, 229n104
Hawi, Sami, 47, 233n61
Ḥay ben Meqitz, 12, 22, 67, 75, 77, 109, 119, 169; as character, 38, 39, 61, 63, 64, 78–79, 110–111, 119–125, 136–137, 172, 173, 181; different from *Ḥayy ibn Yaqẓān*, 23, 38, 39, 96–97, 126, 135; English translation of, 189–207; as part of *Ḥayy ibn Yaqẓān* cycle, 209n1; as personification of Active Intellect, 61, 98, 110
Ḥayy ibn Yaqẓān, 5, 7, 8, 13, 15, 19–25, 26, 35, 40, 41, 45, 47, 54, 57, 60, 61, 65, 66, 100, 102, 103, 106, 109, 112, 115, 116, 125, 134, 185–187; and aesthetics, 106–112; as character, 20–21, 24–25, 38, 46, 54, 56, 61, 63, 64, 77, 80, 101, 107, 118, 126–133, 137, 139–143, 173, 175, 178–180, 182–183; different names given to, 17; as a genre, 2–3, 17, 19, 35–40; maximalist versus minimalist reading of, 7, 13, 40, 48, 61; Neoplatonic context of, 15–17, 62–63, 64, 68–70; and non-discursivity, 69; personification of Active Intellect, 61, 64; relationship to other Islamicate literature, 25–30; ritual component of, 119–145. *See also* initiatory tale
Heath, Peter, 37, 66, 72, 108, 222n67
heavenly ascent, 44, 48
Hebrew, 14; polemics with Arabic, 2, 11–12. *See also* Arabic; Ḥay ben Meqitz; ibn Ezra, Abraham
Heidegger, Martin, 8, 32–33, 49, 50, 84, 113–114, 147
hekhalot (palaces), 43, 44
hekhalot literature, 44, 121
Hermias, 62
al-ḥikma al-mashriqiyya. *See* oriental wisdom
ḥusn al-niẓām (beauty of order), 104, 165
Husserl, Edmund, 83

Iamblichus, 52, 62
ibn Bājja, 24, 100, 233n51
ibn Daud, Abraham, 22
ibn Ezra, Abraham, 2, 8, 9, 11, 12, 13, 16, 21–23, 30, 38, 46, 50, 54, 63, 66, 97–98, 135, 161, 182; brief biography of, 21–23; difficulty in classifying, 60, 95–96; familiarity with Avicenna, 14, 211n1; *Ḥay ben Meqitz*, 2, 13, 38, 67–68, 77–79, 96, 109–111, 119–125, 136–137, 172–173, 176–178, 181–182, 189–207; *Ḥay ben Meqitz* not simple copy of Avicenna's *Ḥayy ibn Yaqẓān*, 15, 96; as Islamicate Neoplatonist, 60, 210n6; *ha maskil yavin*, 60; problematic nature of, in Jewish philosophy, 22; theory of aesthetics, 166–169; theory of the golden calf, 166–169; theory of the soul, 96–99; use of biblical narrative, 23, 78–79, 110–111, 136, 173, 176–178, 181; *Yesod Mora*, 56, 213n41
ibn Ezra, Moses, 22, 72, 235n11
ibn Gabirol, Shlomo, 75–76; influence on ibn Ezra, 75
ibn Jamʿa, Samuel ben Jacob, 22
ibn Ṭufayl, Abū Bakr, 2, 9, 14, 23–25, 30, 32, 38, 46, 47, 54, 58, 59, 60, 63, 182; brief biography of, 23–24; *Ḥayy ibn Yaqẓān*, 80, 100, 111–112, 128–133, 141–143, 178–179, 182–183; knowledge of Avicenna's *Ḥayy ibn Yaqẓān*, 14; and metaphor of the mirror, 56–57; political dimensions of his *Ḥayy ibn Yaqẓān*, 15, 128–129,

132–133; and "secrets of oriental wisdom," 32, 58, 59; and textual *ḥujub* (veils), 70, 143; theory of aesthetics, 173–174, 178–179 (*see also* oriental wisdom); theory of imagination, 100–102; use of Qurʾānic imagery, 80
ibn Ẓaddik, Joseph ben Jacob, 22, 212n30
ibn Zayla, 30, 77
Ikhwān al-Ṣafāʾ (Brethren of Purity), 26–27, 161, 162–163; initiatory aspects of their *Rasāʾil*, 26–28
images, 1, 3, 6, 8, 34, 40, 43, 46, 50, 55, 56, 66, 77, 79, 81, 82–114 passim, 115, 150, 151, 152, 154, 175, 183; as disclosure of ultimate reality, 4, 49–53, 83–86, 108, 132, 135–136, 147–160, 171, 183–184, 187; epistemological currency of the imagination, 82–86; ibn Ezra on, 167–169; and relationship to Neoplatonic poetics, 73–80. *See also* ibn Ezra, Abraham; imagination
imagination, 2, 3, 4, 5–6, 8, 16, 35, 46, 69, 82–114 passim, 131; Aristotle's theory of, 85, 88–89; Avicenna's theory of, 35, 91–95; and disclosure of ultimate reality, 83–86 (*see also* images); hermeneutical faculty, 6, 82, 83, 85; ibn Ezra's theory of, 95–99; ibn Ṭufayl's theory of, 100–102; and initiatory tales, 86; as inner eye, 82, 99, 102; locus of the divine presence, 2, 8, 39–44, 58, 67, 83, 99, 101, 103, 113, 124, 125, 137, 143, 183, 185–187; and ontology, 7, 9, 15, 18, 49–50, 72–86, 104, 147–149, 158–160, 164–165, 174–175, 177; perceived as unreliable, 3, 82, 83; Plato's theory of, 85, 87–88; Plotinus's theory of, 89–90; and prophecy, 92; relationship to aesthetics, 1–5, 6, 8, 37, 49–51, 89, 90–91, 102–106, 111–112, 149, 150, 154–160, 183, 184, 185–187; relationship to intellect, 16, 37, 57, 82–114 passim, 175; relevance to philosophy, 85; traditionally marginalized in secondary studies of medieval philosophy, 3, 82, 148, 150, 185–186; visual faculty, 6, 82–85, 113
initiation, 19, 64; in Avicenna's *Ḥayy ibn Yaqẓān*, 125–128; as a genre of medieval Islamicate literature, 25–30; in ibn Ezra's *Ḥay ben Meqitz*, 119–125; in ibn Ṭufayl's *Ḥayy ibn Yaqẓān*, 128–133
initiatory tale: definition of, 19; and embodiedness, 50–51; *Ḥayy ibn Yaqẓān* cycle as, 19; and imagination, 86, 171–186; late antique predecessors of, 26, 64–65; as meditation manual, 102–106; more than allegorical, 39; and philosophy, 45–46; and ritual, 117–145; use of myth, 40–44. *See also* Ḥay ben Meqitz; Ḥayy ibn Yaqẓān
inner eye, 82, 98, 181. *See also* imagination
intellect: Avicenna's theory of, 93–95; and the impossibility of imageless thinking, 49. *See also* imagination
ʿirfān (gnosis), 32, 94. *See also* *maʿrifa*
ishāra (allusion). *See* allegory
Ismāʿīlīs, 26–28
isrāʾ (night flight), 41–43. *See also* *miʿrāj*
istiʿāra (metaphor). *See* allegory; metaphor
iʿtidāl (harmony), 104, 160, 165
ittiṣāl (conjunction), 25, 32, 94, 95, 97, 130, 131
Ivry, Alfred, 29

al-Jūzjānī, 30

kabbalah. *See hekhalot; merkabah*
Kahwaji, S., 151

kavod (glory), 96, 97
kisse ha-kavod. See divine throne
Kitāb ma^{c}ānī al-nafs, 224n111

ladhdha (pleasure), 46, 58, 71, 100, 105, 135
language, 1, 15, 38, 47, 49, 73–80, 89; absence and presence in, 7, 49–50, 67, 70, 103, 156; and aesthetics, 148; as delineator of truth, 51, 53, 70–72; and embodiedness, 7, 50, 109, 135, 148, 175–183; and experience, 59, 70, 210n16; and ineffability, 59; limitations of, 16, 51, 53–54, 59–61 (*see also* Neoplatonism); relationship to ontology, 7, 49–51, 90; use in al-Andalus, 10–12. *See also* initiation
Levin, Israel, 189
Lévi-Strauss, Claude, 119
Levy, Ze'ev, 151
literary criticism. *See* Neoplatonism
literature, 18; epistemic significance of, 50; and philosophy, 18, 45, 64–80. *See also* language; Neoplatonism
love of God, 94, 98, 112, 141. *See also* God

Maimonides, 28, 169–170
ma^{c}rifa (gnosis), 26, 32, 94. *See also ^{c}irfān*
Marinus, 57
merkabah (chariot), 43, 44
merkabah literature, 121
metaphor, 70–80, 148–149. *See also* aesthetics; language
Metatron. *See* Enoch
microcosm motif, 54, 60, 162
mi^{c}rāj (ascension), 41–43. *See also isrā$^{\supset}$*
mirror: and imagination, 89–90; medieval composition of, 55–57; metaphor of the soul, 55–56
monotheistic paradox, 4, 44, 75, 149–150. *See also* God
Moses, 41, 45; as prototype for Ḥay ben Meqitz, 38, 61
muhākā (mimesis), 69, 135
Muḥammad, 41, 42, 43, 45
mundus imaginalis, 33
mushāhada (vision), 19, 32, 58, 59, 100, 101, 112, 131, 182
mysticism, 2, 3, 6, 15, 18, 22, 83, 210n16; Avicenna's relationship to, 34–35; ibn Ṭufyal's relationship to, 24, 100–102; and relationship to philosophy, 17, 55, 63–64, 100–102, 174–175
myth, 1, 2, 7, 38, 48, 51, 53, 92, 159; defined, 65; and initiatory tale, 40–45, 76–80, 106–112; and philosophy, 49, 66–68, 74–75, 87, 156–157
mythopoesis, 35, 147–148, 156

Neoplatonism, 5, 18, 34, 40, 47, 48, 51, 54, 80, 116, 134; and aesthetics, 147–149, 153–160, 179–180 (*see also* aesthetics); versus Aristotelianism, 40; and career of the soul, 41, 62–63; 65–68; and contemplative vision, 2, 5–6, 8, 16, 32, 35, 41, 48, 51–61, 81, 102–103, 113, 134, 147–148; difficulty in defining, 51–53; divided loyalties in, 15–17; eclecticism of, 15–16, 51–53; and epistemology, 161; and ineffability of truth, 53, 58, 69; and literary criticism, 49, 66, 68–70; and literature, 64–80; and non-discursivity, 69; and ontology, 15, 18, 48, 50, 52, 54–55, 72, 83, 86, 97, 104, 147–149, 153–154, 158, 160–161, 164–165, 174–175, 177; and poetics, 30, 35, 45–46, 51, 68–70, 71–72, 89, 104–106; relationship to monotheism, 41–45; ritual component of, 54, 69, 114, 116–117; and theurgy, 35, 52; and use of metaphor, 70–80; and visionary experience, 54;

as way of life, 34, 134. *See also* emanation; imagination
niẓām (order), 160. *See also ḥusn al-niẓām*
Nussbaum, Martha, 18, 37, 45–46, 49

Olympiodorus, 68
oriental wisdom: Avicenna and, 30–31, 59, 141; Corbin and, 32–33; Gutas's criticism of, 34–35; ibn Ṭufayl and, 32, 58, 59

Pagis, Dan, 11
"perennial philosophy," 210n16. *See also* oriental wisdom
Philoponus, John, 52
Plato, 4, 8, 52, 58, 65, 68, 103, 146, 153; theory of aesthetics, 154–156; use of myth, 1, 87, 156 (*see also* myth)
Plotinus, 4, 48, 54–55, 57, 65, 146, 153, 160; and influence on medieval thought, 90; and metaphor, 73–74; and mirror, 55; *On Intellectual Beauty*, 103–104; *Theology of Aristotle*, 90, 113, 157–160; theory of aesthetics, 157–160; theory of imagination, 89–90
poetics, 46; and Neoplatonism, 35. *See also* language; literary criticism
Porphyry, 52
Proclus, 57; and aesthetics, 158–159; *Commentary on the Republic*, 159; paideutic versus entheastic myths, 66
Pythagoras, 62, 63

qaṣīda (ode), 119
Qurʾān, 41, 63

ramz (symbol), 34, 37, 59. *See also* allegory
Rappe, Sara, 73, 134–135, 158
ritual, 9, 115–145; defined, 117; liminal dimension of, 117–118, 120, 122, 123, 129; and Neoplatonism, 114; relationship to imagination, 117. *See also* van Gennep; Grimes; Neoplatonism; Turner
Rorty, Richard, 55

sariqa (plagiarism), 23
Schwarzschild, Steven, 150–151
self-knowledge. *See* microcosm motif
Sells, Michael, 43
Smith, Jonathan Z., 14
Socrates, 36, 63; as celestial guide, 62
Song of Songs, 38, 61, 121–122, 173
Sorabji, Richard, 52
soul, 4, 15, 18, 46, 51, 59, 65–68, 75–77, 156, 162–166, 169–170, 181, 187; purification of, 16, 26–27, 55–57, 123–125, 127–128, 130–132, 134–136, 146–158. *See also* body; celestial guide; imagination; Neoplatonism
Stetkevych, Suzanne, 118–119
sufism, 24, 42–43, 131
Suhrawardī, Shihāb al-Dīn Yaḥya, 209n2
Syrianus, 62

taʿajjub (awe), 46, 69, 71, 105
taʿam (taste). *See dhawq*
takhayyul (imagination). *See* imagination
taʾlīf (composition), 104, 160, 165
taṣdīq (assent), 46, 69, 94, 105, 126
tashbīḥ (comparison), 71–72, 101
taʾwīl (allegorical interpretation). *See* allegoresis
textuality: and cosmology, 39; meditative dimension of, 133–143; as metaphor for divine reality, 39; and supertextual experience, 39, 67, 68–70
Theology of Aristotle. *See* Plotinus
theurgy. *See* Neoplatonism
Turner, Victor, 9, 116, 118, 120, 122, 133
al-Ṭūsī, Naṣīr al-Dīn, 27–28
al-Tustarī, 42

visionary experience, 2, 5–6, 16, 48, 51–61, 81, 82, 83, 94, 98–99, 103, 124, 147–148, 154–155; in apocalyptic literature, 44; Daniel's, 43–44; Ezekiel's, 43; in *Ḥayy ibn Yaqẓān* cycle, 18–19, 21, 32, 35, 39–40, 91, 111–112, 172, 182–183; Muḥammad's, 41–43. *See also* imagination; *mushāhada;* Neoplatonism

wahm (estimation), 46
Walbridge, John, 38–40
waṣl (attainment), 58, 59, 101, 112, 131
Wolfson, Elliot R., 6, 43, 54, 83, 84, 147–148

al-Yaman, Ja[c]far ibn Manṣūr, 27
yored merkabah, 44–45

ẓāhir (outer dimension). *See bāṭin*

Aaron W. Hughes is Assistant Professor of Religious Studies at the University of Calgary.